USINESS
RATION

ctory Readings

D I. HARTMAN
NCE P. HOGAN
T. WHOLIHAN

ss Administration
LEY UNIVERSITY

SCOTT, FORESMAN AND COMPANY

To Our Families

Library of Congress Catalog Card No. 68-29375
Copyright © 1969 by Scott, Foresman and Company, Glenview, Illinois 60025
All Rights Reserved. Printed in the United States of America.
Regional offices of Scott, Foresman and Company are located in Atlanta,
Dallas, Glenview, Palo Alto, and Oakland, N. J.

Table of Contents

Preface

The study of business administration at the undergraduate level frequently begins with a course in Introduction to Business. The books written for such a course typically cover a broad range of subjects, often resulting in many topics being dealt with rather summarily.

Modern Business Administration: Introductory Readings was constructed to be used in several different ways. It can be used to supplement standard textbooks written for introductory business courses. The selected readings provide the beginning student with an exposure to the field of business. Through this exposure, the student gains additional breadth, depth, and insight into the area of business administration.

The selections are designed to be challenging, yet comprehensible for the beginning student, and articles of varying degrees of difficulty are included. We have also attempted to include a blend of theoretical and practical approaches to subject areas. In some instances, we have included articles on the same subject in which the points of view differ. It is our hope that this will stimulate students to think about and analyze opposing concepts and philosophies. Questions are included at the end of each article to enhance the student's understanding.

Some instructors may prefer to use the book as their basic textbook. The introduction to each part of the book summarizes and highlights the important areas of business. Individual instructors may wish to expand upon the introductions in order to satisfy course objectives.

The articles have been selected and organized around the basic functional areas of business, in a framework flexible enough to permit individual instructors to adapt the book to their needs. Part One is concerned with the business environment. It deals primarily with the economic and social systems within which businesses operate. Part Two treats the problems, principles, and ideas currently present in the area of management and organization. Part Three deals with the financial aspects of business. Part Four includes articles about the vital area of marketing. Part Five reviews the complexities of the production function, emphasizing the current thinking in the areas of automation, location theory, and research and development. Part Six covers the personnel function. Emphasis is upon the traditional personnel areas, although a strong behavioral flavor is provided. Part Seven, which examines the evolving patterns of business, looks to the future and examines the challenges of the coming decades. It is also concerned with the burgeoning areas of government-business relations and international business.

We would like to thank Professors Douglas of The University of Kentucky, Perlick of Northern Illinois University, and Thompson of Foothill College for their constructive reviews of the manuscript. We, of course, assume full responsibility for the contents of the book.

We would also like to thank Mr. Robert St. Clair, Mr. William Snyder, and Mrs. Carol Embury of the Scott, Foresman and Company staff for their editorial assistance.

We are grateful to the individual authors and publishers who permitted us to reprint their materials.

1

The Business Environment

It is impossible to carry on the routine activities of life without daily involvement with business. Yet, the questions of what business is and what it does are seldom asked and even less frequently answered.

WHAT IS BUSINESS?

In our society business is the supplier of goods and services. It provides the public with the things it needs and wants in order to survive, enjoy life, and improve in a material sense. From the point of view of the consumer, business is the satisfier of needs and desires. What the customer demands is what business should provide.

Business is also the producer of wealth for society. In satisfying demand, business uses the resources of land, labor, and capital. These resources taken separately have little value; but business combines, structures, and refines the resources to produce useful goods and services. Such goods and services are an addition to the value of society. Further, business employs people who exchange their talents for wages and salaries. These people, in turn, exchange their compensation for desired goods and services.

Business is a profit-seeking entity. It supplies goods and services to satisfy demand and adds to society's value by earning a profit. Our society permits business to earn this profit as a reward for assuming the risks of operating a business.

Business is also a participant in society. In satisfying demand, supplying goods and services, and earning profits, business is deeply involved in the most fundamental activities of society. As a result, society looks to business for more than products, services, and profits. It looks to business for leadership and direction in helping to achieve society's objectives. It expects business to assist in the establishment of a better society.

BUSINESS IN SOCIETY

The environment in which business operates is the complex world around us. The economic, legal, social, and political aspects of this world are important to business since they most directly affect and influence the activities of business.

The environment in which business operates is dynamic, that is, continuously changing. Business, too, is dynamic. As business participates in society, it both causes and adapts to changes in the environment. For example, if a business develops a new product or service, openly supports a candidate for public office, is in conflict with a labor union, or acts in collusion with other businesses, it is causing changes in some aspects of the environment. At the same time, business responds and adapts to changes imposed upon it by the environment. Changes in laws or in the economic pace of the economy require business to adjust its performance in order to be able to continue to operate in the society.

Business has not always been as influential as it is today in structuring society. The organized activities of business in the United States date back less than two centuries. Prior to 1800 our society was predominantly agricultural. The production and exchange of goods and services were limited primarily to single-village trade. Lack of transportation and communication facilities encouraged each farm or farm community to achieve a high degree of self-sufficiency. Barter was common as a result of both a shortage and a distrust of currency.

From the beginning of the nineteenth century significant changes are evident in the economic structure of the United States. As markets were slowly linked by improved transportation facilities, large-scale trade began to develop. Small businesses expanded to capture a share of the expanding trade.

Prior to 1812, trade consisted primarily of agricultural products and import products manufactured abroad. The War of 1812 restricted foreign trade and stimulated domestic manufacturing. Once initiated, manufacturing activities expanded to satisfy the almost unlimited demands of a rapidly expanding population. The foundation of our industrial society was being established.

Throughout the decades from the 1820's to the 1850's, business expanded and adjusted to changes in society. Developing and adapting the new mechanical inventions brought about some large industries, primarily in textiles, railroads, and steel. Still the majority were small businesses. Domestic competition increased as these small businesses sought to share in the expanding and changing consumer demand patterns.

Business, particularly in the North, received a great impetus from the Civil War. War materials needed for the army forced the development of production techniques and further organization. By the close of the war the need for large-scale business was a reality. The economy of the southern states had collapsed and was dependent upon the productive capacities of the North. The North's needs were virtually unlimited as a result of the shortages created by the war. The result was the birth of a new era of business in the United States. This era was marked by the rise of industrial capitalists.

Industrial magnates arose: Carnegie in steel; Rockefeller in oil; Harriman, Hill, Gould, and Vanderbilt in railroads; and Morgan in finance. As owners and managers of empires, these men began to seek ways of avoiding competition. Although numerous tactics were used, the major tools for avoiding competition were organizational techniques. These entrepreneurs, often seeking both wealth and notoriety, combined small business firms and created trusts and holding companies. The Standard Oil Trust of the 1880's was one of the early trusts established to reduce competition in that industry. Later, Standard Oil of New Jersey became a holding company which controlled numerous subsidiary companies. These organizations were the forerunners of our modern corporations.

The era of these entrepreneurs, 1870 to 1910, began to reach an end as a result of some of the methods they used to create their industrial empires. The government had, until 1890, followed a philosophy of laissez faire (noninterference in business by government). The role of the government had not been significant either as a taxing agent or a controller of business. However, with the formation of the Interstate Commerce Commission in 1887 to control the railroads and the passage of the Sherman Antitrust Act in 1890, the government gave clear evidence of departing from its laissez-faire philosophy.

The new attitude of the government and the new legal controls tested the creativity of business to adapt to its ever changing environment. Business did not cease to grow but instead discovered new legal means which permitted greater growth.[1] The expansion of business encouraged an expansion of the influence of the government. New legislation was passed to further governmental control.

Among the legislative enactments were the Clayton Act of 1914 and the Federal Trade Commission Act of the same year. The Clayton Act supplemented the Sherman Act and declared price discrimination to be illegal. The Federal Trade Commission Act was passed to enforce fair competitive practices. The government's position in regard to labor was established by the National Labor Relations Act of 1935 (Wagner Act) and the Labor Management Relations Act of 1947 (Taft-Hartley Act). These and numerous other laws have influenced the position of business in society.

BUSINESS AND CAPITALISM

Business in the United States evolved as a part of a new socioeconomic organization of society. This organization included legal, political, social, and economic concepts brought together to form what is called *capitalism.* Capitalism is a system under which the means of production, distribution, and exchange are privately owned and directed. The characteristics of a capitalistic system are: first, private property; second, a free enterprise economy; third, the profit motive; and fourth, competitive free markets.

It should be recognized that no economic system operates in a pure form. For example, Russia does not have a purely communistic economic system nor does Great Britain have a purely socialistic system. The label capitalism is used to identify the system in the United States because the characteristics of capitalism predominate.

Private ownership of property is a basic characteristic of a capitalistic system. It permits the businessman to buy and sell in the market place. Private ownership of resources allows their use in the production of the goods and services desired by consumers. Free enterprise as a characteristic of capitalism means that business can engage in legal activities without direct interference from the government. In other words, a business owning private property cannot be told what or how to use this property in the production of goods and services. Business is free to make such decisions.

---

[1]Adolph Berle and Gardiner Means, *The Modern Corporation and Private Property* (New York: The Macmillan Company, 1933), pp. 36-40.

Business would be unwilling to assume the responsibility for such decisions or to assume the risk of failure if it were not for the *profit* motive. Profit is a strong positive motivator. While businessmen are motivated by other factors as well, the opportunity for economic gain is necessary for business to achieve maximum performance.

It should be obvious that the economic system in the United States is not capitalism in a pure form. In reality the existing system is what is called a *mixed economy*. In a mixed economy the government does involve itself in the regulation, ownership, and operation of some business activities. Through its agencies, such as the Interstate Commerce Commission, the Federal Communication Commission, and the Federal Trade Commission, the government does tell private businessmen what they can and cannot do. Beyond this regulatory function the government also is involved in direct ownership and is in competition with private enterprises. For example, the Tennessee Valley Authority is a government-owned-and-operated utility complex that competes with privately owned utility companies.

THE OBJECTIVES OF BUSINESS

Business in the United States has evolved within the framework of a capitalistic system. This evolution has required business to define its objectives, or reasons for existing—in other words, the nature and purpose of the business.

There is no single statement that explains the nature and purpose of a business. Rather, when establishing objectives, a manager must think in a plural sense. Peter Drucker, a noted management theorist, points out that "objectives are needed in every area where performance and results directly and vitally affect the survival and prosperity of the business."[2] These statements of objectives are needed to organize, test, predict, appraise, and analyze the performance and results of business.

In the businessman's mind the first objective to be defined is profit. This is reasonable since profit is the motivating force of our free enterprise system. However, the establishment of the profit objective is not an easy task. Profit goals differ from business to business and throughout the life of an individual firm. Therefore, a manager must set realistic profit objectives based on his knowledge of such factors as market conditions and competition.

Profit is more than just the final figure on the profit and loss statement. It serves three vital purposes. First, profit is regarded as a measure of operating effectiveness. Second, profit can be regarded as the potential premium for the risk assumed by owning or operating a business. Third, profit may be seen as a source of capital needed for the future of the business.[3]

In considering profit as the first objective of a business, many businessmen have come to consider it the only objective. However, another objective of business is service. The service objective refers to the ability of the business to satisfy the needs and wants of the consumer through the creation and distribution of

---

[2] *The Practice of Management* (New York: Harper & Brothers Publishers, 1954), p. 63.
[3] *ibid.,* pp. 76, 77.

goods and services. The business firm will not earn a profit unless it produces goods and services desired by the consuming public. Therefore, the profit and service objectives are linked together. A business cannot earn a profit without providing goods and services, and neither can the business continue to provide goods and services without earning a profit.

Profit and service are not the only objectives of business. Peter Drucker states that every business needs objectives in at least eight areas: market standing, innovation, productivity, physical and financial resources, profitability, manager performance and development, worker performance and attitude, and public responsibility.[4]

Market standing and innovation objectives can be used as examples. A business should establish an objective of the share of the market it seeks. This involves defining the nature and composition of the market. The multiplicity of markets complicates the establishment of such objectives. For example, General Motors controls approximately 52 per cent of domestic automobile sales. Each auto division (Chevrolet, Pontiac, Buick, Oldsmobile, and Cadillac) and each model line within the division has a market. General Motors is concerned with its overall market standing. The management of the Chevrolet division, for example, is concerned with the individual share of the markets controlled by Chevrolet, Chevelle, Chevy II, Corvair, and Camaro.

Management must also establish innovation objectives. In our competitive society a business without innovation goals may relinquish its market standing to other firms. Innovation means not only the development of new products and services; the firm must also introduce marketing, finance, production, personnel, and other changes that improve the company's capacity to provide the consumer with the same or more value at less cost.

The objectives of a business cannot be established in a vacuum but must be structured realistically within the framework of our competitive environment of free enterprise. Further, the business objectives cannot be established once and then stored carefully in the company vault. Nor can the objectives of the business be limited to a single time dimension. Instead, objectives must be structured in the light of both long- and short-term factors.

SOCIAL RESPONSIBILITY OF BUSINESS

The debate exists whether business has any responsibility beyond the earning of a maximum profit. The idea of social responsibility for business is based upon the concept that a business is something more than a purely economic institution. Social responsibility is based on the premise that business has a greater impact on society than can be measured by profit or loss. As a participant in society, business should contribute to the humane and constructive social policies that guide society. The rise of the social responsibility creed is a result of changes in our society. Having moved through eras of rugged individualism and laissez-faire competition, society's value system now emphasizes greater protection and freedom for individuals and groups.

---

[4] *ibid.*, p. 63.

Business has multiple responsibilities. However, it is impossible to determine in universal terms the extent of these responsibilities. The nature of the company, including its size, products, and financial resources, influences the level or degree of social responsibility. The recognition of social responsibility by business has been termed the emergence of a *corporate conscience*. The corporate conscience is significantly influenced by the professional managers who control business. The evolution of the concept of social responsibility in the United States is the result of increasing governmental regulation and increasing business sensitivity to the changing values of American society.

BUSINESS ETHICS

Business ethics deals with morality in the business environment. It involves moral judgments based on an understanding of the norms of society.

The issue of ethical activity goes beyond the question of legality. The legality of an action depends upon its rightness or wrongness and is based on societal norms. However, ethics extends beyond the legal question and involves the goodness or badness of an act. Therefore, an action may be legally right, but ethically wrong. For example, a small community located fifteen miles from the closest shopping area has a single supermarket. The manager of the supermarket can legally charge any price for his products. This price is usually referred to as "what the traffic will bear." It is the highest price that customers will pay rather than drive fifteen miles to the next supermarket. Morally, what prices should the manager charge? Should the manager charge thirty cents for a can of soup that costs him five cents and sells in the next supermarket for ten cents? What price would *you* charge for the can of soup?

What are the norms of society? Who establishes them? How does the business executive working as a professional manager decide what is ethical or unethical? In part, what is ethical is based on the individual's personal code of behavior. The personal code of behavior is the result of the complex environment that influences one's life. The ethical standards imposed on a manager by his superiors also influence him in his decision as to the morality of his behavior. If the superior condones unethical activities such as padding expense accounts, the subordinate is encouraged to look upon this activity as an acceptable practice.

The policies of the company also influence the determination of ethical conduct. In spite of their personal belief that an act is unethical, numerous managers reply, "Who do I think I am to tell my company what is right or wrong." Standards of behavior in an industry are often influenced greatly by the dominant firms in that industry.

Considerable differences remain among managers as to what they think is ethical or unethical. Business today lacks a code of ethics, and it is questionable whether such a code would improve ethical performance.

In the following articles, an attempt has been made to establish the framework within which business operates. The article by Dow Votaw explains the evolution of power and politics in an evolving corporate society. John Mee defines business objectives and explains the importance of objectives in formulating a management philosophy. Charles Huston, president of Lukens Steel Company, presents his personal experience in developing corporate objectives. Leonard J. Konopa defends the honor of the profit concept in our society. *Business Week* defines the ideological conflict existing regarding the social responsibility of business. James C. Worthy integrates the earlier themes of profit and professional management, showing how these factors within the corporation can foster a balance to protect and serve the public interest. George Fitzpatrick asks the question, "Can good business and good ethics co-exist?" He suggests that if they cannot, it is because top management does not assume an "ethical posture." Willis W. Hagen discusses how business ethics need to be established and clarified to protect management rights.

The Politics of a Changing Corporate Society

DOW VOTAW

Politics is a broad, and perhaps even classical, term for the customs, usages and traditions, for the policies, relationships and arrangements through which men and societies live and are governed and by which men work at shaping their destinies. Partisan politics are a part of this broader term, but not the part with which this paper is primarily concerned.

A hundred years ago, the term "political economy" could have been used to describe the aspects of "politics" which constitute the focus of this article, but that term, unfortunately, has had to be abandoned. Once the economists, the political scientists and the sociologists went their separate ways, "political economy" was left with nothing it could call its own.

This fragmentation has had some unhappy consequences, especially in making it difficult to get an over-all view of our society or of any of its major parts. Some fraternization takes place, of course—in recent years, an increasing amount, but fraternizing is not yet the natural thing to do.

Our knowledge and understanding of the corporate segment of the society have been profoundly influenced by the lack of any interdisciplinary studies of the corporation. We know the corporation reasonably well as an economic institution, and the sociologists are beginning to take an interest in it as a social institution. The political scientists, oddly enough, have largely ignored it.

The result is a rather lopsided and misleading picture of corporate society. The large corporation is certainly one of the dominant features, if not the dom-

Reprinted from the *California Management Review,* Vol. III, No. 3, Spring 1961. Copyright 1961 by the Regents of the University of California.

inant feature, of our society and, as such, cannot be properly appraised or understood in economic terms alone. Only if we have a thorough familiarity with the corporation as a political institution, as well as an economic and social one, can we hope even to recognize the effects that it has had and will have on the rest of society.

The purposes of this paper are to consider the characteristics which the large corporation has in common with other political institutions and to offer some suggestions as to the kinds of issues which are raised when the corporation is examined in a political frame of reference. Before this can be done profitably, however, it will be necessary to review briefly the historical development of our corporate society.

EVOLUTION OF THE CORPORATE SOCIETY

In the year 1553, a group of London merchants financed an exploratory voyage by Sebastian Cabot, the son of John Cabot, for the purpose of opening up trade relations with the Russians through the port of Archangel. When one of the three original vessels returned safely to England with a report that the Russians were receptive, the London merchants obtained from Bloody Mary a royal charter as a corporation "as one bodie and perpetuall fellowship and commaltie" known as the "Russia Company" or, more extensively, as the "Merchant Adventurers of England for the Discovery of Lands, Territories, Isles, Dominions and Seignories, unknown and not before that late adventure or enterprise by sea or navigation commonly frequented."

This was the first English company intended to operate on a joint stock. The charter did not even mention it, but the agreement for the expedition in 1553 had mentioned it, and "joint stock" is the way the company actually operated.

ADAM SMITH DID NOT APPROVE

The next two and one-half centuries witnessed the greatly increased use of the joint stock and the gradual evolution of the legal forms facilitating its employment. Permanent capital, limited liability and legal personality became characteristics of the corporation, but the corporate device played a minimal role in society. Most corporations, both in America or abroad, were public or quasi-public in nature and often, especially in England, were actually arms of the state concerned with foreign exploration or exploitation.

Adam Smith did not approve of corporations and did not believe that they had any future. "The pretence that corporations are necessary for the better government of the trade, is without foundation," he wrote in *The Wealth of Nations*. Even the enactment of the first general incorporation law in Massachusetts in 1809, organization theretofore having been by royal charter or by special act of the legislature, did not for a long time spread the use of the corporate device much beyond the quasi-public areas.

The corporation was ready for its new role, but society and the economy had not yet provided the necessary climate. While the corporation bided its time, society had an opportunity to get used to it in small doses. Our ancestors became accustomed to corporate personality and immortality and to a small, mostly illusory, separation of the ownership of property from its control.

There was plenty of time to adjust to new ideas, and most of these ideas did not seem very important anyway. The building of the railroads, the rapid expansion of the economy and the country after the Civil War, the appearance of national markets and mass production, and the need for vast amounts of capital changed all of that.

Adam Smith was correct; the corporation was not necessary in 1776. But a century later, in America at least, the corporation was necessary. Within a very short period of time, the need, the desire and the technique all came together, and the large business corporation became one of the major landmarks on the American scene.

IMMORTAL AND UNTRAMMELED

The implications of corporate characteristics did not go unnoticed during the early years of the 19th century. Immortality and personality were easily acceptable when possessed by a city or by a university but were something quite different when possessed by a private profit business corporation. Adam Smith was not the only one who saw threats to the liberty and opportunity of the individual businessman or who feared the growth of monopoly.

The draftsmen of the early incorporation laws were afraid of the perpetual and unlimited accumulation of property by the corporation. Perhaps some of these draftsmen remembered their English history and recognized the parallel with Edward I and the statute of Mortmain. Others were concerned about creating non-human persons who, without soul or conscience or morals, could roam the world as they wish, beholden to none and immortal to boot.

Most of the early statutes tried to limit the life of a corporation to 25 or 30 years, to limit the accumulations of capital and property, especially land, and to limit the powers and activities of these organizations. All of these pathetic limitations have been swept away. Corporate life is perpetual; there are no effective statutory limits on accumulations; and the limits on power and activity are remembered now only by legal scholars interested in the quaint old doctrine of ultra vires. Chartermongering and the needs of the economy brought an end to these methods of allaying the fears and suspicions of a century ago.

Interestingly enough, most of the fearful predictions of the 1800's have come to pass, but how different they look today! The highest standard of living in history, the broadest distribution of wealth in the memory of mankind, spectacular achievements in science and in commerce so commonplace we hardly pay any attention to them, and all of these things made possible, to some degree, by a society dominated by large corporations.

Tremendous benefits have softened the consequences that our ancestors predicted for us. Some dangers that our ancestors never dreamed of have also appeared on the scene, and the benefits are not entirely unmitigated, but we have learned new ways of dealing with some of the problems and we have learned that what may have appeared to be an evil result in 1860 may turn out to be a blessing a hundred years later.

For better or for worse, we cannot go backward and we cannot very materially change the course on which we are now embarked. We can seek to discover the implications of what is going on; we can foresee the dangers that are being created and take steps to avoid them. We can and should re-examine the premises on which we base our political decisions and reappraise the goals toward which we are striving.

CORPORATE MYTHOLOGY

Until very recently, we were not doing any of these things. We have been enacting statutes and making decisions with regard to the corporate segment of our society in terms of the fears, the premises and the goals of a hundred years ago. The legislators, the professors and the corporate spokesmen have all been guilty of this intellectual error. We have created a kind of corporate mythology under which we try to explain events we do not understand in terms of things that no longer exist.

Most attacks on the corporation are still based on the 19th century fears. The language used by most critics of the large corporation is straight out of the 19th century: "heartless," "inhuman," "big," "stifles small business," "separates owners and managers," "massive," "monopoly," "without conscience or soul" and many other examples.

Oddly enough, most defenses against these attacks on the corporate system are in the same vernacular and often attempt to take on a rather folksy air. It is difficult in this atmosphere to think clearly about the real problems of our corporate society. The 19th century fears must be forgotten, and the completely individualistic approach to society that condemns every organization beyond the family must be abandoned.

We must accept the large corporation as an important, proper and probably permanent factor in our environment. It is time to re-examine the premises and deal with the situation as it is rather than as it was a hundred years ago.

CORPORATION AS POLITICAL INSTITUTION

If we want to examine wide ranges of the broader politics of a corporate society, and if we want to look objectively at the position of the corporation in our society and eventually give consideration to some of the implications of what we find, our first step is to recognize the large corporation and the corporate system as political institutions and appraise them as such.

What we must be concerned with is the political nature of the large corporation, individually and collectively. The visitor from a small planet would probably not attach much importance to the small corporation in our society, but he would certainly be impressed by the part played in every phase of American life by the large corporation. The dominant feature in our society, in other words, is not the corporate form itself but the adaptations of that form in the very large scale enterprise.

In rough outline, the incorporated corner grocery and General Motors look very much alike, but in the actual use of the corporate form they are farther apart than are the corner grocery of 1960 and its predecessor of a hundred years ago. The use of the corporate form by the large corporation is no more like the use by the corner grocery than the use of crude oil by Standard of California is like its use by an Indian medicine man. There are vast discrepancies between the legal structure of large business corporations and their real structure.

If we go back to our original explanation of the word "politics" in its broad sense, it becomes very easy to see the corporation as a political institution. The corporation is certainly one of the most important relationships or arrangements through which we and our society live and through which we seek to shape our destinies.

Every day in a thousand ways, corporate activity, both individual and aggregate, affects our lives. Price decisions, collective bargaining agreements, market and product decisions, personnel policies, plant locations and relocations, mergers and consolidations will touch almost every segment of our society. A price increase or decrease by General Motors or United States Steel often has more influence on our economy than does a state or federal budget or a change in the rediscount rate by the Federal Reserve.

BIG AND INFLUENTIAL

The influence goes far beyond the strictly economic sector also and may show up in foreign policy, space and rocket research, the internal stability of an African republic, or even American social attitudes and customs.

Every organization, whether it be a church, a social club or a corporation, has an internal political order, and in that sense is a political institution, but the organization becomes of interest to us in our present discussion only if it has wide and profound influence on society as a whole and thus is a political institution externally as well as internally.

A large corporation satisfies this criterion; an industry consisting of a few large corporations satisfies it even more clearly; and an economic system characterized and dominated by large corporations satisfies it most clearly of all. This is not suggesting collusion in any legal sense, but merely pointing out that all large corporations have many inherent characteristics in common and that in the aggregate these characteristics have aggregative effects, some of them so important that in these respects the corporate system is a more important political institution than the government itself.

FATHERED NEW MIDDLE CLASS

Individual income and college enrollment statistics are all the evidence we need of the vast explosion that is now going on in the American middle class. From a small fraction of the population in 1850, the middle classes have grown to a point where they now represent well over one-half the population. The sheer size of the middle class is not as important as the fact that it is still growing very rapidly, especially the intermediate ranges represented by the junior executives, professionals and those in managerial capacities below the policy level. Perhaps a third of our population already falls into this "middle-middle" category.

It is the large national corporation, more than anything else, that has brought about this middle class explosion. The corporation has brought millions of new white collar employees into its ranks and bestowed upon them middle class status. The managerial and technical specialist groups have expanded tremendously and now make up a far larger portion of the working force than they did even 25 years ago.

Other factors have contributed to these changes, but the corporation, as the characteristic institution of our age, has shaped and guided the changes and controls their final form. Some effects of the middle class explosion are only too obvious. Even without the work of Riesman, Lynes, White, Parsons, Spectorsky, Mills, Wilson and many others, we would have recognized many of these effects. We still do not know what they will bring in the long run.

Some of the characteristics of the new middle class are worth noting here because they are fast becoming the characteristics of our changing corporate society. The new middle class is not only large, it is national and transient. The man who once called Springfield "home" is now more likely to live in one indistinguishable suburb after another on his climb up the corporate ladder.

The sense of belonging to a local or regional community rarely has time to develop. There is good evidence that corporate citizenship is replacing local citizenship among large segments of this middle class, with deep ramifications for a democracy built on the assumption of local loyalties.

CORPORATE CITIZENSHIP

The need for the feeling of belonging is strong in all of us, and it is easy to see why, with corporate encouragement, the transient middle class adopts corporate citizenship. David Riesman sees the effects of this already in the loss of political commitment in local, state and federal elections, a commitment which was traditional in the older middle class.

The New middle class is propertyless. With this condition may go the destruction of what has been an integral part of political theory over the last several hundred years. Property provides the little area of freedom where one can say what he believes without being afraid of losing his livelihood. The argument for private property is based in large part on this idea. This is why Jefferson wanted every man to be a property owner.

ROOTLESS AND PROPERTYLESS WORKERS

The vigor and the power of the middle class of the past was due to the fact it was a property owning class. For the individual, corporate citizenship and status may provide a kind of substitute for property, but for a political system created by property owners for property owners on the assumption of widespread property owning, the change may bring unexpected and perhaps unpleasant consequences.

Not all of these characteristics of the new middle class contain danger signals, but all of them do indicate a need for re-examination of our assumptions and basic premises. Our present situation may be much like having unexpectedly fallen heir to a million dollars. We are not going to return the money just because we have a few qualms about the responsibility involved, but if we do not learn to recognize and accept the responsibility, we will not enjoy the benefits of the inheritance and may lose it altogether.

One of the greatest benefits that the modern corporate system has provided, and is now providing more than ever, is that of filling the vacuum left between the much more slowly evolving art known as "statecraft" and the amazing expansion and improvement of technology.

FILLING POLITICAL VACUUM

In an age when no point on earth is more than a few hours, or even a few minutes, from any other point, when the whole world is so closely and irrevocably linked together that even the remotest corners are affected by the acts of Congress, of Standard Oil, or of Lever House, when almost no trade or industry can be confined within existing national boundaries, our past failures and present lack of progress in statecraft are creating new and independent nations along ethnic, cultural, territorial and even tribal lines which have not made sense for a thousand years and which will make nothing but trouble for a thousand more.

Into this incredible vacuum between political frontiers on one hand and the advances of science and commerce on the other has moved the corporation. Our ancestors were worried about corporations roaming the world at will; we are lucky they do.

CORPORATE DIPLOMACY

It has been said recently, and I think accurately, that for the last century, the novel, the brilliant, the daring innovations in the field of politics have come largely from business enterprise. Chief among these innovations has been the adaptation of the corporate technique to penetrate political barriers. The personality of the corporation makes it possible for it to be a citizen of one country while its stockholders and managers are citizens of other countries, and, thus, the corporation can provide the vital link which ties the country of its citizenship to the broader world of commerce and technology.

It becomes an instrument of state without the barriers faced by the political state or its citizens. Just as many of the great English trading companies of three centuries ago were instruments of state to penetrate frontiers, to acquire new lands and to govern them, the modern corporation is such an instrument though without all the overtones of nationalism and conquest.

The old trading companies were English with a capital "E," but the modern corporation is international in character, and some will argue fervently that it is international also in fact, an instrument more of a corporate than of a national state. Throughout the world, the corporation is supplying technology, providing markets, opening up frontiers and tying the world together in a fashion which the political states can only observe in awe.

Occasionally, the policies and activities of the corporate instrument of state conflict with the policies of the political state which has jurisdiction over the corporation, or over one or more of its arms, or over one or more of its human beings.

There is no question but what many large corporations make some foreign policy for the United States. (This is a much broader reference than to the local manufacturer who lobbies a tariff into being.) There is no evidence, however, that these corporate foreign policies are any worse than what the government makes, and there is some evidence that most are better. Usually, the conflicts are serious only in time of war or threatened war, when the choice is obvious. A further danger lies, perhaps, in the possibility that the conflict is not visible.

I think enough has now been said toward establishing the corporation as a political institution. Our next step is to examine the ramifications of this conclusion. If the corporation can properly be examined as a political institution, then the important issues become those which are important in other political institutions: power, legitimacy, accountability, influence, and sanctions, to name a few.

There is no need to look at all of these, but to consider the corporation in the framework of a few of them may be useful. If power is to be possessed and exercised over a period of time, it must be legitimate power, and those who exercise it must be in some way accountable to those whose lives it affects. Most of our discussion will be devoted to a consideration of this simple framework.

CONCENTRATED POWER

I am not going to try to document the concentration of power in the large corporation. The issues with regard to economic power have been well established, and other types of power have received brief comment above. There are heavy concentrations of power in other portions of our society, too, as the government and the labor unions, for example. But the government is circumscribed by constitutions and is more or less responsible to public demand.

Labor union power, while great, is largely a reflection of the corporate power on the other side of the bargaining table and is a relative newcomer to the power elite. Both are also interesting topics, but neither characterizes our modern society the way the great corporation does.

Accepting then the existence of substantial concentrations of power in the corporate system, our first task is to try to establish precisely the location of that power and of those who wield it. The corporate system in this country has gone through several phases of development in this connection, and the location of the power has shifted several times. It may now be in the process of another important shift. As one might expect, the stockholders held the power in the early years when most corporations were small and when the managers and the stockholders were often the same people. Even if they were not the same people, where one person, or a small group of persons, or members of the same family owned a controlling interest in a corporation, they could look upon the property of the corporation as being very little different from their own property and could select and control the managers as they pleased.

The managers simply represented the expressed will of the stockholders. The original corporate device in this country was based on this idea. There are very few large corporations today, Ford and to a limited extent du Pont, where this stockholder control idea provides an accurate picture. Unfortunately, a lot of our thinking about corporations is still based upon this misleading premise.

MANAGERS EXERCISE POWER

As the size of corporations increased and as their shares were more and more widely held, it became impossible, as a practical matter, for large numbers of uninformed stockholders to exercise any real control or influence over the managers or even, in most cases, to choose them. It was inevitable, under these circumstances, that the power should shift to the managers themselves and that the shareholders should become, as a whole, passive.

At annual meeting time, however, the corporation, its managers and shareholders, all participate in a quaint tribal ritual during which shareholders are referred to as "owners," the company as "your company," and the directors as "your directors," but the shareholder must look elsewhere for reassurance during the rest of the year. The managers like this ceremony too, because they still want to feel that their positions and their power are made legitimate on the ground that they represent the will of the stockholders.

Can it not be argued, however, that the managers do represent the stockholders' will most of the time, simply because the stockholders agree with what the managers are doing and that if the stockholders do not agree, they can throw the rascals out? Several recent, notorious and successful proxy fights would seem to suggest an affirmative answer, although in some cases it was difficult to tell which group contained the rascals.

Actually, however, these proxy fights only support the original statement that power in the large corporations rests with the managers. It cost the Robert Young group, which started with 20% of the stock, $1,500,000 to throw out a New York Central management owning only 2% of the stock of a corporation with relatively few (41,000) shareholders.

PROXY FIGHTS INSIGNIFICANT

The proxy fights one reads about in the papers involve struggles for the control of small, or at most, medium-sized corporations. Is there likely to be a proxy fight for control of General Motors, American Telephone or Standard of New Jersey? Practically impossible!

There is considerable additional evidence, from the inside and from the outside, that in many large corporations it is not even the directors in whom the corporate power rests but the officers, who select their own boards of directors, often on the basis of reward for faithful service.

Legitimacy would be a greater problem for the management in this sort of situation. Adolph Berle has called the present phase of corporate power an "automatic self-perpetuating oligarchy." But there is no point in getting too excited about the present phase, because the indications are strong that it is on its way out too.

SHIFT IN POWER AXIS DUE

Just as Henry Ford's Model T transportation eventually revamped America's cultural patterns and redistributed the population, a movement originally unrelated to corporate power may now be signalling the end of the manager's phase. I do not suppose that anyone who participated in the early growth of the pension plans during and after the First World War could have guessed that what he was starting would in less than forty years cover more than a quarter of the entire American working population, amass assets of more than $35 billion, and threaten to make basic changes in the whole economic system.

There is nothing new in personal savings or in a government pension, but the pension funds are new in that they are neither personal savings nor state-controlled funds but are vast aggregations of wealth upon which many have claims of greater or lesser enforceability and which nobody owns. Originally, these funds were looked upon as gifts by employers to their workers in recognition of long and faithful service, and most of them could not be enforced in any way.

More recently, as the unions have included pension plans in their war-induced search for fringe benefits, the arrangements have become more formal, but not as formal, especially in terms of management and enforceability of the plans, as one might suppose. There appears also to be the strong possibility that in the future these funds will be looked upon legally more as compensation than as gifts.

Although many of the early pension plans had no "fund" at all, almost all of the modern plans call for the actual accumulation of funds for the payment of future pensions. A few of the funds are managed by the employers themselves, but most are turned over to banks and other professional trustees under a trust indenture giving the trustee full investment powers.

It is obvious that a pension fund will grow very rapidly during its first years and then tend to level off as the number of claimants reaching retirement age increases and finally stabilizes. Very few of the pension funds in this country are old enough to have reached the leveling-off stage. Most estimates do not see any aggregative leveling until well into the 1970's.

PENSION TRUSTS MAY EVENTUALLY INHERIT CORPORATE POWER

The significance of these funds in terms of corporate power is simply that they are heavy buyers and holders of common stock. Thirty per cent of the value of all new issues of common stock in 1958 was purchased by pension trusts. At present, about 30% of the pension funds' investment is in common stocks, but this figure is increasing. In 1958, 43% of the purchases were in equities.

More significant perhaps is the fact that the funds tend to concentrate on certain high quality common stocks, as would be expected of responsible trustees. In the period 1953-55, almost one-third of all pension fund stock purchases was in only 25 stocks, and 90% in a list of 200 stocks.

All of which means that the holdings are concentrated in relatively few corporations. The pension trusts now hold a total of something like $12 billion in common stock and each year buy as much common stock as all individual buyers combined, and have 10-20 years of growth yet to go. There have been predictions that in 25 years the pension trusts may hold 30% or even larger percentages of all the good equities.

There are other factors which must be taken into account also. The pension trustees are almost all banks or insurance companies who also have vast quantities of additional capital to invest. The place of the institutional investor in the securities markets was cause for considerable wonder even before the pension funds became important. It is estimated that in 1955, 31% of the shares on the New York Stock Exchange were held by institutions, with another 30% held by individuals who do not hold long enough to be a factor in corporate control.

"MY MANAGEMENT, RIGHT OR WRONG"

The last, and in some ways most interesting, factor is that the institutional holders and pension trustees are themselves heavily concentrated, the heaviest concentration being among a handful of New York banks. All of this raises some interesting questions: Can the trustees or other institutional investors fail or refuse to exercise the power they may eventually possess? Can they continue, for example, a rather common policy at present of voting with management in all cases except where there are serious disagreements, in which case the policy is to sell the stock rather than to vote against the management?

What is happening is that the trend toward dispersion of share ownership, the trend that brought about the managers' phase of corporate power, appears to be reversing itself, and it is possible that we will see in the next decade or so a shift of corporate power from the managers to the pension trustees and institutional investors, one degree further removed from ownership in any real sense of the word and much more heavily concentrated.

LEGITIMACY OF POWER

The second issue of importance to an appraisal of political institutions and their power is that of legitimacy, a highly developed field among students of government and of public institutions but only beginning its development in other political institutions. Legitimacy involves the capacity of a political institution or system to create and maintain the belief that existing political institutions are the most appropriate for the society at a particular time.

Many factors are important here: the way the institution came into existence, how the institution has survived a crisis, how it has handled the key issues that have arisen in the society, how the values of the institution conform to the basic values of the society, and others. Social values change with time, and the legitimacy of a political institution may depend on how the institution adapts itself to changing values of society.

SELF-PERPETUATING

The corporate institution in the United States has done a good job on most counts of keeping its legitimacy. It had a close call during the 1930's when it appeared to be failing the crisis test and when it appeared not to be adapting to changes in social values. It rode out that storm and performed remarkably well during the crisis of World War II. A weakness now, on this score, may result from the location of power that we have just been discussing, and a crisis might be required before that can really be put to the test.

The symbol and ritual of shareholder control is important here, as similar symbols are important in maintaining the legitimacy of governmental institutions. It is interesting to note that 10 of the 12 stable European and English-speaking democracies are monarchies, thus preserving a thread of legitimacy for political institutions that in some instances approach the far limits of the welfare state. Yet, the loyalty of conservative and aristocratic elements is held by the thread to the past while the institutions are substantially changed. The French Revolution cut this thread so thoroughly that none of the French Republics has had the loyalty of the conservative, aristocratic or clerical elements, and the result has been the worst sort of instability.

ACCOUNTABLE TO WHOM?

The third issue is that of accountability. The wielder of political power over the society or its members must be accountable in some way to those affected by the power. For much of the power that corporations wield, there is accountability in the market place, but for some of the newer forms of political power, especially that wielded over the individual, accountability, if present at all, is only in its most rudimentary form.

If the industrial system had originated in a political process, there probably would have been a constitution for it, and legitimacy and accountability would have had tangible foundations. Because the corporate system was not the product of political processes, it has no ready-made constitution. Instead, the "constitution" must evolve slowly as the system itself evolves. We are in a transitional stage right now and cannot expect to see a full blown constitution emerge overnight. There are signs that the constitution is taking shape. There may be times when the natural processes are found to be too slow or heading in the wrong direction, and it may become necessary to use the political power of the state to protect the individual. This has already occurred in a few areas.

THE ISSUES

We now turn our attention to a brief examination of some of the issues which the discussion of the changing corporate society has revealed.

Where the power of government is limited by the constitution and by responsibility to the electorate, the limitations on corporate power are more informal in nature, for example: having to obtain funds in the capital market, competition, public opinion, and the overriding political power of the state.

Public opinion is not a very satisfactory limitation because it is very slow to act and because, when it does act, it usually tends to be extreme. The political power of the state can and will be used in emergencies, but, otherwise, when used by itself, is not a very effective instrument for dealing with many of the day-to-day problems arising out of heavy concentrations of corporate power.

The capital market appears not to be the regulator it once was. From 1946 to 1953, 64% of corporate expenditures for capital improvements came from internal sources; in 1958, this figure was 82%.

Competition is still relied on as the chief limitation on corporate power, with important assists from the antitrust laws. However, in the oligopolistic industries dominated by a few giants, competition does not operate in the way one might expect and often becomes more like war or collusion than like a competitive struggle.

TRUST BUSTING FAILED

The antitrust laws have not proved to be effective tools in this connection. "Countervailing power," or the self-regulating effects of competitive power centers, has been suggested as a substitute for the classical forms of competition, but this view does not contain sufficient assurance to society or to individuals to be more than a transitional limitation. In other words, as the nature and extent of the concentration of corporate power have changed, many of the traditional restraints have weakened or disappeared. Are there any restraints in sight with which to fill the gap?

There are a number of possibilities. Let us look at an example or two. The automobile industry is characterized by a very few giants at the manufacturing level and by a very large number of small organizations at the dealer level. The cancellation or failure to renew a dealer franchise can wipe out a large personal investment and a lifetime of hard work, and the dealer is at the mercy of the giant organization from which he purchases his stock in trade.

A dealer whose franchise is revoked or cancelled or not renewed had no review, no appeal, no court action, no nothing. A few years ago, General Motors set up its own review board to hear complaints from dealers who felt they had been unjustly treated. General Motors did not have to set up the board, and there is no guarantee that a dealer will get a fair hearing if he does appeal to the board, but it is something, perhaps a rudimentary beginning for what may become an internal constitutional law.

Rhode Island, a few years ago, set up a public administrative body to review automobile dealers' appeals, and in 1958, Congress passed the Automobile Dealers' Franchise Act permitting a dealer to sue in federal court if he feels he has been aggrieved by the failure of a manufacturer to act in good faith in terminating, cancelling or not renewing a franchise.

CORPORATE CONSTITUTIONAL LAW?

Here we have evidence of the development in and around the corporate system of formal and informal procedure usually characteristic of governmental institutions. It has been argued that this trend will continue and that certain constitutional limitations on power, especially due process, may eventually be applied directly to the great corporations on three grounds: that they are instruments of the state, that they are acting under the requirements of the government, and that they have the economic and political power to invade materially a constitutional right.

The Supreme Court in *Marsh* v. *Alabama,* held a private corporation to constitutional limitations on its public function when the right of free speech was invaded in a company owned town. How much farther is it to the application of the minimum standards of due process where constitutional rights are invaded or threatened? What is or is not a "public function" is only a matter of degree and interpretation.

Or is this the right approach? Do constitutional limitations bring rigidity, and might not this line of reasoning be inconsistent with what has been said about the daring and the innovative in politics having come from business enterprise?

The idea of due process is so deeply rooted in our social conscience as to make it unlikely that due process will be innovated out of existence. The innovation may well be the development of a corporate due process.

SIGNS OF SCHIZOPHRENIA

One thing is clear, however; corporate schizophrenia is rather prevalent in the land, especially among the larger corporations whose managers want to be identified with the private sector of the society yet feel a strong responsibility for education, government, slum clearance, civic welfare, foreign policy and other areas heretofore almost exclusively in the public domain.

Furthermore, it is rather difficult to classify as entirely private an organization whose annual budget is greater than that of most states, whose decisions affect every part of the society, whose employees are numbered in the hundreds of thousands and whose activities abroad may make up an important portion of American relations with other countries.

In which direction does the answer lie? The corporate system now represents one of the greatest concentrations of power, both economic and political, since the beginning of organized society. This power and its exercise have brought many benefits to mankind and will probably bring many more, but power also brings problems of control, of responsibility, and of human rights.

Our constitutional system implies that the conscience of the state cannot be relied on when it comes to the exercise of power affecting the rights of individuals.

Can we rely any more safely on the corporate conscience in the matter of power affecting individuals and other parts of society?

I believe that the answer lies in improving the art of statecraft to the point where it reflects our progress in technology and commerce and where it can cope with the unique and rapidly changing issues of modern society.

In the meantime, however, we must rely on the traditional limitations, especially those of the market place, and most important, must keep ourselves aware of the changes taking place and of the ramifications of those changes. This is not an easy task. History is not history when it is being made, and it takes a great deal of ingenuity and objectivity to be able to appraise one's own time and decide how best to assure a good life for those to come.

QUESTIONS

1. What is meant by the term *politics?*

2. Compare the current attitudes toward corporations with the attitudes toward business companies one hundred, two hundred, and three hundred years ago.

3. In what ways are corporations seen as political institutions?

4. What is the extent of corporate power? What is meant by legitimacy of power?

5. Discuss the similarities between corporations and political institutions.

Management Philosophy
for Professional Executives

JOHN F. MEE

Interest in management philosophy and practice has steadily increased during the present century. Since World War II, students of business and public administration have joined efforts with administrators in business and government to formulate an acceptable philosophy of management as a guide both for modern management practice and for the education of those who aspire to a career in the field.

From *Business Horizons*, December 1956, pp. 5-7. Reprinted by permission of Indiana University.

Professor Ralph C. Davis[1] offers the following comment concerning the problems of management philosophy.

> *The problem of greatest importance in the field of management is and probably will continue to be the further development of the philosophy of management. A philosophy is a system of thought. It is based on some orderly, logical statements of objectives, principles, policies and general methods of approach to the solution of some set of problems . . . .*
>
> *Business objectives involve the public interest as well as the interests of customers, dealers, bankers, owners and employees. They affect everyone in an industrial economy. A managerial philosophy cannot supply a basis of effective thinking for the solution of business problems, if it is satisfactory only to owners and employees. A managerial philosophy that is commonly accepted is a requisite for a common scale of values in an economy. It is necessary, therefore, for unity of thought and action in the accomplishment of economic objectives. We cannot have an effective industrial economy without effective industrial leadership. We cannot have an effective leadership without a sound managerial philosophy.*
>
> *Industrial leaders without such a philosophy are business mechanics rather than professional executives. . . .* [2]

The main reasons for the continued interest in management philosophy among educators, public administrators, and progressive businessmen are:

1. The increasing trend toward decentralization of operating responsibilities and decision-making in business and governmental organizations.

2. The increasing numbers of professional executives required in business and government for growth and decentralization of operations.

3. The necessity for a logical framework of management philosophy and practice as a basis for training in executive-development programs and college curricula.

OBJECTIVES

In current thinking and writing, the starting point for either a philosophy or the practice of management seems to center around predetermined objectives. The entire management process concerns itself with ways and means to realize predetermined results and with the intelligent use of people whose efforts must be properly motivated and guided. Objectives may be general or specific; they may concern the organization as a whole, a segment of it within a decentralized unit, or even a particular function such as production, sales, or personnel.

---

[1] Dr. R. C. Davis is Professor of Management at The Ohio State University.

[2] "Research in Management During the '50s," in Arthur E. Warner, ed., *Research Needs in Business During the '50s* (Indiana Business Report No. 13; Bloomington: School of Business, Indiana University, 1950), p. 32.

What are or should be the objectives of management in our industrial economy? A study of current management literature and the published objectives of business firms provide some revealing and interesting concepts from recognized authorities. Here are some selected statements:

> *The goal of the organization must be this—to make a better and better product to be sold at a lower and lower price. Profit cannot be the goal. Profit must be a by-product. This is a state of mind and a philosophy. Actually an organization doing this job as it can be done will make large profits which must be properly divided between user, worker, and stockholder. This takes ability and character.*[3]
>
> *If we were to isolate the one factor, above all others, that transformed the tiny company of 1902 into the industrial giant of 1952, while hundreds of competitors failed and are forgotten, I should say that it has been Texaco's settled policy of thinking first of quality of product and service to the customer, and only second to the size of its profit. To some of you, this may sound somewhat trite. But it is the starkest kind of business realism. In a highly competitive industry such as ours, the highest rewards are reserved for those who render the greatest service.*[4]
>
> *To make and sell quality products competitively and to perform those functions at the lowest attainable cost consistent with sound management policies, so as to return an adequate profit after taxes for services rendered. As a corollary objective, the corporation must be the low-cost producer of the product it offers for sale. (United States Steel Corporation statement of general company objectives.)*
>
> *The mission of the business organization is to acquire, produce and distribute certain values. The business objective, therefore, is the starting point for business thinking. The primary objectives of a business organization are always those economic values with which we serve the customer. The principle objective of a businessman, naturally, is a profit. And a profit is merely an academic consideration, nevertheless, until we get the customer's dollar.*[5]

Numerous further examples of published and stated objectives of modern business management could be presented. However, all of them could be summarized with the conclusion that: (1) *Profit* is the motivating force for managers. (2) *Service* to customers by the provision of desired economic values (goods and services) justifies the existence of the business. (3) *Social responsibilities* do exist for managers in accordance with ethical and moral codes established by the

---

[3] James F. Lincoln, *Intelligent Selfishness and Manufacturing* (Bulletin 434; New York: Lincoln Electric Co.).

[4] Harry T. Klein, *The Way Ahead* (New York: The Texas Co., 1952), p. 14.

[5] Ralph C. Davis, "What the Staff Function Actually Is," *Advanced Management,* XIX (May, 1954), p. 13.

society in which the industry resides. The economic values with which customers are served include increased values at lower costs through innovation and creativity over a period time.

In formulating and developing a modern management philosophy for successful practice, a combination of the above objectives in the correct proportion is required. Every decentralized organization unit and essential function must contribute to the realization of the general objectives by attaining the organizational, functional, and operational objectives. Unless predetermined objectives are set and accepted, little or no basis exists for measuring the success and effectiveness of those who perform the management functions.

The importance of predetermining the objectives desired has resulted in the formulation of the management principle of the objective. This principle may be stated as follows: Before initiating any course of action, the objectives in view must be clearly determined, understood, and stated.

QUESTIONS

1. Why has interest in management philosophy increased so rapidly?

2. Why are objectives so vital in formulating a managerial philosophy?

3. Explain why profit and service objectives are so closely related.

Setting Corporate Objectives

CHARLES L. HUSTON, JR.

In any progressive company, many ideas are generated for corporate improvement throughout the firm which find their way into marketing, plant facility method and procedure, and personnel improvements. In the flow of these ideas some years ago in our company, one such suggestion was directed to me as president: "What are our corporate objectives?"

Maybe you can imagine your reaction to such a question within the area of your responsibility. Frankly, I was startled.

Surely, I thought, corporate objectives had been dealt with over the years

From *Dun's Review*, (October, 1962, pages 62-63, 122, 124, 126.) Reprinted by permission.

through meetings, speeches and letters. It did not take me long to realize, however, that there really was no adequate but concise statement of objectives readily available for use as reference and for review for change as necessary.

Our company, in the same fashion as many others, had its annual financial forecasts and budgets, its long- and short-term goals for attractive markets, its long-term plans for capital expenditures and its personnel and executive development programs looking to the future.

In these are involved the important questions requiring constant and careful consideration by general management: Where is the company going? How does it propose to get there? In the light of worldwide and local, political and competitive developments, should the direction of the company's path be altered? If the conclusion is reached that the direction should be altered, how should the change be accomplished?

Sound answers to all of these questions require comprehensive and reliable information and judgment, supported by an innate sensing and awareness. First, however, the enterprise needs pertinent aims or goals in order to set its course and realistically check its progress.

Somehow, in our case, it was simply assumed that these aims or goals—the corporative objectives—were common knowledge. So in line with our policy and practice of delegation, I asked my senior associates to come up with a tangible statement of objectives. Shortly, however, it was evident that the starting job was in my lap.

There followed laborious hours of searching and evaluation to develop a few down-to-earth fundamentals which resulted in the bedrock objectives. The first of these bedrock objectives is to promote reasonable and improving corporate earnings through productive effort applied primarily, but not limited to, the manufacture and sale of our existing products. The second is to conduct the business as a constructive and honorable corporate citizen in its relations—designed to be mutually profitable—with shareowners, employees, customers, suppliers, community and government.

In considering these objectives, there are two important philosophies influencing the conduct of business. One is the emphasis on "profit motive." The other is emphasis on "good relations" based on mutual profitability. I believe these to be fundamental to the long-term success of any business.

The bedrock objectives are only the first step. To make them effective, more detailed basic objectives are needed for each of the company's organizations plus the indicated means to accomplish them.

THE SECOND STEP

Thus was evolved Step Two, the administrative organization objectives. Here we start with objective "A"—to establish and periodically re-evaluate the following broad basic objectives for corporate guidance:

☐ To plan, direct and coordinate the various company organizations, programs and activities for comprehensive balanced accomplishment.

☐ To secure a reasonable return on company investments in markets, plant facilities, products and manpower.

☐ To build good, mutually profitable relations with all who help make the company a constructive and successful enterprise.

These we thought sufficient as broad guidelines by which to direct a future course: they highlighted the things we generally considered to insure progressive improvement. But we also felt that we needed to go further and cover the basic objectives in the area of people. This became administrative objective "B"—to develop and maintain sound, clearly understood organization structure and personnel designed to meet the needs of the business.

Essentially, Objective B has to do with developing and maintaining the right organization and personnel to meet the needs of business now and in the future. As a company progresses and the nature of its business changes, the organization structure must change too.

To provide for these changes, a separate department in the industrial relations department studies organization structure constantly, both within and without the company. It assists in the setting up of new units as well as in the periodic appraisal of established ones. For example,

☐ For the proper placement of qualified personnel, there must be a constant effort to learn more clearly the comprehensive requirements of a given job, and then to fill the position with the man or woman who shows the promise of giving a better than average performance.

☐ Setting the climate for cooperation occurs when a business relationship promises to be mutually profitable and is clearly understood. "Objective evaluation" and "communication" are the tools to produce the cooperative climate.

☐ With realization that salesmindedness expands as communications improve, there must be a positive effort to broaden the knowledge of people throughout the company on relationship with customers.

☐ The implementation of health and safety requires a comprehensive program that starts with and is a part of the engineering and planning stage for equipment and processes. It continues through individual indoctrination and day-to-day supervisory-employee relationships supported by educational and promotional media. In my own experience, a lost-time accident reduction program begins to be really effective only when top-level management evidences sincere determination for results and participates itself in carrying out the effort.

With the bedrock and administrative objectives put together, it is now up to the organization heads to come up with their objectives and the means of accomplishing them.

HOW TO DO IT

The results outlined here are, of course, applicable to the operations of a particular company, but I believe they are equally adaptable in setting the corporate objectives in almost any field. Sales and marketing, for instance, aim "to set sales and marketing objectives, within broad corporate aims, for improvement of company earnings and acceptance." This is a three-way approach, which begins with the development of new markets and new products. We believe that the best way to do this is to recognize the unmet needs of our customers and the industries they serve.

The field sales force in its daily contact with customers, obviously, can provide the primary means of transmitting those needs to us. In addition, marketing, engineering and service personnel who travel frequently also help to sense out interesting market needs and at times furnish the motivation for new and improved products.

The second approach is to sell company products and services at prices which will yield a reasonable and improving return over costs. As every corporate executive well knows, this goal is becoming more and more of a challenge.

Comprehensive sales standards and controls to guide the field sales force in improved efficiency are among the ways to minimize sales costs, insure adequate attention to prospective purchasers and focus a critical light upon various expenses. Increasingly keen competition among both home and foreign suppliers, the never-ending upward movement of direct and indirect labor costs and the higher prices for goods and services highlight the extreme importance of making progress toward fulfillment of these objectives.

The third sales approach is to help customers develop and service their own markets to the benefit of the company. In an operation in which a great number of existing products reach end-use markets only after fabrication and assembly by customers, to the extent that a portion of merchandising effort is directed to the customer's customer, the customer himself is tied closer to the company as a source of supply.

IMPROVING OPERATIONS

In the operating organization, the mission is to set objectives for improvement of business. To accomplish this, detailed standards and controls must be developed to improve the quality of products, reduce the costs of their manufacture and provide added insurance for on-time deliveries to customers.

As a case in point, a medium-sized producer, in competition with larger companies which offer a greater variety of products, develops ready acceptance of its products and services only to the extent that it can be counted upon for superior quality, service and delivery.

The use of expanded statistical quality controls helps indicate where method changes can be made, resulting in improved quality. Of course, it can result in decreased costs, too. Thus it is a means of accomplishing another operating objective—to strive for both major and minor economies in operations and procedures, for increased savings and improved earnings.

Specific cost-reduction goals for each operating department, the application of engineering to methods and procedures, new or improved operating facilities and the wider use of incentives are additional aids to the development of economies.

A third operating objective is to undertake developments that promise new and improved products, together with appropriate facilities for their manufacture. To this end, contributing ideas must be cultivated from sales representatives, outside consultants, customer contacts, and from the company's own research and engineering departments. An internal suggestion system, properly encouraged and promoted, can produce a promising number of improvement recommendations.

Moving from operations to finance, the controller's aim is to set objectives for adequate record and control of costs, a basic goal which is certainly nothing spectacular or unusual. Yet a company's management depends on the effective attainment of this goal to know where it has been and where it is going.

Periodically, inventory must be taken of how efficient an organization has been, either by a self-audit or with the assistance of competent consulting firms. A year's exhaustive review and appraisal by an outside firm, for instance, comparing the controller's organization against the standard of the most modern practices appropriate to the company's operations, can result in innumerable steps to implement the department's corporate objectives more effectively.

To cite our own example, budgeting has been raised to full department status, and a systems and procedures department has been established to search out and develop economies in office work and procedures throughout the company. Profit goals are assigned on the assets used in the business, and management responsibility for income, cost and profit now are defined more clearly. Recognizing that the controller's organization is essentially a service unit, research has been undertaken on the most effective method of presenting financial information.

In the industrial relations organization, a major category in the objective for the most effective development and application of human resources is to stimulate recognition of every employee as an individual. The recognition involves the employee's dignity, his status and service in the organization and his contribution to the success of the enterprise.

The breakdown of organizational objectives includes those of purchasing, which must maintain a continuity of satisfactory supply with a minimum of investment; the secretary's office, which is the company's memory, watchdog, family ambassador and a sort of philanthropist; and the treasurer's department. All of them hinge on the bedrock objectives and on the two important philosophies I mentioned earlier—the emphasis on profit motive and on good relations based on mutual profitability.

A MATTER OF RECORD

Are such objectives really meaningful, or are they fine-sounding words that, having been agreed upon, are set aside to gather dust? I will have to admit that in my own organization, enthusiasm for the objectives was less than intense at the time of their inception. But interest grew with exposure. Before long the organizational heads asked the managers of their respective divisions to draw up divisional objectives.

Finally, all the objectives—bedrock, organization and division—were printed in one book for management distribution and information. Today reference to objectives at all levels is the norm rather than the exception. They provide continuity of planning, programming and operation.

The bedrock objectives—and all the objectives stemming from them—are a constant reminder that the company's various publics have a right to hold the company accountable in the areas where it has elected to go on record.

QUESTIONS

1. What are "bedrock" objectives?

2. Explain the relationships that exist among the different levels of objectives.

Is Profit a Dirty Word?

LEONARD J. KONOPA

A full-page magazine advertisement shows the caricature of an individual surreptitiously drawing a dollar sign on a board fence and beneath it appears the question: *Is profit a dirty word?* The ad has been run nationally several times by Marsteller, Inc. In the same vein, Bradford B. Smith, U.S. Steel Corp. economist, gave a speech in which he said in part, "I read recently that 'profit' has now become a dirty word. The assault on the profit and loss system has been embroidered by such slogans and phrases as 'production for use and not for profit,' 'controlled economy,' and so on."

A cursory search of recent business publications unearthed a score of articles by various executives defining profit as the *sine qua non* of our economic system. Is this defense of profit really necessary? Is the public ill informed about profit?

THE MAJORITY OPINION

Evidently so, according to Opinion Research Corp., which says their surveys show more than half of the American voting public are of the opinion that profits result from exploitation. Walter Barlow, president of Opinion Research Corp., further reports ". . . a continuing survey indicates an inching year by year toward a belief that Government should control the profits of large corporations. In 1961 there were 43% of those scientifically polled who wanted 'a great deal' or 'a fair amount' of such control. Amazingly enough, this included 28% of those earning over $15,000 a year, 35% of the stockholders, and 37% of the professional men and managers."

In 1960 the Lamp Division of General Electric ran a survey in which a 10%

From *Banking,* Journal of The American Bankers Association, April 1964, pp. 112, 114, 116, 118. Reprinted by permission.

sample of its employees were asked: "Of each dollar GE took in this year, what is your guess as to how much the company made as profit after costs and taxes?" The average estimate of net profit after tax was 22 cents on each sales dollar whereas the actual profit was 6 cents. This survey is not atypical. Others show similar results with many people estimating profits as high as 25% to 50% of sales.

BUSINESSMEN TO BLAME

Businessmen, unfortunately, have contributed to this erroneous estimate by playing down their profits or referring to them in an apologetic tone. The attitude of "the less said about profit the better" stems from management's belief that a discussion of profits encourages employees to demand more wages, customers to ask for lower prices, and the Government to increase taxes or control over business.

Management's attempt to obscure its profit, however, has not had any salutory effects nor has it forestalled any of these groups. Union negotiators continue to unearth the profit figures of successful companies and treat them as justification for higher wages as well as a readily available source. Whether profits are adequate or inadequate, consumers still are chagrined whenever the price of a product goes up. Finally, the Government's intervention in the price increase proposed by U.S. Steel in 1962 provides ample evidence that an apologetic attitude about profits has hindered and hurt industry more than it has helped. As a matter of fact, this latter experience is primarily responsible for management's change of heart and its desire to discuss profit with the public.

Now that management is willing to discuss profit, how are they going about the task of enlightening the public? The first step in the process is a careful explanation of the true nature of profit.

THE BASIC FACTS

Only when a company successfully sells its products at a higher price than it spends or allots for such things as raw materials, labor, light, heat, power, interest, depreciation, and real estate or use taxes does it have a profit. If it is unsuccessful in any given year, it has a loss. Companies that are consistently unsuccessful eventually die.

Once the public is apprised of the true nature of profit, the next step is an analysis of its functions or role in our economy. That is, having seen what profit is, the emphasis shifts to seeing what profit does. Rather than discuss all of its functions, only its role in (1) allocating resources, (2) providing jobs, and (3) supplying tax revenue are covered here.

BASIC FUNCTIONS

(1) *Allocation of resources.* Profit is the indispensable ingredient that makes our economic system operate. In the attempt to earn profit, entrepreneurs allocate

resources in such a way as to maximize utility and provide consumers with the most favorable mix of goods and services. When an entrepreneur accurately anticipates future needs, he is rewarded with an economic profit. Should he misinterpret these needs, he sustains an economic loss. Resorting to another analogy, we find that money is the lubricant keeping the inputs and outputs flowing smoothly in our economic machine while profit is the control mechanism that regulates these inputs and outputs.

(2) *Profit provides jobs.* It does this in at least five different ways. If prospects of deriving a profit are good, then production and employment increase. When the outlook for profit from new investment is favorable, gross national product and total employment react accordingly as new investment is injected into the economy in the form of new businesses, new plants, and additions to existing facilities. It is through profits that enormous sums are secured and spent annually to replace worn out or obsolete equipment and insure jobs for the future. Profits also supply the additional sums that must be obtained to provide the necessary equipment for those entering the labor force. Finally, research and development funds come from profits and are the seed corn that provide new products and ultimately new jobs.

DOUBLE-EDGED WEAPON

Actually, profit affects jobs in two different ways. First of all, it supplies the incentive to invest substantial sums in new products, plants, or equipment when the return (actual or anticipated) is attractive. Secondly, funds to finance such investments are derived in part from profit. Profit, therefore, is like a double-edged weapon. One edge may be labeled "incentive" and the other "funds for reinvestment."

With respect to incentive, historical data suggest that incentive to invest is strongest when corporate profits (after tax) run 8% or more on invested capital. Because many corporations retain 40% to 50% of their after-tax profit, the actual dividend return to stockholders may total only 4% or 5% on their invested capital. The yield on many long-term minimum risk bonds is approximately 4% at this time. With such attractive low risk alternative investment opportunities available, incentive to invest in new plant and equipment is lacking unless there is some intimation net profit will total 8% or more.

Turning to profit as a source of funds for reinvestment, we find profits are reinvested in two ways. As suggested above, one method is to withhold part of the after-tax earnings instead of paying them out as dividends. This is the "captive" method. Estimates show retained profit accounted for $82-billion worth of new investment in plants and equipment this past decade. Stockholders ordinarily forego these sums on the premise that their abstinence will not only enhance their opportunity of earning larger dividends in the future, but also increase the value of their investment.

The second method of reinvesting profit is indirect and occurs when some of the dividend expenditures are "recaptured" by issuing additional stock.

Just how important the task of providing new funds has become is shown by a recent publication of the U.S. Department of Commerce, *Investing in Jobs.*

Estimates based on limited data indicate that the minimum amount needed to provide jobs for 10,000,000 new workers during the decade is $163-billion. If the cost of capital were to rise another one-third by 1970, at least $200-billion would be required.

Inflation, of course, also affects the cost of replacing equipment. When amounts allotted to depreciation for this purpose are insufficient because of inflation as well as the higher price of more sophisticated replacement equipment, industry must secure additional outside capital or use some of its profit to make up the deficiency.

Totaling the funds needed to provide equipment for new job holders as well as to replace machinery which is currently obsolescent or will become obsolescent, a figure ranging from $330- to $380-billion is derived depending on how well the nation arrests inflation.

Because there are few industries in which one can manufacture an identical product indefinitely, expenditures for product improvement, research and development are mandatory. Industry supplied $2.24-billion for research and development in 1953-54. By 1960-61 the sum had doubled to $4.49-billion. During the 8-year period, 1953-60, a research and development fund totaling nearly $26-billion was provided by industry. Once again, it is obvious that some of this money came from profit.

In a sense, research and development expenditures are similar to buying insurance. Companies are spending these sums to improve their chances of producing desirable products economically. If successful, they survive and thereby continue to provide employment.

A REAL TAX PLUM

(3) Profit also provides tax revenue. Perhaps the Federal, state, and local governments should finance an extensive campaign emphasizing the desirability of corporate profit since corporations supply nearly one-third of their revenue. In 1961, for instance, corporations paid approximately $42-billion in various forms of Federal and state taxes. Interestingly, this is almost twice the amount of net corporate profits after tax.

Just where the incidence of corporate income tax rests is difficult to determine. Although some economists argue that it is passed on either to consumers in higher prices or to labor in lower wages, especially in the long run, others disagree. It is evident, though, that there is a direct relationship between the degree of business prosperity and governmental tax receipts.

As we have seen, profits are essential to our economy; but there are many responsible citizens who are embarrassed by profit, apologize for it, or believe it should be closely regulated (even abolished in some instances) by the Government. To overcome the enigma of the need for profit but opposition to profit, an economic education campaign is being waged.

All forms of media and avenues of communication are utilized to convince the public of the desirability of profit. In the past, executives often gave speeches on the role of profit to management groups which already appreciated its function. Rather than "talking to each other," they are now cultivating opportunities to address various professional groups, women's organizations, fraternal associations, high school assemblies, and PTA meetings.

Advertisements such as "Is Profit a Dirty Word?" or "Profit? Who Needs It?" are a part of this campaign. Upon occasion, sponsors of radio and TV programs promote profit instead of their particular products. Annual reports also make excellent vehicles.

The techniques adopted to explain and create a favorable image for profit vary widely. Among the more successful ones are such practices as:

(1) Putting price tags on new equipment and showing how profit helped buy it. The story is carried in the company's publications and local media as well.

(2) Dramatizing the large amount of capital investment needed for each job. This is done occasionally by posting jobs or running ads for a skilled operator at $5 an hour. To secure employment, he must furnish his personal machine costing $20,000 or more.

(3) Showing that two of every five employees are working on products created since World War II from research funds provided by profit.

(4) Having facsimiles of checks inserted in annual reports. Sums representing cost of labor, supplies, income taxes, social security, and so forth are torn out as these items are discussed with employees and stockholders.

(5) Giving the names of retired employees, widows, children, or institutions who are stockholders in the company, thus helping to dispel the belief "profit is for the few" or "all profit goes to bloated capitalists living off the sweat of labor." The technique used in emphasizing the fact there are approximately 15,000,000 stockholders varies, but the theme itself is very popular.

(6) Publicizing business failures to illustrate the significance of profit to employees, stockholders, dealers, and suppliers.

These are but a few of the approaches developed to visualize the significance of profit. The outspoken advocates of profit are increasing, but it is neither an easy nor a popular project. Many people, moreover, will never be reached, while others will still regard profit as distasteful. If this latter group prefers to alter our economic system, they should have the fortitude to do so overtly rather than by subtly taxing away profit or eroding management's control through various laws which seem innocuous in themselves, but are devastating as a whole.

Profit is not a dirty word unless we make it so through ignorance, indifference, or inertia.

QUESTIONS

1. Why is the defense of profit necessary in our society?

2. What are the basic functions of profit?

3. How does profit affect the availability of jobs?

4. What techniques can be used to create a favorable image of profit?

The Ideological Debate Dividing Businessmen

Kremlinologists are accustomed to periodic outbursts over Communist ideology. As theoretical or abstruse as these debates sound to those unschooled in Marxist-Leninist lingo, they usually reflect—and sometimes foreshadow—major historical developments.

Thus, the debates between Stalinism and Trotskyism of the 1920s were essentially about whether Communism should settle down to grow within Russia's borders or keep pushing for external expansion; Stalin's settle-down line won—until World War II opened fresh opportunities for expansion. The current debate between Khrushchev's peaceful co-existence policy and Mao's militant anti-Western line is, in effect, a modern replay of the Stalin-Trotsky debate.

WESTERN APPROACH

By comparison, debates among capitalists over their ideology seem mild—and are often neglected as tiresome academic exercises with little or no real-world significance.

Yet it suddenly is becoming apparent that an ideological controversy that in recent years has been agitating professors and the more articulate businessmen (and their still more articulate speech writers) is no mere semantic tempest in a teapot, but reflects a central political, economic, and business issue of our time: Whether business is going to settle down to live in the mixed economy, cooperating with big government and big labor, or is going to reverse this trend and do battle to regain greater independence from government control or labor interference.

TWO SCHOOLS

On the ideological level, the debate has taken the form of an argument between proponents of the traditional "free enterprise" creed and the more recent "social responsibilities" creed. Although millions of words have flowed on this issue in scholarly and business journals, company advertisements, university lecture halls, and even some board rooms, a new book—The Business Establishment, edited by Prof. Earl F. Cheit of the University of California (John Wiley & Sons) —sharply reveals much of the sense and nonsense in this windy debate.

The book grew out of a symposium staged earlier this year at the Berkeley campus. Its participants included a number of distinguished American and European scholars, none flagrantly hostile to business, but all hypersensitive to the sham, empty cliches, evasions, and false rationalizations that in the past have typified efforts to develop a business creed. The issue between the two main business creeds boils down to this:

☐ The free-enterprise creed holds that the aim of business is and should be to maximize profits. In the words of a 1926 disciple, quoted by economist Robert L. Heilbroner: "It is inconceivable to a 100% American that anyone except a nut should give something for nothing." Put more politely—as it is by such contemporary economists as the University of Chicago's Milton Friedman, an adviser to Sen. Barry Goldwater—this creed maintains that the pursuit of self-interest, i.e., maximum profits, is today—as in Adam Smith's day—the only logical or efficient way to run a business. Likewise, it is the only way to preserve a free and economically progressive society.

☐ The social-responsibility creed, by contrast, holds that this free-enterprise, maximum-profit philosophy is an anachronism. It made more sense in the old days of smaller companies, something closer to free competition, and foolish, tyrannical kings; it makes little sense in today's society where huge corporations play not only a vital economic role, but also an important political and social role. These corporations cannot avoid having a major and conspicuous impact on society, which society will either approve or disapprove, permit or prevent.

Hence, proponents of this creed hold that if business wants to retain its autonomy it must be prepared to assume certain social responsibilities, not just go after the maximum profit. Holders of this view constitute the liberal wing of business ideologists. Although, like other big businessmen, they mostly are Republicans, many champions of this view today are among the businessmen for Pres. Johnson.

LITTLE LOVE

However, liberal scholars contemplating the business spokesmen of the social-responsibilities creed do not necessarily regard them with fraternal love and charity. Heilbroner, for example, dissects the speeches of some businessmen holding to the social-responsibilities line and declares they are offering a "more or less transparent defense of privilege masquerading as philosophy, the search for sanction cloaked as a search for truth, the little evasions and whitewashings that cheapen what purports to be a fearless confrontation of great issues."

Critics of the new business liberalism apparently regard the social-responsibility ideology as essentially a device for rationalizing and retaining the autonomy of business managers from control by government.

TOO EXTREME

Cheit suggests that skeptics like Heilbroner go much too far. He uses statistical evidence to cast doubt on the commonly held assumption (first promulgated by lawyer Adolph A. Berle and economist Gardiner Means in 1932) that there has been vast separation between corporate ownership and control. Managers are not fearful of the "legitimacy" of their control through ownership, says Cheit, nor are they afraid they do not command public acceptance. Yet heavier demands are being made upon management to meet social obligations—in fields ranging from race relations, to wage and price policy, to international trade and investment.

Sensitive managements of large corporations, he suggests, know well that in daily affairs they confront—and even create—a wide range of complex issues, solutions to which require managerial freedom. They realize that when that freedom is abused, society will intervene, as it has in the past in labor and financial matters.

HANDS OFF

Still it's better, Cheit suggests, if society doesn't have to intervene. He notes that J. Kenneth Galbraith, as ambassador to India, urged developing nations to resist the temptation to interfere with corporate autonomy, and that not only Germany and Britain, but even Russia have been adjusting their national ideologies to permit wider degrees of corporate independence.

Cheit sees the new Gospel of Social Responsibility as a basically conservative business response to a changing environment. Just as England's aristocrats during the rise of capitalism retained their dominant social position by marrying the daughters of wealthy merchants, he sees smart managers of big companies today marrying big government and labor, and thus keeping control over the system.

LILLIPUTIANS

Paul A. Samuelson of Massachusetts Institute of Technology isn't sure big business sees it that way. "Business is allegedly in the saddle," he says, "although that isn't how I hear it down at the Union League Club." Samuelson suggests that big business is constantly on the defensive because it knows it lacks political power, even compared to the masses of small businessmen.

"Big outfits are less able to break the law and resist the social pressures of democracy," says Samuelson. "The family farmer can and will cheat where the vast corporate farmer will not. Altruism is a scarce good, and corporations may help society economize on its use."

FADED AFFAIR

In the view of Columbia University's distinguished historian Richard Hofstadter, trustbusting has become a "faded passion of American reform." This ho-hum attitude toward public control of monopoly seems to some observers to make it all the more necessary for business to assume a sense of social responsibility. Thus, Cheit insists that we should welcome the Gospel of Social Responsibility, because "at a minimum, it has replaced the free-enterprise campaign with a new cliche, and depending on our response to it, may provide the basis for a more flexible use of private enterprise in our mixed economy."

FROM ABROAD

Two European scholars present at the California symposium—Philippe de Woot and Gilbert M. Sauvage—seconded Cheit's motion. De Woot noted that, although he found the U. S. ahead in the field of individual opportunity and achievement, he felt the Europeans were putting greater stress on organizing a good society. "We have received so much from you," he said, "that you must understand that we are longing for the time when we will be able to show our gratitude in some concrete way."

In particular, Sauvage suggested that his French countrymen could teach U. S. businessmen something through their experiment in economic planning. The Plan, he said, shouldn't frighten U. S. businessmen; it eliminates much risk and uncertainty and makes French businessmen bolder. Then, he said, social responsibility is effectively married to profit. He quotes a French economist as saying that "the Monnet plan was designed to limit the economic freedom of the entrepreneur and, if necessary, to increase it."

EASY NOW

However, such talk is still too rich for the blood of even the most ardent American champions of the social-responsibility school. They retain a wariness of government controls that draws them much closer to their free-enterprise colleagues in the U. S. than to the business planners of France. When in France, however, the American businessmen think like the French. "At home," said one, "we think about autonomy. Over here we look for influence."

Still, in the U. S. the split between the social-responsibility school and the free-enterprisers is all too real. Some businessmen fear, as does Robert Heilbroner, that if the free-enterprise ideology were to prevail, business and the economy would suffer a "serious inability to cope with reality." Champions of the free-enterprise ideology, however, still agree with Prof. F. A. Hayek that temporizing with the enemy and abandoning the classic market freedoms inevitably is "the road to serfdom."

THE BATTLE LINES

Thus the issue seems clearly drawn—but politics and demands for salesmanship muddy the waters. Author George Lichtheim notes that in the most backward countries, the answer to how to sell capitalism to the masses is obviously "by calling it socialism."

And in our own country? Says Prof. Cheit: "By calling it social responsibility."

QUESTIONS

1. What is the free-enterprise creed?

2. What is the social-responsibility creed?

3. Where does the government fit in between these two creeds?

Business and the Good Society

JAMES C. WORTHY

What is presented here is not a balanced thesis, but a series of notes on certain characteristics of business life. These notes are not intended to be argumentative but are to provide a framework for discussing the role of the businessman in our society, and the kinds of ethical and moral problems with which he must deal.

THE ROLE OF PROFIT IN THE MODERN CORPORATION

Any adequate understanding of the role and problems of the businessman today must take into account the rise of the large, publicly-owned corporation. Big business is not merely small business writ large; it is a new order of being and cannot be intelligently explained by concepts drawn from the experience of a small enterprise economy. Two points in particular require attention: the drastic modification of the role of profit and the emergence of professional management.

The greater part of economic activity today is carried on by corporations rather than by a large number of individual entrepreneurs. Five hundred corporations in the manufacturing and extractive industries, for example, employ 48 percent of all workers in those industries. Ours is a large-business economy, not only in terms of the share of the total economy accounted for by big business, but in terms of the influence of big business in all phases of our economic life. The large enterprise is the prototype, the representative institution of the economy today.

One of the most significant consequences of this development is the separation of ownership from control in the affairs of enterprise. Owners, i.e., stock-

From *The Christian in Business,* ed. Andrew J. Buehner, copyright 1966, pp. 70-82. Reprinted by permission of the Lutheran Academy for Scholarship.

holders, generally are too widely diffused to exercise control of the corporation. Legally, of course, they have the final say, and management is accountable *pro forma* to its stockholders for its stewardship. Actually, as anyone who has ever attended a stockholders' meeting can testify, their degree of control is tenuous.

In practice the typical stockholder of a major corporation seldom behaves like an owner. This is particularly true of institutional investors such as pension trusts, mutual funds, insurance companies, and universities. The investor, whether individual or institutional, is a necessary figure in corporate life but not an active participant. He does not have the sense of responsibility that is generally associated with ownership, as in the case of a house or a farm or a small, one-man business. His interest is chiefly an investment interest: he is concerned with the rate of dividend, the prospects for capital appreciation, and the degree of speculative risk. He has little loyalty for any particular corporation, and readily shifts his investments from one to another as his own judgment or his investment advisor's counsel may dictate. The shareholder prospers largely by knowing when to buy or sell, and is only indirectly concerned with profits as such. He may be said to operate in terms of a profit motive, but the profits are his, not the corporation's.

The managers of the corporation, on their part, cannot be said to be actuated by the profit motive in the classical sense because of their relatively small ownership. A recent survey, for example, disclosed that typically managements of major corporations hold substantially less than one percent of the stock of their own companies. While the managers are responsible for the profits of their corporations, these profits accrue to the business and not to the managers except to the extent of their usually minor ownership interests. The corporation is a legal entity without psychological motivations. It is the managers who have motives, but under modern corporate organization these can be described as "profit motives" only by doing violence to the term itself.

This is not to suggest that managers are not interested in profits; quite the contrary. The corporation may not have motives, but it certainly has needs, and one of the most important of these is for an adequate rate of profit. Managers as custodians of the corporation have primary responsibility for serving this as well as other needs of the corporation. But the point to be emphasized is that profits are essentially institutional rather than personal.

In the modern corporation profit is no longer a reward to one of the factors of production. Typically only a portion of earnings is paid out to stockholders. The amount set aside for dividends is likely to be determined on the basis of "socially approved" rates of return, i.e., enough to maintain stockholder interest and preserve a ready market for the corporation's securities. A major portion of earnings is usually retained to aid in meeting the company's capital needs, among the most important of which are expansion, replacement, and improvement of productive facilities. Profits are thus a means for providing for the future —not merely the future of the corporation, but of society. And because the needs of the future are great, profits must be correspondingly large if the corporation is to continue to perform its economic function effectively.

Unfortunately, this relationship between profits and survival is not generally understood. The social stake in profits is heavily obscured by the implicit equating of profit with self-interest. This confusion of the two concepts is not only inaccurate; it places the business system in a vulnerable moral position and seriously weakens the claims of business for social policies that will foster its efficient performance. A more realistic and more defensible doctrine of profits will have to be built around the survival needs of the enterprise as an instrumentality of social service.

THE RISE OF PROFESSIONAL MANAGEMENT

The separation of ownership and control has profoundly altered the role of the manager. As noted, he typically has only a minor ownership interest, but for all practical purposes he exercises complete control. As distinct from the owners, i.e., the stockholders, he has a great sense of loyalty to the corporation and a keen sense of responsibility for its welfare. In a very literal sense, he is the only one in a position to assume and exercise effective responsibility. Recognition of responsibility not rooted in ownership has given rise to a growing sense of professionalism in management.

The manager in the modern corporation wields power and exercises authority not by virtue of ownership but of position. The circumstances of the enterprise necessarily emphasize the concepts of managerial trusteeship, service, and long-range planning and at the same time minimize personal acquisition and self-aggrandizement. Individual cleverness and ingenuity no longer win immediate cash rewards, as was often the case with owner-managers. The important considerations are necessarily long-term, both for the corporation and the individual. This is a tendency and not an absolute condition. But even as a tendency it is a change of major significance.

Managers are not uninterested in the material returns of their work, and by and large they are paid very well, particularly as they rise to the higher levels of the organization. Also, their rewards are not limited to money but include the satisfactions which come from improvements in position and status as well as from a sense of achievement, power, and responsibility.

It should be recognized, however, that while advancement in the hierarchy carries with it improvements in the manager's income—with all that means in terms of economic security and creature comforts—wealth as such no longer enjoys the prestige or exerts the attraction it once did. The phenomenon of "conspicuous consumption" is much less apparent today than it was in Thorstein Veblen's time, when the businessman, generally lacking a place within a stable and established hierarchy that would help define his status, turned to flamboyant ways to demonstrate his achievement and establish his position. This kind of behavior is no longer necessary, and would be out of place among executives in most modern corporations. Now that the larger enterprise has become the dominant form of economic organization, position in the community is determined not so much by wealth as by position in the enterprise.

In the broadly-owned, professionally-managed enterprise people hold their positions and win advancement on a basis of merit and competence rather than through nepotism or ownership. This is an important change, for the fact—sometimes the accident—of kinship or ownership does not necessarily imply ability. The practices of the modern corporation are more likely than traditional arrangements to place high responsibility in the hands best qualified to exercise it.

In a certain sense it may be said that position and preferment in business are "inherited." Sons of presidents and vice-presidents are more likely than the sons of mechanics to become presidents and vice-presidents themselves—usually not in their fathers' companies but in others. This, however, is chiefly a function of differences in educational opportunities and career expectations, rather than of nepotism. And the fact that little actual ownership is required of managers means that men are not unduly handicapped by lack of wealth in their struggle to rise to high positions in the enterprise. Together with freer access to educational opportunities this means that business careers are becoming increasingly open as compared with an earlier day, and more and more they depend on "what you are" rather than "who you are."

An essential characteristic of any profession is recognition of responsibility beyond immediate personal interests. As management has grown more professional, it too is growing increasingly aware of its responsibilities. Unfortunately there is considerable confusion, both in the minds of managers and of students of management, as to the nature and extent of managerial responsibility. A frequently recurring item on the agenda of management conferences is management's responsibility for this or that—for profits, for better quality goods and services, for good employee relations, for education, for community welfare, and so on ad infinitum. As a part of its growing sense of professionalism, management is becoming increasingly conscious of a sense of responsibility, but to some degree this remains diffuse and ill-defined.

THE ENTERPRISE: FOCUS OF MANAGEMENT RESPONSIBILITY

It is important to know to whom and for what management is responsible. Obviously management cannot be responsible to everyone for everything. It must be careful not to accept, or seem to accept, responsibilities that go beyond its managerial role—as is implicit in some of the looser talk now current about management's responsibilities for education, welfare, government, and the like. There is always the danger of taking on responsibilities that are beyond one's capacity to perform—either because of limitation of resources or because of inherent conflicts in institutional roles.

On the other hand, there are certain types of responsibility which are an integral part of the managerial role, and management must be alert to these and ready to assume them to the extent of its resources. To avoid the two dangers of taking on too much or too little, there is need to define more realistically the "to whom" and "for what" of managerial responsibility.

In an earlier day the businessman's role and its attendant responsibilities were fairly clear-cut. These could be summed up succinctly as the successful conduct of his business, and this was easily measured by his balance sheet and profit and loss statement. Anything that contributed to or interfered with sales and profits was rightfully a part of the businessman's concern, and anything not fairly directly related to sales and profits was outside his sphere of interest as a businessman, however much it might have occupied his attention as a citizen.

As businesses have grown larger and more complex, these simple criteria and distinctions are no longer an adequate or reliable standard. We are in grave need of a new formulation of the principles of managerial responsibility that will guide and direct the actions and policies of management, and provide a basis of judgment by which the public can evaluate management performance. Because of present fuzzy thinking in this whole area, there is danger that the public will come to expect more than management can possibly deliver. There is also the danger that management, confused as to what its responsibilities really are, may dilute its managerial effectiveness.

Let us address ourselves, therefore, to the question: to whom and for what is management responsible?

To stockholders? Yes, in a legal, *pro forma* sense. Operationally, however, responsibility to stockholders is limited and conditional. It is incumbent upon management to earn a high enough rate of return to attract and retain stockholder investment. But it is the enterprise's need for capital which makes the stockholder necessary. Hence, the responsibility for earnings and dividends is based primarily on the needs of the enterprise and only secondarily on satisfying stockholders.

How about customers? Unquestionably management has a responsibility to its customers—but again, only in a limited sense. Simply stated, without customers there can be no enterprise. But while the enterprise serves customers and exists on their favor, it is the needs of the enterprise that makes the customer important.

Is management responsible to employees? Yes—but again in a limited sense. Employees are essential to the enterprise, and management must pursue policies and practices that will attract and retain an adequate work force. Here again, however, it is the needs of the enterprise that are basic.

What remains? The public, of course. But here too, management is responsible only in a general sense. A certain amount of public acceptance and goodwill is necessary to permit the business system to function, but "the public" is too vague and amorphous to serve as an operative guide.

Management *does* have important responsibilities to stockholders, customers, employees, and the public. Each of these four entities, however, has something the enterprise needs and without which it cannot exist: capital, patronage, work skills, and a suitable legal framework and social climate. The obligations of management to these entities are conditions precedent to their assets being made available to the enterprise; in striving to meet them management fundamentally is seeking to serve the enterprise. Our conclusion is that management's first responsibility is to the enterprise itself and that all other responsibilities are limited and subsidiary.

This is not to postulate any mystical character to the enterprise—that it should be the focus of so much responsibility and concern. I hasten to add that while management exists for the enterprise, the enterprise does not exist for itself.

The enterprise is an organ of society serving a necessary social function. Society has many institutions to serve its many needs: religious, educational, governmental, cultural, etc. As an economic institution the function of the enterprise is to serve society's economic needs. This is its first obligation and only justification. Thus, management's responsibility is to the enterprise, but the enterprise's responsibility is to society, and management as the creator, moulder, and dynamic leadership center of the enterprise is ultimately responsible to society for its stewardship. The service rendered by the enterprise is economic—responsive to one of society's basic needs. The focus of management's responsibility, therefore, must always be the adaptation and improvement of the enterprise as an economic institution.

While this formulation seems fairly precise and rules out many possible areas of concern, on closer examination it will be found to take in a great deal of territory and to include many elements not customarily included within the purview of managerial responsibility. This arises from the changing and growing needs of the enterprise itself.

There is, above all, the need for continuity. To be productive, business organizations must have a high degree of permanence and stability. The modern large-scale enterprise cannot be put together overnight; it takes time to build a complex human and technical organization. An economic enterprise, no less than an educational or religious enterprise, depends for its effectiveness in large part on its ability to maintain itself in time. In this respect the modern, large-scale economy is fundamentally different from the small-scale, owner-managed economy which preceded it. It did not take much to set up in the buggy manufacturing business, or to open a grocery store, but think what it would take to recreate a General Motors or an A & P. In simple truth, if the large, publicly-owned, modern corporation is to serve its economic function, it must be managed with an eye to perpetuity.

Under conditions of rapid technical, economic, and social change, a prime requirement for continuity and survival is adaptability. Management decisions must therefore take into account not only immediate circumstances, but the possible effect of present actions on future eventualities. The results of research, for example, often take from 10 to 20 years to come to fruition. New capital investment typically does not pay out for 10 or 12 years, as against two or three years at the turn of the century. The corporation must be run in such a way as to survive all vicissitudes: technological change, shifting markets, competition, vagaries in demand, inflation and depression, managerial error, legal complications, labor disputes, and management succession. Emphasis must be placed on long-term planning of finance, productive facilities, organization, and marketing. Buying and pricing policies must be devised in terms of the requirements of stability and continuity in buying and selling relationships.

All of these factors have greatly lengthened the time spans in which modern managers must think. They are often called upon to make decisions that will not be carried out fully during the remainder of their working lives. Whereas the effective time span of the owner-manager's thinking is likely to be that of his own lifetime or perhaps his son's, the manager of the large, publicly-owned corporation is more likely to think in terms of much longer time spans. He often reminds his associates that the company will still be here long after all of them are dead and gone.

Management must balance the present and the future. It cannot afford to jeopardize the present in favor of grandiose plans for the future. Neither can it sacrifice the future for immediate profits The needs of both present and future must be served. Peter Drucker has stated the case well:

> *... Management must keep the enterprise successful and prof-*
> *itable in the present—or else there will be no enterprise left to*
> *enjoy in the future. It must simultaneously make the enterprise*
> *capable of growing and prospering, or at least of surviving in*
> *the future—otherwise it has fallen down on its responsibility of*
> *keeping resources productive and unimpaired, has destroyed*
> *capital.* (The Practice of Management, *p. 15*)

This substantial lengthening of the time span of management thinking brings many new considerations within the scope of management's legitimate and necessary concern for the enterprise as an effective, on-going economic institution. Many matters which might once have concerned the businessman as a citizen, if they concerned him at all, are now the proper objects of his concern as a businessman.

Consider education, for example. The enterprise has an important stake in a continuing supply of educated personnel, and, for that matter, in an educated society within which to function. Management must be careful not to infringe on the role and responsibilities of the educator, but there are important ways in which it can help strengthen education to the long-range benefit of society and the enterprise.

Despite the great extension of public welfare services, there is an important place in our society for private charity. Private charity is more adaptive to changing needs, more human, less bound up with red tape, less expensive. If all needed welfare work were left to public agencies, the human and economic costs would be very great, and would represent an excessive burden on the entire community, including business. Charitable giving, therefore, is a proper responsibility of management in the interests of the enterprise.

These are some specific examples of the broadening area of legitimate management concern and responsibility. The point to be made here is simply that while the enterprise itself must be the focus of managerial responsibility, the nature of the modern enterprise is such that its health and capacity for growth are dependent on many factors and influences external to the enterprise proper. The intelligent assessment of these factors and influences, and a prudent response to them, are therefore within the proper and necessary range of managerial responsibility.

We must recognize, however, that in many of these areas we are moving on highly uncertain ground. The profit and loss statement and the balance sheet were once reasonably adequate guides to business policy and action. We have no similar criteria to guide and control managerial activities in areas which are important but external to the enterprise per se, for example: education, charitable giving, and community improvement. But perhaps this is a good thing; at least it places a premium on good judgment, promotes flexibility and adaptivity to changing needs, both in the enterprise and in society, and helps keep business more humane.

One consequence of the broadening needs of the enterprise is that the roles of the citizen and the businessman are no longer as separate and distinct as they once were. This may be illustrated by the examples of the Rosenwald and the Sears Foundations.

The Rosenwald Foundation was established by Julius Rosenwald with resources produced by Sears but by then the private property of Rosenwald and no longer under Sears control. This foundation engaged in many worthwhile programs and made a number of significant contributions, but all of its activities were reflections of Julius Rosenwald's personal interests and concerns as a private citizen. The Sears Roebuck Foundation was likewise created and maintained by Sears-produced resources. It too has engaged in many worthwhile undertakings and made many significant contributions. But these programs have been primarily reflections of business concern and business policy.

Significantly for the present point, Julius Rosenwald's son, Lessing, has engaged in many important philanthropic and cultural activities, but these are different from his father's and are reflections of his own interests and personality. On the other hand, there have been five chairmen of the board of Sears since the Sears Foundation was established in its present form, but the programs and policies of the foundation show great continuity because they grow out of and reflect the needs of the business rather than the personal predilections of its officers.

CONCLUSION

Professional managers are coming to recognize that business can no longer pursue its economic interests regardless of social consequences. The big company in particular has developed into a quasi-public institution and as such has social and economic responsibilities beyond those of small companies. More and more the managers of big business are becoming aware that the welfare of their companies and of the business system itself are indissolubly bound up with that of the American economy and society. When such men express the faith that in the long run the good of society and the good of business go hand in hand, there may sometimes be a certain confusion as to which comes first; but of the strength and reality of the identification there can be no doubt.

Unless the policies of business—especially big business—benefit society they will not in the long run benefit business, no matter how attractive they may be in the short run. Management must find the means for harmonizing the interests of the enterprise with the common good—for making its own self-interest correspond with the public interest. General Robert E. Wood, former chairman of the board of Sears, once put it very well:

> *This company must be so managed as to make everything likely to strengthen our* country, *or to advance its prosperity, add strength to the* company *and advance its prosperity.*

To put it more precisely, what the general was saying is that what is good for the country must be *made to be* good for Sears. This formulation does not assume or imply any preestablished harmony. What is good for the country is not *necessarily* good for the enterprise—and vice versa. To make the good of the enterprise coincide with the good of the country takes hard work, skill, broad understanding, and courage.

Nevertheless, it is basically true that socially irresponsible action is also economically irresponsible action. The reverse is likewise true: economically irresponsible action is socially irresponsible. In either case, irresponsibility not only does not pay but may have disastrous consequences for society *and* the company. Acting responsibly is not merely "doing the right thing," but doing what the needs and interests of the business *as a social institution* demand.

This is a far cry from classical economic theory which looked to the interplay of a multitude of individual self-interests to achieve a balance that would both protect and serve the public interest. A modern theory of enterprise must recognize the manner in which the internal dynamics of the corporation itself tend to foster policies and actions that work toward such a balance. More important, it must emphasize the professional obligations of managers to protect and serve the public interest, not as a fortuitous by-product, but as an integral part of their managerial function.

QUESTIONS

1. What is the role of profit in the modern corporation?

2. How has the separation of ownership and control affected the managers of business?

3. Does the responsibility of management extend beyond simply managing the business? Explain.

Good Business and Good Ethics

GEORGE D. FITZPATRICK, S.J.

One of the most persistent questions of our day asks: Can good business and good ethics co-exist? Despite impressive attempts to bed the question down, just as we are tiptoeing out of the room, the clamor of an electrical price-fixing scandal or of a "salad oil" scandal raises the question with brand new importunacy. And each time the child wakes up yelling, we become less sure that we will succeed in putting it to sleep.

From *Advanced Management Journal*, October 1965, pp. 23–28. Reprinted by permission.

Can good business and good ethics co-exist? Possibly they can; but not as long as we leave unchallenged the ethical philosophy which reasons that the chief allegiance of businessmen is to the dollar. For, this philosophy collides with the teaching of the Gospel: You cannot serve God and mammon. To date, the current national discussion on business ethics has not come to terms with the impasse brought about by the collision of two antinomies, the one materialistic, the other godly. The impasse is inevitable and permanent until businessmen will convince themselves that they just can't have the best part of two worlds; that the only way out of the present standoff lies in a sensible and critical reappraisal of the one motive which has undone many an erstwhile ethical businessman, the profit motive.

The closest we seem to come to a real discussion of ethical issues is a "me too" for good ethics, quickly followed by a spirited defense of the profit motive. Unfortunately, many businessmen feel that somehow they can serve two masters. Because good business and good ethics seem—with few exceptions—to get along compatibly, there is born the *simpliste* attitude that good business equals good ethics and that, moreover, good business could never owe its life to bad ethics. That the majority of businessmen sincerely want both good business and good ethics is transparently clear. However, if they insist on measuring business success solely under the glare of profits, they shall blind themselves from genuine business morality.

If we acquiesce in the philosophy that the businessman's principal devotion is to the dollar, we shall soon find ourselves backed into a neutral corner marked *moral vacuum.* This is nothing more nor less than retreat from the fray. It settles nothing; although it does invite immorality as a business way of life.

The moral-vacuum philosophy has some purchase on modern thought. Profits, so this approach has it, are not moral and they are not immoral. They are, quite simply, necessary to the survival of free enterprise. Therefore, it follows inexorably that the businessman cannot properly apply himself to business unless, as R. Freedman has exhorted in *The Atlanta Economic Review,* the businessman learns "to give up the personal quest for standards of moral action in his role as businessman." ("The Challenge of Business Ethics," May, 1962). That exhortation, remarkable as it sounds in a day when men have actively concerned themselves with the problem of being more ethical, does the service of reminding us of the hard gospel truth: no one can serve two masters.

In an article appearing in the July 1963 issue of *The Atlanta Economic Review,* M. Mescon complains about those who have so built up the case for the "social responsibility of businessmen," that they have lost sight of the fact that "without profit there will be no employees." ("What Kind of Capitalist Are You?") Although I believe the point well taken, it fails to explain, defend, or criticize the mischief that the profit motive inspires when it is not qualified by the demonstrated ethical posture of top management.

Surely, no one of us needs to be persuaded that profits are necessary. They are necessary if we are going to have employees; they are necessary if we are going to have employers. Rather, we should be asking and answering that unanswered question: Will we *serve* profit?

In other words, do we believe that it is impossible to be both good and in business? If we can't be both, do we believe that we can somehow escape to a never-never world where, as businessmen, we don't have to choose between the two? This question cries out for intelligent discussion. For if the profit motive knows no rival in a man's heart, the businessman can permit himself everything under the aegis of profit.

And the rationalization: "it's the only way a business can be run," helps not at all. The very meaning, the very consequence of the national discussion on business ethics must be that we *don't* believe it's the only way a business can be run. Otherwise, we are expending a lot of time and energy in search of the unattainable.

Attempts to preserve business' most sacrosanct canons *and,* at the same time, a meaningful ethic will sooner or later abort. T. Levitt, writing in the Sep-Oct, 1958, number of the *Harvard Business Review,* pointing out business' responsibilities both to honesty and to profit, finds himself finessed into a moral absurdity: "Instead of fighting for its survival by means of strategic retreats masquerading as industrial statesmanship, business must fight as if it were at war. And, like a good war, it should be fought gallantly, daringly, and, above all, *not* morally" ("The Dangers of Social Responsibility").

The foregoing "position" unwittingly testifies to the impasse in the present national discussion on business ethics. Although most men probably agree that business does have two responsibilities—honesty and material gain—these same men hesitate to agree that business sometimes cannot live up to both. Or, if they suspect that on occasion you can't live up to both, they become tongue-tied at the prospect of saying anything unkind about the profit motive. And in so defaulting, they leave the way clear for a type of intellectual foot-stomping which clouds rather than clarifies the real moral issues.

If we genuinely want solutions to moral problems, we cannot seriously expect to solve them with principles nonmoral, no matter how peculiar the business context. And no business problem, let us hope, is so peculiar that it can elevate business immorality to a way of life. Tragically, many of the hard-headed businessmen who defend most strenuously our free, competitive enterprise system exempt themselves—thanks to a flexible morality—from the vicissitudes of free, open and honest competition.

However, although some men actually talk and act as if business morals differed from "ordinary" morals, many businessmen cannot accept such a dichotomy. My own research convinces me of this hopeful fact. For the past two years I have been conducting a study on *executive success.* Although the research has nothing to do with business ethics, some of the results lend themselves to the present discussion.

I have the data from forty interviews with business presidents in the Greater Boston area, plus the data from over one-hundred essay-type questionnaires returned to me from business presidents from all parts of the country.

I wish to mention the results of one question: "What one thing would you like to be remembered for after your death?" Twenty-five per cent of the answers had to do with honesty; twenty-three per cent had to do with service to others; fifteen per cent with having successful families; fifteen per cent with running successful businesses.

Since I asked this question in a context of executive success, I will make no effort to give the answers an accommodated meaning. Whatever else these answers indicate, however, they do not support the notion that businessmen abdicate all value systems when they go to work. Nor has it ever appeared, in personal interview or in written questionnaire, that a majority of businessmen carry split-level living into the moral order.

I cite these data because they have given me evidence (that I was in no way looking for) that most men believe their lives, their business lives included, are more refined and complex than some popular writing would allow. These data convince me that businessmen, as men, hold to values.

And yet, we might wish that these data revealed something about businessmen's attitudes regarding their subordinates. For, conceivably, these same men, however integral their own lives, have not made it equally possible for their employees to aspire to a similar fullness of life. In other words, maybe these high-minded executives, by demanding *results,* by judging subordinates according to "the argument that works best," have made it practically impossible for a man to take a religious view and at the same time command the support of his company.

This confronts us with one of the great unanswered questions in the whole area of business ethics: must a man opt between a religious view and the support of his company? Does management dare to tell the subordinate what he may and may not do in the name of management, or will management conveniently turn its mind from the *personal* conflicts of employees?

Repeated vaporings by management about the "American Dream" and "Free Enterprise" and "Fair Play" do nothing to solve the very real pressures that subordinates experience in the area of ethics. Father R. Baumhart, S.J., writing in the July-August, 1961, issue of the *Harvard Business Review,* has reported the fact of these pressures as convincingly as can be done ("How Ethical Are Businessmen?").

And the editors of *Chemical Engineering* (Dec. 9, 1963) have corroborated the undermining role of such pressures in the field of engineering. The comments of six-hundred and fifty-two *CE* readers confirm that, "economic pressures on the individual and the company that employs him sometimes make an engineer act in ways that he feels are unethical."

Statistical studies, however interesting and useful, only reinforce what we already know about the tyranny of business pressures. And management can relieve these pressures only through a less myopic view of profit.

J. Worthy, in the *Christian Century* of October 8, 1963, has said, in a gentle rejoinder to the clergy, that "In their evaluation of business profits, some clergymen evidence a lack of appreciation for its primary function: as providing the means for financing any continuing business enterprise in its purpose to produce goods or services and thereby provide jobs for people." I agree. Unhappily, many of the people who rush to defend the "primary function" of profits misread any and all criticism of profits as an onslaught by do-gooders against the very concept of profit. This interpretation is true in some instances.

But it hardly justifies the hypersensitivity of many businessmen concerning profits. Probity does not spell the demise of profits. The two need not fight to the death, not if there obtains a proper relationship between them.

However, the two are certainly doomed to enmity if management refuses to establish the relationship between them by realistic moral commitment. Business leaders have to abandon their unrealistic moral retreat. They have to hold their ground and face up to the conflict between rival obligations which beckon a man in two opposite directions.

Any earnest quest for a moral solution must debouch in the sensitive locus where profit and personal rectitude cannot both come away the victors. Morality —need we prove the point?—is born in conflict. It is ratified in challenge. And if we feel that there is some price too dear to pay for moral rectitude, then we surely haven't reckoned the consequences of the quest we have started.

Or else, having understood, we seek to skirt the consequences with morally devoid sloganeering. Because American business has not frankly acknowledged the conflict between the profit motive and the ethical motive, and because, in the electrical industry, the profit motive was not tempered by sincere ethical guidelines, we are unable to write the final chapter to a scandal which still begs for a conclusion.

For, to this writer's mind, that final chapter will have to include management's stated policy towards the conflict enunciated in the words of those who felt that price-fixing was the only way to satisfy top management. The ethical question concerns itself with those norms—knowable and findable by all men— according to which we judge certain actions "good" and other actions "bad." We cannot, any of us, prescind from ethics; for, from the moment we judge an action good or bad, we have stepped into the moral order.

From this moral awareness springs moral obligation, even if this obligation— and here the morally weak and their opposites part company—does not physically coerce. Each of us remains quite free to disregard it, and each of us remains quite free to urge others to disregard it. But we cannot destroy moral obligation.

Whether heeded by the morally responsible or derided by the morally irresponsible, it can be destroyed by no earthly power, since it does not exist by the *fiat* of men. It owes its existence to the moral consciousness imprinted in each man's soul. Without this moral awareness, man could merit neither heaven nor hell, for he could live neither a good life nor an evil life. Without a moral awareness, he would never have to take a stand on business ethics.

The preceding observations are, perhaps, superfluous; they are meant to be a reminder that God strictly obliges man to strive after a morally good life. And a morally good life cannot square with the impoverished ethics of, say, price-fixers. Either collusion is unethical or morality has come completely undone.

If the ethical response at times costs too much (such as it seems to have in the electrical case), the financial response equally costs too much. This brings us back to the crux of the issue. No one finds it onerous to be ethical in the absence of conflict. And no one, to be sure, wants to be evil. But put a man in conflict and he might choose evil as the simple solution of conflict. The proof of morality, the proof of a man's virtue, shows only in time of challenge, in time of moral siege.

In times of moral challenge (subordinates' moral challenge, that is) management has remained struck dumb. Can we wonder that subordinates take the easy way out if management has not taken a clear and unambiguous posture regarding business morality? How many men today, because of the muteness of management, think it necessary to perform unethically in order to keep their jobs?

"We did feel that this was the only way," said one of the defendants in the electrical price-fixing trial. Did top management also feel that it was the only way? If not, why did it not say, why does it not say what you do when profits and probity conflict? Without the answer to this soul-disturbing question, the business-man will always be surprised by and unprepared for moral challenge in the market-place. His response to challenge will always be makeshift.

The question of how long free enterprise in this country can remain free takes on more pertinence with each new scandal. The answer lies squarely in the hearts and hands of those to whom has been entrusted the management of our nation's business. These managers betray their high calling each time they allow our enterprise to become a little less free. The conduct of business, to be free, must be honest. Those people who believe that there are times when one cannot be honest bear the burden of having to prove it. For, the obligations of genuine morality admit of no surcease.

Referring once more to my own evidence, I believe that most businessmen want to be good and that they don't think it possible to be good on a part-time basis. Yet, they might usefully ask themselves if they have permitted their sub-ordinates to enjoy the same fullness of life of which these executives have spoken and written to me.

In a free enterprise system a man should be able to serve honesty as well as his company. But the company must seek to be honestly served. Unfortunately, the electrical companies did not succeed in dispelling the suspicion that the price-fixers were serving in a satisfactory way . . . up to the moment of their detection. How cruelly ironic that these men thought they were serving well while perform-ing a gross disservice to their own personal integrity.

That they did do a disservice to their personal integrity some of the price-fixers admitted. And if others sought to dismiss the moral question by saying that it was "the only way a business can be run," at best they succeeded only in de-positing the question on the doorstep of top management. For, although we toss moral responsibility back and forth much like a ball, sooner or later we have to stop playing catch. And when we stop, somebody has the ball.

Intelligence recoils from the stupid, if comforting, hope that the ball might get stuck in mid-air, thereby enabling the subordinate to affirm that it's the only way a business can be run and enabling the superior to confess that he didn't know the subordinate was acting dishonestly. If, in fact, dishonesty alone can salvage some business situations, then management, through conspicuous silence, must be presumed to condone dishonesty.

Where, then, does management stand when the profit motive and the ethical motive cross swords? In demurral—the electrical scandal proved—lurks disaster. In vapid moralizing lie the seeds of cynicism.

If management barricades itself off from the unpleasant sounds of corporate conflicts, it might, for a while, plead ignorance of the spiritual costs of corporate loyalty. After a while, however, it must fall liable to the taunt: there are none so deaf as those who won't hear.

The facts of business life are hard and the facts of moral life are hard. A man should never be backed into an all-or-nothing choice between the two. Still, it happens that the twin calls of corporate duty and spiritual duty back a man into just such an impossible dilemma. And at these times, only a management which is both hard-headed *and* God-fearing dares resolve the dilemma. In a Christian context this has to mean that morality will prevail.

QUESTIONS

1. What is the conflict between good ethics and the businessman's allegiance to the dollar?

2. Should we serve profits or should profits serve us? How?

3. Are business morals and ordinary morals different?

4. Can business avoid moral issues?

Ethics in Business

WILLIS W. HAGEN

Ray Eppert, president of Burroughs Corporation, has recently observed that "Business leaders lead much more than the companies they represent. Collectively, the business leaders of the free world are the first line of defense of the capitalistic system which the leaders of communism have sworn to humiliate, defeat and destroy. Only as long as we can continue to make capitalism work beneficially can capitalism survive. Only as long as we can make capitalism work beneficially can man's hopes for better living *with* personal liberty and individual dignity remain alive."

In order to survive and deserve survival, he said: "our capitalistic system must continue to work better than any other system in bringing the benefits of civilization to all men everywhere."[1]

In order for free enterprise and the capitalistic system to work better than other systems in bringing benefits to us and thus survive the economic and ideological conflict, what must it do? First, it must produce vast quantities of goods and services. But, the Gross National Product is not *the end* in itself. Business leaders are allocators of scarce resources, they must realize their moral duties in this respect, and must perform their function as allocators wisely and morally. Moreover, as leaders, they have a responsibility for product selectivity. They must do this job better than the dictators of planned economies. They have a moral duty to produce goods and services contributive of the well-being of Man. As Eells said in his book, *The Meaning of Modern Business:*

From *Advanced Management Journal*, April 1965, pp. 14-20. Reprinted by permission.
[1]Ray R. Eppert, "Moral Basis for Business Leadership," *Management Record* (The Conference Board), March, 1962. Vol. XXIV, No. 3, pp. 2-4.

> *Responsible product selectivity may mean the exclusion of prod-*
> *uct lines that promise large returns but would require the use of*
> *capital for socially dubious purposes. A company may choose*
> *among alternatives, none of which will result in socially deleteri-*
> *ous products and services, but some of which may contribute*
> *more substantially to the upbuilding of the kind of community*
> *the responsible executive wants to see.*[2]

To work better than other systems the free enterprise system must cause an equitable and just distribution of its product to the contributors to the system. Communism touts equality of distribution. Capitalism must strive for equity of distribution—just distribution. In its simplest form, this means the equitable distribution to each individual contributor of the greatest quantity of material things in exchange for his or her contributions of services and property to the system. In its broader view, it means a judicial role for management in balancing the claims of all groups and individuals—even of society as a whole, for that matter—for their contributions toward the product of economy. It means the application of ethical calculus in management's decision-making in areas which concern the distribution of the product of economy.

Finally, to work better than other systems the free enterprise system must be able to work within the broader concepts of moral ideals. The business manager cannot relegate concern for morals to the hours of Sunday morning church attendance. As Peter Drucker said in his book, *Concept of the Corporation:*

> *If the big-business corporation is America's representative social*
> *institution it must realize these basic beliefs of American society*
> *—at least enough to satisfy minimum requirements. It must give*
> *status and function to the individual, and it must give him the*
> *justice of equal opportunities. This does not mean that the eco-*
> *nomic purpose of the corporation, efficient production, is to be*
> *subordinated to its social function, or that the fulfillment of*
> *society's basic belief is to be subordinated to the profit and*
> *survival-interest of the individual business. The corporation*
> *can only function as the representative social institution of our*
> *society if it can fulfill its social functions in a manner which*
> *strengthens it as an efficient producer, and vice versa. But as*
> *the representative social institution of our society the corpora-*
> *tion in addition to being an economic tool is a political and social*
> *body; its social function as a community is as important as its*
> *economic function as an efficient producer.*[3]

In summary, then, with respect to our first consideration, namely, concern for business ethics as a factor in the world-wide struggle of free enterprise and democracy with communism, morality becomes action consistent with or leading

---

[2]Richard Eells, *The Meaning of Modern Business,* Columbia University Press, New York, 1960, pp. 230, 231.

[3]Peter F. Drucker, *Concept of the Corporation,* Beacon Press, Beacon Hill, Boston, 1946, 1960, 1962, p. 140.

toward a goal of greatest possible production of goods and services contributive of the well-being of Man with a view to the equitable distribution to individual contributors of the greatest quantity of material things in exchange for his or her contributions of services and property to the system consistent with the attainment of broad, moral values.

BUSINESS ETHICS AND THE PRESERVATION OF MANAGEMENT'S PREROGATIVES

The decision-making areas of management have been seriously encroached upon over the years by both government and labor. Management no longer determines what is a "fair trade practice" or what is a "fair labor practice." These matters are determined for it by the Courts, as a branch of the government. Negotiations with labor have resulted in the constantly increasing paternal role of labor leaders in labor's function in production. Even now, there is pending before the United States Supreme Court a case involving the question of whether it is an unfair labor practice for a private industrial corporation to go out of business and whether a corporation going out of business has a duty to continue compensation to its employees until they find other employment. The ultimate consequence of this erosion of the authority of management is the end of the entrepreneurial corporate business organization which has been the hallmark of free enterprise and capitalism as we have known it in the past.

Henry Ford II, in 1961, said:

> *If we are to preserve the good names of our respective companies, our corporate executives must keep their own house in in order. If and when they fail to do so, the house-cleaning job will certainly be put in less friendly hands. We now run a serious risk of having codes with sharp teeth imposed on business by a federal legislature. Because such codes would further restrict the areas of free business action and decision, we must, in our various companies and industries, see to the establishment of our own formal principles of ethical practice, plus the effective means of self-policing those principles.*
>
> *I would like to suggest that all of us in business management take a new, long look at ourselves and all our business practices. I suggest we look not only at the obvious areas of danger, where we may run afoul of the law, but also at those borderline areas of corporate action that might have unfortunate social consequences for our fellow man.*[4]

Perhaps, Mr. Ford's comments reflect only an attitude of enlightened self-interest and might be looked upon askance by a formal moralist, but, if action dictated by enlightened self-interest can serve to preserve the corporate organization as an instrument of free enterprise, it warrants further attention.

---

[4]Henry Ford II, "Business Ethics and the Law," *Management Review,* August, 1961, Vol. 50, No. 8, pp. 54, 55.

Is the corporation, in its mature years, suffering from the excesses of its youth? Has it failed to grow ideologically along with its physical growth? Had the corporation developed a mature philosophy, an active "corporate conscience" and a social outlook in keeping with its physical growth, would there be the extensive inroads on corporate decision-making areas that there are today? The answer to these questions must necessarily be highly conjectural and subject to wide disagreement. There are some aspects of this subject matter which are quite clear, however. The corporate form of business organization limits the legal liability of its members, but it does not limit the moral and social responsibilities of its management which arise out of the power which it exercises over and the impact which its decisions have upon the lives of persons. The corporate "shield" which protects its members from unlimited legal liability does not protect against unlimited public condemnation for the failure of its management to recognize the social and moral responsibilities which are correlative of its power over persons. The corporation, like all good citizens, is not only expected to "make a living" for itself, but also to contribute to the community and to society. A good citizen concerns himself with social and public matters and does not live in isolation. Surely, the corporation cannot do less if it hopes to retain an image of respectability in society.

Long range profitability remains a prime object of the corporation, but cannot be an exclusive preoccupation. Besides the interests of security holders, the corporation must be concerned with its moral responsibilities to employees, to suppliers, to customers, to the local community, to the national community and to society as a whole. It must be concerned not only with its responsibilities to suppliers of capital, but to the suppliers of services, to the suppliers of revenue (its customers), to the suppliers of trained manpower (the schools), to the suppliers of police and fire protection, of sanitary facilities and, in general, of a local environment in which the business can operate (the community), and to the suppliers of the almost endless factors that merge into its product and enable its continued existence. This it must do in its own interests and to retain the control of the remaining areas of decision-making in its management.

Almost every decision which management makes involves an ethical issue. Management, in effect, is constantly assuming a judicial role in balancing the interests of those who contribute to its product. Its actions are moral when, in a given situation, these varying interests are brought into proper perspective and a decision is reached and an action is taken which is fair *on balance* to all interests concerned.

By way of illustration, we might take the current problem of "runaway industry." Let us suppose that a given corporation is contemplating moving to a new location. What factors are involved from a moral point of view? Clearly, they are the survival of the corporation, long range profitability, the obligation of management to stockholders, the effect its movement will have upon its employees, such as the disruption of their economic and social postures, the effect upon the community from which it has received benefits which enabled it to grow and develop, and the effect upon the total product of economy. If the primary purpose of the movement is to make the corporation a more effective factor in the product of our free enterprise economy by increasing its efficiency through greater proximity to raw materials or its market, although generalizations are dangerous, on balance the movement would contribute to the values of a greater product for economy, greater efficiency of the individual business involved, a contribution toward its survival interest, and a benefit to its stockholders, values which would appear to outweigh the obligations of management to its present employees and the local community. On the other hand, where the sole purpose is to take advantage of non-union labor or escape an "unfavorable" tax climate, the thing directly done is of questionable moral value, the good effects of the action in terms of profitability, survival interest and stockholder interest, which may be only short term and, possibly damaging to the image of the corporation, may well be outweighed by the bad effects of economic waste, employee and community disruption. In terms of the broad responsibilities of management to balance all interests, the action may well be branded as immoral.

MANAGEMENT: THE FOUNTAINHEAD OF ETHICS IN THE FEDERAL REGULATION OF BUSINESS

I recently had the experience of confronting and being confronted by the present Federal Trade Commissioners in Washington, D.C., on a case which I argued on ethical philosophical grounds. In examining the Law in preparation for the case I was quite surprised to find that, in spite of the fact that the Commission administers law as it applies to business morals, no principles of moral philosophy have been developed in the decisions affecting business morality to serve as a foundation for legal argument. As a lawyer, this distressed me. As a matter of fact, I was appalled to think that after 50 years of decisions involving business ethics we are still back in the "what's right is right" era with "right" being determined arbitrarily, capriciously and with unlimited discretion by a small group of political appointees.

The Federal Trade Commission was created in 1914 and given the power by the Federal Trade Commission Act to determine what constitutes an "unfair method of competition in commerce" and to proceed against methods it deemed unfair. While it was not provided with a specific standard of fairness by the Act, it was required, by implication, to judge unfairness in the light of competitive practices in industry. Later, in 1938, the Wheeler-Lea Amendment extended its jurisdiction to "unfair or deceptive acts or practices in commerce." This amendment eliminated the implied requirement that the Commission give consideration to competitive practices in industry. The Commission which, thus, administers law as it applies to business morals, views the 1938 amendment as giving it *carte blanche* to legislate the morals of the business community without the guidance of standards or principles pronounced by Congress and without the benefit of any consideration of prevailing standards in industry. It considers its function to determine morality upon the basis of its own sensibilities.

Morality is more than the shallow concept, what's right is right, as a survey of the literature on the subject will readily reveal. Over the centuries learned men have contemplated the values and obligations of Man in depth and there have developed many schools of ethical thought. An action is right or moral, in the view of a given school of thought if it is consistent with a principle verified to the satisfaction of its adherents. Immorality is action inconsistent with these principles. Obviously, the same action may be moral or immoral depending upon the school of moral thought to which one subscribes.

Business morality is the application of moral principles to business problems. Business practices, therefore, become moral and fair or immoral and unfair if they are consistent or inconsistent with a particular pattern of moral theory. Again, the same business practice may be fair or unfair, depending upon the pattern of moral theory to which one subscribes. The Federal Trade Commission has the power to select whatever moral theory it pleases to apply to business or fly by the seat of its collective pants if it chooses, all with far-reaching legal effect. Such broad power not only violates the United States Constitution, which puts the law-making power of our country in the Congress, but it violates the fundamental principle of our system of government that the rights of men are to be determined by the law itself, and not by the let or leave of administrative agencies. It was the unconstitutional delegation of legislative power of this type that caused the United States Supreme Court to condemn the NIRA, an act which was to give the executive branch of our government the power to establish and impose codes of fair practices upon industry.

While the broad provisions of the Wheeler-Lea Amendment extended the jurisdiction of the Federal Trade Commission to unfair practices irrespective of their effect upon competition, there was nevertheless implicit in the language of the amendment a standard against which unfairness *might* be determined and therefore, the amendment itself *could* be viewed as constitutional. The Commission's administration of the amendment is unconstitutional in any case, however, since it chooses to ignore the standard.

A proper interpretation of the amendment is that it implicitly provides the standard of prevailing practices. It is the Commission's duty to determine prevailing standards by evidence in a given case and to find a respondent unfair only when his practices are below the level of prevailing standards. This may not be expedient, but expedience has never been a justification for the unconstitutional exercise of power. The prevailing standard may not agree with the sensibilities of the members of the Commission, but to determine unfairness otherwise, is to make their sensibilities the standard.

It might be asked: What if deception were the prevailing practice in industry? Would then a respondent who is practicing deception not be acting unfairly? The answer to those questions is that such a condition could not exist, since it would be self-defeating. Under such circumstances, no one would believe representations of businessmen and their efforts to deceive would be futile. Business morality will seek its own level. The practical, "cash," value of the good image, the level of morality in society as a whole, and the policing effect of public opinion will prevent such utter degradation of business morals.

I am making these observations to indicate the state of the Law with respect to business morality, or more particularly, with respect to the regulation of business morals. There is, to my way of thinking, a dilemma in this field of business regulation. Judge Learned Hand wrote: "It is its (the Commission's) duty to discover and make explicit those unexpressed standards of fair dealing which the conscience of the community may progressively develop."[5] Judge

---

[5]Federal Trade Commission v. Standards Education Society, 82 F. 2d 692, 696 (2d Cir. 1936).

Cardozo said: "When the task that is set before one is that of cleaning house, it is prudent as well as usual to take counsel of the dwellers."[6] Judge Stone wrote: "The statute does not authorize . . . censoring the morals of businessmen."[7] It would seem from all of this that the function of the Commission in the field of business morality is to bring the actions of individual businessmen into harmony with the prevailing level of morality. This would mean that in each individual case the Commission would have the burden of adducing evidence of the then state of morality and of then showing that the respondent's practices did not conform. This would be a tremendous burden and, in some cases, perhaps, impossible task. But if there is no developed and accepted ethical philosophy of business, this is the only framework in which administrative law can operate in its present state and still remain within the bounds of the United States Constitution and good conscience.

The type of regulation which now confronts and confounds the businessman was typified by former Commissioner Lowell B. Mason with the following colloquy: "But what if you said to the man next door, 'My friend, what is the boundary line between my property and yours?' and he were to reply, 'I refuse to tell you. But beware if you step over it—I shall shoot.'"[8] There will always be the unscrupulous who will have no regard for anything except immediate profit maximization. There must be a force to bring them into line to make business morality work. But what constitutes moral deviation in business, who is to draw the line and where it is to be drawn are other questions.

If businessmen do not want their ethics dictated to them, they must develop an ethical philosophy of their own. They must familiarize themselves with philosophical thought and they must give substantial attention to the ethical dimensions of business decisions. Perhaps in addition to the legal consultant there should be the ethics consultant. Ethical issues in business must be approached from an ethical, philosophical point of view. Where the litigation of business morality is involved, legal argument must be framed upon ethical, philosophical lines. If the philosophy of American business is to be a matter of law, its philosophical principles must be pondered, argued, litigated and resolved.

QUESTIONS

1. What must we do to make our free enterprise society work?

2. Can the implementation of good ethics help our society to work better? How?

3. With what, in addition to profitability, should the corporation be concerned?

4. How has the federal government become involved in the question of business ethics?

---

[6] A. L. A. Schechter Poultry Corp. v. United States, 295 U.S. 495, 552 (1935).

[7] Federal Trade Commission v. Keppel & Brothers, Inc., 291 U.S. 304, 313 (1934).

[8] Lowell B. Mason, *The Language of Dissent*, The Long House, Inc., New Canaan, Conn., 1959, p. 278.

2

Management and Organization

The task of achieving organizational objectives in a business rests with the managers of the firm.

An understanding of this task can best be accomplished through the study of various management theories. Professor Harold Koontz of the University of California, Los Angeles, identifies the following schools of management thought:[1]

1. *Management Process School.* Identifies and analyzes the process of management and sets forth principles to guide managerial action.

2. *Empirical School.* Analyzes past managerial experiences with the intent of forming generalizations useful in present managerial activities.

3. *Human Behavior School.* Emphasizes interpersonal relations and concentrates on the human element in managerial behavior.

4. *Social Systems School.* Views management as a complex social system composed of cultural interrelationships of various social groups.

5. *Decision Theory School.* Emphasizes rational decision making as the focal point of managerial action.

6. *Mathematical School.* Views management as a system of mathematical models.

A general theory of management acceptable to most management theorists has yet to be written.[2] But perhaps the most widely utilized school of management thought is the management process. In this school, management is defined as the process of achieving some desired objective through the intelligent utilization of human effort. The management process consists of a series of functional activities directed toward the achievement of objectives. A most useful method of classification is to identify the functional activities as planning, organizing, motivating, and controlling.[3]

Planning may be defined as the act of determining courses of action that will lead to the achievement of predetermined objectives. The planning activity provides answers to the following questions: (1) *What* actions are necessary to achieve the desired objectives; (2) *why* are these actions necessary; (3) *who* is

---

[1] "The Management Theory Jungle," *Academy of Management Journal,* December 1961, pp. 174-188.

[2] See William C. Frederick, "The Next Development in Management Science: A General Theory," *Academy of Management Journal,* September 1963, pp. 212-219.

[3] Other authors may use a different classification of functions. For example, see Harold Koontz and Cyril O'Donnell, *Principles of Management,* 4th ed. (New York: McGraw-Hill Book Company, 1968), Chapter 3.

responsible for these actions; (4) *where* will these actions take place; (5) *when* will these actions take place; and (6) *how* will these actions take place.

Planning always involves future action. The manager is forced to think ahead and to anticipate the future environment in which he will be operating. Forecasting involves predicting the future environment. However, "planning" is a more comprehensive term. The manager must go beyond the preliminary stage of forecasting and develop programs of action designed to maximize the firm's future performance. Thus, in the planning activity we are concerned with accomplishing objectives with the greatest certainty, efficiency, and economy.

Perhaps the most significant recent development in planning has been the PERT concept. PERT stands for Program Evaluation Review Technique. It is a technique for planning and controlling nonrepetitive projects.[4] Prof. Harry F. Evarts of Ohio University states that "PERT is designed to evaluate progress toward the attainment of project goals, focus attention on potential and actual problems in projects, provide management with frequent, accurate status reports, predict likelihood of reaching project objectives, and determining the shortest time in which a project can be completed."[5]

Organizing involves the identification and grouping of the work activities essential to the achievement of the objectives and the identification of the proper relationship between persons performing the work activities. In the task of organizing we must make sure that the factors of production (men, money, machines, materials, and markets) are combined and utilized in the most effective and economical manner possible. The end result of the task of organizing is the creation of an organization structure. The structure must not be viewed as an end unto itself, however. It must be viewed as a vehicle for enabling the organization to achieve its objectives.

Motivating involves guiding and directing subordinates' efforts toward the achievement of objectives. Successful motivation of subordinates is dependent upon the manager's ability to know and understand his subordinates, to know the nature and sources of job satisfaction, and to be able to create a work environment that contributes to high productivity and job satisfaction.

Managers may motivate their subordinates through leadership, human relations, training and development, and communication. Motivating must be viewed as a continuous process. People must be continually motivated if the highest possible performance results are to be achieved. Research contributions by behavioral scientists (psychologists, sociologists, social psychologists, and anthropologists) have enabled managers to more effectively motivate their subordinates.[6]

Controlling is regulating business activity so that actual performance takes place according to plans. The manager must realize that deviations from planned

[4]See Richard I. Levin and Charles A. Kirkpatrick, *Planning and Control with PERT/CPM* (New York: McGraw-Hill Book Company, 1966).

[5]*Introduction to PERT* (Boston: Allyn and Bacon, 1964), p. 2.

[6]See, for example, Rensis Likert, *The Human Organization: Its Management and Value* (New York: McGraw-Hill Book Company, 1967); Douglas McGregor, *The Professional Manager* (New York: McGraw-Hill Book Company, 1967); Frederick Herzberg, *Work and the Nature of Man* (Cleveland: The World Publishing Company, 1966).

performance will occur. Consequently, control effort is necessary to correct these deviations.

The control process consists of the following phases: (1) establishing standards of performance (planned performance); (2) measuring actual performance; (3) comparing actual performance with the standards and determining the deviation that exists, if any; and (4) eliminating the deviation by means of corrective or remedial action.

The management process (planning, organizing, motivating, and controlling) is considered to be a universal process.[7] This implies that the process is performed by all managers in the firm. This includes the president, vice-presidents, division managers, department heads, and foremen. Another reason the management process is considered to be universal is because it is performed by managers in various types of institutions (business firms, hospitals, universities, churches, and governmental bodies). The concept of universality implies that managerial knowledge and experience are transferable from one firm to another or from one type of institution to another.

ORGANIZATION STRUCTURES

Organization structures, as was explained earlier, are the end product of the managerial function of organizing. There are two basic types of organization structure—the functional structure and the divisional structure.

The *functional structure* is formed by placing all the work required to achieve organizational objectives into basic functional departments. The organization chart for the Apex Manufacturing Company (Figure 1) shows a typical functional organization structure.

FIGURE 1. FUNCTIONAL ORGANIZATION STRUCTURE OF THE APEX MANUFACTURING COMPANY

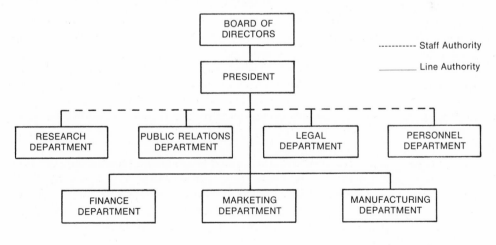

[7]See William V. Muse, "The Universality of Management," *Academy of Management Journal,* June, 1967, pp. 179-184.

In the functional structure all work of a similar nature is placed in one department under the direction of one manager. Thus, the marketing manager is responsible for all marketing activities in the firm. According to Louis Allen, the functional structure has the following advantages: (1) facilitation of specialization; (2) facilitiation of coordination within functional departments; (3) promotion of economy of operation; (4) allowance for economic flexibility; and (5) projection of outstanding leadership skills.[8]

Almost all firms start with a functional organization structure. The advantages of the functional structure are greatest when the firm is small and under the leadership of a limited number of persons. However, if the firm is experiencing growth and is beginning to diversify its product lines, some consideration must be given to a re-examination of the firm's organization structure. Allen indicates that many firms change from a functional to a divisional organization structure when sales are between $25 and $100 million.[9]

The *divisional organization* structure is formed by creating a number of semi-independent units that operate within the organizational framework of the firm. Divisionalization may be either product or geographic in its orientation. The product divisional structure emphasizes the manufacture and distribution of the goods or services being offered for sale. The geographic divisional structure emphasizes the need to structure the divisional unit toward the characteristics of the various market areas being served. The product divisional structure of the Beam Corporation is shown in Figure 2.

In the Beam Corporation example, the corporation is organized for the purpose of manufacturing and marketing aerospace products, agricultural equipment, and marine engine products. In this illustration, each product division has its own manufacturing, marketing, accounting, and personnel groups. Thus, the manufacturing department of the aerospace division is concerned solely with the manufacture of aerospace products. The same would be true of the manufacturing departments in the other two divisions. Above the divisions in the organization structure are a series of staff vice-presidents. These men and their subordinates have the responsibility for helping the president coordinate and manage the entire corporation. The staff vice-presidents will engage in long-range planning and policy formulation, and will provide specialized advice and services to the operating product divisions (aerospace, agricultural equipment, and marine engine). General Motors, General Electric, IBM, American Machine and Foundry Company, and General Dynamics are examples of firms using product divisional organization structures. Product divisionalization is usually selected when product, manufacturing, engineering, and marketing characteristics are critical.

The geographic divisional structure would be created by substituting division managers for the Eastern United States, the Central United States, and the Western United States for the aerospace, agricultural equipment, and marine engine divisions as illustrated in Figure 2. With a geographic divisional structure, each division manager is responsible for manufacturing and marketing all of the com-

---

[8]Louis A. Allen, *Management and Organization* (New York: McGraw-Hill Book Company, 1958), pp. 79-84.
   [9]*ibid.*, p. 86.

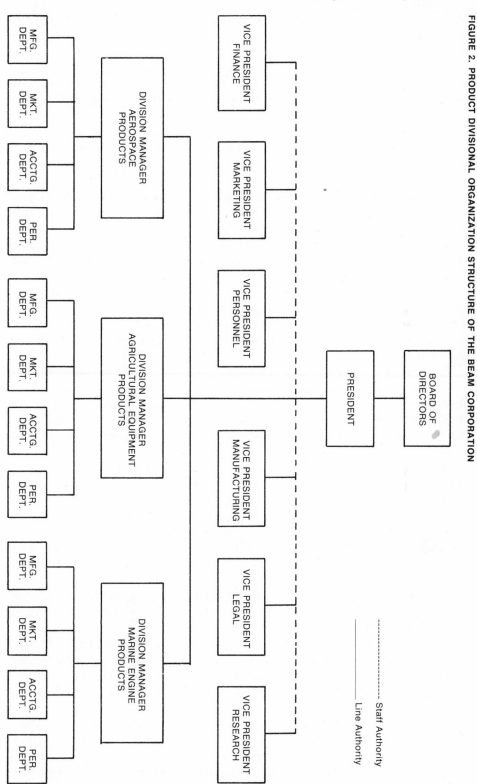

FIGURE 2. PRODUCT DIVISIONAL ORGANIZATION STRUCTURE OF THE BEAM CORPORATION

pany's products or services in his geographic area. Many firms in the public utilities, transportation, insurance, and service industries utilize the geographic divisional structure.

The division manager of the product or geographic division is typically responsible for the profit or loss earned by his division. Hence, in many respects he has the same problems and responsibility as the president of a small or medium-sized firm.

AUTHORITY AND RESPONSIBILITY

Authority is typically defined as the right or power to take action or to command or expect performance from others. The *formal theory* of authority holds that the true source of authority stems from the right to own and use private property. Thus, according to this view, authority flows from the stockholders (owners) to the board of directors to the president and on down the chain of command in the organization.

The *acceptance theory* views the source of authority in a somewhat different light. According to the acceptance theory, the true source of authority is the willingness of subordinates to accept the orders and commands given by their superiors. In the acceptance theory authority flows upward from subordinates to superiors.

If organizations are to accomplish their objectives, managers must delegate a portion of their authority to their subordinates. *Delegation* is defined as the act of passing authority from one manager or organizational unit to another for the purpose of accomplishing work activities. The president of the firm delegates a portion of his authority to the vice-president of manufacturing for the purpose of accomplishing the tasks involved in manufacturing the firm's products. The vice-president will then delegate a portion of his authority to his subordinates. This process continues on down through the organizational structure.

When individuals accept positions in organizations, they assume the responsibility for performing the duties or work activities assigned to their particular position. Thus, *responsibility* is the obligation of an individual to perform his assigned duties to the best of his ability. It is generally agreed that a manager should have sufficient authority to accomplish the work activities for which he is responsible.

An individual who receives authority from his superior has the obligation to keep his superior informed of his use of authority and the accomplishment or lack of accomplishment of assigned work activities. This concept is commonly referred to as *accountability*.

In most business firms a distinction is made between line and staff authority. Positions or organizational units that possess *line authority* are those which make a direct contribution to the achievement of organizational objectives. In a manufacturing firm, marketing, finance, and manufacturing are generally considered to be line functions (see Figure 1).

Staff authority is assigned to those positions or organizational units which make an indirect contribution to the achievement of organizational objectives. Personnel, legal, public relations, and research activities are often considered to be staff functions (see Figure 1). Persons and departments possessing staff authority provide advice, service, and counsel to line departments. The staff makes its contribution to organizational objectives by enabling the line to perform its work functions in a more efficient and economical manner.

PLACEMENT OF AUTHORITY

The top management of every firm must decide whether decision-making authority is to be concentrated in the hands of a small, selective group of top-level managers or whether the decision-making authority is to be delegated down throughout the entire organization. This decision involves the concepts of centralization and decentralization.

Centralization denotes that the majority of major decisions in the firm are made by the president and his key subordinates. Centralization is likely to exist within a small or medium-sized firm dominated by several key individuals. A firm that has a shortage of management talent may have no choice but to centralize decision-making authority.

Decentralization refers to the attempt to delegate decision-making authority to the lowest feasible levels in the organization. The late Alfred P. Sloan is generally credited with pioneering the practice of decentralization in the General Motors Corporation during the 1920's. Decentralization is typically found in firms that use divisional organizational structures (Figure 2). Some degree of centralization is usually found in firms that are characterized as being highly decentralized. Centralization may exist in policy formulation, planning, capital budgeting, and coordination activities.

DECISION MAKING

The manager is constantly making decisions. Professor Herbert Simon of Carnegie Institute of Technology goes so far as to conclude that decision making is synonymous with managing.[10] Decision making may be defined as the selection of one behavior alternative from among two or more alternatives. Many decisions the manager makes are made as a matter of routine or habit. It is important to recognize that decision making takes place in executing the managerial functions of planning, organizing, motivating, and controlling. In addition, decision making occurs in all the operational phases of business.

The quality of the decision can be enhanced if the decision maker follows a rational process. An example of such a process follows.[11] First, the problem must be carefully defined. A problem is any obstacle or barrier in the path of accomplishing an objective. The decision maker must be careful to distinguish between the problem and symptoms of the problem. A symptom is merely a manifestation or indication that a problem does, in fact, exist. For example, if a car is using

---

[10]*The New Science of Management Decision* (New York: Harper & Brothers Publishers, 1960), p. 1.

[11]For a more complete discussion of decision making, see Charles H. Kepner and Benjamin B. Tregoe, *The Rational Manager* (New York: McGraw-Hill Book Company, 1965).

a quart of oil every 100 miles, that is not the problem. The problem is what is causing the engine to burn an excessive amount of oil. The problem might be faulty rings, pistons, or valves.

Consider the business firm that is experiencing a sharp decline in sales. The decline in sales is a symptom, not a problem. The problem may be a faulty market distribution system, a poorly designed product, an unrealistic price, or some other critical factor. The person who can successfully define his problem is well on the way to solving the problem.

The second phase of the decision process is to carefully analyze the problem. This would include gathering, organizing, and evaluating all the information that is needed to solve the problem.

Phase three involves developing alternative solutions. This is perhaps the most creative phase of the decision-making process. The typical manager is prone to propose traditional rather than new, creative solutions. Yet, the creative solution may well hold the greatest promise of success. The manager typically explores only a limited number of alternatives. A quick appraisal of the firm's objectives, resources, and ethical standards will indicate that some alternatives are not feasible.

In the fourth phase the manager must analyze and evaluate the consequences or results of each principal alternative. In this phase the decision maker estimates what will happen if each alternative is selected.

The final phase of the decision-making process is to select one alternative; that is, to pick the most favorable alternative from among those available. The final choice depends on how well the various alternatives serve the objectives of the firm with respect to benefits and costs. It is important to remember that a decision once made is sterile until the time that it is implemented. The objectives of the firm won't be accomplished until decisions are converted into plans of action and then successfully put into effect.

During the past twenty years, tremendous advancements have been made in the field of decision making.[12] Quantitative methods such as linear programing, dynamic programing, game theory, and probability theory use sophisticated mathematical models to solve complex business problems.[13] These operations research techniques were applied to military problems during World War II and have since been applied to the solution of business problems.

INFORMATION SYSTEMS

The quality of the decision made by the manager is in large part determined by the quality and quantity of information the manager has at his disposal. During the past decade a considerable amount of emphasis has been directed toward the development of *management information systems*. Professors Adrian McDonough and Leonard Garrett of the University of Pennsylvania define a management information system as "a communication process in which data are

---

[12]For example, see Simon, *op. cit.*, pp. 14-20.
[13]For example, see Billy E. Goetz, *Quantitative Methods: A Survey and Guide for Managers* (New York: McGraw-Hill Book Company, 1965).

recorded and revised to support management decisions for planning, operating, and controlling."[14] The management information system must be designed to gather, process, analyze, store, and transmit data to various persons in the organization.[15] The data are transmitted to the manager so that he can do a more effective job in discharging his responsibilities as a manager.

The electronic computer has aided in advancing the development of information systems and complex decision-making methods. Electronic data processing equipment makes it possible to process vast amounts of information. The computer has been used to improve payroll procedures, production scheduling operations, inventory control procedures, evaluation of federal income tax returns, law enforcement techniques, medical research, market research techniques, and countless other activities.

The use of the computer has increased at a very rapid rate. For example, it is estimated that in 1956 there were fewer than 1000 computers in the United States. By 1966, there were more than 30,000 computers in operation. R.C.A., a computer manufacturer, estimates that there will be 85,000 in 1975, 150,000 in 1985, and 220,000 in 2000.[16] Needless to say, the computer will bring about many changes in the ways managers and workers go about performing their work activities.

The articles that follow were selected to provide the reader with a greater understanding of management and organization. Robert T. Hof's article examines the role of management; the scientific management, human relations management, and mathematical management theories; and the practice of management. The advantages and disadvantages of functional and divisional organization structures are the subject of Franklin G. Moore's article. Line and staff relationships are analyzed by Louis A. Allen. Ernest Dale compares and contrasts the concepts of centralization and decentralization. John E. Swearingen identifies some of the problems surrounding the executive decision. William R. King discusses the role of the systems concept in management. The *Business Week* article describes one company's approach to the creation of a management information system. Charles Klasson and Kenneth Olm's article explains the nature of the modern approach to creating integrated business operations.

---

[14]*Management Systems: Working Concepts and Practices* (Homewood, Illinois: Richard D. Irwin, Inc., 1965), p. 4.

[15]*ibid.*, p. 4.

[16]Stanley Penn, "Shape of the Future—Computers Will Bring Problems Along with Their Many Benefits," *The Wall Street Journal,* December 20, 1966, p. 14.

Contemporary American Management

ROBERT T. HOF

Greek historians tell us that in ancient Egypt it took 100,000 men to build the great pyramid of Khufu. The builders used 2,300,000 limestone blocks—each weighing 2½ tons. The pyramid was almost as high as the Washington Monument . . . and its base would cover 8 football fields. It took 20 years to build— and that was 5,000 years ago. These ancient people had no machines and no computers—just manpower, motivation, and management.

I mention the Great Pyramid to make the point that management has been with us a long time. And management is what this article is going to discuss— not the management of ancient Egypt but contemporary American management.

We talk a great deal about mineral resources, agriculture, industry, and human resources. We talk about science and technology, and economics and finance, and such things as the gross national product of nations. There is a golden thread that runs through the discussion of all these subjects. That golden thread is *management.*

Perhaps the greatest resource of all in the United States is management skill. Other nations marvel at it. It is perhaps our most important export. In World Wars I and II and the Korean War, the American Economy astonished our allies and confounded our enemies—with the management ability to mobilize industry in support of the war effort. Management was the hero of the logistics efforts.

Putting aside the war record for the moment, let's look at the peacetime record. The United States has only 6 percent of the world's population and 7 percent of the land. Yet the United States produces one-half of the world's output of energy, and Americans consume one-third of all the world's goods and services.

Today, we accept as commonplace things that 50 years ago were not even visible in the fortune teller's crystal ball: Nuclear-powered submarines, space vehicles transmitting close-ups of the moon, aircraft operating at more than twice the speed of sound, and even the everyday household items—air conditioners, television, and frozen foods. Of course, all these things are the brain children of scientists and inventors, and these men are entitled to the highest praise for their work. However, these achievements did not come out of a garage or basement workshop. These are the products of large business—and sometimes government enterprises—with men in charge called managers.

MANAGEMENT AS A RESOURCE

Management is an important economic resource. Management starts with man. Man is a *social* animal. He lives and works together in groups. He specializes in his work. He exchanges the goods and services he produces for other goods

From *Business Perspectives*, Winter 1967, pp. 5-10, 30. Reprinted by permission.

and services which other men produce. He is *not* self-sufficient. He has learned that well-being comes about through specialization of labor and through trade.

On the face of the earth, there are still tribes who avoid trade with the outside world—who produce their own food and clothing and very little else. They find subsistence hard and death comes early.

But men who have joined together in enterprises, exchanging the fruits of their labor with the outside world, have grasped the meaning of a better life for themselves and for their children.

To make the cooperative efforts of men work and prosper *is* the task of management. Someone has to have the vision to conceive the need for an enterprise, the skill to mobilize the means of production, the determination to control the enterprise, the leadership to guide people toward objectives, and the financial genius to meet the bills when due. That someone is called a manager. The quality of management spells the difference between success or failure for a business enterprise or for a society.

In the 1920's General Motors was just one of more than 50 automobile manufacturers. Its product had no unique advantages, yet it emerged as the dominant company in the automobile field. The difference was in the quality of management.

We are accustomed to think of management in terms of industry, but every enterprise—government, national defense, the church—calls for management. History records many great management achievements that were not of a private business nature: Columbus was a manager, our founding fathers were managers, General Goethals who built the Panama Canal, Eisenhower's international team which planned the Normandy Invasion, and the government-industry team which has put men into space, were all managers. And, of course, our Federal government is the largest manager of all.

The Federal budget has grown "a little" since the turn of the century. In 1901, the budget was half a billion dollars. Today, it is about $100 billion and about half of that goes for defense. And the number of employees has grown from 350,000 to five million. Government is certainly big management.

So you see that when we talk about management theory and practice we are talking about concepts that apply to government—including defense—as well as to the industrial segment of the economy.

WHAT IS MANAGEMENT?

At this point, perhaps we should ask ourselves: What *is* management? Is it an art? . . . or a science? A formal definition is "Management is a process of organizing and employing resources to accomplish pre-determined objectives." Another definition is that management is the art of getting things done through people. For this latter definition, we are indebted to Mary Parker Follett, who was a social worker back in the 1920's. In a day of highly autocratic management practices, she made the statement that you can get more work done by exercising power *with* people—rather than power *over* people. She interjected the human element—which we will write more about a little later.

There is, I think, an even better way of describing American management.

Someone has said that one opinion is worth 1,000 definitions. Let me give you an opinion on American management as expressed by a group of British businessmen who visited the states a short while ago. They said

> *If there is one secret, above all, of American achievements in productivity, then it is to be found in the attitude of American management. American management engenders an aggressiveness which believes that methodical planning, energetic training and enthusiastic work can solve any problem.*

They attributed this American attitude to four factors:

The legacy of the frontier.—A spirit that has fostered a sense of opportunity pervading American industrial and community life.

Faith in business and the individual.—A faith reflected in the high esteem with which the businessman is regarded in the American national community.

The ideal of competition.—An ideal which leads even those companies, not operating in a highly competitive community, to run their enterprises as though they were.

Belief in change.—A belief whereby a successful experiment is *not* allowed to crystallize into accepted custom . . . whereas an unsuccessful experiment is accepted as an occupational risk and is set against the experience that has been gained.

THE MANAGER EVOLVES

Having heard that outside opinion, and before we plunge into theory and practice, let's take a brief look at the evolution of the American manager himself. This man is a product of change. One hundred years ago, he was the owner-manager of a small business. The largest businesses of those days were tiny compared to today's giants.

Starting about 1880, the captains of industry appeared. They still owned the business but businesses were getting much, much bigger. Some people called them "robber barons." Some of them deserved it. They were ruthless in dealing with the customers, the public, and each other. But let's give credit where it is due. They founded many of our basic industries. They built industrial empires and railroad and communication systems that joined the East and the West. The old captains or robber barons didn't die—they faded away early in this century, under the onslaught of public opinion and the anti-trust laws and because their business just grew too big for them to handle.

They were followed by the financial managers—the financial wizards, some people called them. Big businesses had grown too big for one-man or one-family ownership. Ownership came to be spread widely among stockholders. The financial wizards ran the business for the stockholders. Unfortunately, many of them were speculators and plungers. Sometimes personal fortunes were made while stockholders lost their collective shirts. This is not to say there were no ethical financial managers; but neither were there many controls over their activities. After the '29 crash, public indignation and government regulation put an end to the heyday of the financial managers.

And then a new man entered the scene—the professional manager, pretty much as we know him today. He is a career man in business. Usually, he doesn't expect to own any large part of the enterprise and he is likely to see more in his career than just making a living. By background and training, he is keenly aware of his stewardship over other people's financial resources and he recognizes responsibilities to employees and to the general public as well as to the stockholders. It is not uncommon for him to seek elective or appointed public office or the job may seek him: Romney of Michigan comes to mind, and there is a man named McNamara.

Now, it is time that we discuss the theory of management. There are two of what I shall call "mainstreams" of modern management theory and one important tributary theory. The mainstreams I shall call, "scientific management" and "human relations." The tributary, I call "the mathematical school," and along with it I will comment on computers.

SCIENTIFIC MANAGEMENT

To begin, scientific management is sometimes called the traditional school. Other people call it "Taylorism," after Fredrick Taylor who is known as the father of the movement. Taylor was a foreman at the Midvale Steel Works in Philadelphia back in the 1880's. He later rose to chief engineer. Two things appalled Taylor: inefficient use of manpower and low wages. He was determined to get a full day's work out of every man on the payroll, to streamline operations, and to raise wages.

The first thing he did was to break each job down into its simplest parts so that each man could specialize in a simple task. Then he experimented with production standards and set quotas for each job. Last, he put the jobs together in a smooth flow of work, anticipating the production line.

Taylor achieved resounding success. He began with the pig iron handlers, and the coal and iron shovelers. He reduced the number of shovelers from 600 to 140 and he raised the output per man from 16 tons a day to 59 tons a day. He cut labor costs from 7 cents a ton to 3 cents a ton. *But mark this:* wages went up from $1.15 a day to $1.85 a day! So, he accomplished everything he had set out to do.

"Taylorism" caught on fast. It marked the end of an era—the end of craft workmanship. It paved the way for the assembly line and mass production. The scientific approach was taken up by the railroads and other industries. Henry Ford was a Taylor man. He believed in job simplification, the assembly line, quotas, and higher wages. Taylor's enthusiastic followers introduced industrial engineering complete with time and motion studies. Scientific management is still with us. Taylor's spirit lives on in the person of every manager who takes a logical approach to getting work done more efficiently. It is implicit in the rapid development of labor-saving devices. Many authorities see automation and electronic data processing as a natural evolution of the scientific management theory.

But Taylor's followers back in the 1920's and 1930's got so enthusiastic about job simplification, work flow charts, and time motion studies that they overlooked people. They figured that pay would take care of people. As Professor Dale of Cornell has said "They took it for granted that human beings will act rationally . . . in their own best economic interest." This has been called the theory of the economic man—or simply, that man does live by bread alone. This neglect of people was a major factor in the rise of labor unions. If Taylor was the father of scientific management, he was also at least an uncle of the labor unions.

HUMAN RELATIONS MANAGEMENT

However, something happened in the early 1930's that was destined to shake scientific management to its very roots. The human relations school of management was born in Chicago. The obstetrician in this case was a man named Elton Mayo, a psychiatrist by profession. Mayo conducted a series of experiments at the Hawthorne Works of the Western Electric Company in Chicago. They have become famous as the "Hawthorne Studies." The experiments took place in the relay assembly room—where girls wired telephone relays together. The experiments started out along traditional scientific management lines. They were to study the effects of fatigue upon production workers. In this case, management wanted to find out if they could increase production by improving working conditions. The first thing that Mayo did was to improve the lighting in the relay room. Sure enough, the girls increased production of relays. Then, to verify his results, Mayo reduced the lighting. Guess what! Production went up again.

Mayo tried several other things. He made working conditions better, then worse. He even changed the rules for going to the powder room. No matter what he did, production went up! Mayo asked himself what this meant—this change to the lights and working conditions in relation to production. He concluded that it meant absolutely nothing. The experiment was a bust! But something *had* happened. There *was* an answer to why production went up in the relay room. I think any woman reader can tell us. The girls in the relay room were getting a little attention! Men were asking them serious questions. They were part of an experiment! They felt wanted. Mayo was not a lady, but he was a scientist. He knew he had something.

This is what scientists call serendipity—the wisdom to discover something good you are not looking for. This is how we got penicillin. And this is how the Human Relations School of Management was born. They discovered that Mary Parker Follett had been right all along.

Human relations brought into the management field, at least in an advisory capacity, a wave of social scientists: psychiatrists, psychologists, sociologists, and anthropologists. Needless to say, management has never been the same. The school of human relations is people-oriented as opposed to scientific management which was work-oriented. Human relations has been defined as the science which studies the activities, attitudes, and interrelationships among people at work. It recognizes that work is done by people—usually in groups. It teaches us that the organizational chart is fiction. It is like a turtle's shell. It covers up what is actually going on inside the animal. It teaches us that the informal organization is a fact with which managers have to cope. Managers may set production quotas—but the informal group sets the production rates.

The human relations school says that managers must seek ways to get people committed to organizational goals. They say that one way to do this is communication, from the bottom up, as well as from the top down—and laterally. They say that participation is another way. People should be allowed to participate in the setting of goals and work standards and decision-making. Hopefully, if we do all these things, individual and organizational goals will be integrated.

We should mention something that the human relations school has done to organizations. It is the genesis of committees as a management technique. Committees are regarded by many people with mixed emotions. For example, when Mr. McNamara took over as Secretary of Defense, he abolished 400 joint committees. In fact, he is reputed to have said that the ideal committee consists of 3 members: one at the North Pole, one at the South Pole, and one at work. However, we still have committees in the Department of Defense. And no one has been able to abolish them in industry. The committee as a management technique appears to be here to stay.

Not all managers accepted the human relations theory with enthusiasm. Some said it gave them schizophrenia. They wound up with split personalities. On the one hand, they tried to be "do-work" managers, with stop watches and production quotas. This manager's motto is, "Get to work or get out!" On the other hand, they tried to be "do-good" managers. Their motto is "Keep warm. Be happy!" Well, perhaps human relations did go too far.

At any rate, in the past decade, the pendulum has swung back to scientific management. Not all the way of course, but to a sort of middle position. This, too, has been supported by experiment. In the early 1950's, the famous Michigan studies (named for the University of Michigan) demonstrated, among other things, that the happiest group is not necessarily the most productive group. (Which should come as no surprise to parents and teachers.)

However, human relations has become part and parcel of contemporary American management theory. The social-psychologist may not have replaced the efficiency expert—but he certainly has joined him.

Today, it is generally accepted that the most successful managers are both work-oriented and people-oriented—even at the risk of schizophrenia. And the combination appears to be profit-oriented.

MATHEMATICAL MANAGEMENT

The basic theory is that all management processes are logical and, therefore, can be expressed in mathematical symbols. This, of course, makes the theory a natural for use with a computer.

The mathematics school takes in such esoteric terms as operations research, linear programming, queueing theory, and model building.

Operations research usually means a balanced team of researchers who make a detailed analysis of military or business problems. They may use computers and they may use models, queueing theory, etc.

By a balanced team, I mean that, depending on the problem, the disciplines represented may include mathematics, chemistry, physics, psychology, and even, believe it or not, business.

Queueing theory, or "waiting line" theory, has been very useful in planning the correct or optimum number of toll booths on turnpikes, the number of tellers' windows in banks, the number of gasoline pumps in filling stations. It has been used to plan the number of loading and unloading docks at transportation terminals and maintenance docks at airports. It is even useful for making up bus schedules.

Without going into all the mathematics involved in linear programming, let me say that it is most helpful in determining the optimum mix of scarce resources —whether they be weapons systems or men or machines.

Model building implies simulation and that is what it is useful for. Mathematical models can be built to resemble a business, an industry situation, or a battlefield. A year's business transactions can be simulated in a minute. A computer can fight 100 land, air, or sea battles in an hour—or at least, simulate them.

Mathematical models are a great aid to business and to military planning, provided numerical values assigned to things like sales projections and casualty rates are valid.

In the Department of Defense we use the whole gambit of these techniques in a process called "systems analysis."

All of these techniques make use of the computer. So, let's talk about the computer. Some people do not appreciate the results obtained from the computer, and it does have its limitations. But, the computer is here to stay.

Computers have vastly increased the amount of information we can store, they recall this information almost instantaneously, and they perform the most complicated mathematical calculations in the twinkling of an eye. There is no question that computers, plus high speed communications, have made a tremendous contribution to the practice of management.

In industry, they have been credited with a major contribution to the current, unprecedented cycle of prosperity. Manufacturers have been able to hold inventories to a minimum while accelerating deliveries. And unprofitable operations can be discovered before serious losses occur. The airlines are using computers to handle reservations much, much faster and more accurately than people ever could do it. Computers are handling payrolls and personnel records centrally, for companies whose operations are spread across the country. In doing this, they read the records, compute the pay, make the deductions, and print and mail the checks. In some cases, computers are running automated factories. This is particularly true of oil refineries which have processes that lend themselves to automatic controls and computer-programmed operations. Tiny computers guide our space satellites in flight.

All of these things they do much faster and much more accurately than people can.

Where the machine extended man's muscle-power, the computer has now extended his brainpower. And, just as we had scientific management and human relations enthusiasts, now we have mathematics and computer enthusiasts. Already some people claim that computers will replace vice-presidents and factory managers.

But those who know the practical application of computers are quick to point out three critical limitations of computers. *First* is the difficulty, and, in some cases, the impossibility, of treating with things that cannot be quantified—things that cannot be dealt with mathematically, such as morale, customer behavior, reaction of business competitors, or the reaction of the Red Chinese for that matter. *Second* is a lack of creativeness. Computers cannot create new ideas or new solutions to new problems. *Finally,* there is a computer's inability to accept responsibility. This third limitation is certainly its most critical.

Even if ways can be found to treat with the first two limitations, only when a computer can be made responsible for success or failure, when it can be fired, will we consider using it to replace our managers.

So now, we are at the point of leaving management theory, the mainstreams of scientific management and human relations plus the wonderful new tools of the mathematical school. It is time to venture into more down-to-earth matters—the practice of management.

THE PRACTICE OF MANAGEMENT

When our bright young men who know all about computers do become managers they will find that they have four major functions to perform: planning, organizing, leading, controlling. These functions, on which there is general agreement, sometimes with minor variations, are a distillation of centuries of experience of men who have had to lead large organizations: prime ministers, governors, princes of the church, generals, admirals and businessmen. As an example, Von Clausewitz's *Vom Krieg (On War)* is almost a textbook for the practice of management.

As we said, the first major function of the management process is planning. Planning is making decisions about the future. The late Charles Kettering once emphasized the importance of planning with an analogy. He said, "One composer can keep 10,000 fiddlers busy."

Setting objectives is the most crucial part of planning. Corporations, governments, armies (and the people in all of them) have to know what their goals are. Objectives or goals range from capturing a larger share of a market or sending a man to the moon down to subgoals such as calling on more customers each month. One thing is certain: people have to have goals. For example, a friend of mine once hired a laborer to dig holes in his front yard. He had him dig one hole, then another, then another. The holes were not in a line or circle—they were scattered around. When my friend asked the laborer to dig another hole, the man said: "I quit. I'm not going to waste my time just digging holes." My friend then explained that he was trying to find a drain pipe that was clogged up. The laborer said, "Why didn't you say so?" and he went back to work.

Short run goals are steps, like the steps of a stairs, leading to the long-run goals at the top. Goals lead to two other kinds of plans: standing plans and single-use plans.

Standing plans simplify the work process and the decision-making process because they decide in advance the what and how of a variety of operations. They are essential for smooth operations. They are called by many names—policies, procedures, standing operating procedures, standard methods, etc.

Standard plans tell us *how* to make up a payroll, *how* to control inventories, *how* to select a mode of shipment; and incidentally, these are the kinds of jobs that are most readily translated into the language of computers.

Standing plans make it possible for managers to spend their most creative efforts on single-use plans.

Under single-use plans we include strategic or long-range plans and all major programs—opening a new plant or buying a new missile system. And here we should note that a program of any magnitude needs to be broken up into time-phased steps. We have to determine the resources needed for each step—men, money, and materials. And we have to assign responsibility for accomplishing each step.

In essence, a well-conceived program covers all actions needed to achieve a specific goal and it shows who does what, and when. For large complex programs, such as planning an annual model change in the auto industry or developing a missile system, there is a hierarchy of supporting programs. And programs, of course, must be priced out. And when you do and put them all together you have the finance plan.

The first year's slice of the financial plan is the budget. In other words, the budget is the sum total of your standing and single-use plans for the next year, expressed in dollars. Or, as the financial experts say, it is next year's profit and loss statement—you hope.

Some people include innovating under planning. Actually, it applies throughout the planning process and the entire management process. If a man just keeps on doing what he always did or what somebody else always did, the competition will pass him by.

Decision making and innovating go together. They both touch all the other parts of planning. Between them they are responsible for Henry Ford saying, "A manager doesn't re-act—he *acts!*" A manager is a man who makes things happen by innovating and decision making.

And the next major step is, of course, *organizing*. Organization has been with us a long time. The Bible, for example, tells us that Moses "chose able men out of all Israel, and made them heads over the people, rulers of thousands, rulers of hundreds, rulers of fifties, and rulers of tens." "And they judged the people at all seasons: the hard cases they brought into Moses, but every small matter they judged themselves."

The problem that faced Moses was the same problem of organization that faces all managers. He had to divide up the work. Moses chose to form a simple line organization—the pyramid of authority. A line organization in industry might look like this. The chain of command runs straight up and down. Each man reports straight up or gives orders straight down—like the rulers of tens, the rulers of hundreds, the rulers of thousands of Moses' organization.

This straight line organization might work in a small business, but, as the business grows in size, the work of the boss has to be divided up too. So, we add a staff to divide up some of the boss's work.

This is the familiar line and staff organization. The church and the military—both large organizations—have used it for centuries. When business got big, it copied the line and staff organization. The role of the staff is to extend the special knowledge required by the executive and to advise and assist him on such matters as sales, engineering, production, finance, and anything else that is required.

The staff has an advisory capacity toward the line managers—outside the command channel. Theoretically, the staff cannot give orders to the line. Staff men are supposed to get things done by persuasion. But staff men are usually selected for their expertise and their intelligence. Such people are likely to be ambitious, and they have the boss's ear. So there is an eternal power struggle between line and staff. But, bear this in mind, no one has found a solution.

Everyone agrees that an organization needs both line and staff. Each needs the other. They are like some married couples you might know—they can't get along without each other—but when they are together, life is apt to be a series of donnybrooks. A few years ago someone hit upon another kind of organization in an attempt to resolve this age-old problem. Here each staff officer has a command line, but only for his own specialty. The plant manager might be responsible to one staff man for marketing, another for production, another for budgeting, another for quality control—and on and on. He has no direct line to the president.

So after planning and organizing we are ready for the next major function of the management process—what Henri Fayol, writing in 1916, called "command." Since that time it has gone through a semantic evolution. In turn, it became "direction," then "coordination," then "leading." And finally, nowadays, most writers refer to it as "motivation." Well, what's in a name?

Call it what you will. It means that after all your planning, all your organizing, it still takes people to get the work done, to make the plans come true. This takes leadership—or motivation. You will recall that we discussed motivation of people under the human relations theory and we concluded that the most successful leadership is both work-oriented and people-oriented.

Our discussion of planning, organizing, and motivating leaves only the fourth major function of the management process.

Controlling.—This is the report card! the howgozit chart! the thermometer! Under planning, we talked about goals. *Control mechanisms* tell us how we are moving toward them. We set standards, we pick control points, we measure and we watch—we do this for each area that impacts on our goal. We do it for sales, costs, quality, profits, and all other major areas. And finally, if we are not moving forward as we planned, we take corrective action. The phrase "management by exception" has come to be associated with this. In other words, we don't worry about everything. We let our control system pick out only those things that are going badly (the exceptions) and we find out why, and then we do what needs to be done. Computers again have been a big help in this area, particularly in large complex programs, such as the development of new weapons systems.

As a matter of fact, control is the essence of a system known as PERT—which is the acronym for Program Evaluation and Review Technique. You will recall that I said a well-conceived program covers all actions required to achieve a goal and tells who does what when. PERT uses computers to control all these actions, in the vast hierarchy of plans involved in developing new weapon systems.

The outstanding case has been the development of the polaris ballistic missile submarine system. Admiral Raborn brought this program to completion 2 years ahead of schedule using PERT with computers for control. The Admiral told a congressional committee that he could not have done it without PERT.

Well, there you have it all, the process of management—planning, organizing, leading, and controlling.

CONCLUSION

In closing let's make one final comment on the manager and what *we* derive from *his* process. We *depend* on him to run our business and our government. We *look* to him for continued prosperity. We expect him to mobilize the resources needed to support our effort in Vietnam—or any other conflict we may get into—as he has done so well in the past. And we depend upon the mightiest array of destructive might the world has ever known . . . which this man's team put together. And we depend on the organization of scientists, engineers, and construction workers (military men and civilians) which this man leads and manages to put Americans on the moon and beyond—before the end of this decade.

He is the contemporary American manager!

QUESTIONS

1. Compare and contrast the scientific management, human relations management, and mathematical management theories.

2. Do you agree or disagree with the author's statement, "Perhaps the greatest resource of all in the United States is management skill." Why?

3. What is the relationship between "the practice of management" and the three management theories?

Is Divisionalization on the Way Out?

FRANKLIN G. MOORE

In January, 1964, the United States Steel Company dissolved seven of its steel-making divisions. Gone are the American Steel & Wire, National Tube, Tennessee Coal & Iron, Oliver Iron Mining, Michigan Limestone, Pittsburgh Steamship, and Columbia-Geneva divisions. Their activities were all merged into two giant manufacturing and sales departments.

This change from a divisional to a functional form of organization structure

Reprinted by permission from the May, 1964, issue of the *Michigan Business Review,* published by the Graduate School of Business Administration, The University of Michigan.

is against all recent trends. Company after company changed from functional to divisional structures in the 1950's and more have changed in the 1960's. But the trend has slowed down and occasionally now we read about a company which has found that, for it, divisionalization didn't pay off. Ampex, for example, decentralized, turned into a money loser, partially recentralized, and got back into the black. Ford Motor eliminated several of its divisions, recentralized them, and saw profits go up to new highs.

DECENTRALIZATION AND DIVISIONALIZATION

Today the words "decentralization" and "divisionalization" are almost interchangeable with each other, but it wasn't always so. "Decentralization" used to mean that you let lower men decide a good many things. It meant that you pushed decision-making power down from the top and that is all that it meant.

Divisionalization also pushes decision-making down; so it is one form of decentralization. But divisionalization is something more. It means decentralization accomplished through divisions instead of through functional departments. In a manufacturing company, divisional structures eliminate the company-wide sales and manufacturing departments characteristic of functional structures. In their place are divisions, usually based on product lines. Each division head is responsible for making and selling its product line and for making money in its sphere. General Motors, a divisional company, does not have one large manufacturing department and one large sales department. Instead Chevrolet is a "division" and Semon Knudsen, Chevrolet head, is responsible for making and selling Chevrolets and for making money on them. And it is the same with Herman Lehman, in charge of Frigidaires. Lehman has charge of everything to do with Frigidaire products.

In department stores, divisionalization is often on a geographical basis. R. H. Macy has a Macy's New York division which operates in New York City. But Macy's Davison-Paxon division operates the company's stores in Georgia. In each case the divisional manager is responsible for the whole operation in his area.

THE DIVISIONALIZATION MOVEMENT

General Motors adopted the divisional form of organization in 1921 and so did DuPont. But, successful as these pioneer decentralizers were, only a few companies followed suit in the next thirty years. In the late 1930's, Westinghouse changed from a functional to a divisional structure, but it was one of few that made such a change. Several other companies, Blaw-Knox, Borg-Warner, Union Carbide, General Dynamics, and General Foods, for example, were, however, put together as divisionalized companies.

Divisionalization really caught on, however, in the late 1950's. General Electric, General Mills, Ford Motor, Continental Can, Monsanto, Carrier Corporation, IBM, and Raytheon, to name a few, changed to divisional structures in the 1950's. Scarcely a month went by without an announcement of another company going divisional.

But, as said above, by the 1960's the movement had lost its steam and slowed down. For one thing there weren't so many companies left which hadn't already joined the rush. But also, disturbing stories of divisionalization that failed began to be heard. Beside the Ford and Ampex stories, several companies that had always been organized on a greatly decentralized basis found that they needed to tighten up their control and to centralize more. Most of them didn't adopt a functional structure but they took away a good bit of decision-making power from their divisions and centralized it in the home office. Blaw-Knox tightened up, for example. So did Borg-Warner, Union Carbide, and General Dynamics. And to top it off comes the U.S. Steel move back almost wholly to a functional structure with one main manufacturing and one main sales department.

Before going into the reasons for all of these changes we should note that not all giant companies have gone divisional. Goodyear, Standard Oil of Ohio, National Cash Register, Massey-Ferguson, Crown Zellerbach, and a good many more giant companies are still organized functionally. Not everyone joined in the rush to divisionalization.

What actually are the merits of functional and divisional structures? What's the matter with functional structures that makes some companies want to give them up? What gains do managers hope to achieve by adopting divisional structures? Why have some companies had trouble? And, finally, why have some companies stayed with functional structures?

FUNCTIONAL STRUCTURES

The move away from functional structures is largely because they have several weaknesses which seem, in giant companies, to outweigh their one big advantage. The big advantage, the great use of specialization that you get in functional structures, seems often to be more than offset by the following weaknesses:

1. Functionalization makes the president, and the president alone, really responsible for profits. Other people are responsible for doing certain work or for producing income or for holding down outgo, but no one besides the president is responsible for total results, making money. This de-emphasizes the company as a whole, and it de-emphasizes total responsibility.

2. You lose emphasis on the product in functional organizations. No one has the job of doing "total thinking" about individual products. No one person has the job of trying to figure out just what the customer wants and to design the product to suit the customer and to manufacture it at a cost that will return a profit. The product thinking that is done is disjointed and uncoordinated. Years ago, before Westinghouse went divisional, the sales department often was selling products made in plants in a completely different line of jurisdiction. The sales department had no influence over engineering, production, or the cost of the product. This is characteristic of functional structures.

3. Functional departments are often uncooperative and think "my department" too much. They become insular, jealous of their prerogatives, and compete with each other in empire building rather than trying to work effectively toward a unified goal.

4. Functionalization tends to force coordinative decisions to the top of the organization. This gets worse with giant size. Because functionalization keeps decision-making of the coordinative type high in the organization, too many problems go up and down through too many levels before you get decisions. Top men get overloaded and this slows down decisions. For instance, before Westinghouse changed to divisions, it took from three to five weeks to get any kind of a cost and delivery time estimate for a customer who wanted a product not in the catalogue.

5. It is difficult, with functional departments, to judge whether activities are worth their cost. You get narrow thinking with no one looking critically at the value of any kind of work compared to its cost. Functional departments emphasize the kind of work, and doing the work well or better, but they don't emphasize cost control or profits.

Even if you want to be cost-conscious, it is hard to be so in functional structures because there is so much "common-pot" accounting. Until the mid 1950's Chrysler had a functional structure, which didn't work very well partly because of this very difficulty. The company could not, for example, find out what it cost to make a Plymouth car. Nor could it find out whether it was making or losing money when it sold a car.

In functional structures it is hard to control costs of both line and staff departments. It would seem to be easy to control the costs of line departments because they are responsible for "end-results." But *what* end-results? When you have only one big manufacturing department that makes all the products you sell, the "end-result" for which it is responsible is the making of products. And the sales department's "end-result" objective is to sell products. Neither department is inherently very cost- or profit-conscious.

Staff work, too, is hard to control. You fall for too many frills (in, for example, such fields as public relations, advertising, and personnel) without adequate tests of their value against their cost. No one below the president asks critically whether each kind of staff work pays its way. And, even if someone does ask, you never can tell very certainly whether staff work pays.

It may be asked, however, aren't these difficulties present in both functional and divisional structures? Will divisional structures solve these problems? Not completely but I list these problems as disadvantages to the functional form because the divisional form seems to handle them a little better. With divisions, profit thinking is pushed down farther in the organization and so is control over expenses. You get better control over expenses by profit-oriented men who are closer to expenses. Divisional staffs, for example, have to render service that appears to pay off in their divisions or the divisional heads will eliminate them.

6. Functional staff departments are cumbersome when they have to be decentralized. Purchasing will illustrate this point. In a big company with plants all over the country, centralized buying of *everything* would be slow and wasteful, so it is better to decentralize and to have purchasing agents at each plant buy almost everything but the biggest items.

But now you have a new problem. Who is each plant's purchasing agent's boss? From whom does he take orders? Is it the company-wide director of purchases at the home office or is it the head operating executive in the plant where he works? Usually, the plant executive is his boss, but actually decentralized purchasing agents have two bosses. The first is the manager of the plant where he works and the second is the director of purchases in the home office.

With partially decentralized purchasing, it is also hard to figure out whether the decentralized purchasing agents are doing good jobs. And it is hard to know what to do about it if they aren't, and who should do what. Admittedly, you have similar problems in divisional organizations, but the functional form seems to make them worse.

7. Functionalization does not develop good managers because there are few over-all managerial jobs. You are likely to have a shortage of well-rounded top men in the future.

DIVISIONAL STRUCTURES

Divisional organizations don't entirely eliminate the weaknesses of functional structures because individual divisions themselves usually have functional structures. Rather, they reduce the bad effects of functional structures because they segmentize giant corporations into several divisions each of which is much smaller than the whole corporation. This reduces the problems created by functionalization to a more manageable size.

In General Motors, the Chevrolet division has to contend with functional problems within its division. So does General Electric's Hotpoint division. And so does the Convair division in General Dynamics and the Maxwell House division in General Foods. All four "Generals" use divisional structures. They gain by confining the problems of functionalization to divisions. None of the four "Generals" has one large manufacturing department, or one large sales department. Instead, in each company, divisional heads are almost wholly responsible for what their divisions do and they have charge of developing, making, and selling the products in their product lines. When divisionalization is on a geographic basis, as it is at Macy's, divisional heads are responsible for operations in their territory.

CENTRAL SUPERVISION

Divisions are not independent companies and they are subject to general company-wide policies. Nearly all divisional companies have home office staffs to look after corporate-wide matters and to help insure that the divisions will be well run. Legal matters such as an anti-trust suit, for example, are often corporate-wide matters and are best handled by a staff in the home office.

Central staff review is also needed for capital expenditures since the company's money should be spent where it will produce the most good for the whole company. Head office managers require divisions to plan for the future and they review such plans with them. And as time goes on they check each division's progress toward its plans. Central office groups also watch over the accounting procedures and the executive development programs of the divisions and other activities of this sort. Central staffs also stand ready to help in such areas as market research, building new factories, and other activities in which some divisions need occasional help.

The assistance that divisional managers get from head offices is usually more in the nature of help than it is restriction. Within the framework of corporate policies, divisional managers have a relatively free hand to operate their divisions as they see fit, *provided they make money.* They are usually judged on the profits they make as a rate of return [on] the capital invested in their divisions more than on any other factor.

ADVANTAGES OF DIVISIONALIZATION

A great deal of decision-making authority is decentralized to division heads. Down within the various divisions, the structure, the delegations, and the further decentralization of decision-making power is much like it is in functional companies. The big difference between functional and divisional companies is in the kinds of major departments and in the degree of freedom that top level managers have. As compared to functional structures, divisions have these advantages:

1. Divisions provide greater motivation to managers because they put men largely on their own and give them whole jobs to do. These men make better decisions in their divisional areas than faraway top men can make. The organization has more life to it and it makes more money than would a giant functional company.

2. The "wholeness" of the work of divisional managers helps develop them into good men. Divisional managers are forced to do "total" thinking. They learn to think about the effects of their decisions upon all parts of their divisions and not just upon narrow functional areas.

3. Divisions help in the appraisal of the performances of your managers. You can compare their performances according to profits, rate of return on investment, market penetration, budget variances, or other bases. When you make such comparisons, your good men usually stand out.

4. Divisional structures reduce the bad effects of the provincial thinking of functional specialists because division heads must do total thinking. Yet down *within* each division there is just as much tendency to be provincial by functions as in functional companies. The gain comes from pushing total thinking down one or two levels in the company, which automatically pushes functional provincialism down still farther. You are better off than when the president tries to handle these same problems at the corporate level.

DISADVANTAGES OF DIVISIONALIZATION

It seems that divisions have several very important advantages so why doesn't divisionalization always work well? What are its disadvantages? There are several:

1. Divisionalization requires good managers and divisionalization helps to develop them. But when a company first changes to a divisional structure,

the men you have are at a disadvantage. The functional form doesn't develop well-rounded middle-level men, so when you first give up the functional form, you don't have as good men as you need. It takes time to develop well-rounded middle-level men and to make divisionalization operate successfully.

2. Divisions help develop well-rounded men, but they know only their own divisions' work. The head of Kelvinator would have a lot to learn if he became head of American Motors. And the head of General Dynamics' Electric Boat division (which makes submarines) would have a lot to learn if he became head of the company and had to direct the making and selling of airplanes, chemicals, and the rest of General Dynamics' products.

3. Divisional companies almost always have more staff men, in total, than do functional companies because each division tends to have a full set of staffs in addition to the home office staffs. When companies first change to divisional structures, staffs tend to grow too much and it usually takes several years for them to shrink back to an economic level.

4. Although I listed the reduction of provincial functional thinking as an advantage of the divisional form of structure, divisionalization does not eliminate it. Divisions generate divisional thinking and this is provincial thinking of another kind. Provincial divisional thinking seems to be not quite so bad, however, as provincial functional thinking. Divisional thinking retains the profit emphasis, which the functional emphasis loses. And it retains a strong product emphasis, which is also good.

Nonetheless, divisional provincial thinking hurts cooperation between divisions. Sometimes a division manager doesn't know what is good for the company, and even if he does, he is motivated to put his division's good above company good. A division manager has, for example, little incentive to give business to a sister division if he can buy better outside.

5. When divisions have to coordinate their work, difficulties sometimes arise because each division is so self-centered. The biggest coordinating job arises when one division supplies parts or materials to another. Their production schedules must be coordinated closely. You also run into transfer price problems. Usually, when you must coordinate the work of different divisions, you will need the help of home office staffs and you will need to give them at least limited authority to make the divisions coordinate their work.

6. When each division does all its own buying, there is too much small-lot buying. Even when your divisions are in unlike industries, there are usually some opportunities for quantity discounts. When you let each division do its own buying, you lose out on the economies that you'd get from the central buying of big items.

7. When each division sells its own products, you have as many sales organizations as you have divisions. There are 30 different General Electric sales organizations listed in the Chicago telephone book! If GE combined them all, it could probably save some salaries and some office rent. (It does combine a few of them; the Chicago telephone book lists only 24 different GE sales addresses and telephone numbers.) But if GE combined all these sales departments, it would be back to one big sales department, and this would be worse than having some duplication.

Warehousing is also likely to be inefficient. Duplicate facilities, not always fully used, are common in divisional companies. Customers who buy from two divisions get separate shipments from each division.

8. Divisions don't coordinate their efforts, as the following incident illustrates. "Is or is not gas the best for heating?" the architect on the telephone demanded, "Your men can't seem to agree." The architect was designing a new factory building in Cincinnati. First, a salesman from Cincinnati Gas & Electric Company's gas division called on him. Gas was best and had it all over electricity. Then a salesman from CG & E's electricity division came around and said that gas was all wrong and that electricity was best. This story isn't so bad, however, as some stories you hear about uncoordinated customer relationships in divisional companies. At least, CG & E was unlikely to lose the customer.

The American Machine & Foundry Company almost got into a much worse spot through its divisions' independence. A division on the West Coast was so unhappy with some steel it had bought that it was going to sue the steel company. The home office heard about it just in time to stop the suit. The steel company was a big customer of two other AMF divisions.

9. Divisional managers, motivated to make good showings in the short range, are likely to decide matters on a short-range profit basis. They won't spend money for research with distant pay-out prospects because this hurts short-range profits. General Electric (where "Progress is our most important product") reports that the central office continually has to prod the divisions into doing more long-range research.

Probably you ought not to expect profit-conscious and profit-driven divisional executives to spend money for blue-sky research. You might be better off to set up a research center (like the General Motors Technical Center in Detroit) for this kind of work. Then either the divisions will not be charged for it at all or each manager will bear only a proportional part of its costs.

General Motors, for example, does its research on a smog control device to solve Los Angeles' smog problem at its Technical Center. At Minnesota Mining & Manufacturing (maker of "Scotch" Tape) the central research group tackles such fundamental problems as "Why do things stick?" And at Procter & Gamble a central research group studies "How does soap get dirt off?"

10. There is a danger that divisional managers will pay more attention to making the record look good than they will to doing a good job. They develop an overriding concern for the good of their department, or at least their department's record, whether it is good for the company or not.

This sometimes makes divisional managers do hasty or wrong things just to show top men that they are doing something about a situation. They may, for instance, fire someone. Desperation firing of men is likely to be indiscriminate firing. At GE in the 1950's one division had three marketing managers in one year. When this happens, it is hard to keep everyone from developing an anxiety neurosis.

In divisional companies with profit centers, budgets are so important that they need very careful making up and you rely heavily on finance division analysts to make sure that performance reports show facts as they are. John Dearden, formerly of the Financial Control Department of Ford Motor Company and now Associate Professor of Business Administration at Harvard Business School, says that a divisional manager in trouble tries to cover up by understating the seriousness of his situation when he explains budget variances.[1] And the more serious it is, the more he wants to cover it up. Yet this is exactly the opposite of what top men want.

Also, because budgets are so important, each division has its own budget setters and they and the central office people are likely to spend endless hours arguing with each other.

Dearden states that "profit decentralization" (divisionalization) has unmerited glamor. He says that decentralization looks better than it is because, (1) it sounds reasonable: decisions are made below the top level by men who are strongly motivated to earn a profit, (2) centralization is old-fashioned, (3) if a little decentralization is good, more is better, and, (4) successful decentralization is publicized because no one wants to admit that the move was wrong.

DIVISIONALIZATION NOT ON THE WAY OUT

Perhaps divisionalization has been oversold. Nevertheless, despite the slowing down of the movement to divisionalization, this form of organization seems to be here to stay. The functional form of organization just doesn't seem suitable to the diversified operations of most giant companies. And since so many giant companies are going in for diversified product lines, it would seem that divisional structures, with a great deal of decentralization of decision-making power, are better suited to the needs of the situation than are functional structures.

QUESTIONS

1. What kind of company could best utilize a divisional organizational structure?

2. What kind of company could best utilize a functional organizational structure?

3. How can a company tell when the disadvantages of divisionalization begin to outweigh the advantages of divisionalization?

4. Explain why Franklin Moore feels that divisionalization is not on the way out.

---

[1]"Mirage of Profit Decentralization," *Harvard Business Review,* November-December, 1962.

The Line-Staff Relationship

LOUIS A. ALLEN

Inadequate working relationships between line and staff departments are one of the most potent sources of friction and inefficiency in many companies. Frequently staff people are confused and uncertain as to what they are supposed to do and what right they have to do it. Just as often, line managers look upon staff specialists as unnecessary impediments in the otherwise simple and efficient administration of production operations.

Unfavorable effects are usually obvious. Decision-making is often slowed to a feeble walk in the unending hassle between line and staff. There is constant jockeying for position and authority. Important deadlines may be missed. And coordination is often inadequate.

The picture is not all black, however. In many companies, staff and line work together as an integrated team. As a result, line management is supported by a highly effective group of experts who are on call to help with the complicated problems that arise in the highly technical operation of modern industry.

Even where line and staff differences are most troublesome, there is no question about the necessity of staff. Basically, the problem is one of how staff and line can learn to work together in helping the company achieve its goals. But preliminary to the solution of this problem is an understanding of what line and staff mean and what they do.

DEFINING LINE AND STAFF

Every company is organized for a specific purpose. This may be to make, invent, or sell a product or service, or any combination of these. But whether it be production, sales, research, or finance, the line component is the one that has direct responsibility for accomplishing the objectives of the enterprise. Organizationally, the line is the chain of command that extends from the board of directors through the various delegations and redelegations of authority and responsibility to the point where the primary activities of the company are performed. The line, then, refers to those departments that have the power to initiate and carry through to conclusion the basic activities of the company.

"Line" Is Identified by the Objectives of the Company

Since the line is directly responsible for accomplishing the objectives of the company, it follows that line elements can be identified most accurately in terms of these objectives.[1]

From *Management Record,* September 1955, © 1955, National Industrial Conference Board, pp. 346-349, 374-376. Reprinted by permission.

NOTE: A detailed analysis of staff and line relationships in terms of the philosophy and practice of seventy-two leading companies was published in THE CONFERENCE BOARD'S *Studies in Personnel Policy* series.

[1] See "Organization Planning," *Management Record,* October, 1954, p. 372.

To the extent that objectives of companies differ, line activities also differ. For example, a steel company has as its primary objectives the manufacture of quality steel products and their sale at a profit. The line functions in this instance are production and sales.

An oil company is organized to develop sources of crude oil and natural gas, to manufacture petroleum products and by-products, to market these products, and to operate transportation facilities. The line departments are production, manufacturing, transportation, and marketing.

In a department store chain success depends as much upon buying as selling. Both the buying or purchasing and the sales functions are line.

Some Functions Are Line in One Company, Staff in Another

There is little uniformity as to what is line and what is staff from one company to another. For example, one eastern company is organized primarily to manufacture and sell machinery. Engineering the product and providing service to customers are important, but only as a means of selling more effectively. Consequently, in this case, manufacturing and sales are line. Engineering operates in an advisory capacity to the line, and the service function supplies parts, training and assistance to the franchised dealers who service the machines. It is noteworthy that in the organizations of the franchised dealers, sales and service are the line function.

These same functions receive different emphasis in an aircraft manufacturing company. Here the enterprise can succeed only if it continually invests a good share of its effort in the complex problems of design and engineering of new aircraft, and the testing, servicing and modification of the aircraft it sells. In this organization, the line departments are engineering, manufacturing, sales and service.

The finance function is considered staff in many companies; in others it is line. In a typical manufacturing company, for example, the finance department operates as a specialized staff department, with responsibility for financing, accounting, and reporting or budgeting and control of expenditures. The performance of these duties is a staff service to other units of the company and does not involve the exercise of authority by the finance department over line departments. Necessary uniformity as to accounting, budgeting and reporting procedures is secured through company policy and procedures, which are issued by top line management.

In some companies, however, finance is line. In an eastern manufacturing company, for instance, about half of the company's business comes from products which are leased to customers instead of being sold outright. Because most lessors pay their rental on a usage basis, the accounting group within the finance department is directly concerned with a substantial amount of the company's income. Finance is therefore set up as a line operation, with authority to make final decisions as to leasing arrangements, in the same fashion that manufacturing and sales have the last word in their functions.

Research is line in some companies, staff in others. Again, the reason for the difference can be found in the objectives of the company. In a typical case, research is responsible for providing advice and recommendations aimed at the improvement and maintenance of products and the development of new products. Manufacturing and sales are the line departments in this case.

Another company, however, considers research of equal importance with sales and manufacturing in achieving its objectives. This company believes its future success depends upon a steady flow of new products and processes. Therefore, it has established research as a line department and gives its research director a place comparable to that of the directors of manufacturing and sales.

Some Functions Are Both Line and Staff in the Same Company

A function may be both line and staff in the same company. For example, in a decentralized business, the chief executive officer may need specialists in sales and production to advise him on matters of over-all planning, policy making and control. Sales and production thus are specialized staff departments at the corporate level. However, within the operating divisions of this same company, sales is responsible for marketing and distributing the product. At this point it is line. Since production handles the manufacturing in the plants, this function is also line at the operating level.

WHAT STAFF IS

Once a line manager's job grows beyond a certain size, he needs help to perform it properly. Staff refers to those elements of the organization which provide advice and service to the line. Actually, staff is best thought of in terms of a relationship. When one *position* exists primarily to provide advice and service to another, it is in a staff relationship. And if the work of a *department* is predominantly that of advice and service to one or more other departments, it is classified as a *staff department*. Staff includes all elements of the organization which are not line.

It is to be noted that a line, or chain of command, runs from the top to the bottom of each staff department, just as it does within each line component. Some positions within the staff department may exist primarily to provide advice and service to other positions within the same department. In this case there is an internal staff and line relationship. For example, in the personnel department in one company the line runs from the manager to the section heads of management development, labor relations and compensation. The personnel department also has a personnel research section which conducts library research and surveys for the management development, labor relations and compensation sections—not for the company as a whole. The personnel research section is staff to the line of the specialized staff department. In the same way, an assistant to the personnel manager is staff to him.

Part of the confusion in identifying staff and in determining its proper relationship to line stems from the failure to recognize that managers need help of two different kinds and that two types of staff provide this help.

Personal staff refers to the positions created primarily to aid the manager in carrying out those parts of his job he cannot, or does not wish to, delegate to others. These reserved responsibilities, which the manager performs personally may include over-all planning for his function, policy making and interpretation, coordination, human relations and control.[2]

Specialized staff helps the line by performing work that requires special skills or more objectivity than the line can normally be expected to possess. This may include help with accounting, personnel, engineering, purchasing, medical and other problems. Work of this type is so highly specialized that it can be delegated as a separate function to the appropriate specialist.

Personal Staff

Personal staff may consist of three kinds of assistants:[3]

> Line assistants
> Staff assistants
> General staff assistants

Line Assistants   The line assistant assists his chief in the whole range of his duties, except where a more limited delegation is made. He helps the principal to manage the function; that is, he assists with over-all planning, organizing, direction, coordination and control. Although the line assistant is in the direct chain of command, he is staff to his superior because he exists only to advise, counsel and act *for* his principal. The line assistant has no responsibility apart from that of his principal; therefore, he has none to redelegate.

Staff Assistants   The staff assistant is also commonly known as the "assistant to." He usually serves in a much more restricted fashion than does the line assistant. The staff assistant is differentiated from the line assistant in that he has no authority over other employees, except in the case of special assignments. Neither does he take over the department in the absence of his principal.

The work of the staff assistant varies widely from one company to another. He may be anything from a glorified secretary to a vice-president. His duties may range from opening the mail and answering the telephone to sitting in on board of directors meetings of subsidiary companies with power to speak for the president of the company.

Staff assistants may also be called "administrative assistants," "special assistants," and "executive assistants," depending upon the kind of work that they actually do.

General Staff Assistants   Some companies use a general staff, which is an adaptation of army practice. This is, in reality, a group of staff assistants functioning at a high level. These staff assistants usually serve as advisors to top management in specified areas. The general staff is used in addition to the regular corporate specialized staff.

---

[2]See "The Art of Delegation," *Management Record* (March, 1955), p. 92.

[3]For a detailed discussion of assistants and how they can be used most effectively, see "The Uses of Assistants," *Management Record* (May, 1955), p. 174.

Specialized Staff

In contrast to personal staff, the specialized staff advises and serves all line and other staff departments in a functional capacity. For instance, the staff finance department reporting to the president is available not only to advise and serve him, but also to serve other departments that need help in financial matters. The specialized staff thus becomes a reservoir of special knowledge, skills and experience which the entire organization can use. The specialized staff has two identifying characteristics:

1. It has no authority over other parts of the organization. The specialized staff advises and serves; it does not direct.

2. It can be used by all line and staff units of the organization, within the limits of company policy or practice. The activities of each specialized staff department are restricted to one specialized area or function. This differentiates it from the personal staff, which exists primarily to help one executive in carrying out his reserved responsibilities.

The specialized staff assists the line and other staff functions in two ways. First, it performs advisory activities—providing advice, counsel, suggestions, and guidance. Second, it performs service activities—specified work *for* the line, which may include making decisions that the line has asked it to make.

Advisory Activities   Specialized staff managers are, by definition, best qualified to advise the line and other staff managers in matters having to do with their specialties. The advice offered by staff may be of several different kinds.

Staff may offer planning advice to managers by undertaking study, research, analysis and the development of alternative courses of action. These can be of invaluable assistance to the line manager who has to make a final decision. This advice may include planning objectives, policies and procedures which will apply to and govern the operations of the line departments. It may cover the explanation and interpretation of objectives, plans and policies to line and other staff departments.

Staff may offer advice as to how decisions can best be put into practice. It may advise the line on planning performance controls. This advice may include assistance in establishing standards or yardsticks, determining the best methods of measuring work in progress, analysis of actual performance compared with the standard, and reporting findings to responsible executives.

Service Activities   Staff may perform service activities by carrying out specified work *for* the line. For example, the personnel department may recruit, select, and employ people for the line and other staff departments. The purchasing department may buy materials and supplies for the line. Finance may install accounting, budgetary and reporting systems for the line organization.

It is to be noted that in each case where staff performs a service for the line, authority for performing that service and final decision as to how it is to be done rests with the line. For example, the accounting department, if it is staff, does not direct the line to conform to standardized accounting procedures necessary for the compilation of a consolidated balance sheet. Such procedures are authorized by the president, who gives either explicit or implied authority to the accounting department to install for *him* the accounting system that will best serve the objectives he has set forth. The personnel manager who recruits college graduates, and who may even hire them, is acting only at the express request of the line departments he serves.

IMPROVING LINE-STAFF RELATIONSHIPS

Study of company organization brings to light frequent instances of friction and conflict between line and staff. What is at the root of the difficulty? Both line and staff have their viewpoints.

The Line Viewpoint

Line managers most often have these complaints about the staff organization:

> *Staff tends to assume line authority*
> *Staff does not give sound advice*
> *Staff steals credit*
> *Staff fails to see the whole picture*

Staff Assumes Line Authority   Line managers are generally keenly aware of their responsibility for results and profits. While they recognize that the staff man is necessary and valuable, they frequently resent what he does, or what they think he is trying to do, because they feel it encroaches upon their duties and prerogatives.

For example, in one company the plant manager had just finished negotiating a contract with a labor union. The central staff labor relations manager had been present all through the proceedings, ostensibly to guide and assist the plant manager in the negotiations.

The plant manager was not complimentary about the staff man's participation. "He knew just what he wanted, and he tried every way he knew to get me to go along. He would have made concessions to the union we didn't have to make at this plant and that we couldn't live with. I know some other plants in the company had to give in on those points, but there is no reason why we should."

Staff Does Not Give Sound Advice   Many managers complain that the counsel and advice staff offers is not always fully considered, well balanced, and soundly tested. In many companies, staff is considered "academic" or "ivory tower." Responsibility for this attitude can sometimes be laid squarely on staff people. For one thing, since staff is not held accountable for ultimate results, some staff managers show a tendency to propose new ideas without thinking them through or testing them. For another, staff specialists sometimes become enthusiastic advocates of ideas or programs because they work well in other companies. They do not always determine whether these ideas are adapted to the operating conditions of their own organization.

The sad fact is that sometimes the staff man is not well enough acquainted with operating conditions or processes in his own company to be able to identify the limiting factors. For instance, in one company the executive development director attended a seminar in which he heard accounts of the effectiveness of the committee method of executive appraisal. He made an enthusiastic recommendation to two division managers that they install this system in their plants. He did not understand why his idea met with a cold reception until he realized, several months later, that both divisions had many small treating plants with fifteen or twenty people and one or, at the most, two supervisors. As a result, committee appraisal was highly impractical.

Staff Steals Credit   Another common complaint is the tendency of staff to assume credit for programs that are successful and to lay the blame on line when they are not.

Staff people usually have a strategic advantage because they are closer to the top line manager and have more frequent access to him. In the nature of things, if a division manager accepts his staff industrial engineer's recommendation for installation of a methods improvement program, he will consult with him frequently on how best to go about it. Since the staff man has his chief's ear, he will be able to inject his own opinions and judgments as to why the program does or does not work. As one production superintendent said, "When things go wrong, those staff engineers make sure we're behind the eight ball. But when things click, every staff man in the shop rushes in to take credit."

Staff Fails to See the Whole Picture   Line managers frequently point out that staff people tend to operate in terms of the limited objectives of their own specialty rather than in the interests of the business as a whole. The difficulty here seems to be that the staff man becomes so involved in his own area that he fails to relate it to the task of the line and to the over-all objectives of the company.

The Staff Viewpoint

Complaints in the staff-line relationship are not entirely one-sided. Many staff men have complaints about the line. These usually center about the following:

> *Line does not make proper use of staff*
> *Line resists new ideas*
> *Line does not give staff enough authority*

Line Does Not Make Proper Use of Staff   In many companies, the advice and help of staff is sought only as a last resort. The line manager possibly prefers to run his own show and does not want to call in a specialist. He may be reluctant to place his actions in public view so they can be criticized. Again, he may distrust the motives of staff, and feel they are trying to usurp his authority. Whatever the cause, staff specialists usually believe that their potential value is minimized if they are only called in when a situation is so far out of hand as to be hopeless.

Most specialized staff managers feel that they should be consulted during the planning stages of a program that involves their own area of specialty. This enables them to anticipate problems and to recommend precautionary measures. As one safety engineer put it: "If I'm called in before machinery or equipment is ordered, I can help specify safety features that the maintenance and purchasing people aren't aware of. It's my business to keep up with our special requirements and new developments in safety engineering. Most times I get in on the show only after accidents have happened."

Line Resists New Ideas   Many staff men feel that line management tends to be shortsighted and resistant to new ideas. Staff men are usually alert to the newest thinking and innovations in the field of their specialties. The public relations man may be enthusiastic about open-house programs; the personnel man may be convinced that psychological testing is a panacea for many of the ills of the plant; the industrial engineer may be certain that statistical quality control is the cure-all for low quality.

Line management, however, is often cautious and slow to accept new ideas. One industrial engineer who was advocating the use of work sampling and meeting with a great deal of resistance from the plant superintendent summed up this point of view when he said, "They preach 'wait and see' while we're wasting thousands of dollars a day. We'd do better with a little gumption and less caution."

Line Does Not Give Staff Enough Authority   A common theme in the staff manager's complaint is lack of authority. As one industrial engineer said: "We're paid to be experts. Most of us know a lot more in our specialty than line people. But we haven't got the authority to make it stick."

Many staff managers feel that if they have the best answer to a problem, they should be able to enforce the solution on the line man involved. To their way of thinking, knowledge is authority, and there is not much point in throwing organizational barriers between the man who knows and the job that has to be done.

Solutions

The answer to better teamwork between staff and line seems to lie, first, in an understanding of their basic relationship. Company experience indicates that the following important points must be observed if effective teamwork is to exist.

1. The units that are designated as line have ultimate responsibility for the successful operation of the company. Therefore, line departments must be responsible for operating decisions.

2. Staff elements contribute by providing advice and service to the line in accomplishing the objectives of the enterprise.

3. Staff is responsible for providing advice and service to appropriate line elements when requested to do so. However, staff also is responsible for proffering advice and service when it is not requested, but where the staff believes it is needed.

4. The solicitation of advice and acceptance of suggestions and counsel is usually at the option of the line organization. However, in some instances it must

be recognized that only the top level of the organization has this option and that top management's decision with respect to the use of staff advice or service is binding throughout lower levels. For instance, if the president decides that all purchasing will be handled by the staff procurement department, an operating department is not at liberty to contract for its own purchases of safety shoes. These decisions may be expressed in company policies or procedures, or they may be conveyed informally.

5. Line is responsible for giving serious consideration to advice and offers of service made by staff units, and should follow the recommendations if it is in the company's best interest to do so. However, except in those cases where the use of staff advice and service is compulsory and subject only to appeal to higher authority, it is not mandatory that the advice of staff be followed. Except as noted above, line managers should have authority to modify, reject or accept such advice.

6. Both line and staff should have the right to appeal to higher authority in case of disagreement on staff recommendations. However, this right to appeal should not be permitted to supersede the line's responsibility for making immediate decisions when required by the operating situation.

How Staff Can Do a Better Job

How can the staff specialist do a better job in terms of these relationships? Many companies find that the following points help facilitate and improve staff operations.

Operate in Terms of Policies and Objectives of the Company As a Whole Written statements of company policy have an important bearing on staff-line relationships. These statements of what the company believes and intends to live by provide guides to both line and staff people over which the staff exercises a watchdog kind of control. In many cases the staff executive is responsible for interpreting these policies with, of course, the final decision resting with the chief executive officer in cases of dispute. Understanding by both line and staff executives of their responsibilities for the development of and adherence to the company policies tends to eliminate much of the friction that can easily develop between line and staff. The objectives of staff departments should be aimed at helping the company accomplish its purposes, and not devoted to the specialized goals of the staff department itself.

For example, the company may not need a program of psychological testing because tests are not capable of identifying the special kinds of talent the company requires. Statistical quality control may not be indicated because the company is trying a new market in which gross tolerances are permissible and in which price is far more important than precise machining. To be able to operate in such terms, the staff man first has to see the over-all picture. He needs to know what the company is trying to accomplish in terms of operations, costs and sales. Then he needs to be able to subordinate his personal and professional interests to the welfare of the company as a whole.

Encourage and Educate Line to Use Staff Effectively   A line manager cannot use a staff specialist effectively unless he knows what that specialist can do for him. The staff man has the responsibility of letting the line know what he has to offer.

In some companies, this is done through training conferences. Each staff manager appears before conference groups of line and other staff personnel and describes his function to them. He points out how he can be helpful in solving specific problems, and answers questions that may come up.

In other companies, staff managers make a point of talking with line managers individually about their operations. The staff man uses this opportunity to outline his own activities and to introduce any ideas he may have as to how he may be useful to the line operator.

Recognize and Overcome Resistance to Change   One of the important reasons for line opposition to ideas presented by staff is the psychological factor of resistance to change. People tend to resist ideas that threaten to change their way of doing things. The fact that a change is even suggested seems to imply that the old way was not good enough.

It is not so commonly recognized that people are even more set against changes that threaten disturbance or alteration in personal relationships. For example, a maintenance supervisor may be moderately opposed to a suggested change in his job responsibilities. He has always been responsible for the installation of new equipment and he does not want to give it up, even though he is being given responsibility for the lubrication program in its place. However, if the change means that he will also have to move to another part of the plant and work with another group of people, his resistance is likely to be greatly intensified.

Staff specialists can anticipate and overcome this natural resistance to proposed changes. Many companies have found these points helpful:

1. Determine to what extent the proposed change will affect personal relationships. Is the staff man advocating a major, sweeping change which will affect the social patterns established in the group? If so, the traumatic effect and accompanying resistance can be diminished if the change is broken into smaller, more numerous moves which will make gradual adjustment possible.

2. When major changes are involved which will modify the relationships between a manager and the people who work for him, opposition from the manager will be minimized if he participates in the preliminary planning. Then, when announcement of the change is made, the principal directly affected can make it as a working partner with the staff, and not as an unwilling associate. In effect, this gives the line manager an opportunity to make the idea his own.

3. People who will be affected by the change will accept it better if:

The change is tied in as closely as possible with their personal goals and interests, their jobs, families, and futures, and if they are convinced it will make their own work easier, faster or safer.

They have an opportunity to offer suggestions, ideas and comments concerning the change as it affects them—provided they are convinced these suggestions are sincerely wanted and will be given serious consideration.

They are kept informed of the results of the change.

They are able to check on how well they are doing in terms of the change.

4. Acquire technical proficiency. The primary reason for the existence of staff is that it is highly informed and capable in a specialized field. It follows that the staff specialist, if he is to merit respect and to do his work properly, must be an expert. He needs a detailed and extensive knowledge of his field, and he needs to be able to convey this knowledge and information convincingly to others.

Technical proficiency in a staff man implies more than specialized knowledge. It also requires that the specialist have a knowledge of the company and its operations. The more he knows of line problems and operations, and those of other staff specialties, the better he can develop effective recommendations in his own area.

How Line Can Make Better Use of Staff

The effectiveness of the line manager depends to a large extent upon how he makes use of staff services. The line manager who wants to make most advantageous use of the staff services at his disposal will find the following points of value:

1. *Make maximum use of staff.* The more the line man makes use of staff, the better acquainted the specialists will become with his problems and his way of working. Many line executives find that it is only common sense to make habitual use of staff. In effect, the line manager has on retainer a consultant who can help him perform better.

2. *Make proper use of staff.* Lost motion, duplication and personal irritation often occur because the line manager hasn't made up his mind what advice or service he needs before he calls in the specialist.

In one case, for example, a plant manager asked the purchasing agent to secure data on the comparative costs of a pusher bar conveyor installation as compared to the existing crane and magnet operation. After the purchasing agent had completed his study at considerable time and effort, the plant manager told him: "We haven't got the money for new equipment. I guess what I really wanted to know was how to operate that crane with two men instead of three." He then called in the industrial engineer to make a new study for him.

3. *Keep staff informed.* Line managers frequently take action directly affecting staff activities without notifying the staff people concerned. For example, in one company the executive vice-president and the manager of one of the operating divisions decided to install a fully automatic assembly line in one plant of the division. This necessitated the use of many more maintenance and technical people over a period of years, together with several additional engineers. The personnel manager found out about the new plan only after the work was completed and a request for additional people came through. Instead of having an opportunity to train and upgrade people from within the company over a period of months, he was forced to hire the additional staff from the outside.

Many companies have found that time and effort spent in training and educating managers in proper line-staff relationships is an excellent investment. Evidence seems to show that this is a direct means of improving teamwork, increasing the productive capacity of members of management and reducing friction in personal relationships.

QUESTIONS

1. Why are some functions line in one company and staff in another?

2. Explain why the role of the staff has become so important in the large corporation during the past several decades.

3. Are conflicts between line and staff inherent in the concepts of their work?

4. What can be done in the way of improving the working relationship between line and staff?

Centralization Versus Decentralization

ERNEST DALE

"Decentralization" like "politeness" means different things to different people, but in no case should it be taken to imply a value judgment. The term itself means the delegation of business decisions by the owners to their immediate representatives (the board of directors and the chief executive), and then to others further down in the management hierarchy. This is done with the aim of furthering the objectives and values of the enterprise; hence decentralization is only a means to an end.

In addition, "decentralization" is not an absolute term. There are varying degrees of decentralized authority, and the extent to which any company is decentralized must be gauged by tests.

The *locus* or *place* of the decision-making authority in the management hierarchy is one criterion. The lower the rank of the executives who make given decisions, the greater the degree of decentralization. For example, decentralization is greater where larger amounts of money can be spent at lower levels for such things as capital equipment, administrative or operating purposes, or salary changes. The degree of authority for decisions that could result in a loss may also be a test. In a carpet factory, a mistake in the weave would not be serious; hence the function of quality control could be placed far down in the management hierarchy without any great degree of decentralization. In a pharmaceutical company, on the other hand, an error might cause a death, and quality decisions need to be made near the top level.

From *Advanced Management Journal*, June 1955, pp. 11-16. Reprinted by permission.

In addition, the *degree* of decision-making power at the lower levels will be a factor. This can be determined by studying the authority which can be exercised (1) without any check with higher authority at all (routinized decisions such as the billing procedure, safety enforcement, purchase of stock orders); (2) with a check or regular report after the decision is made and carried out (engagement of clerical personnel, purchases of equipment covered by budget); or (3) with a check before the decision is made or put into effect (decisions without precedent, special appropriation requests). Or there may be the simple requirement to check with a superior on all matters of policy changes, of financial appropriations, or potential and actual disagreements.

In determining the degree of decentralization, moreover, it must always be remembered that an enterprise has both *formal and informal decision-making* rules. Official policy statements may decree one type of decision-making, but actual practice may be quite different. Thus there may be a high degree of formal centralization, but if successful business conduct is not possible under such circumstances, decisions may be, in fact, made much lower down.

For instance, in one firm with about a billion dollars of sales, all purchases over $2,500 must be submitted to the president; and all changes in salaries above $4,000, all expense accounts and all public appearances of executives have to be approved by the chief. Obviously, this chief executive is unable to handle all these approvals himself. The large majority of the purchasing decisions are, in fact, made by executives lower down the line, because merchandise has to be bought and sold if the business is to continue.

When objectives clash with the assignment of responsibility and authority, one or the other is likely to be disregarded. Thus, informal, centralized controls may make possible over-riding the effectiveness of formally decentralized responsibility and authority.

Again formal centralization may be offset to some extent by physical decentralization. For example, the production of certain products may be undertaken at a separate physical location; accounting records may be assembled and placed next to the immediate user. Thus in decentralization movements, headquarters are sometimes shifted away from the plant to prevent the close control that can come from propinquity.

CURRENT STATUS IN THE UNITED STATES

There is no statistical information on the extent of centralization and its reverse, the decentralization of decision-making, in U.S. industry. Business literature usually carries accounts of corporate decentralization, largely because such moves are considered "progressive" and hence newsworthy (one rarely reads today of a president boasting of centralization). However, general reasoning will show that centralization is still quite widespread. Probably "one-man control" is found in more companies and affects more employees than "control by the few" or "control by the many."

One-man control stems partly from tradition and partly from human nature. Men in commanding positions like to believe that they are indispensable—secretly hope, perhaps, that they may always be there to carry on. They fear that delegation of authority may foster the creation of "empires within the empire," and make them more dependent on others. In addition, it is hard for the one man in control to jettison all his intellectual investments. He may be committed to a belief in the virtues of benevolent dictatorship, and the power of vested ideas may well be stronger than the power of economic interests.

And this may well be a long-run trend. For there may be a difference (and sometimes an appreciable one) between the maximum profit that a company *could* make and the actual profit it must make to keep the stockholders from complaining too loudly. To this extent the compulsion to maximum profits no longer exists to the same degree that it did 50 years ago when owner-management was much more common. Nor is the maximization of profits as advantageous for the individual executive as it used to be, since income taxes, the decline in the value of money, and the long-run decline in the rate of interest all make large accumulations of wealth difficult and often impossible. Andrew Carnegie made many millions of dollars, but the present heads of the Carnegie-Illinois Steel Corporation have no such prospects, even though the job is probably considerably more difficult and complex than in Carnegie's time. For this reason, it may not be worthwhile to risk public opprobrium by squeezing customers or employees, and the consequent trend to "awareness of social responsibilities" may be affecting even family-owned and operated businesses to some extent.

Hence, one may be justified in studying the shift from profit to power as a major business objective and its effect on decentralization. "Power" may be sought in volume of sales or percentage of market, in professional distinction (i.e., the emphasis on "management as a profession," as an "elite," etc.). The chief executive may demonstrate his power by setting the tone in the local community or the industry, by accepting important positions in government or the foreign service. Or he may simply hold on to all major and many minor decisions in the enterprise. Even in allegedly decentralized companies the delegation of powers may go no further than from the chief executive to his vice presidents, and subordinates cannot complain because the holders of power are their immediate superiors.

Factors making for centralization in an enterprise may be many. Most important, perhaps, is the example of the chief executive. To the extent to which he retains powers, his subordinates are likely to imitate him. To the extent that he welcomes "checking," "consultation" and dependence, his subordinates are likely to do the same. Of course, the chief does not actually have to make each decision himself. He merely needs to "spot-check." For example, if he insists on passing on all increases in salaries above $400 a month and 1,000 such applications reach him every month, he needs to pass on only one or a few of them. If he raises a question (or an eyebrow) everyone will be careful to propose only such increases as can be justified under questioning by the chief.

MEASUREMENT OF RESULTS NECESSARY BUT COMPLEX

Then all the devices used to coordinate an enterprise may be used to foster centralization. Such "tools" as organization and policy manuals, methods and procedures manuals, authority limitation manuals (dealing with authority for capital expenditures, salary and personnel changes, etc.) may actually take away more authority than they confer. Sometimes they enforce systems of communication along the lines of a pyramid. Or the chief executive may set up checks and sources of information that nullify the delegation of powers. Measurement of results is, of course, necessary; the chief must know how the delegated powers are exercised. But the controls may bring about so much checking, transmission of so much information so continuously, and so much correction that the "decentralized" operators may spend a considerable part of their time explaining and defending themselves. In some companies, the saying goes: "It takes two tons of paper to make one ton of product." There is also the possibility that the chief's general staff may deliberately force executives to refer many decisions to headquarters or influence decisions without adequate consultation. Or the special staff may exercise central command powers because of actual or assumed technical knowledge, direct operation of services, "concurrent authority," superior articulation, physical proximity to the chief, or simply in default of decision-making elsewhere. There are the possible abuses of group work, the enforcement of compatibility and conformity, the use of manipulative techniques to strengthen centralization.

Finally there are the modern means of communication—telephone, telegraph, teletype, radio, and now television—which make it physically possible for the chief executive to issue direct orders to distant subordinates. And it is even possible that future technical developments may eliminate one of the main reasons for decentralization. If enough information can be brought to a central point quickly enough, there may no longer be a need to have problems settled at a point close to their source. The development of electronic devices, calculators, punch card systems, etc., together with such tools as operations research and Cybernetics, may so greatly and so quickly increase the information available to central management that the basic desire of many chiefs—to continue to make as many decisions as possible or to widen the range of their decision-making—might be gratified.

FORCES BEHIND GREATER DECENTRALIZATION

But even if these powerful factors making for "one-man control" did not exist, extensive delegation might still not be possible. For the personnel who can shoulder the additional responsibilities might not be available. Those who grew up with the chief in the business may not be able (or willing) to take more responsibility. Yet if the chief brings in outside personnel, the newcomers may be thwarted by uncooperative oldtimers.

Thus effective delegation of decision-making may be costly. Difficult personalities may be hard to replace, and both the training of new executives and their initial mistakes may be expensive. Additional functional personnel (accounting, research, industrial relations, etc.) may have to be hired in the now semi-autonomous divisions and branches and the difficult relationship to head-office worked out. Informal work groups and long-established relationships may be upset and destroyed. It is difficult and time-consuming to get executives to assume and exercise additional responsibility.

Finally, hard times and increased competition may foster centralization. When the chief executive feels that the company cannot afford mistakes, he is likely to want more power in his own hands.

So it is clear that the tendencies toward greater centralization or at least preservation of the *status quo* may be strong.

CONTROL BY THE FEW

When the founder or sole directing head of the enterprise passes away, or when there is a reorganization, the struggle for succession may be resolved through the assumption of control by a group whose members have more or less equal status. If the major decisions of the enterprise are made by a small number of men, we speak of "control by the few." Usually each of these men handles one or several management functions and makes the major decisions concerning them. Insofar as a decision affects more than one executive—that is, if it requires coordination or cuts across the business as a whole—several executives may have an important voice and the decision-making power of each may be practically equal. Control is often exercised by informal consultation, but there may be formal meetings held at regular intervals—of executive committees, management committees, etc.

Motives for establishing "control by the few" are varied. Sometimes it is believed that the company is too large to be managed successfully by one man. That is how Myron Taylor is said to have felt, after Judge Gary's death, about the management of the U.S. Steel Corporation. So he brought in Fairless to handle production, gave Olds charge of the legal and public relations functions, and Voorhees responsibility for finance. Each had more or less equal power on intracompany problems. In other cases, equality of decision-making is designed to train successors to the chief executive by inducing a number of senior vice presidents to compete for the top position. With the increasing emphasis on the social responsibility of business, new members of the board of directors or new top operating executives may be added to represent the point of view of some of the various "publics" affected by the enterprise. Finally, control by the few may be the end result of one of the plans of "group dynamics" or executive participation.

Genuine equal control by a group of individuals rarely attains long-run equilibrium, and usually only where there is long experience and training, careful selection, an established tradition and long personal acquaintance and respect such as exists in the Management Committees of the Crown-Zellerbach Company or the Executive Committee of the du Pont Company. If it is to be successful, the group should be homogeneous in outlook, heterogeneous in ability. Objectives and authority must be fairly similar; otherwise disagreements are likely to upset the equilibrium sooner or later. Participants must have a degree of sensitivity toward situations and toward each other, and be broadminded enough to disagree without quarrel, e.g., there must be both informality and careful appreciation of all the usual committee mechanics—definition of functions, agenda, assignment of responsibilities, etc.

The great drawback to control by the few is the potential paralysis of decision-making. It takes time to obtain unanimity, and it may sometimes be achieved only by a compromise that is less effective than the decision of one man; such as agreement on the lowest common denomination. Or the group may split and the majority dominate. The more heterogeneous the composition of the group, the greater the probability of such conflict. For example, the difference in viewpoint between financially minded and production minded executives may make it impossible to arrive at lasting solutions of labor and human problems.

Thus control by the few may be a passing phenomenon. When conditions change to an extent affecting the course of the business perceptibly, one-man control may be restored. Alternately, progress may be made toward "control by the many," that is, participation in important decisions by an increasing number of executives. This tends to develop as members of the "oligarchy" attempt to arrive at genuine joint decisions better than those any one individual or a few of them could reach alone.

CONTROL BY THE MANY

The control-by-many type of decision-making may be called "integrative" or "participative." (These are probably better terms than "democratic," because the latter, taken from political science, assumes an equality of men that usually does not exist in this context, certainly not in terms of status and income, and usually not in terms of power to influence business decisions.)

Most frequently this participation takes the form of informal, friendly consultation among leading executives and possibly their subordinates. This is, however, of a haphazard nature and could be quickly changed or destroyed by the whim of any important executive involved. Informal consultation may be useless as a starting point or as a means of continuing and stabilizing far-reaching control by the many. For this reason formal control by the many, often called "decentralization," may be adopted.

HISTORY OF DECENTRALIZATION IN AMERICA

The decentralization movement in American business was probably begun by Henry V. Poor in the 1850's through his proposals for the reorganization of American railroads, when he sought to help those first large-scale organizations overcome the drawbacks of diminishing returns from management. This remarkable man coined the phrase "the science of management." Poor's suggestions were first applied by Daniel McCallum, General Superintendent on the Erie Railroad 1854 to 1857 and later one of the chief organizers of the American transport system during the Civil War.

The first successful large-scale plan of decentralization in manufacturing industry was probably that presented in 1920 to W. C. Durant, President of General Motors by Alfred P. Sloan, Jr., then G.M. Vice President. This was a most remarkable and far-sighted document, largely formed the basis of the present General Motors organization and was put into effect by many other companies. This was adopted when General Motors was reorganized in 1921. Independently of this, A. W. Robertson, lately Chairman of the Board of the Westinghouse

Electric Corporation; Ralph Kelly, Vice President and F. D. Newbury, Economist (now Assistant Secretary of Defense) developed and carried out such a decentralization program at Westinghouse from 1936 to 1939, and it proved to be extremely successful. Standard Oil of California was a pioneer in systematic organization planning under L. L. Purkey. Outstanding post-war examples of decentralization with a successful record of over seven years include the work of L. F. McCollum at the Continental Oil Co. and the decentralization of the Ford Motor Co. Among successfully decentralized smaller companies the "cooperative capitalism" of the C. J. Bath Company should be mentioned—in this firm all levels of management participate in major policy decisions.

Essentially one or more of the following characteristics mark a program of decentralization in a large corporation.

(1) *The administrative unit that usually covers the company as a whole as well as all its plants is broken into smaller administrative units—often on either a geographical or product basis.* Each is headed by a manager who may be compared to the head of a smaller enterprise. Usually he has fairly complete control over basic line functions, such as manufacturing and marketing; if he also has staff services such as accounting, engineering, research and personnel, the unit may be largely self-contained.

(2) *Provision is made for the effective utilization of a centralized staff of specialists to aid the decentralized operations to increased profitability and better relationships in order to combine the advantages of a large unit of management with those of a small one.* Central staff specialists are said to "advise and assist" the chief executive and the line operators, and perhaps handle certain centralized functions for the company as a whole, such as public relations, law and taxation. In other cases, the centralized staff specialists maintain "functional supervision" over divisional operations in their fields of expertise, such as industrial relations, finance, and possibly manufacturing and sales. Functional supervision may cover formulation of major company objectives, policies, plans and programs for line management's approval and seeing that decisions are carried out, furnishing administrative and technical advice, setting up standards, systems, procedures, controls and measurement of performance, concurring in selection of key personnel and in changes in their assignment.

DELEGATION OF AUTHORITY TO SPECIALISTS

The essential problem in this area of decentralization is the delineation of the authority of the staff specialists. The theoretical "indirect" authority of the central staff may vary in fact from advice to command. For example, the headquarters staff specialist in personnel administration may be an adviser on personality problems, a coordinator of union negotiations, a policy-maker in job and salary evaluation, a researcher on executive development, a statistical compiler of personnel data, an operator of cafeteria services (and of his own department) or he may "concur" on urgent problems of safety (e.g., prohibiting a worker from continuing on a dangerous machine), a controller of the observance of personnel policies. Clearly there are numerous opportunities for widespread participation by "staff" in the decision-making of the enterprise, through the actual use of authority of various kinds, including the "authority" of knowledge.

(3) *A series of general staffs may be provided for the chief executive* to handle the functions which he cannot delegate and which may become increasingly burdensome as the company increases in size. For example, growth of the enterprise requires more attention to the increasing number of people affected by it. When the chief represents the company personally in these contacts, an increasing proportion of his time is spent away from his subordinates. Or it may be difficult or impossible for the chief executive to handle the growing demands of coordination and communication. Hence he may acquire staff assistance in the person of an "assistant to," who has been called "an extension of the personality of his chief," and as such acts in his name.

APPLICATION OF MILITARY TO BUSINESS ORGANIZATION

The use of a general staff, widely and successfully employed in the armed forces of the world, has been urged by President Eisenhower to the author as "the major application of military to business organization." It is interesting to note that a number of business leaders and pioneers of scientific management started out as "assistants to." For example, Gantt, Barth and S. E. Thompson were assistants to Taylor. Alfred P. Sloan, Jr., and Walter P. Chrysler were assistants to W. C. Durant.

Other staff variants are the "Pentagon Staff" which handles long-range planning for the company as a whole (e.g. the Bell Telephone Laboratories) and the "personal staff" whose job is to make the business life of the chief smoother and more convenient.

(4) *Centralized Controls are designed to find out how well the delegated authority and responsibility are exercised.* Controls may include budgets, standards, reports, audits, visits, regular meetings and exchange of information. Instead of measuring results for the company as a whole, an attempt is made to break down profit or (controllable) cost responsibilities by operating units. This is merely a modernization of the practice of some of the great department store founders who let individual managers alone for a year or two, and then "looked at the record." Perhaps the "decentralization of measurement" partly explains the success of the Standard Oil Company of New Jersey's system of "wholly owned subsidiaries." Furthest in this direction went Orlando F. Webber, for some time the chief executive of Allied Chemical and Dye Company who ran the company on the basis of detailed monthly reports brought to him at the Waldorf Towers, his New York hotel. Not only may costs be effectively controlled by "decentralized measurement," but managerial analysis of results and remedial action are facilitated. A closer tie between effort and reward is made possible.

In a more formal sense there may be a "control office" attached to the chief executive to enable him to "manage on the exception principle." This may be supplemented by manpower controls (varying with the state of business), organization, executive development, planning departments. Essentially the task of the control office is to know the multitude of factors, weigh them and present them in an orderly fashion to someone far removed who makes basic decisions and still has the ultimate cost responsibility, yet can decide only by the rule of "exception."

DECIDING THE DEGREE OF DECENTRALIZATION

Decentralization is not an ideal. It is not a series of principles or prescriptions that a businessman ought necessarily to follow. Decentralization is not necessarily good, nor is centralization necessarily bad.

Centralization or decentralization may be, in part, merely the result of circumstances. Many labor problems are handled centrally because the laws of the country require it or the union insists on it. Many operating or sales decisions are decentralized because it would be physically impossible to operate successfully if they were centralized. Frequently, the centralization or decentralization of a decision is merely an accident. Finally, there is an immense variety of possible human behavior, a vast multiplicity of minute, undiscoverable causes and effects that cannot be encompassed in any principle or standard of evaluation. Thus there is a large area in which necessity, intuition, and luck decide the issue between centralization and decentralization.

DECENTRALIZATION BRINGS SPEEDIER DECISIONS

Where a conscious decision to decentralize is made, ideally it should be based on economic factors. The assignment of a management decision, or any part of it, higher or lower in the management hierarchy, should depend on *the additional revenue to be gained as compared to the additional cost.*

Under decentralization, decisions may be made more speedily because problems of communications are minimized. Often the decisions will be wiser also, because the men who make them will be closer to the problems. Other economies may be achieved through better utilization of lower and middle management, greater incentive, more and improved training opportunities, insurance that some products will not be pushed at the expense of others. In addition, when the administrative unit is smaller—absolutely or as a proportion of the employable population of the community—there are likely to be closer and better employee-management and community relations. And for the business as a whole, the decentralization of activities may mean a more widespread distribution of sales and purchases, which may reduce proportionately the unfavorable impact of sales decline.

Finally, decentralization may result in an increase in the marginal social net product—i.e., benefits to the community as distinct from benefits to the company. These general benefits may include more freedom of action for individuals, more widespread opportunity for constructive individual participation, less social stratification within the business.

The contributions of decentralization to profits must be weighed against the costs, both those that can be measured in dollars and cents and those that are more intangible. Easily measurable are the permanent extra costs that result from the larger staffs necessary, and some temporary expenses of introducing the change in management. More intangible costs are the disturbances caused by the change and their possible effects on morale. In addition, there may be "disguised unemployment" (high-priced men not fully utilized) and losses from watertight thinking or over-specialization. Finally, there are the costs (and gains) of destroying or delaying educational and promotional opportunities from some executives and creating them for others in the process of reorganization.

Basically the economic issue between centralization and decentralization is between lower total administrative costs and more effective performance. This is indicated by a quantitative comparison of centralized and decentralized personnel departments in a recent study by E. C. Weiss of the Department of Psychology, University of Maryland. In a small, but apparently not unrepresentative sample of 38 companies, decentralized organizations had a larger ratio of administrative employees to total employment than centralized firms, but lower rates of labor turnover, absenteeism, accident frequencies and severities.

THE STAGES OF DECENTRALIZATION

In reorganization the shift from centralization to decentralization can be compared to a capital investment. There is a heavy initial outlay which may be recovered after some years with a permanent net gain.[1]

In the development of every corporation there comes a point at which the gains of increasing size are such that the still increasing costs of coordination are likely to exceed them. Diminishing returns from the management factor begin to set in when the top executive(s) are no longer intimately acquainted with the major problems of the company and are unable to coordinate them effectively or lose their health in attempting the task. (In this the "managerial optimum" differs from the "technical optimum." The latter merely relates to a minimum scale of operations below which the greatest efficiency cannot be achieved.) But if the managerial optimum is exceeded, costs, through declining managerial efficiency and the need for additional coordination begin to rise. The managerial optimum sets, therefore, an upper limit to the scale of operations unless there is a reorganization and some decentralization.

Reorganization implies an analysis of basic company objectives to determine how well the existing structure meets them, the elimination of existing deficiencies and the introduction of new organizational techniques to overcome the diminishing returns from the factor management. The process of reorganization may perhaps go through the following three stages:

PROCESSES OF REORGANIZATION IN THREE STAGES

The immediate impact of delegation of decision-making tends to bring about economies. At the top management level the need for coordination of all major

---

[1](F. W. Taylor once observed "the building of an efficient organization is necessarily slow and sometimes very expensive", *Shop Management,* p. 62.)

decisions is considerably reduced. Top management's time is freed to some extent for more important activities. In the smaller administrative (product) units responsibility for basic operating costs is more clearly fixed. There is likely to be an immediate reduction of "red tape and bureaucracy," and elimination of duplication. Better dissemination of more nearly correct information is obtained and faster action taken. Joint responsibility for costs is reduced. There is a new spirit about, and there are many other immediate savings.

Some immediate increase in cost also occurs, since there must be some increase in the number of executives and specialists. Headquarters requires a larger staff to provide more expert advice and control the results of delegated responsibility and authority; and the heads of the various administrative units each require staff assistance also. Flexible budgets, standard cost systems, and other means of analyzing results may be introduced.

In the second stage, the increase in controllers and staff specialists leads to a net increase in administrative expenses, part of which is permanent, and part of which is due to the necessity of gaining experience in the new system.

Eventually, however, the controls and the expert counsel from headquarters and field staff specialists are likely to make for greater profitability. In the long run, therefore, the corporation should not only recoup its initial outlay, but achieve gains that more than offset the continuing extra costs.

Thus decentralization is clearly a difficult process. This explains the necessity of considering it in balance with centralization. Even if the effort does not result in actual delegation of decision-making, it may still prevent an increase in centralization and afford prestige and opportunity to those receiving it.

QUESTIONS

1. Why have a number of business firms relied upon centralization of the decision-making function?

2. What are the advantages of decentralizing the decision-making function?

3. Trace the history of decentralization in the United States.

4. How should the manager go about deciding the degree of decentralization to utilize in his firm?

The Nature of the Executive Decision

JOHN E. SWEARINGEN

For some time we have been bombarded by a great number of books, articles, and theories about decision making. Anyone who is interested can find detailed instructions in print telling him how to make bigger decisions, faster decisions, more profitable decisions—almost any kind, in fact, except totally wrong decisions, which are the kind we all make frequently. Much of this is misleading. One of the most popular bits of advice we are apt to get along these lines is to start by determining all the relevant facts. Strictly applied, this injunction would paralyze any major decision. If D-Day had been postponed until all relevant facts were determined, the Normandy invasion would never have been launched.

This is not to belittle everything which has been written on the subject. Even if we do not actually understand how decisions are made, hindsight can at least identify decisions which worked in a given situation and those which did not, and guides can be developed on this basis which are helpful in avoiding mistakes under similar circumstances. But it is still dangerous to assume that anyone can construct a logical blueprint which will lead us to correct decisions.

Particularly in larger organizations, the nature of executive decision-making is often concealed by use of the expression "corporate decision," which suggests the end product of some vast, impersonal process. In spite of a general fondness for the term, there is really no such thing, since a legal abstraction cannot actually come to a conclusion. At the genuine decision-making level, there are only decisions made by human beings, either singly or collectively.

This in itself has some rather significant implications. For one thing, it means that we do not really know how decisions are made, particularly those which are complex, because we do not know enough about the functioning of the human brain. An interesting illustration of this is a recent statement by a contemporary historian who observed that one of the things lost with the death of President Kennedy was his own explanation of the Bay of Pigs decision, since not even the President's closest advisors could know what went through his mind at that time. Further reflection suggests that even the testimony of the man who has made a given decision leaves much to be desired, since none of us is capable of isolating all of the conscious and subconscious factors which go into the process.

THE CRITERION OF DECISIONS

In corporate terms, we do, of course, have an *ex post facto* means of evaluating decisions—by asking whether or not they have furthered the company's objectives, foremost of which must be profitability.

John E. Swearingen, "The Nature of the Executive Decision," *MSU Business Topics,* Spring, 1965. Reprinted by permission of the publisher, the Bureau of Business and Economic Research, Division of Research, Graduate School of Business Administration, Michigan State University.

The corporation has been selected by our society as one of the principal mechanisms whereby wealth is to be created and distributed. The corporation is, in effect, entrusted with different types of assets of a certain current value and told to turn them into something of greater value—that is, to create new wealth.

Since the value that society puts on different forms of wealth is highly subjective and varies with the passage of time, a given corporation may find it hard to determine where it actually stands at a given moment. It might be devoting its major efforts today to the creation of something society will put no value on tomorrow.

The test of the correctness of corporate decisions in this regard is the test of profitability. Profitability is both society's recognition of success in creating new wealth and the chief—although imprecise—measure of how much wealth has in fact been created by the process.

Growth, Survival, Profit

It is obvious that profitability must be the fundamental corporate goal, if only because there is no other satisfactory way to measure what a corporation can or does do. This goal is customarily sandwiched in between two others called "survival" and "growth." There is a neat logic about this, I suppose, if you want three goals rather than one, but the latter two are largely implicit in the first. Profitability pretty clearly demands existence, that is survival; and, particularly in a highly competitive system, growth tends to go along with profitability—assuming it is the right kind of growth. If it is the wrong kind, it can be fatal to both profitability and existence.

However, the end product of successful decisions is a profitable corporation, and customarily, a growing one. It is hardly surprising that corporations have tended to grow in a country which has elevated growth itself to the status of a national goal; and growth we have surely had, ranging from the unprecedented in population to the breath-taking in technology. In the process, corporations —as one of our key social institutions and themselves a prime source of growth in wealth, techniques, and ideas—have also increased in both number and size.

One of the challenging by-products of this history of growth is the multiplication in the volume and complexity of decisions to be made, particularly at the upper levels of management.

The very scope of decisions has tended to escalate. Instead of four or five major competitors, they must take dozens into account; instead of hundreds of employees, they can affect thousands; instead of tens of millions of dollars in assets, they often involve hundreds of millions.

THE SCOPE OF RESPONSIBILITY

The responsibility this focuses on the decision-maker is very great indeed. As an example, my own company has approximately 40,000 employees on its payrolls. This does not include the service station operators who sell our products and their employees, who together comprise easily another 100,000 people with an immediate interest in our operations. If we include the families of these various groups, we find no less than half a million people whose livelihoods are tied in directly with the success or failure of our company and whose lives are affected by the decisions made.

When you add in stockholders, supplying companies, and customers, you begin to get a measure of the range and impact upon human lives which can be embodied in a single major policy decision. Such decisions can affect the economic well-being of entire communities, and whole states, through their influence on employment levels and tax revenues.

Compounding the problem has been a mounting need to make longer-range decisions at a time when exploding technology has made the job of prediction increasingly hazardous. As if this were not quite enough, we have seen accelerating demands to make decisions more quickly, under the pressures of competition and instantaneous communication.

Intellectual Capacity

It is not easy to see just where all these developments are taking us. Some attempts to describe tomorrow's corporate decision-maker suggest a combination of Alexander and Einstein. Since all of history has yielded only a single example of each, it seems less than likely that we are going to be able suddenly to develop managers by the hundreds or thousands who will combine the unusual attributes of such men.

Here we come up against a very hard fact indeed. There is no evidence that man's intellectual capacities have shown either quantitative or qualitative improvement over thousands of years. While we have a larger number of educated minds and more tools, techniques, and knowledge for them to work with, individual reasoning power is no greater than it was at the time of Ptolemy. Yet the body of knowledge in mathematics and astronomy—to take two fields in which he was the leading authority—is today so vast that no one would expect even a man of his genius to master it all.

I do not wish to suggest that the situation is hopeless. There are still no positive signs that we have exhausted our capacity to manage what we have created. Despite the mounting pressures on the corporate decision-maker which I have described, the system has still functioned, and functioned rather well. This is not to deny that there are danger signals flying. We obviously cannot continue multiplying forever the number and complexity of decisions to be made at a given location.

Against this background, it might be helpful to take a closer look at the executive decision itself. In general terms, the decision-maker is given certain elements with which he is supposed to accomplish his objectives: these include people, physical assets, money and credit, and time. All of these have to be employed within a constantly changing environment which includes forces both favorable and unfavorable to the company's goals. In many instances, attainment of a given goal may even necessitate bringing about some alteration in the environment itself. Moreover, all of these elements are interrelated.

This means that the executive decision is very much like a move in a game of three-dimensional chess. A decision either to act or not to act in a given situation will ordinarily have repercussions running well beyond what appears to be the immediate action. A decision of any significance will invite reactions within the company, from competitors, from customers, from the general public, from stockholders, and frequently from organs of government.

The decision-maker also knows from hard experience that important decisions are seldom resolved in clear-cut terms. For one thing, he knows that any complicated problem is undoubtedly susceptible to more than one apparently satisfactory solution, and that a great deal depends on being able to ask the right questions in order to try to arrive at the best solution, assuming there is one.

He is also very conscious of the time factor. He knows that a decision which might have been successful a year ago might be wrong today, and that one which may be right today could be erroneous in six months. He is further plagued by the realization that, since many of his decisions have results running into the future, it may be years before anyone can determine whether the decision taken was good or bad. And, always, there is the haunting question raised by Robert Frost in "The Road Not Taken": what would have happened if we had taken the other road?

A Hypothetical Case

To make some of these points a little more concrete, it might be helpful to take a relatively routine problem from our own business, by way of example. Suppose we have before us a proposal to undertake an oil exploration and development venture in the Land of Oz. Typically, this would involve an agreement to spend a certain amount of money in exploring for oil over a certain period, to be followed by further expenditures in a given time to develop any oil found, plus agreement as to how any profits would be shared. The length of the contract might be 20 or 30 years.

An inspection of this problem will show that it involves more unknown factors than known factors. Some of the unknowns have to do with technology, some with finance, some with people, some with politics, some with economics, some with competition.

Without even attempting to exhaust the list of questions raised, let me note just a few. How reliable are our estimates of oil demand 10, 15, or 20 years ahead? What is the competitive situation likely to be? Does our present planning encompass profitable outlets for any new oil found over this period? Do we have people capable of negotiating a favorable contract with the present government of Oz, and people to guide and run this new operation? Is the present government likely to be replaced in the foreseeable future, and, if so, who would be the successors? Would they be likely to honor our agreement? What is the best evaluation of the probable political complexion of the surrounding area over the period involved? If we should succeed in finding large amounts of oil, will the developmental costs involve cutting back expenditures in another part of our business, and if so, what part? Is the venture consistent with overall corporate objectives? What would be its effect on profitability, whether the venture succeeds or fails?

JUDGMENT AND THE COMPUTER

It seems to me that if this example demonstrates anything, it dramatizes the critical importance of the faculty of judgment in the decision-making process. Regardless of the quantity and sophistication of the data that can be assembled to bear on the problem, the ultimate decision demands the weighing and balancing of a good number of imponderables and unknowns. It cannot be made purely logically; nor can it be made with certainty.

Beyond doubt, there is a promise of some very real assistance to the hard-pressed decision-maker in the form of new developments in such fields as operations research and from the efforts currently under way to duplicate biological functions by unnatural means—whether mechanical, electrical, electronic, or whatever.

My own company is currently—and profitably, we think—employing a good number of techniques from these new areas. These embrace such diverse things as sophisticated methods of investment evaluation and pioneering applications of computers to our business.

Nevertheless, what all these techniques and devices add up to so far are largely aids to decision making. As aids, some of them are very good indeed, but they do not yet show much promise of growing up to make real decisions for us, if only because the quality of judgment is so vitally involved in the process.

A recent article in *Fortune* suggested that this limitation is not confined to corporate activities. The author, chief of space and ballistics missile planning for the Air Force, argued that if computer techniques and the modern theory of games had been employed in the Civil War, Robert E. Lee would have been given no chance of winning one of his major victories (at Chancellorsville) because computers could not have adequately evaluated Lee's initiative, skill, and daring. He further questioned whether human action can really be expressed in mathematical form, or whether strategy—that is, qualitative action—can be expressed quantitatively.

Actualizing Decisions

There is another serious reservation about the extent to which machines are likely to be of assistance to us in decision making. The problem is not resolved when the decision is made. The decision then has to be put into action, through people. And even if we had a machine capable of making all the judgments leading to decision, I do not see how it would go about the all-important job of getting human beings to follow through. We would also be sacrificing the important control of accountability. It is one thing to be able to penalize a man for a bad decision and reward him for a good one, to assist in his development; punishing or rewarding a machine would seem to be relatively pointless.

Many of the new sciences involved are in their infancy, to be sure, and we cannot predict where they will ultimately lead, any more than we could have taken seriously, a few years ago, the prospect of putting men on the moon in this century. I have seen one prediction that a machine to surpass the intellectual activities of any man will be constructed before the year 2000. This could come to pass, but I remain doubtful as to its usefulness as a decision-maker in a complex organization of human beings like a corporation.

OUR URGENT NEED

What we are more likely to need is a continued supply of well-trained human beings, fallible but unique, capable of making judgments, arriving at decisions, skilled in communicating with other human beings and motivating them to carry out the decision, while also training and developing their own replacements in the process—and even capable of playing an occasional round of golf or hand of bridge.

In short, I think the biblical Valley of Decision is going to continue to be largely populated by man. Nor, in calling attention as I have to some of the many difficulties he faces in this capacity, do I wish to appear pessimistic about his ability to surmount them. History has on the whole tended to confound the cynics and the skeptics.

It is my further opinion that decision making will continue to be one of the most important, demanding, exciting, and rewarding activities to be found in the changing world ahead.

Our urgent need is to develop more managers who possess that combination of intelligence, experience, vision, and tenacity which will enable them to make and carry out the many and demanding decisions that are going to have to be made. Here is probably the greatest challenge facing the corporation today, if it is to fulfill its vital role in our society.

QUESTIONS

1. Why is it impossible to get all the relevant facts before making a major decision?

2. How important is judgment in the decision-making process?

3. What role will the computer play in the decision-making process?

4. What does John E. Swearingen mean by *actualizing decisions?*

The Systems Concept in Management

WILLIAM R. KING

The revolutionary changes in technology which have occurred since World War II have been paralleled by equally drastic changes in the theory and practice of management. Although these changes in management are more subtle than are the technological innovations, their impact is potentially greater.

One major concept has been at the root of changes in both the *planning* (deciding what should be done) and *execution* (doing it) functions of management. That idea—the "systems concept"—has come to pervade management to the extent that the word "systems" is a part of the vocabulary of all who have management responsibilities or interests. Yet, the concept is not so widely understood as it is discussed.[1]

SYSTEMS AND THE SYSTEMS CONCEPT

A system may be defined in dictionary terms as "an organized or complex whole; an assemblage or combination of things or parts forming a complex or unitary whole." The utility of the idea of a system to managing an enterprise may be viewed in terms of two elements of the manager's job. First, he desires to achieve *overall effectiveness* of his organization—not to have the parochial interests of one organizational element distort overall performance. Second, he must do this in an organizational environment which invariably involves *conflicting organizational objectives*.

To demonstrate this, consider the corporate viewpoint involved in the "simple" decision concerning which products are to be produced and in what quantities. The production department of the enterprise would undoubtedly prefer that few products be produced in rather large quantities so that the number of costly machine setups which are necessary to convert from production of one product to production of another are minimized. Such a policy would lead to large inventories of a few products. Sales personnel, on the other hand, desire to have many different products in inventory so that they may promise early delivery on any product. Financial managers recognize that large inventories tie up money which could be invested elsewhere—hence, they want low total inventories. The personnel manager desires constant production levels so that he will

Reprinted from the May, 1967 issue of *The Journal of Industrial Engineering,* Official Publication of the American Institute of Industrial Engineers, Inc., 345 East 47th Street, New York, New York 10017.

[1]A referee for this article has made this point succinctly by saying: "The idea of the 'total systems concept' is one which has been entirely overworked by computer oriented people. Relying heavily on computer jargon, these other authors have tended to cover these fairly straightforward ideas with a cloud of mystery, resulting in a certain lack of acceptance by operating management people."

not constantly be hiring new workers for short periods of peak production and laying them off in slack periods. One could go on to identify objectives of almost every functional unit of an organization relative to this simple tactical decision problem. As demonstrated, these objectives each conflict to some greater or lesser degree: low inventory levels versus high inventories, production of many products versus production of only a few products, and so forth.

The same variety of situation can exist at every other level of the enterprise. The production department must constantly balance the speed of production with the proportion of rejects and the proportion of defective products which are not detected. The marketing function becomes involved when defective products cause complaints and lost sales. Indeed, wherever the "labor" has been divided in an organization, the management task of effectively integrating the various elements is paramount, and this can be effectively accomplished only if the responsible manager adopts the systems approach to the "system" which is his domain.

The systems concept or viewpoint is the simple recognition that any organization is a system which is made up of segments, each of which has its parochial goals. Recognizing this, one can set out to achieve the overall objectives of the organization only by viewing the entire system and seeking to understand and measure the interrelationships, and to integrate them in a fashion which enables the organization to pursue *its* strategic goals effectively.

Of course, this means that some functional unit within an organization may not achieve its parochial objectives, for what is best for the whole is not necessarily best for each component of the system. Thus, when a wide variety of products are produced in relatively small quantities, the apparent performance of the production department may suffer. Yet, if this leads to greater total revenues because no sales are lost, the overall result may be positive. This simple realization is the essence of the systems viewpoint. Its acceptance and utilization has led many organizations to more effective management decisions and to organizing for the efficient execution of those decisions.

SYSTEMS AND PLANNING

The application of the systems concept in management decision-making is closely related to the scientific analysis of decision problems. The reason for this is pragmatic rather than conceptual. The human mind is quite capable of performing analysis. Hence, it is possible that an individual could apply the systems concept and perform a total systems analysis on a totally subjective basis. However, it is unlikely that anyone could actually do so in any but the most elemental variety of system. The human mind, as presently developed, can comprehend only so much at one time, and the application of the systems concept in decision analysis requires that many complexities and interrelationships between problem elements be considered. Even if the manager were able to reduce the complexities to manageable proportions by abstracting out all but the salient aspects, he has no guarantee that he can subjectively relate them in a fashion which is either logical or consistent.

The fields called "operations research," "management science," and "systems analysis" are those whose scopes encompass the application of objective scientific methods to the solution of management decision problems.[2] Practitioners in each of these fields rely on models—formal abstractions of real-world systems—to predict the outcomes of the various available alternatives in complex decision problems.

Because these models are usually symbolic, it is possible to reduce complex relationships to paper and, using techniques of logic and mathematics, to consider interrelationships and combinations of circumstances which would be beyond the scope of any human. Models permit experimentation of a kind which is unavailable in many environments; one may experiment on the model which describes a system without experimenting on the system itself.

Of course, this does not mean that the decision-maker cedes his responsibility for making decisions to some mystical scientific process or that his judgment and intuition do not play a major role in decision-making. By the nature of the mathematics which are available, models have one of the same "deficiencies" as does the human brain in that they are able to consider only a part of the real-world decision problem. Other parts are omitted either as being relatively unimportant, or because they cannot be handled using existing techniques. The difference between explicit models and subjective decision analysis using nebulous "models" which exist in the mind of the manager is one of degree. The *process* is very similar, but explicit models formalize salient characteristics and relationships which may be blurred in the mind of a man. Explicit consideration is given to those aspects of the real-world which should be included in the model and those which should be abstracted out. Men tend to include in their "mental models" the first (or last) aspects which occur to them and to exclude others which stretch the bounds of their comprehension. Moreover, once the explicit model has been constructed, the objective approach has the guarantee of logic and consistency which is not usually a feature of the application of judgment and intuition to problem-solving.

The role of the manager's judgment and intuition is merely refocused by the systems approach. It is directed toward those aspects of problems which are best handled subjectively. The factors in an objectively viewed decision problem which must be handled subjectively are usually separate and distinct. This permits calm expert judgment on each specific aspect, rather than gross judgments encompassing factors related to wide varieties of disciplines and areas of experience. The best illustration of this value of scientific problem analysis involves the *evaluative* and *predictive* judgments which are a part of most complex problems. The objective approach clearly separates those judgments related to *the worth of a state of affairs* (evaluative) and those related to *the future course of events* (predictive). In the mind of a decision-maker, such judgments often become indistinguishable.

Another aspect of the refocusing of the manager's judgment through scien-

---

[2]The author views these three terms as alternative descriptions of a single methodology. This view is not accepted by those who seek to distinguish between different fields of inquiry. The question is entirely one of semantics, however.

tific analysis is that this approach involves utilizing judgment in integrating the results of objective analysis with the predicted effect of unconsidered problem elements, and arriving at a decision based on the totality of available information. In effect, the systems approach to planning may be viewed as a logically consistent method of reducing a large part of a complex problem to a simple output which can be used by the decision-maker in conjunction with other considerations, in arriving at a "best" decision. It permits him to focus his attention on the aspects of the problem which are most deserving and to restrict the attention which he allocates to those things which are best handled more formally. Such an integration of science and intuition permits consideration of the interrelationships of functional activities. In simple terms, it enables the manager to get the "big picture" in its proper perspective, rather than requiring (or permitting) him to devote attention to relatively minor aspects of the total system.

SYSTEMS AND EXECUTION

The systems concept has not only caused great changes in the planning or strategic decision-making portion of the manager's function. So, too, has it caused revolutionary changes in the fashion in which decisions are executed. The most striking example of this is the emergence of the *project manager*.[3]

The project manager's position is based on the realization that modern organizations are so complex as to preclude effective management using traditional organizational structure and relationships. Top management cannot be expected to comprehend all of the details and intricacies involved in the management of each activity, be they weapons systems which are under development, product being marketed, or clients being serviced. Functional units properly give greater concern to their function than they do to individual products or projects. Thus, the need for a manager who can cut across traditional functional lines to bring together the resources required to achieve *project goals* is clear.

Just as the systems viewpoint necessitates consideration of the combined effect and interrelationships of various organizational functions in the manager's planning task, so, too, does it require integration of these functions at the execution level. The project manager is able to operate through the various functional managers in directing the resources which are necessary to the effective pursuance of a project. He is thereby able to focus his attention on *project goals* rather than on parochial production, marketing, or financial goals. As such, he serves as the instrument for implementing decisions in terms of the same structure in which they are made—the system.

IMPLICATIONS OF THE SYSTEMS CONCEPT

The systems concept has already had great impact on management. In the future, the impact will be even greater however, for all of the forces which have nur-

---

[3]Sometimes referred to as a "systems manager" or, in the marketing milieu, a "product manager."

tured the systems approach are still acting to change the management environment. Indeed, they appear to be acting to effect an increasing rate of change.

The implications to the interests and capabilities of the modern manager seem apparent. The modern manager must take the systems viewpoint in all that he does. He must have an analytical orientation and he must be able to operate effectively in organizations which are structured along something other than the old line-staff basis.

However, although these basic qualities are required, their meanings, in terms of degree, are imprecise. Perhaps the most important of these is the often used term "analytic-orientation." Does this mean a claim is being made that only professional operations researchers can become effective modern managers? The answer, of course, is negative.[4] The modern manager need not be a mathematician, nor need he even have extensive mathematical training. The manager need only have a basic understanding of, and appreciation for, the methodology of scientific analysis. If he has this, he will be able to utilize professional analysts and, knowing the strengths and limitations of their procedures, make intelligent use of the results which they achieve in his behalf.

The other important aspect of the qualifications which a modern manager must possess has to do with the environment in which he must operate. Since the people with whom he deals are usually professionals who are not necessarily his subordinates, greater reliance must be placed on motivation to achieve desired goals. The project manager cannot fall back on a superior-subordinate relationship to insure that others will perform as he desires.

The implications of these managerial qualifications are critical to management education. Management education must seek to develop the elusive "ability to work with and motivate others" and the open-mindedness to new ideas which is a prerequisite to an "analytic orientation."

In particular, a field such as Industrial Engineering, because of the organizational overviews which are necessary to conduct its traditional activities, should seek to become more productive of "modern" managerial talent than it has been. To achieve this, it will be necessary for educators and practitioners to de-emphasize the parochial functional viewpoint which is so pervasive, and to emphasize the systems viewpoint more strongly. Perhaps, this will require new academic boundary lines, such as are currently being drawn in a number of institutions. But, most importantly, it will require a change in the attitudes of the people who are involved. And, since such things come only slowly and painstakingly, one is led to conclude that the optimal time to begin is already past.

---

[4]Although the author knows of industrial concerns who are seeking professional operations researchers to become product managers.

REFERENCES: CLELAND, D. I., "Why Project Management?" *Business Horizons,* Winter, 1964, pp. 81-88; KING, W. R., *Quantitative Analysis for Marketing Management,* McGraw-Hill Book Company, New York, 1967, Chapters 1-4; KOONTZ, H. AND O'DONNELL, C., *Principles of Management,* Third Edition, McGraw-Hill Book Company, New York, 1964; LUCK, D. J. AND NOWAK, T., "Product Management—Vision Unfilled," *Harvard Business Review,* May-June, 1965, pp. 143-154.

QUESTIONS

1. Explain why overall organizational effectiveness will be adversely affected if each department blindly pursues its own objectives.

2. Explain how the manager can use the systems concept in preparing the plans of the organization.

3. How do the duties of the project manager differ from those of the typical manager?

Meshing Managers and Computers

The computerization of industry has been rolling along for more than a decade. As computer systems have grown bigger, faster and more sophisticated, many companies have answered pressing problems of information control by putting up large, centralized computer facilities. But no one has yet found a definitive answer to a nagging question: How will all this affect the inner workings of a company's management, from top to bottom?

The latest company to grapple with this question is Deering Milliken, Inc. Last week, Milliken threw an outdoor buffet-luncheon for 1,200 guests to add some festivity to the official opening of its new management information center in Spartanburg, S. C. On the surface, President Roger Milliken appeared to be simply toasting another new addition to his growing textile empire. But, for many, it was a farewell party to "business-as-usual" at Deering Milliken.

A NEW TEAM

Milliken's information center is devoted entirely to processing company data. The windowless building has 94,000 sq. ft. of carpeted office space, including a glassed-in section housing all of the company's computer hardware and a 100-seat chart- and slide-viewing room. To staff the center, Milliken has hand-picked a team of 250 information specialists, operations experts and administrative personnel. It has also created a dozen new management posts to oversee the new staff, and has tacked the whole group on to the organization chart just two steps below the president.

According to Roger Milliken, the new information center will have no real effect on the company's structure. "There has been no organizational change," he insists. But the question still has to be answered: Will a new staff function that controls vital corporate data create a new power center for ambitious executives?

Milliken himself admits that things will be different. From now on, all of the company's information and administrative paperwork, which had been handled at almost 50 mill and sales office locations, will now be turned over to the new management group at Spartanburg.

MEETING FUTURE DEMAND

The move puts Deering Milliken solidly in line with other computer-conscious companies, both in and out of the textiles, that are committed to the "total information system." This system provides an all-inclusive network for gathering, storing, and processing all company data. At the same time, it offers a mechanism for rapidly giving managers just the right kind and amount of decision-making information.

But Deering Milliken takes the process one step further—and it's this step that will be closely watched by other companies. Essentially, Milliken has built into its system the ability to meet any future demands on its new information capabilities. By centralizing its information under a new staff, Milliken hopes to have the flexibility to anticipate all of its future information needs for the entire company.

Before the decision to go to a total information system, Milliken had satellite computer facilities scattered at five locations. Squabbles were developing over whose programs had machine priority. There was no uniformity in divisional computer programs. And information was taking longer to reach the executive's desk. For example, "Inventory reports used to be two weeks late," says Milliken. "Now, each Monday morning we'll know how we stand on inventory as of Friday midnight."

RECRUIT FROM WITHIN

To get the 250-man staff that runs the new information center, Milliken scoured its mill operations and recruited plant-level people handling such local problems as plant control, accounting, inventory, profit analysis and billing.

At the new center, the staff was split into 10 functional areas, each covering a broad piece of the business. The new staff's dozen managers—who average less than 40 years in age—were drawn from group staff offices and from the Deering Milliken Service Corp., a captive consulting arm of the parent company. New management titles were created for each of the 10 areas such as financial planning, manufacturing services, general accounting, inventory allocation, and production planning and scheduling.

THE INTENT

Milliken hopes to use this new group to tie together its diverse operations. Deering Milliken is one of the few really big privately owned companies operating in the U.S. today. After 100 years of making textiles, the company still is controlled by owner-managers from the Milliken family. Business figures are jealously guarded, but textile experts rank Milliken in fourth place in the industry. Sales are close to $500-million, and pre-tax profits are probably in line with the industry average of 5%.

To produce these sales and profit figures, Milliken operates some 40 mills turning out unfinished gray goods, semifinished textiles and finished fabrics. These are sold through seven regional sales offices to apparel makers, home furnishers, and industrial users.

METHOD OF OPERATION

Here's how the new information system works. The raw data from the mills and sales offices come to the center where the facts are screened, studied and stored. Reports and other decision-making information are channeled to all top executives, mill managers, and sales managers as needed.

Each day's flow of information is handled by one of the 10 new functional departments, which are each split into several sections. In production control, for instance, each section is made up of three or four analysts who screen information from each of Milliken's 40 mills. As trouble spots crop up, appropriate reports are fed back to the managers involved.

SMOOTHING THE WRINKLES

The new management team at Milliken is as self-contained as possible. It reports to the president through the financial vice-president and is responsible to no one else. However, it services all areas and levels of management in the company.

The center these men will operate is now running, but not so smoothly and quickly as it will be before long. Terrell Sovey, vice-president of financial planning, who heads it admits, "We're still two years away from the system as we've planned it"; that is, with a capacity to work on a "real time" basis, producing immediate answers.

The main problem facing the planners is fitting new equipment into the system and writing new programs to get it functioning properly. Right now, Milliken's old equipment delivers a "batch" of information on a particular subject, and executives must hunt and pick through it for specifics. When random access storage units come in next year, single facts will be retrieved in microseconds.

Also, much information must now be trucked into information headquarters. By the time the system is complete, however, input terminals will pipe the data from point of origin directly to the computer. And Milliken's new "third generation" IBM 360 computer—to replace the 7010 now in use—won't arrive until early next year. "But," says Sovey, "it's just a question of speed. Right now we're handling all bills, all payrolls, all purchasing, in fact, everything."

FORECASTING THE EFFECT

The advantages of such a system seem obvious to Roger Milliken. For one, rental costs for computer equipment will dip from their present levels—even after the IBM 360 takes over. And administrative costs should drop.

But the big value is in the new standardization of forms and procedures that will be forced on the company. "Computers are strict disciplinarians," says Milliken. "We had 40 different invoices in 40 mills each with different information on it. Now, every form will be the same. We'll all be working from the same piece of paper."

What's more, Milliken sees new flexibility and freedom for decision-making for his executives. "We'll be able to act on fact, rather than intuition," he says.

Actually, Milliken views the new information center as a spur to management at all levels. "We're going to have to have managers. This will give them the information, but they will have to make the decisions," he says. And since Milliken managers "don't have the problem of supervising their own information and paperwork," says Milliken, they should have a lot more time for decisions, and for planning.

QUESTIONS

1. How will Deering Milliken's total information center change the way in which executives operate?

2. What kind of data will be processed by the information center?

3. What kind of problems are the managers of Deering Milliken facing in installing their information center?

Managerial Implications of Integrated Business Operations

CHARLES R. KLASSON AND KENNETH W. OLM

An old and continuing key problem confronting American business executives is the development of an integrated management effort capable of maintaining and improving the productivity and profitability of company operations. Recent

Reprinted from the *California Management Review*, Vol. VIII, No. 1, Fall 1965. Copyright 1965 by the Regents of the University of California.

attempts at integrating over-all business operations are causing a transition in management practices which portends as great an impact upon management as did the "scientific management era" at the turn of this century. Many theorists and practitioners alike have identified this as a transition from the "Age of Analysis" to the "Age of Synthesis." James C. Culliton states:

> *In the Age of Analysis, men were taking knowledge apart, sorting it into manageable portions, and struggling, almost desperately, to keep it in understandable, isolated parts. Now, however, the driving force of actual fact is pulling things back together. Man may resist, but he is powerless to hold back the force which is producing the Age of Synthesis.*[1]

In the business world this synthesis has been identified variously as the total systems concept, integrated business operations, and/or unified operations management.[2] Clearly, the emerging focus is now upon the whole business as an operating entity that has tangible characteristics and qualities as opposed to its functional segmented parts. As a business evolves into more complex sets of activities, with numerous decisions involving many people frequently separated by many miles, inevitably task specialization and departmentation result in an attempt to improve the efficiency of operation. Managers for years have attempted to structure people, work, and necessary facilities so as to create conditions which will result in coordinated and balanced operation. Organizing efforts have concentrated on establishing organizational responsibility and authority relationships which were intended to enhance the attainment of stated objectives at all levels in the company.

Ideally, such working relationships within a company would permit both individuals and groups to work effectively together, thus achieving a higher level of over-all company performance. Unfortunately, however, business history reveals that many of these organizational efforts fell far short of their objective. Even when individual managers were mindful of their coordinative and cooperative responsibilities, the existence of formal authority patterns, planning and operational procedures, performance standards, and incentive systems was more conducive to the development of strong departments than of strong organizations.

While recognizing that a completely integrated business operation will not be achieved in the immediate future, Peter F. Drucker in his article "Long-Range Planning—Challenge to Management Science"[3] stresses the value of both

---

[1]James C. Culliton, "Age of Synthesis," *Harvard Business Review*, XI:4 (Sept.-Oct. 1962), 181.

[2]For a representative sample of current thinking in this area, please see the following references: James M. Ewell, "How to Organize for a Total System," *Systems and Procedures*, XII:6 (Nov.-Dec. 1961), 4-8; Richard A. Johnson, *et al., The Theory and Management of Systems* (New York: McGraw-Hill Book Co., 1963); Adrian M. McDonough, *Information Economics and Management Systems* (New York: McGraw-Hill Book Co., 1963); Richard F. Neuschel, *Management by System* (New York: McGraw-Hill Book Co., 1960); James D. Gallegher, *Management Information Systems and The Computer*, American Management Association, Research Study Series, No. 51 (New York: 1961); Arnold O. Putman, *et al., Unified Operations Management* (New York: McGraw-Hill Book Co., 1963).

[3]Peter Drucker, "Long-Range Planning—Challenge to Management Science," *Management Science*, V:3 (April 1959), 238-249.

the concept of functional organization and unified business operations and the requirement that all managers in a firm try to find ways of enjoying the advantages of both. He comments:

> *We need to know how to translate from business needs, business results, and business decisions into functional capacity and specialized effort. There is, after all, no functional decision, there is not even functional data, just as there is no functional profit, no functional loss, no functional investment, no functional risk, no functional customer, no functional product, and no functional image of a company. There is only a unified company product, risk, investment, and so on, hence only company performance and company results. Yet, at the same time, the work obviously has to be done by persons, each of whom has to be specialized. Hence, for a decision to be possible, we must be able to integrate divergent individual knowledges and capacities into one organization potential; and for a decision to be effective, we must be able to translate it into a diversity of individual and expert, yet focused efforts.*

THREE KEY QUESTIONS

Today, while managers do not and cannot view their business solely as a group of separate functions, they are confronted with the problem of finding better ways and means of developing an integrated management structure and operational philosophy which more precisely and effectively tie together the functional knowledges, efforts, and contributions of all levels of management. In an effort to bring together current business thinking and practices relevant to this problem, this article discusses three key aspects which are pertinent to a viable solution:

1. What is meant by integrated business operations? A brief look at the literature can cause consternation for the business executive who is presently involved in a wide range of actions designed to tighten up his company's operations. Before worthwhile changes can be made, the executive, regardless of level, had better know what he is seeking to accomplish or what effect these changes will have on him and his organization unit. Then, the first purpose is to define and explain in some detail the concept of integrated business operation.

2. Why all the concern and increased research efforts in this area? While the basic problems of business are essentially the same today as fifty years ago, as so many executives proclaim, the techniques and approaches to their solutions have changed. This being so, the second purpose here is to review the obvious in order to point out the less obvious reasons for simultaneously streamlining all phases of business operations.

3. What does this mean for company management? Perhaps the most startling aspect of finding ways of competing more efficiently and creatively involves both the immediate and long-run effect on traditional managerial practices, organization, and development. Finally, this paper probes into some ramifications of integrated operations and the managerial implications associated with them. Un-

less key executives anticipate what may result from major administrative and operational changes, their efforts at improvement may be far more crippling than their failure to make necessary changes required to stay competitive within a particular industry.

THE BASIC CONCEPT

The concept of "integrated business operations" has been described in many different ways. Some authorities emphasize system performance requirements or technical and informational requirements, while still others emphasize managerial planning and control requirements. Finally, some stress decision-making and problem-solving requirements, and others, organizational requirements.

Taken together, these requirements describe the top management operating philosophy of a growing number of U.S. corporations that prefer to view their businesses as a functioning, integrated whole, or total, system. While unanimous agreement does not exist today among business executives about the "integrated business operation" concept or exact methods for its implementation, a number of essential characteristics have been identified, developed, and applied as a result of specific company research and applications.

In Procter and Gamble, for example, James Ewell stated that:

> *The total systems concept truly encompasses the entire business. It involves the parent company and subsidiaries made up of many line-and-staff divisions located throughout the world. It could be argued that this concept does not go far enough; that there are multiple interrelationships between our company and other companies which should be included. Our actions directly affect our suppliers of raw materials or packaging supplies, and the distributing operations of the railroad and trucking industries. Then there are the interrelationships with our numerous customers and the increasingly active interrelationship with all three levels of government—Federal, state, and local. Although such interrelations may eventually be included in a total systems concept, such an all-encompassing system would, at this time, be too big for us to handle effectively. As yet, we do not know enough to install such a system. Just developing a system for the operation of the company itself provides myriad patterns of interlocking data and information flow. One cannot get his arms around anything so complex, taken as an entity, so the total system must, for analysis and handling at this time, be broken into major systems and subsystems . . . too many approaches to total system design put too much stress on specific applications and not enough on interrelationship of systems.*[4]

---

[4]James M. Ewell, "How to Organize for a Total System," *loc. cit.*, 6.

Mr. George Chane noted that:

> *RCA has put into effect what I believe is one of the most advanced systems of integrated administrative management controls in existence today. Under the vice-president for finance and administration, the controller's office, the treasurer's office, the personnel function, and the management engineering function operate as a completely integrated planning and monitoring unit, working closely with the operating division heads in accordance with policy objectives established by the president and chairman of the board.*
>
> *Thus, for example, management engineering and the controller's office identify the areas of greatest potential cost reduction and profit improvement.*
>
> *Management engineering sets up reasonable systems, standards and schedules of accomplishment, and establishes variance limits for "above-the-line" direct production areas. The controller's office is responsible for full implementation of the program in such areas as credit policy, assets and capital, and cash forecasting. Personnel oversees all aspects of the program affecting industrial relations and the span of control for management and supervisory personnel. All four groups interlock with one another and with the management engineering, controllership, and personnel functions of each division.*[5]

In a similar manner, James W. Smith of the Martin Marietta Company reports that:

> *Our objective was and still is company-wide systems to communicate with each other . . . the accomplishments and short range objectives of the Martin Company relate primarily to the task of systems integration—which is catch-all terminology for cleaning house. The longer term-objective—which is the scientific manipulation and utilization of management information to plan, direct, and control the company business.*[6]

ESSENTIAL CHARACTERISTICS

The previously mentioned comments are suggestive of some major features of the total systems approach to management. Six major characteristics common to any operational total systems concept are presented below.

---

[5]George W. Chane, "Centralized Administrative Management; the Need, the Promise, the Challenge," *Shaping a New Concept of Administrative Management,* American Management Association (New York: 1961), p. 12.

[6]James W. Smith, "A General Management Computer System," *Computer Based Management for Information and Control,* American Management Association, Management Bulletin 36 (New York: 1963), pp. 12-13.

Performance Objective

The ultimate goal of integrated business operations must be to achieve a higher level of operating efficiency and administrative control of over-all firm performance as well as functional performance of operating departments or divisions. Realizing the impossibility of attaining optimal conditions regarding every action taken in a company, the integrating philosophy attempts to use techniques which consider the potential effects of proposed decisions on other directly related aspects of a firm's operation or on all parts of the operation and to make final decisions that tend to maximize profits or other objectives of the company as a whole.

With organizational growth, it becomes increasingly difficult to minimize those conditions which tend to promote a high degree of departmental or functional performance with little or no regard for over-all company performance. Not infrequently, inadequate review of programs at the top occurs simply because the executive has relatively little knowledge about the inherent variability, potential, or interaction of the many functional company activities in his organization. Traditional coordinating and controlling techniques in the areas of budgeting, costing, and responsibility accounting that deal primarily with historical performance by collecting, tabulating, and presenting operating information in encyclopedic form to executives contemplating future possible courses of action have failed to function as an effective integrating tool.

Integrated Management Structure

To achieve a higher total performance level, an integrated management structure must exist so that functional contributions of managers at all levels will serve to eliminate many of the traditional day-to-day bottlenecks of operations, as well as enabling them to exceed and not merely meet expected performance levels. With organizational growth, the firm is literally disintegrated into functional areas of specializations to enhance efficiency of operations. As each functional work area grows, it tends to create:
☐ Its own planning and operating systems.
☐ Its own technical language.
☐ Its own working internal relationships through system studies and applications.
☐ Its own informational requirements.
☐ Its own performance requirements to service its own special interests which may be inconsistent with the best interests of the business as a whole.

Figure 1 illustrates a typical organizational structure pointing out separate organizational units and their vertical and horizontal relationships. It also demonstrates some of the weaknesses that seem to attend organizational growth as mentioned above.

An integrated management structure seeks to minimize the adverse side effects mentioned above that are associated with growth of any organizational unit. Such a structure comes into being when each organizational unit is conceived and developed in full recognition of the capabilities, functional goals, and perform-

FIGURE 1. DISINTEGRATION OF ORGANIZATION

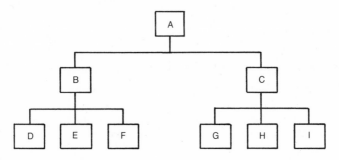

ance requirements of other related units. In brief, managers are forced to design a system of management planning and control which possesses common characteristics and minimizes unique organizational requirements.

Figure 2 portrays what reintegration should do for a company by way of maintaining a tightly functioning unit. It indicates a continuous management action system that provides a complete set of schedules and operating procedures to insure coordinated action of the system as a totality. The distinctive feature of this structure is that it considers opportunities and problem solutions to strategic, structural, and operational problems of management within one framework as a continuous process. Present organization technology does not lend itself to continuous analysis of action alternatives of the whole firm.

Integrated Decision Making

An integrated management effort can only come into being when precise decision-making criteria exist which, when followed, lead to decisions in all parts of the organization which are most desirable for the total organization. Production decisions must be consistent with engineering, marketing, and financial decisions. Manpower procurement and development decisions must align with output decisions. In brief, the firm is viewed as a complex interlocking network of decision-making points which function to control various physical and informational processes associated with producing and distributing goods or services. Integrated operations assure that a large number of key decision points are tied together into a continuous action-oriented operating organization.

One of the few published empirical studies of complex decision systems was conducted by Professor Jay W. Forrester at the Sprague Electric Company. Forrester clearly states that his work is directed toward the goal of "enterprise

FIGURE 2. REINTEGRATION OF ORGANIZATION

A					
B			C		
D	E	F	G	H	I

design"—to create more successful policies and organizational structures which permit more efficient total firm operations:

> *Industrial dynamics is a way of studying the behavior of industrial systems to show how policies, decisions, structure, and delays are interrelated to influence growth and stability. It integrates the separate functional areas of management—marketing, investment, research, personnel, production, and accounting. Each of these functions is reduced to a common basis by recognizing that any economic or corporate activity consists of flows of money, orders, materials, personnel, and capital equipment. These five flows are integrated by an information network.*[7]

Integrated decision making is becoming more of a reality as a result of research like that of Forrester and the advanced work at the System Development Corporation. Major operational breakthroughs which are required for more effective decision-making networks will follow the answers to such questions as:
☐ What relationships exist between organizational structure and decision making?
☐ How many and what types of decisions are made at various organizational levels?
☐ What judgment criteria are used?
☐ Which strategic decisions are related?
☐ Where are decisions made?
☐ What kinds of induced delays exist in informational flow due to decision making and processing?

Integrated Management Information System

Optimizing managerial decisions that are highly interdependent hinges upon the existence of an integrated management information system that is both representative and responsive to actual business operations. In past years, the assumption was widely held that each manager was capable of creating his own system of generating meaningful information.

If management is viewed as the process of converting information into action through the decision-making process as controlled by various policy directives, stated or implied, it is apparent that management success depends in large measure on the availability and timely use of specific classes of information at all organizational levels. Information—meaningful and useful data—or its lack unquestionably is the crucial integrating or disintegrating element in business operations today. Samuel N. Alexander, while chief of Data Processing System of the National Bureau of Standards, described the essential role of information when he said:

> *It is the binding together of the entire organization into an effective, integrated whole, through the flow of information,*

---

[7]Jay W. Forrester, *Industrial Dynamics* (New York: John Wiley & Sons, 1961), p. vii.

that permits the information channel to serve as a means of improving not only the day-to-day operations but the projected operations as well.[8]

It is apparent that many companies take great pains to improve their manufacturing technology and marketing while disregarding information processing almost entirely.[9] The serious effect of inadequate information processing comes into clear focus when such corporate problems as excess inventory investment, high clerical costs, rush manufacturing orders, low labor productivity, and poor utilization of plant and equipment are caused by inadequate managerial information. Most large firms have taken major steps to alleviate the adverse effects of "blunt information tools" through the introduction of electronic data processing systems, additional systems and procedures studies, and the establishment of information departments. Not uncommonly, such efforts, at least initially, represent "patchwork" to an old system, thus resulting in the persistence of the problem of poor and costly management information.

Today, a number of research studies have revealed that the sources and uses of information are still highly compartmentalized with little regard for the total information requirments of the firm.[10] However, with the advent of integrated data processing systems, many firms have been forced to consider total information systems requirements because of the potential adverse impact if they failed to stay in step with their competitors who might adopt new control systems.

While any attempt to describe a total information system admittedly is an ambitious undertaking, the present state of the art has identified a number of key requirements.

These must include a managerial requirement, which means that the system must insure timely, accurate, and useful management planning and controlling information to facilitate achieving corporate goals and make maximum use of the exception principle in reporting to management. Also there is an information flow requirement, designed to permit free flow of formal and informal information from sources of origin or storage to required end-users. The types of information transferred through channels would be standardized as specified by operating policy and requirements.[11] Another would include an information analysis requirement, which increases effectiveness through more valuable analysis of a higher quality of information and through greater coordination of effort made possible by a continuous flow of information conceived out of a need for an interdepartmental viewpoint.[12] In addition, the system should convert information into machine language as near to the origin as possible, permitting its

---

[8]Samuel N. Alexander, "A Progress Report," *Office Management Series No. 144,* American Management Association (New York: 1956), p. 6.

[9]Neil Milroy, "The Disintegration of an Information System," *The Canadian Chartered Accountant* (May 1963).

[10]Adrian M. McDonough, *Information Economics and Management Systems, loc. cit.,* p. 14.

[11]See George Kozmetsky and Paul Kircher, *Electronic Computers and Management Control* (New York: McGraw-Hill Book Co., 1956), pp. 172-173, for comments regarding the inclusion of informal information within a formal system of communication.

[12]See H. Simon, H. Guetzkow, G. Kozmetsky, and G. Tyndall, *Centralization v. Decentralization in Organizing the Controller's Department* (New York: Controllership Foundation, Inc., 1954).

subsequent flow through the processing system automatically, so as to minimize duplication and use of data, yet supply needed information to users.

In summary, an integrated management information system seeks to provide a firm's managers with all necessary information required to create operating statistics which indicate deviations between planned and actual performance.[13]

Programming, Scheduling, and Monitoring Operations

Once top management commits limited resources to various product-market opportunities, some means must exist for insuring that potential returns from these resources are optimized. Over-all programming, scheduling, and monitoring of all company activities are required. Operational programming involves identifying the best course of action from several alternative combinations of basic planning factors and limited resources of the firm. As a more formal technique for preparing operational plans and policies in relation to stated corporate goals, programming is based upon a more objective approach to defining and analyzing major variables and their relationships in a given business situation.

Having selected an operational plan, management then must specify precise times and responsibilities for executing the plan. Scheduling, like programming, represents a more analytical approach to examining the numerous interrelationships among the many problem variables involved. The capability of scheduling techniques to reschedule programs that do not proceed as planned is important. Scheduling techniques such as PERT can provide answers for such questions as to what should be done when manufacturing orders fall behind schedule, when parts are not available, when manufacturing requests engineering change proposals, and when key machinery breaks down. The ability to trace through the effects of such delays on potential profits of the firm and to reschedule operations to minimize losses represents a key advantage of over-all scheduling.

Monitoring is selectively gathering data relevant to actual operations to enable managers to control specific programs. Monitoring seeks to provide managers with sufficient operational information for necessary reprogramming or rescheduling of operations; it thus seeks to provide information for constantly evaluating programs and schedules. Production and cost reports are usually available to individual managers but are not usually documented to reflect total functioning of a system.

Computer Techniques and Applications

It may now be apparent that the characteristics of integrated operations depend largely upon model building and computer techniques that quantify problem variables. If, for example, a company wants to use programming techniques to allo-

---

[13]For illustrative example of requirements of a management information system, see: M. K. Evans and L. R. Hayne, "Master Plan for Information System," *Harvard Business Review,* XL:1 (1962), 92-98.

cate limited resources among competing projects in order to optimize return on investment, company goals likewise must be quantified so they can be inter-related. For comprehensive communication networks to exist which can transmit operational information rapidly and efficiently to required levels of management, a computer to process masses of data is a necessity. A large number of planning factors must be systematically reduced to basic forms in order that useful analyses can be achieved. Computers are needed to program operations initially and to generate alternative programs to reflect changes in over-all situations confronting a company. To date, the major stumbling blocks to programming over-all opera-tions seem to have been a lack of information about the internal requirements for management decisions and control information; about present information flow systems and their interaction; about how the company would fare under alternative courses of action or policies; and how presently constituted manage-ment teams would react under new organizational patterns and plans. The absence of such information has been crucial to planners. With the aid of computers and problem-solving techniques that can simulate business operations, useful insights and answers to the above problems are now possible.[14]

Advanced quantitative and model-building techniques such as mathematical programming, Monte Carlo analysis, game theory, critical path method, and mul-tiple applications method will continue to play a key role in our attempts to under-stand and control better the interaction between various main line elements in a business organization. As businesses become more complicated, the problems of coordinating various operations multiply quickly and almost geometrically. Electronic data processing systems coupled with the above mathematical tech-niques provide a feasible vehicle for attacking the formidable problem of attempt-ing to gain greater control over business affairs.

EXAMPLES OF APPLICATION

The following are brief descriptions of actual applications of integrated business operations:

The Management Operating System Concept[15]

In an attempt to provide a system capable of integrating all functional aspects of a manufacturing operation, IBM developed the MOS concept. The system can control the entire manufacturing cycle (forecasting, material and planning. inven-tory management, scheduling, dispatching, and operations evaluation) from be-ginning to end with only management exception decision changes. Each functional part of the system is considered in relation to all others with changes in one

---

[14]M. A. Geisler and W. A. Steger, "How to Plan for Management in New Systems," *Harvard Business Review,* XL:5 (1962), 103-110.

[15]For a detailed description, see *General Information Manual Management Operating System for Manufacturing Industries,* International Business Machines Corporation (1960).

reflected in all others in order to achieve effective utilization of assigned man-power, machines, materials, and money. The system is designed so that information flows through all related functions, with data furnished to management for decisions concerning programmed work flow. Quality and timeliness of decisions are improved vastly since control information is made available on the whole operation as well as each independent function. Thus, a plant is able to operate on a manufacturing plan which is adjusted each day with each adjustment affecting all related activities.

Remote Data Control System[16]

In the functional area of production, remote data gathering systems (RDC) provide plant management with almost instantaneous information about opera-tions. Emergencies such as machine breakdowns, stockouts of critical inventory items, and serious quality defects are brought to management attention.

Total Integration for R&D[17]

Another example of seeking to create over-all program control in the field of research and development is Sperry Rand Corporation's data processing system called Product Administration and Contract Control (PACC). In concept, PACC is an integrated data-processing system designed to provide management with required tools for controlling over-all program operations. A computer system supports a complex of information and control, subsystems that design and support the mainstream activities of the organization by determining alternate program plans and monitoring program progress. It provides operating tools necessary to coordinate engineering, manufacturing, financial, and marketing flow.

A NUMBER OF CAUSES

A number of factors, other than the usual economic and competitive forces, have brought increased pressures on management groups to find more effective means of integrating their management structure so that contributions of various levels of management can be integrated in accordance with their individual responsibility requirements. These factors include:

☐ Expansion of paperwork and clerical costs.
☐ Increased complexity of operations.
☐ Diversification programs.

---

[16]For a detailed description, see H. E. Klein, "Production's New Brew: Instant Data," *Dun's Review and Modern Industry,* LXXXII:4 (Oct. 1963). 38-113.

[17]Martin J. Cream, "The Total-Integration Approach in Business Systems for R & S," *Control Through Information,* American Management Association, Management Bulletin 24, pp. 28-36.

☐ Forward corporate planning.
☐ Restrictive management control philosophies.

Paperwork

Perhaps the initial impetus to establish integrated business operations came from attempts to find ways to control rapidly expanding paperwork and clerical costs associated with processing the documents necessary to keep a firm functioning. During the past fifty years, while industrial production has increased approximately 700 per cent, the number of office workers increased over $5\frac{1}{2}$ times the number of production workers.[18] An acceptable solution to this problem seemed to be the application of high-speed electronic data processing equipment. After some sobering and costly experiences with a limited approach, many firms realized that insufficient attention has been devoted to determining objectively the informational requirements of the business. Some of these firms then began to examine all operational functions from an integrated viewpoint in order to justify costly EDP systems and to facilitate corporate-wide decision-making procedures.

Increased Complexity of Operations

Expanded sales volume, product lines, and geographical distribution, along with multiple plants, mean more complex operations. Corporate officers tended to find themselves removed from a first-hand knowledge of operations. To compensate, some attempted to decentralize operations and retain centralized control. Others added new staff units to facilitate coordination requirements, further complicating the situation by interposing additional layers of management. Still others have recognized that the growing complexities of internal management environment represented a new problem of developing an integrated management structure quite different from traditional corporate structures.

Diversification

Diversification programs, especially those involving acquisitions, have intensified management problems. Considerable difficulty is usually encountered when associating companies attempt to integrate their operations administratively or functionally. Discovering the incompatibilities between various recording and reporting systems has forced management teams to examine more closely the joint requirements of an integrated management system. Such studies have ventured far beyond the flow of traditional accounting and financial data and lead to the sudden realization that more profound changes are required in the organizational structures of the associating firms in order to insure compatibility.

---

[18]Theodore A. Smith, "From Burden to Opportunity: The Revolution in Data Processing," *The Changing Dimensions of Official Management,* American Management Association, Management Report 41 (New York: 1960), pp. 27-28.

Forward Corporate Planning

Product obsolescence and accelerated technological change have made the need for advanced corporate-wide planning obvious to most observers. Jay W. Forrester of the Massachusetts Institute of Technology identified the need for such planning when he noted that:

> *As the pace of warfare has quickened, there has of necessity been a shift of emphasis from the tactical decision (moment-by-moment direction of battle) to strategic planning (preparing for possible eventualities, establishing policy, and determining in advance how tactical decisions will be made . . .). Likewise in business: as the pace of technological change quickens, corporate management, even at lower levels, must focus more and more on the strategic problems of running the business and less and less on the everyday operating problems.*[19]

To become more sophisticated in advanced corporate planning, management has been forced to examine the problem-solving and decision-making procedures of the company through advanced computer programming and business simulation procedures. System Development Corporation, for example, has devoted significant effort to designing techniques and models to simulate various phases of corporation operation and planning processes. As a result, an increasing number of companies maintain a "corporate management laboratory" with which to evaluate and compare risk feasibility and consequences of various courses of action.[20]

Restrictive Management Control Philosophies

In attempting to control operational and managerial performance, many companies have been victimized by their own internal control systems which have had restrictive and in some cases deleterious effects on the organization. Instead of functioning as enabling devices that would facilitate and insure coordinative organizational thought and action, minimize deviation from planned action, and correct deviations from plans, many of these control systems function largely as negative restraints.

Such restrictive managerial control philosophies are easily identified because they tend to specify rigid standards of performance, functional goals, operating budgets, and report procedures, which quickly report significant variations from

---

[19]J. W. Forrester, "Industrial Dynamics: A Major Breakthrough for Decision Makers," *Harvard Business Review*, XXXVI:4 (1958), 39. Additional insight may be obtained by reviewing the latest developments in industrial dynamics as reported by E. B. Roberts, "New Directions in Industrial Dynamics," *Industrial Management Review*, VI:1 (Fall 1964).

[20]See, for example, J. Kagdis and M. R. Lackner, "A Management Control Systems Simulation Model," *Management Technology*, III:2 (Dec. 1963), 145-159.

planned performance, usually in measurable terms of quantity, quality, time, and cost. They are more concerned with maintaining planned progress than with underlying causes of delay or better methods of operations. Characteristically, restrictive systems also tend to prevent a free flow of information and ideas throughout the organization, to stifle initiative, and to result in departmental self-interest becoming paramount.

Critical examination of existing management control systems reveals such shortcomings, and today managers are seeking new ways of welding together strong organizations that are more concerned about why they are not exceeding planned performance than about concentrating on merely checking for deviations from plans. Comparatively little knowledge existed a decade ago relative to the management information networks and control systems that form the central communication and decision-making network of any organization. Command control systems capable of regulating a dynamic system did not exist. They are now becoming a reality.

MANAGERIAL IMPLICATIONS

Some long-standing managerial practices and concepts are being, or will be, challenged as research continues into the problems of designing integrated business operations.
☐ What types of changes can be expected?
☐ What organizational changes will be required?
☐ How well are managers prepared to cope with these changes?
These and other questions must be answered if management teams are to avoid traumatic reactions which can seriously damage the competitive position of any company. Organizational and managerial changes that merit attention are discussed next.

ORGANIZATIONAL CHANGES

Perhaps the most dramatic changes will be experienced in the content and structure of managerial jobs.

Job Content

Managerial jobs at all organizational levels will be subject to responsibility, authority, and status changes. The prediction made some four years ago that some first-line and middle supervisory tasks could be programmed effectively has proven correct. For example, in the areas of purchasing, inventory control, billing, transportation, production scheduling, and warehousing, routine tasks have been largely eliminated from various managerial positions. In the process of programming managerial tasks, managerial positions were subjected to more intensive analysis and evaluation. Some jobs have been eliminated, others recombined, and in the process, more accurate executive position guides have been developed. With many routine decision tasks now eliminated, the "valued nonroutine decision task"—the essence of any manager's job—is now more clearly identified. New position descriptions and attending authority, responsibility, and status relationships will come to be based on the known, unprogrammable aspects of a manager's job.

Compact Organizations

Through improved information flow, fewer managerial levels are necessary to control effectively complex operations. Programming many day-to-day decisions of middle managers has resulted in a definite reduction in required managerial levels. A number of case studies provide evidence to support this contention. Obviously, new organizational structures yet unknown to the executive can be expected. Major management reorganizations accompanied by the creation of new positions, the elimination of old ones, and combinations of still others are definitely coming.

The important question is not recentralization of control, but rather how can intelligent free-form organizational changes be achieved. A good starting point would be the development of a new and more appropriate organizational vocabulary representative of new operational practices and relationships. Traditional organization charts describing functional and authority relationships must be supplemented with new flow chart concepts which describe more aptly required decision-making and communication relationships. New terminology must be developed to enable those concerned to discuss new organizational concepts which may follow emerging patterns of work, decision, and information flow so common to the total systems concept. An interesting example of such thinking is presented by Henry M. Boettinger:

> . . . *future organization structure may center about three basic categories (aside from strictly staff function): (1) those people who process data, (2) those people who do things for customers, and (3) those people who plan things for the company and the customers.*[21]

The computer, in his opinion, makes that sort of thing possible, wherein you deal with customers as data, as individuals, and as aggregate groups.

Executive Compensation

Integrated operations will require changes in traditional executive compensation plans. Most executives are compensated largely for their individual performances

---

[21]"Some Reflections on Computers and History," *Bell Telephone Magazine,* Spring 1964, p. 11.

(or for the performance of a profit center) and not generally for their concern for other managers and their respective problems. While most performance evaluation forms include quality factors to measure cooperative attributes, experience has taught the executive that he usually receives little apparent tangible remuneration for such concern. Competitive rather than cooperative actions tend to predominate. The implication is that any attempt to integrate once separate functional activities through closer working association of an enlarged group of staff and line managers will require new systems of compensation if it is to succeed. The answer will not be as simple as suggestions for team compensation or group bonuses indicate. Neither executive orders nor programmed activities can compel effective executive cooperation. Personal initiative and creativity must continue to flourish for any executive organization to function productively.

An attending observation involves the traditional salary differential between line and staff managers. As highly trained staff specialists continue in high demand and in short supply, new criteria will be required to maintain equitable compensation plans.

Linking Department

Wherever advanced systems concepts are used, the management service concept becomes an organizational requirement. A management services organization is basically a staff unit assisting top management with problems involving the planning, conducting, and controlling of traditional functional areas of business. These groups bridge operating gaps between functional subdivisions of a company without encroachment on traditional line management authority. Gradual evolution of these groups and line acceptance of their presence indicate that a significant potential for improving over-all productivity of the firm via total systems concept exists. In general, management services groups have consolidated many special talents, such as industrial engineering, electronic data processing, organizational planning, records administration, systems planning, operational and scientific analysis, and electronic computation and retrieval functions that formerly were literally adrift in most organizations.

New Role of Staff

With greater knowledge of divisional activities and performance, corporate staff specialists in the area of market forecasting, product development, and engineering will share activities or even assume those once performed solely by autonomous operating divisions. Sophisticated teleprocessing systems, which permit rapid collection of data from remote operating divisions for forwarding to central processing computers, provide central staffs with very comprehensive information useful in corporate-wide planning. As a consequence, more central staff units possess *de facto* line authority over certain divisional operations. Such functional relationships will tend to increase as communication and computing capacities improve and are more widely adopted.

New Information Function

Information production will be recognized as an important company function deserving of top management attention and approval. The ultimate integration of information flowing from and to various functional departments of the firm will depend upon the establishment of a central information center. In most organizations, the economics of information is not yet recognized as an organic corporate function like production or marketing.

The drive for instantaneous information has led to the creation of positions for staff information specialists. These new specialists are not without their problems. First, acceptance by the practicing line manager (generally a realist) of the usually theoretical and idealistic information specialist has not been easy to come by. Confronted with day-to-day problems requiring quick decisions, the line manager not infrequently has reason to resent the intrusion of a staff specialist.

Second, information specialists are often scattered throughout the organization, reporting to different managers. With accounting, manufacturing, and engineering groups tackling data processing problems, each with different equipment and procedures, uneconomical practices flourish.

Third, the two general types of computer operations—computational and storage-retrieval are not especially compatible. It is not feasible for accounting processing groups to function as information retrieval centers. Information retrieval runs subject control files to constant search which necessarily is disruptive to computational runs. Subject and numerical classifications require switching programs as well.

Fourth, information centers, as is true of many staff functions, tend to be inefficient. Profit-responsible managers are not sure what level of productivity they can expect from personnel performing information work, generally remote from customer contact. Work measurement and incentives may be necessary to insure efficient performance in this area.

Fifth, in order to bring all data processing personnel and equipment together under one department to achieve an optimal total management information system that ignores organizational barriers, particular departments may of necessity be eliminated or greatly reduced. Such action undoubtedly will result in strong resistance to change.

Sixth, if a central information office is to be successful, it must integrate its activities with the operational activities of the company it services. It cannot operate at an optimum level strictly as a separate service unit with little concern for customer requirements.

Shifts in Control

Changes of the magnitude discussed above will result in shifts in corporate control. Regardless of where control should reside in any company, traditional power centers are gradually shifting, and systems planners and responsible line executives must be aware of the fact that positions are at stake. Initially, many of these changes will be *de facto* until retirements provide more freedom for action.

MANAGERIAL CHANGES

The extent of technical progress achieved in planning and controlling over-all business operations, no matter how impressive in terms of potential, will require managerial changes if progress is to be achieved in fact.

Managerial Adjustments

Just as skilled workers were forced to adjust to severe limitations caused by a high degree of task specialization in the interest of efficiency, many managers will be forced to accept limitations in their freedom to act or decide as a result of greater programming of operations. Managers must accept the fact that during the past decade ways have been found to program a large variety of activities previously requiring individual managerial action. Even though routine aspects of jobs have been largely eliminated, many managers will now have time to tackle unprogrammable aspects of their jobs.

Managerial Obsolescence

With an accelerated rate of technical knowledge and resulting task specialization, the threat of professional obsolescence has become a reality. The relative advantage of experience over knowledge seems to be rapidly declining.[22] Early retirements, separations, or demotions as solutions to this problem are not always the equitable solution. Firms must seek practical ways of using human talent, wherein they have their greatest investment. Re-education is a feasible alternative now followed by a growing number of companies. It is possible that the criterion for advancement in the future may rest less on a specific expertise and more on the ability to keep learning in the face of continually obsoleted skills.

Management Training

Integrated operations to achieve any measure of success will require integrated management team effort. If management decisions need to be integrated, so do management teams. In theory this notion is accepted by industry, but in practice much is still to be desired. A number of major U.S. corporations today are actively developing training programs which include vertical cross-sections of management personnel in order to improve team effectiveness by:

1. Establishing criteria for measuring quality of team performance.
2. Perfecting interdepartmental coordination and decision making.
3. Integrating rather than controlling field relations.
4. Achieving greater participation in setting organizational goals through leveling which permits openness and conditions of mutual confidence and trust.

---

[22]H. J. Leavitt, "Dealing with Management Obsolescence," *Computer-Based Management for Information and Control,* American Management Association, Management Bulletin 31 (New York: 1964), p. 51.

Need for Research in Decision Making and Motivation

Resources must be allocated for studying how each organizational unit interacts and functions. Management groups recognize the importance and necessity for product research and development activities, but they must also recognize the need to invest in gaining information about the processes and systems they use to manufacture these products and how they manage the firm itself. Less than adequate attention has been given to a comprehensive analysis and synthesis of the entire management process. Some U.S. corporations have assumed the bulk of this responsibility but they often are reluctant to divulge their findings for competitive reasons. Even though some top executives may question the merit of depth studies of organizational decision-making processes, they also seem to have recognized the potential of such studies and are now beginning to support needed research in their budgets.

CONCLUSION

While we can take a customer's preference and create an automatic chain reaction through sales, credit, engineering, production, personnel, and accounting, the state of the science needs much development before it can be practiced with precision. The manager is the vital catalyst required for successful operations regardless of the industry. Decisions to use innovational techniques often are difficult to make. The preceding remarks may serve to clarify some of what is involved in *a major transition in American management—the integrated business operation.*

QUESTIONS

1. What is meant by the concept *integrated business operations?*

2. What are the six major characteristics common to any operational total systems concept?

3. What factors caused management to find more effective means of integrating their business operations?

4. Explain the organizational changes that will occur due to the use of integrated business operations.

5. What is meant by the term *managerial obsolescence?*

3

The Finance Function

Among the most difficult problems encountered by the average businessman are those involved in financing his business. Planning short-term needs, acquiring long-term capital, budgeting for the coming year, and solving problems of credit are all crucial concerns of the businessman.

Capital generally includes two types of funds: the first, called *working capital,* refers to the money and credit necessary for the day-to-day operation of the business; *fixed capital,* on the other hand, includes the fixed assets of the firm such as land, buildings, and equipment. The successful manager must be able to determine his capital needs and the sources available for satisfying them.

SOURCES OF CAPITAL

Sources of capital are classified according to the length of time the business requires funds. *Long-term financing* refers to a need for funds extending from five to fifteen or more years. *Short-term capital,* on the other hand, refers to funds needed for one year or less. Capital needed for between one and five years is often referred to as *intermediate-term funds.*

Long-Term Financing

Long-term capital can be obtained from both internal and external sources. In those cases where the business is owned by a sole proprietor or where it is a partnership, the personal funds of the owners are an important source of internal funds. These funds have the advantage of incurring no obligation to pay a fixed return on the funds. Also, there is no fixed date upon which the funds must be repaid. The major disadvantage of using personal funds is that these funds are often quite limited, depending on the personal savings of the owner or partners.

Both privately and publicly held firms have a second form of internal funding available to them: the investment of *retained earnings.* Retained earnings are profits of the business not distributed to the owners. The reinvestment of profits can be an important source of long-term capital. The decision whether to retain earnings or to distribute them to the owners is one of financial policy. The owners or stockholders may be interested in the largest possible distribution of earnings. However, they should understand that reinvestment of profits may increase both the long-range growth of the company and the return on their original investment.

External sources of long-term capital are usually available only to corporations. Three major alternatives are open to the corporate firm seeking long-term funding: common stocks, preferred stocks, and bonds.

Common stock is the basic source of capital for most corporations. It represents simple ownership in the corporation, with certain limited rights going to the owner. It usually gives the owner the privilege of voting in the election of directors of the company and other matters presented by management to the stockholders. Many stockholders delegate their vote to an agent (usually called a *proxy*) who is a major stockholder or officer of the company. In addition to having the right to vote, common stockholders also may have the pre-emptory right, or the right to purchase new issues of stock.

Stockholders also have a right to dividends or distributed profits, but this right is limited. The corporation has no obligation to declare dividends. When it does, common stockholders receive dividends only after preferred stockholders have received their return. The final major right accruing to common stockholders is that common stock has final and complete claims on the assets of a company after it has been liquidated or dissolved. Again, this claim is limited to assets remaining after all debts have been paid and the claims of preferred stockholders and bondholders have been settled. Common stock is considered the most risky of securities investments because its value is tied to the immediate and future success of the corporation.

Preferred stock also represents ownership in the company. It is called preferred because it contains certain preferences over common stock. As noted above, preferred stock usually has priority in the areas of dividend distribution and in the distribution of company assets following corporate liquidation. Preferred stock has stated dividend rates, but it typically does not carry voting privileges. Because of the preferences involved and the limited possible return on preferred stock, it is considered less risky than common stock. The possibility of greater return on common stock counterbalances the greater risk for many investors.

A third alternative for acquiring long-term funds is through borrowing. The primary vehicle used for this purpose is the sale of *bonds*. A bond is a certificate of debt which promises to pay a certain amount, called the *principal,* to the bondholder at a certain date in the future and at a specified rate of interest until the principal is redeemed. Thus a bondholder is a creditor, not an owner, of the company. For example, the Ajax Company would issue a $10,000 bond, paying $6\frac{3}{4}$ per cent interest yearly until 1978 when the principal would be repaid. In this example, 1978 would be the maturity date.

Bonds differ from stocks in several ways. The interest due on bonds must be paid even if the issuing company is not earning a profit. *Secured bonds* are often supported by pledges of company assets such as mortgages and equipment. The most common type of unsecured bonds are called *debenture bonds.* They are backed only by the general credit of the company. Because of their relative security and fixed rate of return, bonds are considered by many persons to be a safe, conservative investment.

Short-Term Financing

Sources of funds for short-term use differ from those used for long-term purposes. *Short-term* or *working capital* is used to meet the current obligations of the company. These funds are usually procured through the borrowing of cash or buying on credit. Short-term capital may be differentiated as secured or unsecured. Two of the most commonly used forms of unsecured short-term financing are promissory notes and trade credit.

Promissory notes are unconditional promises to pay a certain sum, either on demand or at a specified time. Notes are often negotiable (transferable or salable). Commercial banks frequently own notes signed by business firms. *Trade (open-account) credit* supplies the bulk of working capital for most business firms. In granting credit on an open-account basis, a firm normally sets certain rules called *credit terms*. These terms include: 1) the length of the credit period and 2) a reward, called the *cash discount,* for prompt or early payment of the bill. Open-account credit is very similar to that credit granted daily to millions of Americans using credit cards or charge accounts.

Secured sources of credit include short-term loans supported by collateral. These loans, typically from banks, are secured by inventories, stocks, bonds, or equipment. Other sources include the factoring of accounts receivable. A credit company called a *factor* may make loans on accounts receivable or purchase the receivables. Thus, the factor provides the firm with an immediate source of short-term funds. Another type of collateral used for short-term loans are *chattel mortgages*. Any piece of movable equipment could be used as security. Motor vehicles in particular are used to secure this type of loan.

The needs of business for both long- and short-term funding are easily seen. Supporting business in its efforts to acquire the necessary capital are the financial institutions, particularly banks, and the securities markets.[1]

Banking

Among the many specialized financial institutions serving business today are the banks. The type of bank best known to the average person is the *commercial bank*. Commercial banks differ from other banks in two ways: first, they accept demand deposits which can be withdrawn at any time (on demand) by the depositor; secondly, they specialize in making short-term loans. Loans made by commercial banks typically require both collateral (in the form of marketable assets) and a good credit rating. On relatively rare occasions unsecured loans are made to firms with excellent credit ratings. Other services frequently offered by the commercial bank include: 1) savings accounts, 2) personal loans, 3) a source of specialized checks, and 4) business and financial advice.

Another type of bank is the *investment bank*. Investment banks specialize in selling long-term securities for business and governmental bodies. In doing

---

[1]For a discussion of all types of financial institutions see Loring C. Farwell, *et. al., Financial Institutions,* 4th ed., (Homewood, Illinois: Richard D. Irwin, Inc., 1966).

this, the investment bank purchases the securities and resells them, taking their profit either from commissions or from the spread between their purchase price and the selling price. *Mutual savings banks,* found in seventeen states, accept savings deposits and then reinvest the funds in securities and real estate mortgages. *Savings and loan associations* operate similarly to savings banks, accepting savings deposits. However, the bulk of this money is invested in real estate mortgages, particularly home loans.

Supporting the banking system in the United States is the Federal Reserve System. Serving as the central bank of the country, similar to the Bank of England and the Reichsbank in Germany, the Federal Reserve System includes twelve regional Federal Reserve Banks located geographically to serve the entire country. The Federal Reserve Banks have two primary functions: first, they supply certain banking services to member banks and the government, including serving as clearing houses for checks and distributing currency and coins; secondly, they regulate money and credit in an attempt to lessen the effects of business cycles, thereby controlling inflationary and deflationary pressures. Most commercial banks in the United States are members of the Federal Reserve System.

Security Exchanges

Security exchanges, often referred to as stock exchanges, comprise the market where stocks and bonds can be purchased or sold. The largest and most important exchange is the New York Stock Exchange. Other exchanges include the American Stock Exchange in New York, the Midwest Stock Exchange in Chicago, and smaller exchanges in fifteen other major American cities.

The New York Stock Exchange, founded in 1792, currently limits its membership to 1375. Only these members can transact business on the exchange. The members, who are said to hold "seats" on the exchange, are partners or officers of brokerage firms doing business with the public. The brokerage firms are known as member firms and many have branches in cities throughout the country.

The primary function of an exchange is to make available an instant market for the sale or purchase of securities. The New York Stock Exchange allows trading in stocks and bonds listed on the exchange by over thirteen hundred of the nation's largest firms. In order to be listed on the exchange, these firms have to meet rigid standards set by the exchange. The other exchanges throughout the country typically list the securities of smaller and lesser-known corporations.

An example of a typical stock transaction on the New York Stock Exchange would go as follows. Mr. Jones, in Peoria, would call his local member brokerage firm. After discussing things with his local broker, he might decide to buy shares in The Color Corporation. His broker would "quote" him the current selling price received by direct wire from the floor of the exchange. The broker would quote the stock as "73 to a quarter." This means the highest offer to buy the stock was $73 a share and the lowest offer to sell the stock was $73.25 a share. If Mr. Jones decided this quote were satisfactory, he would tell his broker to buy one hundred shares at market (the current market price).

At the same time, in Cincinnati, Mr. Thomas, after a similar discussion with his broker, decides to sell one hundred shares of stock in The Color Corporation at market. These two orders—one to buy, the other to sell—reach the member firms' representatives on the floor of the exchange at about the same time. Mr. Jones' and Mr. Thomas' representatives immediately take their orders to the trading post on the floor of the exchange where The Color Corporation stock is traded. There are eighteen of these trading posts on the floor, each handling around eighty stocks. At the trading post the current quote is still "73 to a quarter." This means that Jones' broker could immediately buy at $73.25 per share, and Thomas' broker could sell at $73 per share. However, if this would happen, the customers of both brokers could ask why a better price was not found.

Actually, Jones' broker knows that someone else has bid $73 per share for one hundred shares and has been unable to find a seller at that price. He then raises his offer to buy to $73\frac{1}{8}$ (as all stock prices are quoted at intervals of $\frac{1}{8}$ of a dollar). Thomas' representative, also knowing that no one is willing to buy shares at $73\frac{1}{4}$, hearing Jones' offer of $73\frac{1}{8}$, instantly takes the offer, shouting, "Sold one hundred at $73\frac{1}{8}$." Once the representatives have agreed verbally on price, the transaction takes place, the entire process lasting only a few minutes. The representatives then return to inform their customers of the transaction. Both the buyer and the seller are charged a set commission by the brokers for their services. While this example refers to the New York Stock Exchange, trading in listed stocks on other exchanges would be handled in a similar manner.

Stock which is not listed on an exchange is traded on the *over-the-counter market*. Over-the-counter trading takes place through private transactions among brokers. The stock of 90 per cent of the corporations in the United States is traded on this market. The bulk of the corporations traded in this way are small and relatively unknown. However, the stock of some major corporations, particularly that of banks and insurance companies, is traded on this market. There is also over-the-counter trade in bonds. According to Professors J. F. Weston and E. F. Brigham of UCLA, "the over-the-counter market provides the main outlet for securities being offered to the public for the first time."[2]

BUDGETING

Financial planning and control are among the most important functions of the business manager. A basic device used by a manager to aid himself in performing these functions is the *budget*.[3] A budget is a financial plan showing expected income and expenses for a specified period of time. A budget is *balanced* when income equals expenditures. When income is less than expenses, a *deficit* results; when income exceeds expenditures, a *surplus* exists. Budgets may be expressed in terms of dollars or physical units. A year is the most typical time period for a budget.

A budget serves several purposes for a company: first, it establishes business goals and sets limits for expenditures; second, it aids in planning financial opera-

[2]*Managerial Finance,* 2nd ed., (New York: Holt, Rinehart and Winston, Inc., 1966), p. 591.
[3]See W. D. Knight and E. H. Weinwurm, *Managerial Budgeting* (New York: The Macmillan Company, 1964), for a thorough discussion of budgeting.

tions; third, it serves as a control device against which the company may compare actual performance with budgeted objectives (planned performance).

Most firms prepare several types of budgets. Budgets prepared for planning purposes include those for sales, production, and advertising. The *sales budget* estimates the total expected sales in units and dollars during the budget period. Through the *production budget,* the company sets forth the number of units it expects to produce and the cost involved. The *advertising budget* specifies the amount to be spent for advertising, the media (newspaper, television, or outdoor) to be used, and the time planned for the release of the advertising.

Among the important types of control budgets are the cash, income and expense, and capital budgets. The *cash budget* estimates the cash receipts for the budget period and the estimated cash disbursements during the period. The *income and expense budget* forecasts expected income from sales, rentals, royalties, or other miscellaneous sources, and the expected expenses involved in producing the anticipated income. *Capital budgets* estimate expenditures for plant, machinery, and equipment. These budgets have been arbitrarily classified into planning and control categories. However, in reality, all budgets may be utilized in the managerial functions of planning and controlling.

The preparation of budgets requires the contributions of many persons. Because each department in a company is affected by the budgetary process, managers from each department contribute to budgetary development. However, the final responsibility for the budget lies with the president of the company.

The following articles attempt to show the role of the finance function in a modern business. The *Monthly Business Review* article discusses the internal and external sources of capital used by business in the last decade. Credit terms are the major topic of the Hamel and Thompson article. Paul S. Nadler investigates the many changing services of the commercial banks. John A. Prestbo shows the procedures involved in developing a budget for a major corporation. In the final article, authored by John R. Moore, the focus is on the role of the financial manager in the complex, changing world of business.

Financing Manufacturing Corporations, 1950-1960

New capital for the expansion of fixed assets of a manufacturing corporation as well as for working capital needs may be obtained either from the income gener-

From *Monthly Business Review,* February 1962. Reprinted with the permission of the Federal Reserve Bank of Cleveland.

ated by the operations of an enterprise or from external sources, i.e., money and capital markets. In the period between 1950 and 1960, inclusive, manufacturing corporations in the U. S. acquired $229 billion in new capital.[1] The bulk of this capital was obtained from "inside" the manufacturing corporations, while the remainder was obtained from the "outside".

The acquisition of new capital in the past decade seems to have been a prime requisite for manufacturing corporations attempting to stay in step with the constantly increasing demands of a high-level and expanding economy. Thus, a substantial part of new capital obtained was directed toward increasing productive capacity, the carrying of larger inventories, and the providing of greater amounts of trade credit. At the same time, the burgeoning scientific and technological advances of the past decade implied that, in order to stay competitive, new capital had to be obtained to finance research and development facilities and to introduce new and more efficient methods of production and distribution, so that manufacturing corporations could realize certain economies of scale and other competitive advantages.

A build-up of the capital requirements of manufacturing corporations in the past decade suggests immediately a number of pertinent questions. For example, what sources of capital are available? How do corporations decide which of the alternative sources should be tapped? What are the criteria for making such judgments? In the pages that follow, we attempt to answer these and other questions by reviewing the sources of capital utilized by manufacturing corporations in the U.S. between 1950 and 1960, inclusive, and to suggest some of the reasons these sources were selected. It should be remembered, however, that in all cases the ultimate sources of capital which are tapped will depend on the cost and availability of capital, the purpose for which it is to be used, the capital structure of the acquiring firm, and the general outlook for business conditions.

INTERNAL SOURCES

During 1950-1960, inclusive, approximately $161 billion, or nearly 70 percent, of the total amount of new capital acquired by manufacturing corporations was derived from corporate income. Putting it another way, in the same 11-year period, the amounts of internal capital generated annually by manufacturing corporations expanded by approximately 60 percent.

A primary reason for the growing reliance upon internal funds is the stability associated with this source of capital. The growing dependence upon internal funds may thus reflect management's desire to avoid some of the restrictions associated with the use of external sources.

Internal sources of capital are derived entirely from the gross income of manufacturing corporations. Due to common corporate accounting practice, however, it is necessary to separate internal sources into depreciation and retained earnings.

---

[1] All data used in this article are taken directly or derived from figures published by the Federal Trade Commission and the Securities and Exchange Commission.

Depreciation

The major importance of depreciation allowances as a source of capital for manufacturing corporations is readily discernible in the accompanying chart. From 1950 through 1960 the annual amounts of capital generated by depreciation charges advanced from $4 to $11 billion. As a proportion of the total internal sources of capital for manufacturing corporations, depreciation increased from 36 percent to 60 percent during the same 11-year period.

The concept of depreciation as a source of capital is sometimes confusing to the casual observer due to the fact that depreciation is also treated as a business expense. To the accountant, depreciation is recognized as the loss in value of certain fixed assets, resulting from physical deterioration and normal obsolescence over time. Theoretically, depreciation allowances during a given accounting period should equal the reduction in the value of fixed assets which occurred within that period.

Although depreciation is listed as an expense, and is deducted from gross income, unlike other business expenses, a corporation does not surrender any cash in connection with depreciation expense. Depreciation is thus often referred to as a "noncash" expense. Furthermore, the inclusion of depreciation as a business expense reduces the taxable income of a corporation by an equal amount. As a result, the corporation is permitted to retain a larger portion of its total cash intake, so that the "cash flow" of a business enterprise is enlarged through the inclusion of depreciation charges.

The increase in cash flow resulting from depreciation allowances permits the recovery of all or part of past investments in certain fixed assets. Corporate management may elect, in turn, to reinvest the recovered capital in fixed assets

FIGURE 1. SOURCES OF INTERNAL CAPITAL

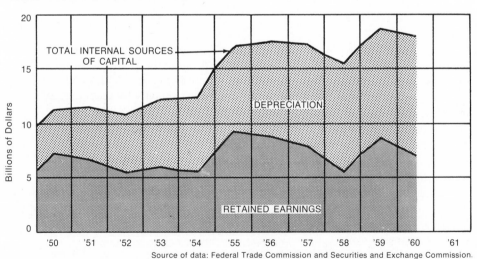

Source of data: Federal Trade Commission and Securities and Exchange Commission.

From 1950 through 1960, the annual amounts of capital generated by depreciation charges advanced from $4 billion to $11 billion, or from 36 percent to 60 percent of total internal sources. Over the same period, retained earnings as a percent of the total declined correspondingly.

or increased working capital; or it may decide to return the capital to the original suppliers, i.e., creditors and stockholders. In most instances, however, funds generated through depreciation are used either to replace or expand corporate assets.

The Growth of Depreciation Allowances

The increase in the volume of depreciation allowances of manufacturing corporations from 1950 through 1960 was due in part to the expansion of the asset base upon which depreciation charges are determined.

In addition, the increase in depreciation allowances beginning in 1950 also reflected the rapid amortization privileges granted on defense facilities during the Korean conflict. In an effort to induce a quick expansion of industrial capacity for defense purposes, the Internal Revenue Act was amended in 1950 to permit corporations to "write off" specific facilities within a five-year period. The law required that the National Security Resources Board determine whether rapid amortization privileges would be granted to an applicant, and in those cases where the Board approved, a Certificate of Necessity was issued. The annual amounts of depreciation resulting from this legislation steadily declined, however, after reaching a peak in 1957.

Another reason for the expansion of depreciation allowances from 1950 through 1960 is connected with the speeding-up of depreciation, i.e., accelerated depreciation. Throughout the postwar period, a great deal of discussion has centered on the adequacy of the methods of determining depreciation allowances as required by the Internal Revenue Code. Those who have proposed liberalization of depreciation allowances have advocated over the years a number of changes in methods of determination, some of which have already been legislated. These proposals have included: (1) the abandonment of the use of "original cost" and the adoption of "replacement cost" as the base for depreciation; (2) a reduction in the number of years over which all assets may be fully depreciated regardless of their connection with national defense; (3) permitting corporations to "charge off" a significant part of the total depreciation allowance at the time of installation or during the early stages of the life of an asset, an approach commonly referred to as accelerated depreciation; and (4) introduction of investment tax allowances which would permit a corporation to deduct directly a portion of the cost of a newly acquired asset from its liability at the time of installation without reducing the amount of depreciation allowance which is usually permitted for tax purposes.

In 1954, the Internal Revenue Code was amended to permit corporations to deduct a larger amount of depreciation during the initial years of the life of an asset. At that time, however, the length of time over which assets could be fully "written off" and the methods for determining the total amount of depreciation expense on various assets were not altered. Nevertheless, the adoption of accelerated methods of depreciation resulted in a closer alignment of annual depreciation charges with the decline in the productive efficiency of equipment.[2]

---

[2]For a discussion of accelerated depreciation methods adopted in 1954, see "Depreciation Allowances as a Source of Corporate Funds," this *Review*, September 1957.

In 1958, the Internal Revenue Code was again amended to permit a corporation to charge off 20 percent of the value of newly acquired equipment, in addition to the regular annual depreciation charge, during the first year in which the equipment is used. However, the legislation limited the 20-percent write-off to an annual investment of $10,000 in additional equipment with a life of six years or more, thereby providing assistance mainly to small business firms.

In recent years, discussion has intensified among businessmen, government officials, and professional economists concerning the liberalization of depreciation allowances as one means of encouraging increased productivity among U. S. manufacturing firms. As part of a program to shorten the depreciable life of many types of assets, one industry was permitted recently to write off specific assets over a shorter period of time than the Internal Revenue Code usually allows; the possibility of extending such a program to other industries is currently being considered. In addition, legislation was proposed in the Congress last year which would have permitted a tax credit, or investment allowance, against new investments in productive equipment. The proposed investment allowance was a part of a larger proposal for changes in the tax laws which was deferred until the current session of the Congress.

Retained Earnings

Unlike depreciation, retained earnings between 1950 and 1960, inclusive, were a relatively volatile source of capital for manufacturing corporations, ranging from a low of $5.2 billion in 1952 to a high of $9.3 billion in 1955. In addition, during the period under review, retained earnings declined steadily as a proportion of total internal capital for manufacturing corporations.

The declining importance of retained earnings as a source of new capital may be explained in part by the failure of corporate profit margins to remain at early postwar levels. From 1950 through 1960 the net income of manufacturing corporations fell from 7.1 percent to 4.4 percent of total sales. Putting it another way, while the sales of all manufacturing corporations increased approximately 90 percent between 1950 and 1960, inclusive, the "after-tax", or net, income of these same firms advanced only 19 percent.

On the other hand, the dividend policy pursued by boards of directors of manufacturing corporations has served, in many instances, to limit the amount of net income available for reinvestment. While the proportion of net income devoted to cash dividend payments during any particular period may be affected by various internal considerations, the cash needs of the organization during the subsequent period, the success of corporate operations in the preceding period, and a desire on the part of management to pay a stable dividend—the policies adopted by many manufacturing corporations during the period under review resulted in a larger relative amount of net income being devoted to cash dividends. For example, while from 1950 through 1955, the cash dividend payments of manufacturing corporations averaged 48.1 percent of total net income, in the period from 1955 through 1960, the proportion of net income allocated to dividend payments averaged 51.1 percent. Thus, the net income retained for reinvestment purposes was reduced by corporate policy.

These two factors—narrower profit margins and larger dividend ratios—combined with the steady increase in depreciation allowances to reduce the relative share of retained earnings as a source of internal capital—from 64 percent to 40 percent—between 1950 and 1960, inclusive.

EXTERNAL SOURCES

The utilization of external sources of capital by manufacturing corporations followed an uneven pattern during the period under review. It is apparent, however, that outside capital was far less important to manufacturing corporations than internal sources, as only 30 percent of the additional capital acquired during the 11-year period was provided by external sources.

External sources of capital tapped by manufacturing corporations may be classified in a number of ways: (1) on the basis of "venture capital" (which represents a part of the equity component of the financial structure) versus borrowed capital; (2) by distinguishing between the flow of funds directly from owner to user and the flow of funds to a financial intermediary which, in turn, supplies the user; and (3) by the length of time over which the capital will be employed. In this discussion, the third alternative is used, i.e., short-term credit as contrasted with intermediate- and long-term capital.

Short-Term Credit

Short-term borrowing is usually defined as any credit transaction in which the borrower agrees to return the funds within a period of 12 months. The ebb and flow of short-term credit between corporate users and the money market is closely related to both the seasonal and cyclical patterns of business activity which most manufacturing corporations experience. During periods of seasonal or cyclical expansion, manufacturing firms may depend heavily on the money market to finance temporary increases in working capital, e.g., larger inventories and higher levels of trade credit. Conversely, as the period of expansion passes and working capital needs decline, manufacturing firms will return the short-term funds to the suppliers in order to avoid the cost of holding such funds.

The importance of short-term credit to manufacturing corporations is reflected in the fact that, between 1950 and 1960, inclusive, approximately 14 percent of the additions to total capital, and nearly one-half of the external sources of capital utilized, were provided by short-term borrowing.

The principal sources of short-term credit for manufacturing corporations are trade credit, commercial bank loans, the issuance of commercial paper, and accruals of tax liabilities.

Trade credit remained the primary source of short-term credit for manufacturing corporations from 1950 through 1960. During that period, credit extended by the suppliers of manufacturing corporations, most of whom were also manufacturing firms, provided roughly 45 percent of the short-term capital needs of the users. The bulk of short-term credit for manufacturing corporations is thus, in a sense, an inter-industry supply of capital. Heavy reliance upon trade credit

FIGURE 2. SOURCES OF EXTERNAL CAPITAL

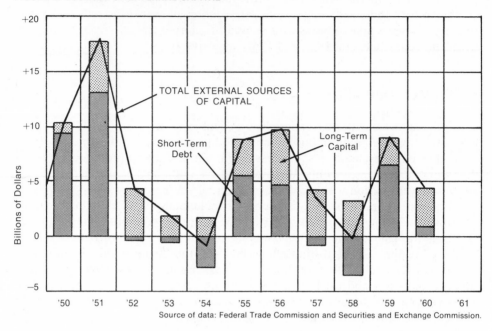

Source of data: Federal Trade Commission and Securities and Exchange Commission.

Short-term debt and long-term capital each accounted for roughly half of the total external capital acquired by manufacturing corporations during 1950-1960, inclusive. The use of long-term capital, however, was characterized by greater stability.

is due mainly to its availability, the lack of an explicit cost connected with its use, and a usual flexibility in credit terms.

Commercial banks provide both direct and indirect short-term credit for manufacturing corporations. Bank loans provided 15 percent of the additional short-term capital for manufacturing corporations between 1950 and 1960, inclusive. Short-term business loans usually carry a maturity ranging from 30 to 90 days, although many are extended for as long as 12 months. In addition, commercial banks may permit the borrower to renew the loan at maturity which, in turn, could carry the extension of credit beyond the 12-month definition of short-term borrowing. Since commercial banks also invest in commercial paper issued by manufacturing corporations, the former also serve as a source of indirect credit.

Manufacturing corporations have found commercial paper a convenient and economical method of acquiring short-term funds. In recent years such corporations have accounted for approximately 40 percent of all corporate organizations issuing commercial paper. The preference for this method of short-term borrowing may stem from an opportunity to borrow at a lower effective rate of interest. The cost advantage derived from the issuance of commercial paper is a result of the differential between the stated rate of interest on commercial bank loans and the money market rates which apply to commercial paper; it may also result from an opportunity to avoid the maintenance of compensating balances which usually accompany commercial bank loans. It should be remembered, however, that the ability to acquire short-term funds through the issuance of commercial paper is limited to large manufacturing corporations with good credit ratings.[3]

Reserves for accrued taxes constitute another source of short-term credit for manufacturing corporations. Because corporations are required to pay income taxes quarterly, they are able to employ the accrued taxes to meet very short-term capital needs until the income tax payment period arrives. From 1950 through 1960, income tax accruals provided a little over $3 billion in short-term funds for manufacturing corporations.

Long-Term Capital

Long-term capital acquired from external sources by manufacturing corporations between 1950 and 1960, inclusive, amounted to approximately $36 billion, or nearly 16 percent of total capital additions. As indicated in the accompanying chart, the demand for long-term capital by manufacturing corporations was characterized by greater stability than the demand for short-term credit. Such stability is due in part to the relative absence of seasonal and other short-term factors in determining long-term capital needs; it is also due to the fact that long-term funds are used primarily to acquire fixed assets and provide additions to permanent working capital.

Although the postwar period has witnessed the introduction of several new methods by which corporations may acquire intermediate and long-term capital, the *sale of securities* has remained the major means used by manufacturing corporations. In the years 1950 to 1960, inclusive, manufacturing corporations attracted nearly 80 percent of their long-term capital through the sale of new securities. Although total new security sales include both bonds and stocks, approximately 70 percent of the securities issued by manufacturing corporations in the period under review were in the form of bonds.

There are a number of factors which help to explain the predominance of bonds in corporate security issues. While both types of securities (bonds and stocks) involve payments to security holders, i.e., dividend payments to stockholders and interest payments to bondholders, corporations are permitted to treat interest payments on bonds as a business expense. Interest payments are thus deducted before the taxable income of a corporation is determined. Dividend payments to stockholders, however, may not be treated as a "before-tax" expense, and can be paid only from the net income or the retained earnings of the corporation. On the other hand, the payment of interest is usually a legal obligation of the corporation, whereas the payment of dividends is left to the discretion of the board of directors. In practice, however, dividends have increasingly become a fixed payment which management views as another cost of capital.

The nature of capital markets in the postwar period has also been an influencing factor in the predominance of bonds in the security issues of manufacturing corporations. The rapid growth of financial intermediaries, e.g., life insurance companies, pension funds, fire and casualty insurance companies, and investment

---

[3]For a discussion of the use of commercial paper as a source of short-term credit, see "Commercial Paper to the Fore," this *Review*, October 1960.

FIGURE 3. TOTAL NEW SECURITIES ISSUED BY MANUFACTURING CORPORATIONS

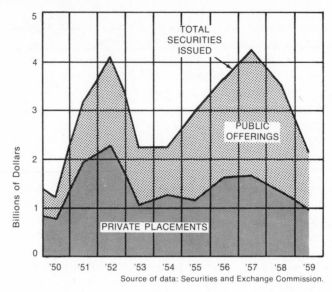

Source of data: Securities and Exchange Commission.

trusts, is perhaps one of the most significant changes in the structure of capital markets. As these financial intermediaries have increased in both size and number they have, in turn, become a major source of capital for business enterprise. Due to various legal restrictions covering the investment activity of many financial intermediaries, some invest heavily in corporate bonds while being permitted to hold only limited amounts of corporate stock.

An indication of the appetite of many of these financial institutions for investment outlets is that, in many instances, they have purchased entire flotations of corporate bonds. Such a situation may reduce for a manufacturing corporation the expense associated with marketing securities; it may also permit the issuing corporation to avoid the loss of time and expense involved in meeting the legal requirements necessary for a large public issue of securities and to reach agreements on covenants within the bond indenture which would not be possible when dealing with many public security holders.

It is not surprising, therefore, that many manufacturing corporations have tailored their new bond issues to meet the standards of various financial intermediaries. According to estimates of the Securities and Exchange Commission, approximately 50 percent of all securities issued by manufacturing corporations during 1950-1959, inclusive, were direct or private placements, i.e., the entire issue was sold to a financial intermediary.

Finally, although the relatively high price which investors have been willing to pay for corporate stocks in recent years has encouraged the sale of additional stock, the desire on the part of management to limit the number of stockholders and the demands upon corporate earnings may also have prompted the use of bonds as the primary means of acquiring long-term capital.

Another means used to acquire external capital by manufacturing corporations is the *term loan*. Term lending has become increasingly popular as a way of financing the purchase of additional plant and equipment. Such loans extend usually from one to ten years, and perhaps can be best described as an intermediate-term source of funds. Repayment of the loan is arranged usually on an instalment basis, which provides both a lower cost of capital for the borrower and increased security for the lender. In addition, the use of the proceeds of the loan usually increases the productive and earning capacity of the borrower which, in turn, generates the income necessary for the payment of both interest and principal. As a result, commercial banks have been attracted to making term loans from the standpoint of security as well as the higher yield which accompanies a loan of longer duration.

Large manufacturing corporations have, in many instances, found term loans a more economical and convenient means of raising capital than the flotation of additional securities. For the small manufacturing firm with little or no access to capital markets, the term loan may be the only means of acquiring long-term capital. Finally, since term loan agreements are determined through direct negotiation between lender and borrower, the borrower has an opportunity to tailor the loan contract to permit a more efficient use of the loan proceeds.

In seeking new sources of intermediate- and long-term capital, manufacturing firms have also turned to the use of *"rented capital"*, i.e., assets acquired by the means of lease arrangements. Although lease financing involves borrowing physical assets, it results in a contractual obligation which is essentially the same as that incurred in borrowing funds. As a recent innovation in external financing for manufacturing corporations, equipment leasing makes available the use of up-to-date production, office, and transportation equipment while permitting a company to purchase the use of these assets in a manner similar to the purchase of electric power and telephone services. A firm is thus able to avoid the immobilization of capital which ownership entails.

Leasing has been especially attractive to small manufacturers and to firms competing in industries in which the equipment used is subject to fast obsolescence because of rapid improvements in design and operation. The need for additional capital is a common characteristic among such organizations, and often they are further handicapped by limited sources of external capital. Leasing arrangements permit the use of necessary equipment while at the same time conserving the limited capital sources at their disposal.[4]

QUESTIONS

1. Discuss depreciation and retained earnings as two different types of internal sources of capital funding.

2. Short-term credit is an important external source of capital. Discuss the principal sources of short-term funds.

3. Why were bonds used to a greater degree than new issues of stock in the period discussed in the article?

4. How do term loans differ from other types of loans?

---

[4]For a review of leasing, see "Leasing's Role in Machinery Financing," *New England Business Review*, Federal Reserve Bank of Boston, September 1961.

When It Comes to Credit and Collections . . .
Most Companies Say It's O.K. to Compromise

HENRY G. HAMEL AND G. CLARK THOMPSON

To meet pressures exerted by competitors or customers, nine out of ten of the 196 manufacturing companies participating in this month's *Survey of Business Opinion and Experience* are willing to compromise on their stated credit terms or on timely collection of accounts receivable, or both, providing the business gained or held thereby is desirable. "Our position has been to meet competitive situations with our significantly important customers," says a financial executive of a construction materials firm. Similarly, a paper company reports that it "attempts to meet competition both in the domestic market and the foreign market by matching the easier terms offered by our competitors." And, in the opinion of a chemical company's treasurer, "competitive term situations cannot be ignored any more than competitive price situations." Likewise, most of the respondents who offer cash discounts for prompt payment of their invoices are not completely rigid in demanding reimbursement for unearned cash discounts taken by their customers.

A number of the survey participants who refuse to bend to pressure for easier credit maintain that their customers' as well as their own interests are best served by their steadfastness. And one of these firms, a producer of specialized industrial machinery, suggests that in today's economy it is not enough to hold the line on credit. According to this company: "In prosperous times like these, terms should be tightened and we are doing so. If you tighten up on terms now, you can afford to slacken up on a sound basis when the economic boom wanes. Competitors who must grant easier terms in times like these are in trouble and will get in more trouble."

RECEIVABLES TODAY VS. A YEAR AGO

Whatever the long-range pros and cons of flexibility vs. firmness in credit and collection practices, the commitment of company funds to accounts receivable is relatively no greater today than it was a year ago, according to most of the participants submitting comparative data. Nor is collection more difficult now than it was then. Although for these 135 firms as a whole there have been slight increases in both the average number of days' billing outstanding and in the average percentage of accounts receivable overdue, in both cases the increases are less than one percentage point. And less than half of the respondents furnishing information on this score report that these indicators are greater now than they were a year ago. The actual figures are presented in the table on the next page.

For the most part, moreover, the increases and decreases since last year

From *Conference Board Record,* November 1965, © 1965, National Industrial Conference Board, pp. 7-14. Reprinted by permission.

TABLE 1. CHANGES IN ACCOUNTS RECEIVABLE OUTSTANDING

A—CHANGES IN NUMBER OF DAYS' BILLING OUTSTANDING

			Today		A Year Ago
Average Number of Days for 135 Companies			40.4		39.6
	Increases in Days' Billing Outstanding	Decreases in Days' Billing Outstanding	No Change		Total
Number of Companies	64	34	46		144
Per Cent of Total	44.4	23.6	32.0		100.0

B—CHANGES IN PERCENTAGE OF ACCOUNTS RECEIVABLE OVERDUE

			Today		A Year Ago
Average Percentage for 135 Companies			18.9%		18.3%
	Increases in Percentage of Receivables Overdue	Decreases in Percentage of Receivables Overdue	No Change		Total
Number of Companies	73	52	49		174
Per Cent of Total	41.9	30.0	28.1		100.0

Note: The total number of companies reporting increases, decreases, and no change in (A) and (B) exceeds 135 in each case because some respondents indicate only the direction but not the magnitude of change.

have not been substantial. In the case of days' billing outstanding, the bulk of the changes, either upward or downward, has been three days or less. As for the percentage of accounts receivable overdue, the fluctuation has been less than plus or minus two percentage points for a majority of the firms.

Of the companies indicating that they have had substantial increases in one or both indicators, most express no alarm about the increases. Several attribute today's larger figures to changes in their activities (e.g., entering into a new type of business, or selling more goods in foreign markets). Other firms report that satisfactory results in collecting receivables renders increases in days' billing outstanding or in the relative number of past-due accounts of little moment. A few of the respondents who are concerned with their relatively greater investment of funds in receivables make the point that large customers have been the principal culprits in pushing up this investment.

YARDSTICKS FOR DETERMINING INVESTMENT IN ACCOUNTS RECEIVABLE

Less than half the participating companies employ some sort of yardstick to determine whether the relative size of the investment in accounts receivable is within acceptable limits. Often deriving from the company's long-range plans, or its own experience, or the experience of other companies in the same industry, the yardsticks are related to sales volume, or, less frequently, to the company's financial position.

Sales-Related Yardsticks

Virtually every survey participant who evaluates accounts receivable in terms of sales regularly computes the number of days' billings or number of days' sales outstanding that are tied up in this asset account. In addition, several firms put emphasis on related ratios, such as the annual turnover of receivables (that is, annual sales divided by average amount of accounts receivable) and the ratio of receivables to sales (the inverse of the foregoing ratio, which expresses receivables in cents per dollar of sales). A chemical company executive explains how his concern applies the receivables-to-sales ratio in evaluating its investment in receivables:

> *We constantly review our accounts receivable in relation to annual sales. Our measurement includes a moving twelve-months' average of monthly accounts receivable balances as related to current twelve-months' sales. When receivables appear excessive in a given segment of our operations, we call this to the attention of the local management.*

A few companies report that their sales-related ratios for appraising investment in receivables vary widely from product to product because market conditions make it necessary to set different credit terms for different products.

Financial Yardsticks

Financial measures for gauging investment in receivables find favor with a number of survey respondents because of the importance they attach to the relationship of this investment with alternative uses of company funds. The financial vice president of a textile company gives expression to this viewpoint as follows:

> *The investment in accounts receivable that we can afford to carry is governed by the availability of funds, the return on investment of the particular business related to the segment of receivables in question, and alternative uses of funds. Thus the problem becomes one of how will available funds be used; should we stay in this trade area or explore other opportunities?*

The principal financial yardsticks employed by participating companies are:
☐ The ratio between receivables and the company's total working capital
☐ The ratio of receivables to fixed assets or to total assets
☐ Cost of borrowing money
☐ The potential return on alternative uses of funds tied up in receivables
☐ Profit margins on the various goods sold by the company
☐ Present and anticipated cash requirements

An apparel company states that it relates receivables to inventories and current profits in assessing its investment in receivables. According to the firm:

Our yardstick is 25 per cent pretax income on a combination of accounts receivable and all inventories. A judgmental factor is involved in determining when to extend receivables or to build inventory in stabilizing production.

Dissenting Opinions

A number of participating companies question the applicability of financial yardsticks to receivables investment. Executives of some of these firms argue that they must accept whatever level of receivables is required to achieve sales objectives. The president of a steel company puts the point this way:

Receivables are the direct result of sales, and once the order has been classified as desirable, based on such considerations as customer relations, production, profit, and risk, we are pleased to have the resulting account on our books. From a financial viewpoint, there has never been a need to restrict selling efforts or our investment in receivables, and we would not do so unless our financial resources and lines of credit were so strained that we could not care for other commitments to conduct our business properly.

A few other companies contend that financing costs in particular should not be considered as a yardstick to determine a proper level of accounts receivable; for, in the words of a textile manufacturer, "it is always cheaper to borrow than to cut back on receivables and lose sales."

WHEN YARDSTICKS ARE NOT USED

Of the companies that do not use any specific yardsticks for gauging the level of their accounts-receivable investment, some say such yardsticks are not needed; a lesser number, that they would not be appropriate; and a very few, that yardsticks have been or would be ineffective.

No Need

Three reasons are given why no standard for appraising investment in receivables is needed. For certain companies, neither the amount of funds tied up in receivables nor the timely conversion of receivables to cash has presented any significant difficulty. Several others find that they do run into late-payers among their customers, but by taking such action as charging interest on past due accounts they automatically keep funds committed to receivables under control. And a small number of respondents report that since they have ample working capital they don't have to be concerned about their investment in receivables.

Not Appropriate

A common objection to the appropriateness of yardsticks for deciding whether the amount of money committed to receivables is acceptable is that careful sales forecasting, financial planning, and production scheduling automatically provide a properly controlled investment in receivables. Moreover, so long as sales are profitable, some respondents aver, it is quite beside the point to be concerned with the level of receivables. An oil company states, for instance, that "no limitation has been put on receivables growth and probably would not be as long as such growth is supported by increasing profitable sales."

Other companies say that their primary concerns are (1) the certainty that outstanding receivables will be converted to cash and (2) the rapidity with which this is done, rather than the relative size of their investment in accounts receivable. Still other firms comment on the difficulty of determining an affordable investment in receivables. According to a financial vice-president of a chemical company, "the maximum investment in accounts receivable that we can 'afford' is extremely hard to pin down, because it is always possible to cut back on funds committed to other assets."

Yet another argument against the appropriateness of setting an affordable amount for receivables is the belief shared by a handful of executives that their credit policies should be heavily influenced by their customers' legitimate needs. One of these executives, the general credit manager of a construction materials company, states: "We attempt to provide sufficient credit to our customers in order that they may fully exploit the market opportunities available to them."

Not Effective

Competitive pressure has made yardsticks for the control of investment in accounts receivable ineffective for certain concerns. Thus a chemical company controller reports:

> *The yardsticks we would like to use, opposed to those we do use, are two different things. Theoretically, we look upon the investment in accounts receivable as part of our investment in a product or a project and consider it capital on which we must earn a return. In recent years, however, we have found that to remain competitive we must follow the trend which is, of course, to be much more liberal in our credit policies.*

A similar view is expressed by the vice-president of a machinery company:

> *Frankly, we have no yardstick to determine how large an investment in accounts receivable our company can afford to carry, for the simple reason that we are going to meet competition in order to maintain a normal sales growth almost regardless of how large accounts receivable grow.*

BRINGING RECEIVABLES INTO LINE

Whether or not a firm formally determines what investment in receivables it can afford, virtually every survey respondent applies one or more of four techniques to reduce receivables if or when management believes that such investment is excessive. These techniques are:

☐ Extra efforts to collect from all delinquent accounts
☐ Putting pressure to pay on selected delinquent accounts
☐ Cutting off shipments or credit to delinquent accounts
☐ Restricting credit terms

Across-the-Board Campaigns

Faced with excessive receivables, almost all companies intensify efforts to obtain payments from all their delinquent accounts. "Having decided to live with our present terms," says the treasurer of a textile company, "the only step we can take when receivables are large is to watch collections closely and put pressure on those people not paying promptly." Specific methods mentioned include making more frequent reminders by mail and by telephone that payments are past due and couching such reminders in stronger language.

Putting Pressure on Individual Accounts

Fearing that an across-the-board dunning campaign is likely to cause unnecessary customer resentment and possible loss of business, other companies prefer to correct excessive investments in receivables by means of a selective effort to secure collections. This entails analyzing every delinquent account and applying the appropriate degree of pressure on each one. In certain circumstances such an analysis leads a company to counsel with customers who have run into financial difficulty, with the aim of overcoming the causes of their late payments. Thus a shoe manufacturer reports: "When a merchant is missing discounts and is requesting extra time, we make it a point to analyze his operation completely to determine just what is causing his request. In many cases we find it to be a problem of poor merchandising practices, and by assisting the dealer to lay out an intelligent six-months' merchandising program we have quite often been able to help him back on sound ground."

In some cases an account-by-account analysis of delinquent customers results in more drastic action with respect to collection. A chemical company reports that "where special requirements and problems of the customer preclude payment on established terms, interest bearing notes are taken." And a company in the metal-stamping industry seeks to persuade badly delinquent customers to obtain outside debt or equity financing when the sums they owe it become excessive. Several companies have resorted to the services of collection agencies or to legal action to secure collection.

Restricting Credit Terms

Practices in restricting credit terms when receivables become excessive vary. A few companies apply restrictions to all customers and keep such restrictions in force until conditions improve. In one firm, however, restrictions on credit terms are placed only on new customers. Other firms eliminate only special terms previously granted to individual accounts.

Suspending Shipments or Credit

To curtain an excessive investment in accounts receivable, a number of respondents have had occasion to cut off or stop shipments to slow-paying customers until these customers have paid their bills. In some cases this step is not taken until several warnings have been given, while in others the procedure is automatic. A lumber company vice-president, for example, says that "we suspend shipments when receivables become from ten to fifteen days past due."

Another practice followed by several companies is to withdraw approved credit lines to delinquent accounts when receivables become excessive. Alternatively, an instrument manufacturing company insists on C.O.D. terms for such accounts when efforts to collect have failed.

"An Ounce of Prevention" . . .

A number of companies control their investment in accounts receivable primarily by taking steps to prevent it from becoming excessive. This tack is described by the controller of an industrial machinery company as follows:

> *Our primary approach is not to let accounts receivable become excessive in the first place. Terms must be competitive but no more than that. Credit must be carefully screened and collection control strictly maintained. Periodic reviews of past due accounts point out areas where greater concentration is required.*

In a similar vein, the financial vice-president of an electrical equipment company states:

> *Our principal line of attack is before the fact, refusing to grant terms which will extend receivables balance and offering credit only to customers whose credit record is satisfactory.*

This executive goes on to say:

> *We review our receivables at the end of each month, keeping both top management and sales managers informed as to the number of days of receivables outstanding. And we keep pressure on sales personnel not to offer extended terms to customers.*

> *At times we make special drives through specific letters to customers requesting satisfaction of outstanding balances.*

In several companies, keeping local managers aware of the cost of funds tied up in receivables has also proved to be effective in preventing accounts receivable from getting out of hand.

PROBLEMS WITH CASH DISCOUNTS

Two thirds of the survey participants give cash discounts on some or all of the products they sell. A number of these companies find that customers who take cash discounts on late payments aggravate the problem of holding down to proper levels their investments in receivables. Indeed, a few companies volunteer the comment that they have abandoned the cash discount system entirely rather than endure its abuses.

Virtually every cooperating company makes an effort to collect, sooner or later, unearned discounts taken by customers. If first efforts fail, such as billing back the discount or returning the customer's check (a preferable procedure, in the opinion of several contributors, because, as one of them puts it, "once you accept the check and set up on your books a balance for the late discount, you have a very difficult time in making collection"), more drastic steps are taken (e.g., suspending shipments or credit). On the other hand, only a few survey participants insist that they be reimbursed for every unearned discount taken. Most of them find it desirable to exhibit some degree of leniency about such offenses. As a paper company treasurer puts it:

> *Many judgements must be made in reaching a decision to allow or disallow a particular unearned discount, such as the amount of the discount, the length of time past the discount period, whether it is a new or old account and whether the customer is a continual discount violator.*

Leniency towards customers who take unearned discounts takes three principal forms. One is to give the customer a few days of grace (usually without the customer's knowing it) beyond the due date before disallowing a cash discount. In some cases the aim of such a period is simply to allow for delays in the mail; but in others the intention is to make a formal, if unannounced, extension of the discount period. For instance, a food processor reports: "We have a five-day unpublicized grace period. Customers whose remittances are not postmarked prior to the expiration of that grace period are billed back for the unearned cash discount."

Another common practice is to forgive the cash discount taken on the customer's first late payment and then dun the customer for unearned discounts taken on subsequent late payments. For example, an oil company's credit manager reports:

> *The first time that a discount is taken beyond the terms, we acknowledge the customer's payment, remind him of terms, and*

> *advise him that we have allowed the discount in this particular instance. If it occurs again, we issue a debit memo for the amount of the shortage.*

Several companies are even more lenient before they refuse to allow discounts on late payments. A lumber company, for one, permits up to three violations of cash discount terms. According to a company vice-president:

> *The first violation is not discussed with the customer but when the second violation occurs, the lateness on that occasion plus the previous lateness are reviewed in a letter with a firm request for payment on time. When the third lateness occurs, a letter is written calling attention to the previous letter and it is then pointed out that no further lateness will be permitted if cash discount is deducted.*

The third form of leniency towards customers who take unearned cash discounts is to make exceptions to stated discount terms for special groups or classes of customers or for minor infractions. Many companies ignore these offenses when the offenders are unusually important customers, or customers that normally pay promptly, or customers that are likely to be upset by dunning letters. Other respondents forego attempts at obtaining reimbursement whenever the customer has some plausible excuse for taking a discount to which it wasn't entitled. If the amount of the discount is small (five dollars or less is a figure mentioned by several survey participants), a number of companies overlook the discount even though it has not been earned. Similarly, a hardware firm reports that it allows unearned cash discounts when the sum does not exceed the cost of processing a collection.

Several respondents that grant exceptions call them to the attention of beneficiary customers. This practice, it is claimed, makes the customer realize that the infraction has not gone unnoticed, serves as a gentle warning that future violations will not be permitted, and at the same time cements relations with the customer.

DEALING WITH PRESSURE FOR EASIER CREDIT

Survey respondents adopt three basic approaches to the problem of reconciling sound credit and collection policies with pressures for easier terms. Some participants insist that rigorous enforcement of such policies is essential to continued corporate well-being and say they consistently give effect to their views, even at the risk of losing business. A great many more, however, compromise on enforcement of their stated terms or relax the terms when confronted with pressures from customers or competitors. A third group of cooperating companies, fewer in number than the other two, say they aggressively use credit as a sales tool.

Reasons for Firmness

The companies indicating that they do not compromise either their stated credit terms or their efforts to collect on time all sums due them from customers have several explanations for adhering to this practice. For a handful, there has been no pressure in the marketplace to do otherwise. But for most, the policy of firmness has been decided upon as being superior to that of deferring to the expressed wishes of customers or matching the action of competitors. According to a credit manager in an industrial machinery company, "While adherence to a sound credit policy brings a problem of threats of loss of business from weak customers, it does prove to be better than a weak or lax credit policy."

A number of respondents make the point that they cannot afford to depart from established terms or collection procedures. The chairman of another industrial machinery firm speaks of the "unbearable burden" that would result "if credit and payment terms deteriorated to the point at which we had to finance not only our own business but our customer's business." Similarly the executive vice president of a construction materials company observes that "a sound credit and collection policy is a prerequisite to survival."

The belief that failure to be firm about credit is tantamount to price-cutting weighs heavily with some survey participants. A lumber company executive, for instance, contends that "longer terms or easier discount policies are in effect a reduction of price; and since we do not permit deviations from our published prices, we do not permit deviations from our standard terms."

Another reason cited for strictly maintaining credit terms and collection procedures is that to do otherwise would entail compromising product quality or service, or both, which would be adverse to the company's interests and its customers' interests as well.

Departure from stated terms can be harmful to customers in other ways, in the opinion of several respondents. An apparel company, for instance, has this to say:

> *Our basic approach to credit is customer's interest. Extended terms build large inventories which breed obsolescence, higher mark-downs, and poorer profit performance for the retailer. Easier terms are generally contrary to the customer's interest and generally represent the efforts of marginal producers to sell an otherwise non-competitive product.*

One company reports that its adherence to a policy of firmness is in part influenced by a desire to assume a position of industry leadership and set an example that competitors will follow.

On occasion, companies have sacrificed business as a result of sticking to such a policy. But in the experience of several respondents, loss of business from this cause is often a threat that does not materialize. According to a chemical company executive:

> *It is often difficult to hold the line on sound credit terms when competition undertakes to offer better, or extended, terms for a*

comparable product. However, our policy is to maintain estab-
lished terms and to sacrifice, if necessary, the business which
can only be 'bought' by these or other discriminatory practices.
Despite the frequent apprehension of our sales department, our
experience has been that we have actually lost very few accounts
as a consequence of pursuing this policy.

And a credit manager in an oil company offers a similar comment:

We have liberalized neither our terms of sale nor our collection
procedures over the past several years. While it is true that we
hear of isolated cases where competitors are 'reported' to be
allowing easier terms we do not find this to be sufficiently signifi-
cant to make any changes in our policies.

The Case for Compromising

Among the survey respondents, it is more common practice, however, to compromise in the enforcement of credit terms or to extend stated terms when market
pressures make such steps essential to gain or hold desired business. Often, of
course, these pressures are reported to emanate from competitors, most frequently from smaller firms trying to gain the patronage of a company's established
account or entering the market for the first time, but sometimes from industry
leaders. But a good number of respondents have found that customers have
actively sought more generous terms or deferments of their payments in order
to ease the strain on their own straitened finances.

The circumstances in which concessions in terms, or postponement of customer payments are made are several. Quite a few companies report they simply
follow industry patterns, making such compromises whenever competition forces
them to do so. Although this practice sometimes leads to the acceptance of poor
credit risks it does not necessarily result in an overall weakening of credit standards. For instance, an instruments company vice-president makes this observation:

We meet the credit and collection terms advanced by our
competitors. This does not always mean the terms provide for
a sound credit and collection policy. Generally speaking, how-
ever, others in the fields in which we compete are just as inter-
ested in making money as we are, and there has been no whole-
sale erosion of credit and collection policies.

Often the degree of risk is the decisive factor. For example, a nonferrous
metals company's vice-president reports: "We endeavor to judge the risk carefully and not compete on credit and terms where risk is out of line. Where the
credit department is satisfied as to safety of our money, the sales department
determines where to meet competitive terms." To prevent undue risk, a paper

company requires the joint approval of requests for special terms by the sales manager, the credit manager, and the division manager. Another practice, followed by several respondents, is to grant special terms if bad-debt losses can be kept at an acceptably low level.

A few other companies relax credit policy or its enforcement only in exceptional circumstances. The financial vice-president of a chemical company says: "We maintain a flexible position only where a justifiable condition of a temporarily financially embarrassed customer of long standing is involved." Other types of situations in which respondents make exceptions to their customary terms include:

☐ When highly profitable business is involved.
☐ When a major competitor is involved.
☐ When allegedly lower competitive offers can be verified.

A hardware company indicates that it is most reluctant ever to relax its credit policy. Its president states:

> *Although competition is a fact of life in credit as well as in pricing, delivery, and all other aspects of business, the extension of credit beyond normal acceptable terms or relaxation of credit policies is used only as a last resort.*

Credit as a Sales Tool

A few respondents regard a highly flexible credit policy as an important means of promoting sales. A financial officer of a chemical company, for instance, says that because his company is engaged in a competitive business it will adjust credit and collective terms whenever it seems necessary to do so. Similarly a construction materials company notes that its corporate planning calls for the judicious use of credit terms as one part of a merchandising package that includes service, quality, advertising support, and other factors. And a third firm, an iron and steel foundry, reports:

> *We feel that our credit terms can and should be sold to our customers by our salesmen and our credit people, just as we sell our product for a particular price. We have the conviction that our policy is sound.*

How credit is used to achieve sales objectives is illustrated in the practice of a metals company. According to its credit manager: "We would attempt to 'buy' large orders from selected accounts by allowing extra time if there were no other solution to obtaining a reasonable share of the market in a given product line." Similarly, if this company's backlog of orders in a critical production area falls, orders are re-screened and credit inducements offered on a selective basis "in an effort to establish a more reasonable flow of business." The credit manager does note, though, that loosening credit in such circumstances has an untoward effect, namely "the difficulty in getting customers back to published terms."

Top Management's Responsibility

A paper company president, who is worried about deviations from stated credit terms in his industry, lays responsibility for taking corrective action at the door of top management. His view is as follows:

> *While the problem of lengthening credit terms is generally attributed to competitive practices, it is our opinion that an underlying force is the misconception that longer terms will generate greater sales. This fallacy falls in the same category as price-cutting, from which everyone in an industry eventually stands to lose. The situation will not be corrected until top management voices its disapproval and formally denounces the practice, thus leaving no doubt in the minds of both sales and credit people that extended terms and loose credit policies are not in the best interest of either a company or an industry.*

QUESTIONS

1. Discuss sales-related and financial yardsticks used to evaluate the investment in accounts receivable.

2. How can a company bring its accounts receivable into line?

3. What problems are the companies surveyed in the article having with the granting of cash discounts?

4. In what ways are firms dealing with the increasing pressure for easier credit?

5. What do the authors mean when they say, "It's O.K. to compromise"?

Why Banking Is Changing

PAUL S. NADLER

When the story of banking in the 1960s has been fully told, the most effective force for change in services and methods of operation in many banks may well turn out to have been the spare time available on bank computers.

From *Banking,* Journal of The American Bankers Association, December 1963, pp. 46-47. Reprinted by permission.

On looking at a bank determining for the local electric company how much power demand it should expect that week or helping a manufacturing company program and establish controls over inventories and receivables, one might wonder whether this is banking or sheer madness.

Yet those who have started to offer these customer services, as well as the less radical new services such as payroll preparation and freight bill payment plans, can argue in return that these new services are just as much a part of banking as accepting deposits and lending customers money.

WELL QUALIFIED

Banks are used to being informed of the confidential data of their customers and have earned their customers' trust that they will keep this information to themselves. Banks specialize in work that involves an ability to handle data in large volumes quickly and efficiently. And banking is the one industry that needs to understand thoroughly the insides and outsides of all other industries.

Thus one might wonder whether there is anyone else other than the commercial bank that is as fully prepared to offer these new services that the public is beginning to demand and depend upon.

As is the case with every other industry, there is a natural hesitancy for most bankers to expand their operations to include new services that look so alien to traditional bank operations on the surface.

Yet there is now more bank interest in the offering of services that differ from traditional ones than at any time in the history of the industry. More banks are actually breaking new ground in service provision than in any previous decade.

To find the reason for this, one must look at the economic environment in which banking must now operate and the tremendous new competitive pressures that have developed in practically all traditional banking spheres. But in addition, one must not overlook that nagging situation preying on the minds of so many bank officials—the availability of spare, unused computer time. For the efforts to make expensive computers as profitable as possible have served as the final motivating force pushing many otherwise reluctant banks into these new realms of bank service.

ECONOMIC ENVIRONMENT

A changed economic environment hardly ever is as strong a direct force leading to change as is some more dramatic although less significant development that strikes closer to home. Yet the changed environment is really the reason why the immediate dramatic development is felt to be so significant.

For example, the liberalization of Regulation Q at the start of 1962 and the resultant advance in the cost of attracting time and savings deposits was the dramatic development leading to a sharp increase in the aggressiveness of bank lending and investment policies. Yet behind this change in Regulation Q was really a new squeeze on bank earnings resulting from lessened demand deposit growth and the realization that future bank expansion would have to come from costly time and savings deposits. Had banking not been ripe for a change in lending and investing policies, no mere liberalization of the ceiling on savings deposit interest could have brought such a drastic reaction in bank operations as the change in Regulation Q did.

A CASE OF NECESSITY

Similarly the growing interest in offering new bank services may appear to many banks to stem solely from the need to utilize spare computer time. Yet analysis of the present economic environment indicates that new banking services were bound to come whether computers had spare time or not. The spare computer time, therefore, simply serves to dramatize a need for diversification that has been present in banking anyway.

The problem the commercial banks face today is simply this: Customers are less and less willing to leave demand deposits in the banks so that deposits must now be bought and paid for through the time and savings deposit route. This many banks realized by the time Regulation Q was changed. Yet at the same time, because of more cash from retained earnings and depreciation in the hands of big companies and greater competition from other lenders in providing the credit needs of smaller borrowers, banks find that they must not only pay more for their deposit funds, but once they have obtained them they must often lend them out for less return than was formerly the case.

When Regulation Q's ceiling was raised, for example, the banks found themselves forced to pay higher rates for savings funds or face considerably slower growth. Yet when they tried to lend and invest these savings funds profitably in mortgages and tax-exempt bonds, they pushed down the yields on these investments, doubling the squeeze on profits! The source of this double profit squeeze is as simple to find as the reason why automobile manufacturers were forced to develop the compact car—growing competition in the face of less strong demand. But the difference is that in banking, the new competition has been more intense and has come from a far more diverse group of rivals than was the case with automobiles.

THE NEW COMPETITION

The basic reason why banking has become so competitive is that the backlogs of demand for goods, built up during the depression and World War II, have now been completely met.

To any other industry, the end of demand backlogs would normally just mean less demand for available productive potential. But in finance, the end of backlogs of demand has a double impact. First, it means the demands for credit have slackened. But in addition, money lent and spent in the past when demands were stronger now is coming back through debt repayment and heavy cash throw-off from depreciation, and these funds must be put to work again.

This largely explains why, at the present, money is so readily available and financial institutions can not utilize all available funds without accepting lower rates of return.

VARIOUS PRESSURES

To commercial banking in particular, this squeeze of lessened demands for credit and greater supplies is felt in a number of ways:

☐ Whereas in the past larger companies relied on bank credit, now many of them have enough cash from retained earnings and depreciation fund flows to meet the demands that formerly required bank loans.

☐ Some other companies that used to rely more heavily on banks now borrow the surplus funds of others through the commercial paper market.

☐ Many large companies are using their surplus funds from depreciation and retained earnings to finance their own customers and, as a result, accounts payable have replaced bank loans as the major short-term liability of a number of smaller firms.

☐ Savings banks and savings and loan associations, facing the same curtailment of demand and heavy flow of repayments in the housing market that banks have felt in the business market, have in many cases entered the commercial banks' sphere of consumer credit lending, either directly or through the indirect method of mortgage refinancing.

Meanwhile, as credit demands have slackened and the banks face greater competition in lending, they also must face the slackened growth of demand deposits that has forced them to buy more of the deposit funds that they need in their lending and investing operations.

EXCESS FUNDS USED

With short-term interest rates maintained at attractive levels both in boom years and recession periods for balance-of-payments reasons, former holders of demand deposits have been finding it worthwhile to reduce their checking account balances and place excess funds in earning assets such as Treasury bills and commercial paper.

Meanwhile new procedures such as wire transfer of funds and the lock box have helped to improve money mobilization, which in turn has enabled depositors to cut their balances further. Finally, individuals have found that they too can earn a return on excess funds that formerly were left in demand deposits; for now many banks will pay them instant interest on their funds. Many more also will arrange check credit accounts that serve as stand-by balances and reduce the amount that individuals feel they must maintain in checking account deposits.

The highly competitive environment in which banking now operates has thus brought new competition and new substitutes for bank credit and bank services in virtually every traditional area of bank operations. Faced with this situation, banks endeavoring to maintain their profitability have had to look to new areas where income could be earned. And with the high cost of deposits and heavy competition in the credit markets reducing the profit opportunities from lending and investing funds, many institutions have had to turn to providing services that do not involve lending and investing of money, but that involve rather the receipt of direct compensation for specific services rendered.

In one instance, the Citizens and Southern National Bank of Georgia, new services for income have taken on such importance that C. & S. stated in its 1961 annual report that it has even set its sights on one-half of total income coming from services within ten years.

In accomplishing such a transformation in the sources of bank income, it is obvious that not all of the new services for fees or, older fee services now being given more stress, will involve automated data processing or the use of computers.

NON-AUTOMATED SERVICES

Some, such as international banking, bond trading departments, and leasing of equipment, have little to do with computer operations. But a large number of others—including mortgage servicing, accounting work for businesses and other banks, freight and travel payment plans, and charge account services—are integrally involved with use of data processing equipment. And it is in these areas of automated data processing that much of the potential for expansion of bank services, and bank income, seems to lie.

Thus, as of this date in many banks, the spare computer time is serving mainly as the nagging catalyst making bankers examine present earning trends and consider new possibilities for income.

But viewed with the perspective that only the future can provide, it may well be that the pressure to utilize spare computer time will have actually served as a significant and dramatic force saving the banks much valuable time in moving in the direction of new services,—a direction toward which basic underlying economic forces would eventually have forced banking anyway.

QUESTIONS

1. Why are banks well qualified to offer varied financial services?

2. How does lessened demand for credit affect the commercial bank?

3. What changes are seen in banking today? Are these changes happening to banks in your home community?

Budgeting Business: How a Corporate Giant Draws Up Its Forecasts of 1966 Sales, Spending

JOHN A. PRESTBO

For Edward J. Kane, this is Judgment Day.

Today, his bosses will appraise his 1965 performance as a businessman in a highly competitive field, and question sharply his predictions of how well he will do next year, and why. Ed, 55 and a divisional vice president of Minnesota Mining & Manufacturing Co., has faced their inquisition before each of the past 15 Christmases, but he still can't take it calmly. He feels a butterfly in his stomach, and rubs his hands a little more often as the hour approaches for him to submit the 1966 budget of his printing product division.

Ed's moment of truth is being widely shared this month. At 3M alone, 44 other operating division and staff department heads are being called before the 17-man management committee this month to help nail down decisions on how much money the company can expect to make next year, and how much it ought to spend to reach that target.

A VIEW OF 1966

At thousands of other companies, other executives are going through the same procedure. Today, one corporate authority estimates, about 80% of all companies with sales of over $10 million a year, or with more than 500 employees, have some type of formal budget, up from only a handful in 1940. If all their documents could be scanned, a comprehensive view would emerge of how much corporate spending will contribute to the economy in 1966, in outlays for new plants and equipment, purchases of raw materials and hiring of men.

Each company has its own budgeting style, and they vary widely. Du Pont Co., at one extreme, doesn't have a company-wide budget. Each of its 12 industrial departments draws a 12-month budget quarterly, and Du Pont doesn't balance their claims against each other in the interests of an over-all plan.

The process at 3M, which in 1965 expects to sell $1 billion worth of such products as Scotch tape and Thermofax copiers, is more typical. It's winding up in a 14-story glass and steel administration building, flanked by research labs and a shallow pond, just outside St. Paul. But it has been under way since August in offices around the world.

Some 4,000 people, or 8% of 3M's work force, have had a hand in the forecasting, questioning, revising and "go" or "no-go" decisions that make the budget. Though not all figures are final, their labors have yielded a 15-inch stack of paper weighing 30 pounds. This pile of paper reveals that 3M in 1966 will spend about $46 million for research and about $70 million in capital outlays, and will buy, among other things, 60 million pounds of paper and 140,000 light bulbs.

Reprinted with permission of *The Wall Street Journal,* December 20, 1965, pp. 1, 8.

WHAT IT ISN'T

Still, 3M's budget, or that of any major company, isn't exactly a bigger version of the housewife's list of expenses subtracted from income. Nor does it pose quite the same problems that budget-makers of the Federal Government or a local hospital face in searching for ways to raise cash to meet spending commitments, or for ways to cut spending to bring it closer to anticipated revenue.

"We don't like the word budget," says 3M President Bert S. Cross. "It sounds as if we sit around and give each division so much money and the authority to spend it come hell or high water. Planning next year's operations is really a series of forecasts—what condition the economy will be in, how much our divisions can sell and how much profit we can make on those sales. If any of these conditions change, we have to revise our forecast of everything from sales volume to manufacturing costs."

The system for making these forecasts, which took its present form in the late 1940s, follows the pyramid-shaped 3M organization chart. Plans start at the plant-foreman level and filter up through narrowing layers of supervisors, managers and executives. At each major level—division, group of divisions, and total company—competing claims for each dollar are refereed and balanced.

The process pivots around the general managers, who run 3M divisions almost like independent companies, serving different markets and facing different competition. Minnesota Mining makes 35,000 products, including tape recorders, cameras, film, gift wrap, sandpaper and industrial adhesives, besides Scotch tape. It also operates the Mutual Broadcasting System, a billboard advertising concern, and a company producing TV commercials.

THE PROFIT YARDSTICK

Despite these diversities, the general managers approach budgeting from a common angle: Profit. Each division is given a profit target—expressed both as a percentage of sales, which are expected to increase each year to maintain 3M's reputation as a growth company, and as a percentage of earnings on the division's invested capital. How to go about hitting these targets is left up to the general managers, provided they can convince management of the short and long-range validity of their plans.

Thus, the general manager's chair is a two-way hot seat. He must work with his own management team to formulate a set of working plans that seem realistic to him. Then, he must sell the package to the upper echelon brass.

"Every division wants to at least triple its research and double its sales force," says 3M Controller Donald P. Selleck. "If we let them get away with it, we'd have the damndest profit and loss statements you ever saw." But, he explains, company ground rules head off a battle royal. "Profit is the game we're playing, and the profit target is the par for the course."

If it is to play at par, a division normally can't double its sales force—not even if it could get some other division's sales force cut in half. Thus, 3M says it avoids the backstabbing and bloodletting that occur in some companies (and in Washington) when the irresistible force of expansion-minded department heads hits the immovable object of a limit on spending.

"Without a profit target, the only way we could settle differences would be by dictating who gets what," says Mr. Selleck. "And we don't like dictators."

A division, however, can balloon spending in one of its departments beyond the normal ratio to sales, by short-changing other departments. This is frequently done, particularly to push new products. (3M, whose advertising slogan is "What Won't They Think of Next?" is getting about a fourth of its 1965 sales from products developed in the past five years).

Even then, the division head must show management that long-range opportunities in the department benefited outweigh short-range belt-tightening in the departments held down. If the extra spending will cause division profit to fall even slightly below target, he also must tell management how and when profits will again reach par, and back up his contention. And that's why Ed Kane is nervous today.

Ed, a tall, baldish man with a slow, broad smile, who always keeps his desk neat, joined the then new 3M printing products division as a salesman in 1944. Within a decade he rose to general manager of the rapidly growing division, which now sells over 30 products.

A TRIPLE BUDGET

He draws three budgets. The biggest is an "operations budget," composed of a sales forecast, the basic strategy for achieving it, and the cost of carrying out that strategy. This budget covers both 1966 operations and those of the next five years.

Ed also must budget "cash flow," meaning he must correlate monthly expenses with income brought in by sales so that he isn't "overdrawn" at the 3M treasury. Finally, he must plan capital spending three years ahead, quarter by quarter.

Ed went over his plans with top aides for four hours Sept. 20. Believing that zooming sales will push output at one plant to capacity sooner than expected, the group moved construction of a new plant up one year in the capital budget. That finished the plans—but left a problem. For 1966, Ed is forecasting profit lower than in 1965.

The reason: Next fall, Ed plans to introduce a new product aimed at a market almost wholly new to the division. Before then, he plans to spend $2 million for machinery, raw materials, advertising and other introductory expenses. The resulting drop in profit is expected to be small. But Ed knows it will raise management eyebrows today, because it will interrupt a steady profit growth in his division. So he has to justify it.

FIRST ROUND WON

It took him only a half hour to win over his group vice president, Raymond H. Herzog of the graphic systems group (this comprises five divisions bringing in

13% of 3M's sales and profit). Mr. Herzog sliced some dollars off Ed's figure for product introduction costs, in part by reducing the number of hand-made proto-types for a test marketing program. But he believed Ed's estimate that the new product will be a solid money-maker in two or three years. Mr. Herzog vetoed a plan by another division to introduce a new product next year "because I'd grow old before I knew if it ever made a profit."

After Mr. Herzog and other group heads okayed division budgets, Controller Selleck consolidated them into a company-wide budget for the management committee. At 3M this is the court of last budgetary appeal; 9 of its members sit on the 15-man board of directors, making budget approval there a formality. (At some other companies it isn't. At Halliburton Co., corporate officers fill only 6 of the 16 board seats, and executives who had already approved a budget spent two hours last month justifying it before getting board approval.)

Until two years ago, each 3M division pleaded its case to the management committee before a company-wide budget took shape. So, says one officer, sessions dragged into January as the divisions "used every trick in the book to snow the brass into approving their requests." And the divisional trees blocked management's view of the budgetary forest. "How come I like each division but I don't like the total?" a vice president asked one year.

OK IN GENERAL—NEXT . . .

Now the committee—President Cross, seven group vice presidents and nine vice presidents of staff departments such as finance—approves a 3M-wide budget before starting sessions with the division heads. On Dec. 8 it approved the 1966 budget as one that would meet the goals of keeping 3M sales rising about 10% a year, and of netting pre-tax profit of 20% to 25% on both sales and net worth. So division heads have had relatively easy sledding in their appearances before the committee.

Still, says Ed Kane, "it's like getting a physical checkup. You know you're healthy, but you imagine all sorts of ills you could have and don't know about."

The committee meets in a windowless, 40-by-70-foot room on the adminis-tration building's 14th floor. Members sit in soft, reddish-brown armchairs around a U-shaped arrangement of desks facing a podium and movie screen. Along the gray, cloth-paneled walls, in less comfortable chairs, sit division heads of the group being reviewed, and their aides.

The executives are convivial as they select chairs (cigar smokers clustering along one arm of the U). But when the heavy doors close precisely at 9 a.m., "Hiya, Bert," yields to "Yes, Mr. Cross."

PROBING FOR "WEAKNESSES"

Division heads don't present their own budgets. Controller Selleck does, pointing out "weaknesses"—such as Ed Kane's forecast of a profit decline, perhaps—and he doesn't tell the divisions what he will say. The committee seeks not to review details but to ferret out problems from the rows of antiseptic figures.

"It's like trying to spot a swindle in an expense account," says Mr. Herzog, a committee member. "If you've done it yourself, you know where to look."

When Mr. Selleck's Midwestern twang stops, a division manager takes the podium and committee questions fly. At a session last week, members noted one division was forecasting a sales gain below the 10%-a-year target. Why?

Well, the division head replied, his already oversized research budget was being used up to improve existing products, just to stay ahead of competition. He didn't think he could ask for more to bring two promising new products out of the laboratory. After all, he had his profit target to meet.

That's no excuse, committee members replied in effect. "We'll go along with a reduced profit margin for a couple of years if you can get out some new products that will bring your growth rate back in line," one summarized. "Come back with your product ideas. If they're as good as you say, we'll take your budget apart in the middle of the year and put it back together again if necessary."

ED KANE TO THE PODIUM

Today, Ed Kane expects to be asked: Does the expected profit drop indicate your division's growth rate has peaked out? How fast do you expect to pick up sales on this new product? When do you expect profit to equal or better the 1965 level?

Ed has answers, illustrated by a bundle of transparencies of tables and charts to be flashed on the screen (with a 3M overhead projector, naturally) as he talks. "A little chuckle goes up from the committee when an old pro like Ed reaches for his transparencies," says one member. "It's as if he's saying: 'I'm glad you asked.'"

This readiness comes from three rehearsals by Ed and his aides. At these, Ed runs through his presentation and his aides, playing committee members, fire questions. If one stumps him, all search for an answer, which Ed notes in his "script." But for the toughest question—will this product sell?—he admits there is no answer. He thinks it will, and has a transparency showing his reasons. But he adds: "We really won't know until somebody pays hard cash for one of these things."

Ed won't be long in doubt about what impression he makes. Committee members shoot questions fairly rapidly, and since Ed is ready for them, he probably will be on the podium only 10 to 15 minutes.

Tension can build in these quick exchanges, but there are lighter moments, too. One year a division head brought in a sample of a product containing radioactive material. He insisted it wasn't radioactive, but President Cross still wouldn't let anybody touch it. "What a way to wipe us out at the top!" he shuddered, as laughter exploded.

ROUND-THE-WORLD BUDGETING

Other sessions end less happily for the men quizzed. In the last half of November eight committee members and international department executives set out to review the budgets of 3M's foreign units, which contribute 22% of 3M sales. Splitting into teams they traveled 88,000 miles, visiting factories in 16 countries and sales subsidiaries in 13, spread through Europe, the Far East, Latin America and Africa. At each stop they went through a budget review much like those in St. Paul, but with plant tours and product displays added.

This year the teams rejected four of the 29 foreign budgets. In one country a team member took a subsidiary's sales forecast, divided it by the number of salesmen, and came up with a volume-per-salesman figure far above anything the subsidiary had ever achieved. The team asked for a revised forecast.

Ed Kane's chances today? When considering a new product, says President Cross, "we frequently gamble on the man who's going to do the job. We take his word, rather than rely entirely on statistics which might indicate the odds are against his selling as much of a new product as he forecasts. After all, he's putting his reputation as a businessman on the block when he commits himself to a forecast. And he knows we have good memories."

QUESTIONS

1. Compare the budgeting methods of Minnesota Mining and Manufacturing Company with those of Dupont.

2. Discuss the 3M budgeting process from its beginning to end.

3. What is the role of profit in the budgeting process?

4. How do the three budgets drawn up by Ed Kane differ?

The Financial Executive in the 1970s

JOHN R. MOORE

Pierre du Pont once wrote: "One cannot expect to know what is going to happen. One can only consider himself fortunate if he is able to find out what *has* happened."

My crystal ball is at least as cloudy as Mr. du Pont's. However, from partial

From *Financial Executive*, January 1967, pp. 28-29, 32, 34, 36. Reprinted by permission.

knowledge of what has been happening lately, I think we can identify trends which will put much greater requirements, opportunities, and responsibilities on financial executives in the 1970s. These future responsibilities will be added to all those which the executives carry today. Many routine duties may be turned over to machines, but the financial executives will still be responsible for them.

The traditional recording and reporting parts of his job seem unlikely to be eliminated even by sweeping changes in technology and in governmental requirements. In fact, I cannot visualize anything ever changing the need for accuracy and thoroughness in keeping a company's tabulation of past performance. The measurement and control of company resources have given the financial profession its historic professional hallmarks of independence, integrity, objectivity, and technical competence. These functions will always be vital to a successful business. Similarly, the financial executive's role in obtaining and watch-dogging working and expansion capital will continue undiminished.

But a business has other needs too. Some of its needs are changing drastically. Out of the changes, a larger role is emerging for the financial staff. In the last 20 years, top management attention has been concentrated chiefly on marketing, manufacturing, and technology. Technological progress is encountering explosive growth. But brilliance in research and development and in production and distribution must be balanced by corresponding brilliance in resource management in order to capitalize on the opportunities of the 1970s.

Decisions about commitments of company resources will be harder to make. Why? Because it is very difficult to set a dollar value on the most precious of these resources—readily accessible knowledge and competent people. Because more key factors and information will be available to management than ever before. Because of the need for understanding long-term trends that could avalanche and cripple a company if undetected. Because there will be increasing numbers of financial opportunities and challenges without prior precedent for evaluation. Because new tools will be available for making financial decisions. Woe betide the company that does not know how to use them. Because mergers and acquisitions are growing in frequency, and while a company might be a useful acquisition to one buyer, it may be a costly nuisance to another. The financial executive should know which and why. And finally, because the 1970s will be the decade when business and government will be called on to plan for and initiate programs of very long range significance aimed at facing up to and overcoming the onrushing consequences of world population explosion, resource depletion, contamination of our land, our waters, our air, and the increasing complexity of business, government, and society.

FUTURE-ORIENTED FINANCE MAN

The traditional role of the financial man has been past-oriented. His new role will be future-oriented. The old-fashioned controller with the sharp pencil was concerned chiefly with records. Tomorrow's finance man must be a forecaster as well as a keeper of records. He will help the company make crucial internal and external decisions governing its future life.

The firm of the 1970s will be searching continuously for new opportunities abroad as well as at home. It will seek not only attractive acquisitions but also new markets and new products. It will have to face the opportunities of business in the emerging nations and competition from both sides of the iron curtain as well as from United States enterprises. Therefore, critical questions will arise concerning the commitment of corporate resources to new areas with new customers, new customs, new laws, new partners, new money markets, and new competition. I recently heard of a U.S. firm of the highest integrity which rejected a controlling ownership in a foreign acquisition because the business methods which this firm had to use to prosper in its environment could never be condoned under the U.S. firm's business ethics.

INTERPRETER OF MULTINATIONAL COMPANY FINANCES

By the 1970s many thousands of U.S. firms will operate in truly international markets. Many firms will be multinational. According to a survey reported by the Indiana University Graduate School of Business, up to now most international finance executives seem to be playing by ear. They need more knowledge now. They will need far more in the 1970s, particularly if lessening tensions with the Soviets open up the communist countries as markets and business areas.

While direct costs are identifiable and measurable, the Indiana report shows that most companies selling abroad have not analyzed the indirect costs of their foreign operations. Nor are they often as familiar as they need to be with the accounting practices and cartel environment which foreign laws require or permit. The 1970 financial executive should know how to analyze and distribute all costs of international operation, because this knowledge will enable him to adjust to variables such as currency fluctuations and differing tax laws. These can make a big difference in net profits.

A multinational company may find its subsidiaries borrowing locally at high costs rather than taking advantage of the parent corporation's access to low-cost funds elsewhere. It may find itself paying interest on bank overdrafts in one country while it has idle money in another.

Multinational company financial executives must certainly learn how to interpret the financial reports of their foreign subsidiaries, partners, or potential acquisitions. They must learn what unfamiliar agreements among competitors can do to market forecasts and profits.

SHORTER PROFITABLE LIFESPAN OF PRODUCTS

I have already touched briefly on product diversification. It will present both opportunities and problems to the man who holds the purse strings. On one hand, new products can open new markets. On the other, invasion of established product lines by new competitors can bring early obsolescence or can saturate a previously profitable market. This will force many more companies to commit major funds to research and development not only to improve established products, but to seek a succession of new products which will be developed and introduced with a rapidity considered impossible today.

American industry now puts out 500 different new products every week— more than 10 every hour of every working day. Some of these inevitably force older products into discard. Some compete directly with each other, others hit the market too soon. Meanwhile the cost of innovation is rising steeply. Early in World War II my company entered about 42,000 engineering manhours to design a new aircraft, the P-51 fighter. Ten years later, it entered about 27 times as many engineering manhours—or more than 1,100,000—to design its F-86. And in this decade, it used 16,000 computer hours and paid engineers for 24 million hours of work in designing its XB-70. In the past, management could finance and build a new plant with reasonable assurance that it would have a working life of 20 years or more. Today, with obsolescence an imminent threat, a company must begin to modernize a plant almost as soon as it opens.

Delay in introducing new products is costly. A major heavy equipment manufacturer recently discovered that if a competitor beat him to market with a new product by only one peak selling season, he would lose at least 14 per cent of his share of the market. In the 1930s Du Pont introduced nylon and had no competition for many years; but recently when it invested $40 million in bringing out delrin, an equally dramatic new product, it found that a competitor got a similar item onto the market within a month, and prices dropped almost 20 per cent during the next few weeks.

So we can look for a continuous shortening of the profitable lifespan of products with a consequent premium on rapidity of new product development and marketing and the necessity of making the right decision to commit company resources within an ever narrowing span of time. Fortunately, the increase in standardization of engineering procedures and application of computers to data retrieval, engineering design, and control of manufacturing processes will greatly reduce the time required to bring out a new product and thereby reduce the quantity necessary to achieve acceptable cost and profitability. For example, Autonetics lead times from go-ahead to production of complex new electronic and electromechanical equipment has dropped 50 per cent since 1963.

This means that in the 1970s a good financial executive will have to keep a sharp eye on product planning and marketing. It will be as important to know when to eliminate unprofitable products as to bring out new ones. Thus, in the past three years, one company dropped 16 of its products. These represented sales of several million dollars, or nearly 10 per cent of its total volume. Nevertheless, the company's net profits increased 20-fold, largely because the discarded products had diverted manpower from more profitable items.

SHORTAGE OF VENTURESOME MONEY

The combination of a steady trend of rising prices with physical growth could mean that corporate business will find its needs for working capital rising at an average rate of perhaps five per cent a year over the long term. At the same time, interest rates are going up while the wage-cost-price spiral places a tightening squeeze on the company's liquidity. Already some signs indicate that the economy may be under-supplied with venture capital. As a wire-service news story stated, "Banks are for the first time in this decade distinguishing between productive and nonproductive loans. There is no money now available, for example, to finance the acquisition of another company."

Savings available for investment are in comparatively short supply throughout most of the world. One reason seems to be that the only really big investors left in America are the investment trusts, pension funds, banks, and insurance companies. These fiduciary investors now hold almost one-third of all the marketable common shares of American business. As you are well aware, the managers of these funds represent vastly more financial power than did the famous tycoons of a half-century ago.

Of all the savings the American people can afford to set aside for new investment, a full third goes into pension funds. These funds are accumulating assets at an estimated rate of a half-billion dollars per month, with a total of $165 billion predicted for 1970. It is clear that all those billions must be invested cautiously rather than venturesomely, since they represent retirement money. The financial executive of the 1970s will have to be a better planner and forecaster, an evaluator of proposed innovations, in order to make the company more profitable and more attractive to investors.

COMMITTING RESOURCES TO CHANGE

Of course this is not a new problem. We might even define economic progress as a process of continually buying more productivity for less money. We make such progress through innovation. Let's define innovation as does Dr. Peter Drucker, the well known writer and professor of economics: "Innovation is *not* invention and discovery. It may require either but the focus is on performance rather than knowledge." Without incessant innovation, all the capital invested in this country since its beginning might have been barely enough to keep our steadily growing population up to a 1776 scale of living. The entire improvement in living standards since then is the result of innovation. Likewise, what now characterizes an under-developed country, and keeps it under-developed, is not so much a shortage of capital as a shortage of innovation. The needs for innovation in the 1970s seem likely to be felt as acutely in the field of management as in technology.

Companies will have to make bold but well-considered decisions in areas outside their traditional fields of operation. Most of these decisions will hinge on money. Tomorrow's financial executive must be as willing to commit company resources in response to changed conditions as he is careful in safeguarding the solvency of the enterprise. His accounting, information, and control systems must be oriented toward future prospects rather than past results. His office may well become the information and intelligence center for the whole business. After all, the most effective control of planning and building for the future is through the allocation of capital, just as the most effective control of all types of cost is the well-conceived budget.

We all are aware of the tremendous advances in energy production and use, in the promises of rich rewards in the oceans, of the problems and opportunities associated with the population explosion, including those of polluted air and water, mass transportation, and just plain existing with fellow human beings in urban beehives. At the same time, we are witnessing great leaps forward in the material sciences, in the medico-psychological field, in every phase of knowledge.

In just one of these—electronics—many are used to thinking of advances in terms of transistor radios made in Japan which can be bought for very few dollars. Transistors did make possible more complex, reliable electronics than had been possible before their invention. The same principles which produced transistors are now being applied to produce whole circuits no larger than the transistors themselves. These circuits are being called first-generation microelectronics. They are relatively large—one tenth by two tenths of an inch—and contain the equivalent of 15 to 30 of the elements which you will find in radios, resistors, capacitors, diodes, and transistors. As the first-generation microelectronics is just going into operational use, the second generation is making its appearance. It is giving promise of being far more sensational than the first generation. The second generation already permits us to build 200,000 equivalent components into a piece of material one inch square by one sixty-fourth of an inch thick, and we have in our laboratories means for increasing this by a factor of 25 to one.

To give you some idea of what this means, we could store five, 350-page novels in one cubic inch. If we assume that the basic company management library contains between 500 and 1000 volumes, we could store that whole library in 100 cubic inches and, more importantly, call for any passage in less than a second. We could put all the circuits of a television, except for the picture tube, on a chip one tenth of an inch by two tenths of an inch by fifteen thousandths of an inch thick; that is, we could put the control and amplifying circuits for 3300 TV sets in a cubic inch. But the most important use of second-generation microelectronics will be in computers.

MANAGING THE INFORMATION EXPLOSION

The uses of computers are boundless. They will be important tools for management, banking, engineering, ground and air traffic control, complex process control, machine control, equipment trouble shooting, communication switching, coding and decoding, and—that one that I always come back to—accessible storage. With such storage we can file and use the information which we are generating and which the future generation will develop.

But more sensationally, computers are beginning to be adapted to machines which seem to think and to earn. These machines can be "taught" to be experts in many narrow fields, such as certain specialized law, specialized medicine, specialized engineering, physics, and chemistry, and specialized finance. They will have infallible memories with tremendous capacity, a capacity which begins to approach that of the human brain. And they are not coming any too soon. One of the most challenging problems of the foreseeable future is how to store, recall, and use all of the information which people and machines are generating at a frighteningly increasing rate.

The 1970 financial executive will help his company make many hard choices, and he will have to call on modern computers for help. For example, he may have to recommend or evaluate one of several plans for expanding capacity in order to supply anticipated market growth. The profitability of the alternative plans may be affected by many long-term factors, such as the market's future growth rate, its future geographical distribution, future price levels, future production costs, future labor costs, future material costs, the company's share of the market, and so on.

DECISION MAKING WITH STATISTICAL TECHNIQUES

Fortunately, computer technology is making new methods of mathematical analysis available to the financial executive to improve his decisions. The aerospace industry and the government already are deeply involved in such analysis on every major new program. Literally hundreds and often thousands of hours of computer time go into analysis of the many possible configurations and operational uses to determine the most efficient system. Similar methods not only enable the financial man to analyze a wide range of alternatives, but also to speed up the decision process.

When factors cannot be predicted precisely, probability theory must be invoked. It has been used to determine how many spare parts should be ordered with a new machine. Too few spares might keep the machine idle for costly periods, and too many would be wasteful. If past records indicate the approximate frequency of part failure and the approximate longevity of the machine, then probability theory can minimize the total costs of spares and the costs of running short. The solution takes into account not only the price of parts, but also the costs of storage and maintenance, the costs of shutting down a machine or a whole line for lack of a spare, the costs of a special order for more spares, and the length of time needed to obtain them.

In more complex situations where management needs to predict the most profitable compromise between the risks of over supply and under supply in meeting a demand that fluctuates unpredictably, another concept known as queuing or waiting-line theory can be used. It can determine the optimum capacity for airport facilities to service aircraft arriving at unpredictable times or the optimum size of a maintenance force that handles emergency repairs or whether a job shop should expand to handle peak loads.

Still another concept, linear programming, is an algebraic technique used for finding the most productive uses of limited resources. Consider the problems of a food manufacturer trying to decide how to assign production of different items to different plants and then stock different warehouses so that salesmen can serve customers most efficiently and profitably. I know of one such manufacturer who actually had more than 700,000 alternatives, yet only one combination would yield the greatest profit. Linear programming cut his number of warehouses by 10, added more than $800,000 a year to profits, and opened up the prospect of further savings by reducing other costs without any impairment of service.

Quadratic programming, like linear programming, is an algebraic technique, but it can be used in problems involving more uncertainty. One paint company uses it in scheduling operations when future orders are unknown. It has thereby saved 8.5 per cent of total direct costs. This technique has several applications in financial programming, including cash flow, short-term borrowing, and long-term financing; the programming of equipment expansion and replacement; and the scheduling of various types of transportation. Companies committed to guaranteed annual wage plans but which must adjust to fluctuating sales may find quadratic programming especially profitable in stabilizing production and employment levels.

A technique known as mathematical simulation can be used to compare alternative investment plans, to schedule the movement of hundreds of vehicles, or to analyze the entire operations of a company. One manufacturer had been allocating production among five plants on the basis of transportation costs, which were thought to be the most critical factor. But when operations were simulated, the mathematical model showed that productivity per worker and utilization of space differed widely from plant to plant. Using this model, a wide range of alternatives was tested, and the most profitable turned out to be closing two of the five plants. Although this did raise transportation costs, it brought much greater savings in equipment and manpower. The manufacturer's profits increased by more than $9 million a year.

These are some of the tools of analysis which the financial executive of the 1970s will have at hand. Other such tools, to list them briefly, are: the method called dynamic programming for deciding exactly when and where to build a series of new plants in a capital expansion program; input-output analysis for analyzing interrelated changes, such as calculating all the effects on a given industry of a new highway program; search theory for allocating research funds; and game theory for deciding optimum strategy to meet unknown moves by competitors.

ADVANCES IN SCIENCE OF MANAGING

The availability of such new methods may mean that an expert in mathematical analysis of financial problems will have to move next door to the president's office. Whether it involves cutting back research, building a new plant, establishing a new marketing organization, introducing a new product, or buying an old company, practically every basic management decision is a long-range decision which turns on the question of how profitable it will be.

Until recently such decisions were made largely by subjective judgment, and the financial executive's guess might be no better than the next man's. But today, in one company after another, better information and better methods are enabling financial men to make decisions that will begin to pay off handsomely about four years from now.

COMPLEX AGE OF "GENERALIST"

Advances in the science of managing complex programs have been a necessary, albeit unsensational, ingredient in our well-publicized military and space programs. The requirement for team effort involving specialists in diverse activity will continue and expand. Our programs have and are continuing to build the management resources to go with our scientific advances. These resources are being generated just in time to give us the tools to cope with the many problems of this Age of Complexity.

Progress in the physical and medical sciences and in management can help us solve the problems of the Age of Complexity, but these in themselves are not enough. We need to discover and to develop people, who for lack of a better word, we are calling these days "generalists." The generalist is the opposite of the "specialist." He is the jack of many trades and master of several. He is characterized by an ability to switch rapidly from one to another of widely diverse problems and widely diverse disciplines, but it is important to note that he must be able to concentrate; he must be objective; he must be an expert in communication both in transmitting and receiving; and he must be able to evaluate the credibility of information which he receives. He must be a man of unusual physical stamina and dedication, and he must be possessed of a very understanding family and group of friends. The capabilities and numbers of such generalists, especially those with an understanding of financial management, will establish the ultimate limit of all of our progress in this Age of Complexity.

Thus, the financial executive of today can face the prospects of the 1970s with the certain knowledge that technology stands at his elbow—like the Genie of Aladdin—only waiting to be called to do his bidding, and that his opportunities will be limited only by his ability and the horizons on which he sets his goals.

QUESTIONS

1. Why will decisions about the commitment of company financial resources be harder to make in the future?

2. How do financial executives function differently in multinational firms as compared to domestic firms?

3. Technology is constantly expanding. How will technological changes affect the financial manager?

4. Will new mathematical techniques aid the executive in his decision-making role? Give examples.

4

The Marketing Function

Management's attitude toward marketing has undergone several significant changes during the past two decades. First, management is far more customer oriented today than it was twenty years ago. The needs of the consumer have become the focal point of action in the marketing function. Second, there is increased emphasis upon the profit objective. Profit has replaced sales volume as the major objective of the marketing function.

The American Marketing Association's Committee on Definitions has defined marketing as "The performance of business activities that direct the flow of goods and services from producer to consumer or user."[1]

SALES PLANNING AND CONTROL

The first step in planning the marketing activities of a firm is to prepare a *forecast of sales*. A sales forecast is an estimate of the volume of sales that the firm can expect to achieve during the forecasted period. The firm will usually forecast sales for two distinct time periods. The short-run sales forecast will typically consist of one year, while the long-run sales forecast may be for five or more years.

The sales forecast serves as a basis for planning and coordinating many activities within the firm. Professor Fred Jones of the University of Illinois suggests that the sales forecast may be used to plan production, manpower, equipment and supplies, inventories, and sales promotion activities. It is also used to prepare expense budgets and to forecast profits.[2]

After the sales forecast has been prepared, management must design a comprehensive *marketing plan* capable of accomplishing the planned volume of sales. In the marketing plan special emphasis is given to the firm's product lines, prices, customers, and promotional efforts.

The determination of product lines and product policy is an important part of the marketing plan. The ultimate objective is to develop and maintain the most profitable product line, while constantly attempting to improve products. Product

---

[1]Ralph S. Alexander, Chairman, *Marketing Definitions, A Glossary of Marketing Terms* (Chicago: American Marketing Association, 1960).

[2]Fred M. Jones, *Introduction to Marketing Management* (New York: Appleton-Century-Crofts, 1964), pp. 112-113.

planning includes the addition of new products and product lines and the elimination of nonprofitable existing products. The Camaro, for example, is a recent addition to the product line of the Chevrolet Division of General Motors.

As was mentioned earlier, marketing has in recent years become far more customer oriented than it once was. The marketing plan of the firm seeks answers to the following questions: Who are their customers? What do their customers want? How do their customers buy? Where do their customers buy? Why do their customers buy? When do their customers buy? The answers to these questions can be provided through marketing and motivational research.

Pricing is another key aspect of the marketing plan. The firm typically attempts to set its prices so that profits are at a maximum level. More will be said about pricing in the next section.

The last aspect of the marketing plan has to do with *determining promotional effort.* If the planned sales volume is to be achieved, sufficient promotional activity must take place. Most firms use two basic types of promotional effort— advertising and personal selling. The firm must decide how much to spend for advertising, what media to use, and when the advertising messages should appear. Personal selling is the responsibility of the sales organization. This organization is necessary if the firm's products are to be distributed in an economical manner. Management therefore has the responsibility of selecting, developing, and maintaining a good sales force. Firms typically divide the sales goal of the firm into *sales quotas* for their salesmen. The sales quota is the volume of sales that the salesman is expected to achieve in his sales territory. The salesman's performance is judged according to how well he achieves his individual sales quota.

The best sales and marketing plan is useless unless it is properly executed. The vice-president in charge of marketing or sales has the responsibility for making sure that the plan leads to the successful achievement of marketing goals. To aid in the achievement of objectives, sales and marketing control must be used. Many firms use sales reports, analysis of sales quotas, managerial supervision, analysis of sales expenses, and customer reports to achieve sales control.

PRICING

The pricing decision is one of the most important decisions that the manager must make. Prices must be set at the appropriate level so that sufficient sales income is achieved. Sales income must exceed the total cost of doing business if the firm is to earn a profit. The firm should make its pricing decisions on the basis of costs, the market, actions of competitors, legislation, and economic conditions.[3] The businessman frequently calculates the cost of the product to his firm and then adds a certain percentage to cover expenses and profits. This method of pricing is called *cost-plus pricing.* A hardware store operator, for example, may buy a power lawnmower for $70 and add 50 per cent to cover his operating expenses and profit. He will then sell the mower for $105. This is probably the most common method of pricing.

[3]Richard R. Still and Edward W. Cundiff, *Essentials of Marketing,* (Englewood Cliffs, N.J.: Prentice-Hall, Inc., 1966), p. 154-159.

The nature of the market also affects the firm's pricing policies. Many manufacturers successfully compete on the basis of the characteristics of their products rather than on the price of their products. One customer may prefer an RCA color television set because of RCA's nationwide factory service organization. Another customer may prefer to buy a Zenith color television set because of its hand-wired circuitry. Neither customer will change brands unless he feels that a significant price difference exists.

Very few businessmen can afford to ignore the prices charged by their competitors. If the businessman sets his prices too much higher than his competitors, he is likely to experience a decline in sales. If an industry is dominated by one or two firms, a *follow-the-leader* pricing policy is likely to be adopted by the other firms in the industry. For example, if the largest zinc producer increases its price, the other firms in the industry are likely to raise their prices. Conversely, if the dominant firm lowers prices, the other firms in the industry will usually follow.

Federal and state legislation also influences the pricing policies established by business firms. For example, the Robinson-Patman Act prohibits price discrimination between purchasers of similar quality goods where the effect is to lessen competition. Purchasers of large volumes of products may still receive quantity discounts if the lower price is based upon savings in manufacturing or distributing the product. Also, a number of states have established "fair trade" laws. Where applicable, the manufacturer establishes the minimum or actual price at which the product must be resold at the retail level.

The level of economic activity also affects the pricing policies of business firms. If the level of economic activity is declining, the sales of many firms are also likely to fall. Consequently, a firm's inventory of finished products is likely to rise. In order to reduce its inventory the firm may cut prices. Conversely, if the level of business activity is expanding rapidly, selected products may be in short supply. The prices of these products are likely to rise.

CHANNELS OF DISTRIBUTION

The business firm must decide how to transfer ownership from the producer to the consumer. This decision involves the selection of a *channel of distribution*. The channel of distribution is the route along which goods move from producers to consumers. There are a number of different channels of distribution available to the producer or manufacturer of products. In selecting a channel of distribution, the manufacturer will typically consider the nature of the product, the financial resources of the firm, the marketing skills of the firm, customer preferences, and the channels used by competitors.

Three major channels of distribution can be identified. The simplest channel involves the producer and the consumer. The baker who sells his product directly to the housewife is a typical example. The Fuller Brush Company, Avon Products, Inc., and Watkins Products, Inc., are other examples of producers who sell directly to the consumer.

The second channel of distribution involves the producer, the retailer, and the consumer. In this channel the retailer purchases goods from producers and resells them to consumers. The Kroger Company and Sears, Roebuck and Co. are examples of large retail concerns that buy directly from the manufacturer and sell to the consumer.

The producer, wholesaler, retailer, and consumer are involved in the third channel of distribution. In this case the producer sells his products to a wholesaler. The wholesaler distributes his products to retailers. The retailer then makes the goods available to the consumer. An auto supply parts wholesaler, for example, buys auto parts from a number of auto parts manufacturing firms. The wholesaler's salesmen attempt to sell their firm's products to retail auto parts stores, gas stations, and other retailers. These retailers will then sell their auto parts to consumers. The wholesaler provides important marketing functions by taking title to the auto parts, extending credit to the retailers, delivering the parts to the retailers, and providing a sales force. Food, drugs, and hardware are commonly distributed through this channel.

In actual practice there are several variations of the three basic channels. The marketing manager must constantly evaluate the success achieved by the selected channel of distribution. He will want to determine whether the selected channel provides his product with adequate market coverage. In addition, the manager will want to be sure that the middlemen (wholesalers and retailers) are aggressively promoting his product. Finally, the manufacturer must consider the costs associated with the alternative channels of distribution.

ADVERTISING

American business firms spend billions of dollars each year on advertising. The advertiser attempts to stimulate sales. Advertising tries to influence customer behavior by providing information, by changing desires, and by altering brand preferences.[4]

Advertisements provide customers with information concerning what goods are available, where they are available, when they will be available, and for what price they are available. Thus, the advertisement provides customers and potential customers with information that is helpful in purchasing goods and services.

Advertising also attempts to create or change the desires of the consuming public. This aspect of advertising is particularly important when the manufacturer is introducing a new, unique product. The advertiser tries to convince the potential customer that the advertised product is highly desirable.

In many instances, the potential consumer already has the desire to purchase a product. The task in this situation is to persuade the consumer to buy the advertiser's brand rather than the brand offered by the competitor.

The advertiser must decide how much money to spend for advertising. The size of the advertising budget should be based upon the effectiveness of advertising; that is, how effective advertising is in increasing the sales and profits of the firm. Many advertisers determine their advertising expenditures by the

---

[4]Alfred R. Oxenfeldt and Carroll Swan, *Management of the Advertising Function* (Belmont, California: Wadsworth Publishing Company, Inc., 1964), p. 8.

per-cent-of-sales method: in this approach a selected percentage of past or forecasted sales is used to calculate the advertising expenditure. An alternative approach is the *objective-and-task method:* in this approach the firm decides upon its desired sales objective and then estimates how much money will have to be spent on advertising to achieve the objective.

The advertising function may either be performed by the firm's advertising department or assigned to an *advertising agency.* The advertising agency is an organization that prepares and places advertisements for a number of different firms. The agency is composed of a group of persons who are knowledgeable concerning the various aspects of advertising. The agencies receive commissions for the services that they render to business.

The advertising department of the firm or the advertising agency must decide the appropriate media for the advertiser's message. Newspaper, television, magazines, direct mail, radio, billboards, and handbills are the most important media available. The advertiser must then allocate the advertising budget among the various media. The objective is to obtain the greatest increase in sales and profits.

MARKETING RESEARCH

Marketing research involves collecting and analyzing data useful in solving marketing problems. Marketing research, if properly conducted, can help solve marketing problems in the following areas: forecasting, product planning, customer attitudes and opinions, pricing, sales analysis, sales control, advertising, merchandising, and competition.[5]

Marketing research is performed by many different groups. Many large business firms have their own marketing research department. Smaller firms, on the other hand, may have their marketing research activities performed by marketing research consultants. These consultants charge the firm a fee for the services they render. In addition, marketing research activities are performed by communications media, banks, universities, and government agencies. These organizations typically have a significant amount of data that the market researcher can use in solving his problems. Data from these sources are called *secondary data.*

In many instances the market researcher will have to collect his data first-hand. This type of data are called *primary data.* The primary data can be collected by the survey, experimental, or observational methods of marketing research.[6] The *survey method* uses personal and telephone interviews and questionnaires to obtain information. The researcher may be attempting to gather factual information concerning magazine readership. The researcher might ask: How many magazines do you read? What magazines do you read? Where do you buy these magazines? In addition, the researcher may be attempting to obtain personal opinions on a wide range of subjects.

[5]Myron S. Heidingsfield and Frank H. Eby, Jr., *Marketing and Business Research* (New York: Holt, Rinehart and Winston, Inc., 1962), pp. 8-10.

[6]Still and Cundiff, *op. cit.*, pp. 116-119.

The *experimental method* of marketing research utilizes the scientific method in solving marketing problems. A firm that plans to introduce a new liquid detergent on the market may decide to test experimentally the effectiveness of two alternative bottle shapes. Through a scientifically controlled experiment the researcher will be able to decide which bottle does the most effective job in promoting the new product.

In the *observational method,* the market researcher actually observes the behavior of the consumer or potential consumer. The researcher will then record this data for later analysis and use.

The market researcher should attempt to collect, analyze, and communicate data that are most useful in solving marketing problems. The firm that neglects its marketing research activities may be making many incorrect decisions due to the lack of appropriate information. Too many incorrect decisions could seriously jeopardize the survival of the firm.

MOTIVATIONAL THEORY

Businessmen traditionally have been interested in why consumers buy. It has been only in recent years that motivational theory has been used to help answer the question. Originally, consumer motivation and behavior were explained in terms of economic self-interest. Thus, man was viewed as being rational or logical in the purchase of goods and services. We are, at times, rational or logical in our behavior; however, we often tend to be irrational in our consumer behavior.

To gain greater insight into consumer behavior, marketing managers began to utilize certain psychological and sociological findings and techniques. For example, many psychologists agree that man has certain basic needs. These needs, such as food, security, and sex, lead to strong drives (motivators) in the individual. These drives can, at least in part, be satisfied by the purchase of goods and services offered by business. Psychologists believe that human behavior is directed toward the satisfaction of these needs. Consequently, our consumer behavior is motivated by our desire to satisfy our needs. Thus, the manufacturer is concerned with the ability of his product to satisfy consumers' needs.

Recent contributions from sociologists also have enabled businessmen to better understand consumer behavior. The consumer is very sensitive to the social environment in which he operates. For example, a consumer of upper-class social standing is typically influenced in his consumer behavior by the values and opinions of others in his social class.

The marketing manager should use motivational theory and motivational research as an aid in making important marketing decisions. The results of motivational research can be used in product, pricing, channel-of-distribution, and promotional decisions. These are the decisions that are critical in the achievement of the profit objectives of the marketing function.

RECENT DEVELOPMENTS

The quality of decision making within the marketing function has been enhanced in recent years due to the use of quantitative decision-making techniques. For example, linear programing techniques are used to determine the proper assignment of sales personnel to sales territories so that sales volume is maximized.[7]

The application of the systems approach to marketing is another important development. The marketing system is viewed as consisting of a set of interacting variables.[8] These variables include distribution channels, sales planning and control, pricing, advertising, sales promotion, and sales personnel. The marketing system is designed to improve the marketing efforts of the firm.

The articles that follow were selected because they provide additional insight into the marketing function of business. Leon Winer explains how to plan the firm's marketing activities. The article by the distinguished economist Joel Dean explains how to price a new product. Jon Udell's article presents the results of a survey designed to identify the policy areas most important to marketing success. Phillip McVey in "Are Channels of Distribution What the Textbooks Say?" challenges some widely accepted views on channels of distribution. Jules Backman's article analyzes the criticism that advertising is economically wasteful. The *Business Week* article explains the growing importance of the marketing research function. Audrey Langdon describes the use of motivational research within the marketing function. Lee Adler's article describes the modern systems approach to marketing.

Are You Really Planning Your Marketing?

LEON WINER

The biggest problem in marketing planning is the *planning*. Many companies have a marketing "plan," yet few of these plans represent any real planning. To demonstrate this point, five steps will describe practices encountered frequently. These practices were observed through intensive interviews with manufacturing firms and their advertising agencies, and have been reported by executives at meetings and seminars attended by the author.

Step 1: Set the market share objective of your brand by adding to its present market share, depending on how ambitious you are.

Step 2: Project total sales volume, for *all* brands of the product, in dollars, for the following year.

---

[7]See Louis J. Rago, "New Techniques for Marketing Management," *Business Perspectives,* Spring, 1966, pp. 29-35.

[8]See George Fisk, *Marketing Systems,* (New York: Harper & Row, Publishers, 1967).

From *Journal of Marketing,* XXIX (January 1965), 1-8. Reprinted by permission of the American Marketing Association.

Step 3: Multiply the result of Step 1 by the result of Step 2. (Market share objective X projected total dollar market.) This gives the dollar sales objective for the brand.

Step 4: Subtract from the dollar sales objective: (a) total factory cost, (b) an allocated portion of the company's fixed marketing costs, and (c) desired profit. What is left, if anything, is "planned" marketing expenditure.

Step 5: Compose a "marketing mix" of advertising, marketing research, personal selling, price concessions, public relations, package design, point of sales materials, dealer aids, and so on, that will (a) just use up all the marketing funds and (b) yield exactly the forecasted sales volume.

These five steps represent the procedures of many companies, yet they are thoroughly unsound, for three reasons:

First, this procedure assumes that an increase in market share is profitable or, for that matter, possible. By definition, not *all* brands of a product can increase their market shares.

Second, this method of marketing planning reverses the cause-and-effect relationship between marketing effort and sales volume. Clearly, the sales volume forecast should depend on the amount of effort expended on marketing, not the other way around.

Third, this method requires the manager to select the "right" marketing mix from among the hundreds, or thousands, of possible marketing mixes. In other words, the manager is given a sales volume objective and a fixed amount of money for marketing, and he is expected to devise the combination of advertising, price reductions, personal selling, marketing research, public relations, point of sale materials, and so on, that will just use up the available money and will attain the sales objective. No human being has the knowledge or the calculating ability to do this, even if it were *theoretically* possible.

If the argument presented above is correct, and widely-followed practice is inadequate, what alternatives are available?

To answer this question, a study was made of the marketing planning practices of companies recognized as leaders in this area, and of planning books and articles. The conclusion was that while a certain amount of adaptation is required in each case, a general procedure exists that is applicable to marketing planning. This procedure is presented as a flow model in Figure 1. The discussion of the steps in the model will follow the sequence shown, except that "assigning responsibility for planning" will be discussed last instead of first.

SETTING MARKETING OBJECTIVES

In setting marketing objectives, planners should keep in mind three properties of objectives: (1) multiplicity, the fact that organizations have many objectives; (2) time, objectives need to be set for varying lengths of time; and (3) level, the firm should have many levels of objectives, or a hierarchy of objectives.

Multiplicity

Generally speaking, marketers tend to focus on maximizing next year's profits as being the only proper objective for their efforts. Actually a company may be

FIGURE 1. FLOW MODEL OF A MARKETING PLANNING PROCEDURE

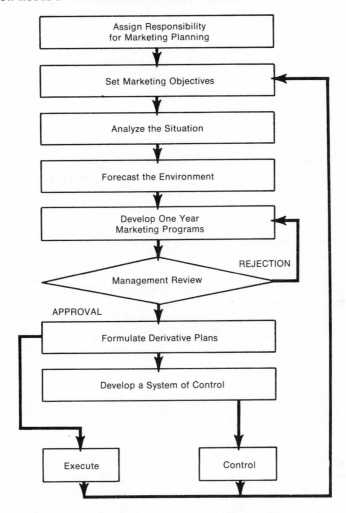

equally interested in stabilizing profits, or in seeking opportunities for investments for the longer term. Therefore, before doing any marketing planning, it is necessary to explore thoroughly with the company's management what *it* views the company's objectives to be and to derive marketing objectives from those of the company.

Objectives and Time

Given the company's objectives, it does not necessarily follow that these can be realized directly. A firm may not be able to capture a larger share of the market, economically, unless it has an improved product. Therefore, in order to attain a more distant objective of increasing its market share, it will set an intermediate objective of developing an improved product.

Since the firm possesses only limited management and financial resources, in setting the objectives described above, it will very probably have to forsake such alternative objectives as entering a foreign market or acquiring a potentially profitable competitor.

Therefore, in setting long-range objectives, and the intermediate objectives that will lead to their attainment, the firm must consider the alternatives it is forsaking, and select those most suitable to its circumstances.

Hierarchy of Objectives

Even though a firm sets long-term objectives and determines the appropriate intermediate objectives, that may not be enough. It does not do much good to tell the advertising department that the objective of the company is to increase its rate of return on investment unless this objective is translated into specific strategies. Therefore, it is necessary to develop a hierarchy of objectives.

Development of such a hierarchy of objectives is not a simple task. Careful study is required to make sure that sufficient alternatives are considered at each level and that suitable criteria are discovered for deciding which alternatives are to be selected, or emphasized.

An example, showing how a hierarchy of objectives may be derived through flow-modeling, is shown in Figure 2. This is the case of the business market (offices, factories, stores, hospitals, and so on) of the Interstate Telephone Company (a fictitious name for a real company). At the top of the chart is one of the Company's permanent objectives, that of increasing return on invested capital. A rate of return of $7\frac{1}{2}\%$ is believed to be attainable. Two possible objectives were derived from this one: (1) increase return, or net profit, and (2) reduce the investment base on which return is computed. The second possibility was not believed to be attainable because of (1) population growth, (2) rapidly growing communication needs, and (3) trend toward mechanization and automation. Therefore, attention was focused on the first.

To increase profits, two objectives may be set, following the reasoning of the Interstate Company: (1) increase billings, or (2) reduce costs. Again, the second objective is unlikely to be attained because one of the important sources of the return on investment problem is the rising cost of labor and materials. (One exception should be noted, however. Costs may be reduced by reducing the rate of disconnections due to customer dissatisfaction, since the cost of installing complex equipment often exceeds installation charges.) This leaves the alternative of increasing billings.

To increase billings, the Interstate Company may (1) try to raise rates and risk reduction in usage, (2) persuade customers to increase usage of existing equipment, or (3) sell additional equipment and services in order to increase equipment rentals and, to some extent, usage. However, a public service commission will not grant a rate increase unless return on investment is *below* a certain minimum, say $5\frac{1}{2}\%$. Then a commission is not likely to grant a raise that will increase return by as much as two percentage points. The next alternative objective, persuading customers to increase usage, has been used as an objective for promotional efforts of the Company. The third objective, that of selling additional equipment and services, has been selected for particular emphasis. In particular, because of the saturation of the business market with respect to basic

FIGURE 2. HIERARCHY OF OBJECTIVES FOR THE INTERSTATE TELEPHONE COMPANY

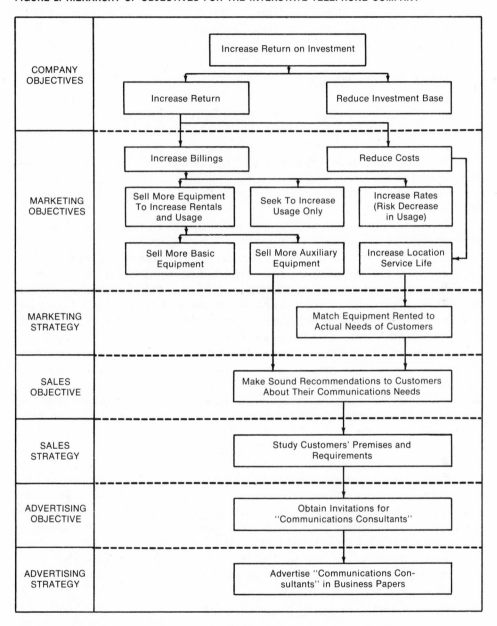

equipment, the marketing effort has focused on the sale of auxiliary services and equipment, such as "Call Directors," teletype units, modern switchboards, and interior dialing.

To achieve the objective of selling more auxiliary services and equipment, and reducing disconnections due to customer dissatisfaction, the Company needs to match equipment and services to the *needs* of the customers, by making recommendations based on careful study of these needs. To do this, it seeks to persuade customers, through advertising, to invite "Communications Consultants" to survey their communications problems. In this way, by deriving a hierarchy of objectives, Interstate identifies the specific marketing strategies that will lead to attainment of the Company's highest objectives.

ANALYZING THE SITUATION

Once the planner has a well-developed set of objectives, the next step is to begin discovering ways of attaining them. To do this, he has to form some ideas about what *actions* of the firm, under what *environmental conditions,* have brought about the *present* situation. He will then be able to identify courses of action that may be used in the future.

Logan[1] has suggested a four-step procedure for conducting the situation analysis:

Investigation—A wide range of data that may be relevant should be sought, with care being taken to distinguish between facts and opinions.

Classification—The planner sorts the data collected during the investigation.

Generalization—Classes of data are studied to discover relationships. Statistical techniques such as correlation analysis are used to determine whether dependable associations exist between types of events. For example, a distributor may find that leased outlets are more profitable than owned outlets to a degree that prevents attributing the differences to chance.

Estimate of the Situation—Causes are sought for the associations discovered in the previous step. The planner now has some ideas about what actions under past conditions have resulted in the present situation. In this way he has learned several courses of action that he may follow to achieve his objectives. In the example cited previously, the distributor may find, on searching further, that the higher profitability of leased outlets is caused by the superior location of the leased outlets. In other words, the fact that the outlet was leased was *not* the cause of the higher profitability. Rather *both* the leasing *and* the higher profitability were caused by a third factor—superior location. (Owners of well-located outlets were not willing to sell them and therefore the distributor had been forced to lease.) Consequently, the appropriate strategy for the future would not be to prefer leasing to owning, but to seek good locations and leasing, if necessary. Inadequate search for causes might have led to very poor results.

Ideally, the situation analysis should cover other firms in the industry, so that the company may benefit from their experiences, both successes and failures.

FORECASTING THE FUTURE ENVIRONMENT

The forecasting problem, from the viewpoint of the planner, is to determine *what* conditions he should forecast and *how* to do it. In this article we will limit ourselves to the first part of the problem because the literature of forecasting techniques is too vast to be reviewed adequately here.

---

[1]James P. Logan, "Economic Forecasts, Decision Processes, and Types of Plans" (unpublished doctoral dissertation, Columbia University, 1960), pp. 14-19, 76.

Frey[2] has listed five factors that may affect purchases of a product:

1. Population changes.
2. Improvements in, and new-use discoveries for competing types of products.
3. Improvements in, and new-use discoveries for the company's own type of product.
4. Changed consumer attitudes and habits.
5. Changes in general business conditions.

Howard[3] suggests four criteria for identifying *key* factors:

1. Variability. If a factor is stable over time, there is no need to make a forecast of it.
2. Co-variation. There must be a relationship between changes in the factor and changes in demand.
3. Measurability.
4. Independence. The factor must not be closely related to another factor already considered.

Essentially, this means that the planner has to find out *which* uncontrollable factors, such as personal income, occupation of consumers, educational level, attitudes, affect sales of his brand, and then he has to forecast the future of these factors. Here, as in situation analysis, statistical methods must be used with care, to avoid erroneous conclusions.

DEVELOPING ONE-YEAR MARKETING PROGRAMS

Development of marketing programs requires three steps: (a) formulating alternative courses of action, (b) examining these alternatives, (c) comparing alternatives and selecting the ones to be recommended.

Formulating Alternatives

The first step in conceiving alternative courses of action was described in an earlier section on situation analysis. We reviewed a four-step process for discovering factors that had brought about the present situation, and presumably could be manipulated to achieve future objectives.

However, in addition to the cause-and-effect relationships discovered in situation analysis, there is usually room for innovation, or the development of new courses of action.

The importance of the creative process cannot be under-estimated, because a plan can only be as good as the best of the alternatives considered. Therefore, it is highly rewarding to spend time evolving alternatives. Unfortunately, there is a strong human tendency to stop the search for alternatives as soon as an

---

[2]Albert W. Frey, *The Effective Marketing Mix: Programming for Optimum Results* (Hanover, New Hampshire: The Amos Tuck School of Business Administration, 1956), p. 11.
[3]John Howard, *Marketing Management* (Homewood, Illinois: R. D. Irwin, Inc., 1957), Chapter VI.

apparently acceptable course of action is discovered. This is a tendency that planners must guard against.

Examining Alternatives

This step consists of projecting all the outcomes of each alternative course of action evolved above. The outcomes considered should include (1) desirable and undesirable; (2) immediate and long range; (3) tangible and intangible; and (4) certain and only possible.[4]

Clearly, one of the outcomes that must be projected in every case is sales volume and/or profit. In making this projection, errors in both directions are possible. Eldridge[5] discusses the probable consequences of these errors and suggests a solution to the problem.

"If (the marketing manager) overestimates his sales volume and gross profit, and bases his marketing expenditures on that overestimate . . . he is likely to find . . . that profits are running well below the forecast. . . .

"If he underestimates his volume and gross profit, he runs the risk of spending less than the product needs—and thereby . . . makes certain that the results are less than hoped for.

"Nevertheless, it is probably preferable for the marketing manager, when weaving his way perilously between the devil and the deep sea, to err on the side of conservatism in budgeting sales, his marketing expenditures, and his profits. . . .

"For himself, his associates, the advertising agency, and the field sales department, it is wholly desirable that objectives should be set on the high side, in order that the attainment of those objectives shall require 'reaching . . .'"

In other words, Eldridge suggests "keeping two sets of books." The implications of this suggestion will be discussed subsequently.

Comparing and Selecting Alternatives

In this step the planner compares the projected outcomes of the various alternative courses of action. The purpose is to rank the alternatives on the basis of the extent to which they achieve objectives and avoid undesirable results. Then the most desirable alternatives are recommended to management.

This point, after programs are prepared, and before they are reviewed by top management, is suitable for writing down the plans.

On the basis of the argument presented here, the written plan should discuss the following topics, if it is to enable management to evaluate it:

1. Specific objective(s) of the plan.
2. Relationship between the specific objective(s) and the objectives of the firm, or an explanation of the extent to which this plan will advance the

---

[4]William H. Newman and Charles E. Summer, Jr., *The Process of Management* (Englewood Cliffs, New Jersey: Prentice Hall, Inc., 1961), p. 302.

[5]Clarence E. Eldridge, "Marketing Plans," in E. R. French (editor), *The Copywriter's Guide* (New York: Harper & Bros., 1958), pp. 3-28, on pp. 24-25.

higher-level and longer-term objectives of the firm. Quantitative measures should be included, if possible.

3. Other specific objectives considered, and the planner's opinion of the relative values of these specific objectives. This evaluation should also include quantitative measures, if possible.

4. Costs of executing the plan.

5. Forecasts of the firm's environment.

6. Course of action recommended: first, briefly, then in detail.

7. Alternative courses of action and reasons why they were considered inferior to the action recommended.

8. Projected results of the plan, if it is executed.

9. Listing of control standards and procedures to be used for controlling execution of the plan.

Before leaving this discussion of preparation of programs, an important point should be emphasized:

Marketing planning should not be done function by function, as has been the tradition for a long time and still is the practice in many firms. (By "functions" we mean the activities normally performed by a marketing department, such as advertising, personal selling, pricing, marketing research, and product and package development. *Within* these functions are many sub-functions. For example, within personal selling is recruitment, selection, and training of salesmen; assignment of territories; design of compensation systems; sales analysis, and so on. At least 50 functions and sub-functions could easily be listed.)

Marketing planning should be oriented to achieving objectives. Of course, if objectives may be fulfilled entirely within one function, the objective-directed plan will also be "functional." But the approach, even then, will still be from objectives to means rather than from means to objectives.

MANAGEMENT REVIEW

Criteria of reviewing executives may be grouped conveniently as follows: (1) economic, or financial; and (2) subjective.

Economic or financial criteria, such as return on investment, present discounted value of future income, alternative uses of funds, and cut-off rates, are sufficiently well known that they do not require comment here.

Subjective criteria, on the other hand, may require some discussion. Smith[6] has commented on the role of management as follows: "Management may simply accept the goals indicated. . . . More frequently . . . management's reaction will be one expressed by such comment as: 'Surely we can do better than that. . . .'"

In the case of the National Paper Company (a fictitious name for a real firm), during one year, management reduced the recommended marketing expenditures by 23%, *without* reducing the sales volume objective. Other, similar, reviewing actions could be cited. Therefore, it appears that management, in reviewing marketing plans, asks itself: "How much 'fat' does this plan contain?" and answers the question somehow, probably subjectively.

---

[6]Wendell R. Smith, "A Rational Approach to Marketing Management," in Eugene J. Kelley and William Lazer (editors), *Managerial Marketing* (Homewood, Illinois: R. D. Irwin & Co., 1958), p. 154.

Are such reviewing actions justified? In other words, is it fair to the planner to suspect him of "padding" his plan? We have noted earlier the view that: ". . . when it comes to budgeting (setting sales, profit and marketing expenditure goals), the situation is different (from setting objectives for the advertising agency, the sales force, and the like). The forecasts for financial budgeting should be sufficiently conservative that . . . they are certain to be made. . . ."[7] This commentator appears to be suggesting that the planner should overstate consistently the expenditure needed to achieve the goals of the plan. This appears to recognize that a conflict may exist between the objectives of the planner and those of the firm.

The management literature has emphasized repeatedly that differences exist between the objectives of the employee and those of the employing organization. Therefore, it seems fair to conclude that the planner, in trying to achieve his personal goals of continued employment and approval of his superiors, may undermine organizational objectives such as maximum return on marketing expenditures. Following this, the problem of the reviewing manager would then appear to be not to decide *whether* there is "fat" in the plan, but rather to estimate the percentage.

FORMULATING DERIVATIVE PLANS

Ultimately, at the lowest level in the hierarchy, the result of planning has to be a list of actions, or a program, to be carried out.

For drawing up this program, Newman and Summer[8] suggest six steps:
1. Divide into steps the activities necessary to achieve the objective.
2. Note relations between each of the steps, especially necessary sequences.
3. Decide who is to be responsible for each step.
4. Determine the resources needed for each step.
5. Estimate the time required for each step.
6. Assign definite dates for each part.

In formulating its derivative plans, the Finchley (a fictitious name for a real company) Drug Company, uses the individual plans prepared for each of 50 products. The pertinent information is pulled out of each product plan and reassembled in three derivative plans: (a) detailing (personal selling) schedule, (b) advertising program, and (c) financial summary. These derivative plans are described below:

Detailing Schedule—The Detailing Schedule is structured very much like a calendar. For each month, three products are listed in the order in which they are to be presented to physicians. The schedule serves as a working document for the sales force. As the year passes, 500 copies of each page are made and distributed to Finchley's detail men to be carried out.

Advertising Program—The Advertising Program describes several thousand items of direct mail and journal advertising to be prepared during the course of the year. The items are arranged by month and by day of the month when they

---

[7]Eldridge, same reference as footnote 5, p. 25.
[8]Newman and Summer, same reference as footnote 4, pp. 415-416.

are to appear, or to be mailed. As the year progresses, this information is used by technicians and artists in the Advertising Department and the Company's agency to prepare advertisements, buy space and materials, and so on.

Financial Summary—The Financial Summary, unlike the other two documents, is not used by any functional department as a basis for action. Instead, it is essentially a communication and control device. Probably the best way to describe the contents of this document is to list the information presented for *each* actively promoted product:

1. Total market ($).
2. Company's share (%).
3. Company's sales ($).
4. Advertising expenditure ($).
5. Allocated detailing cost ($).
6. Total marketing cost ($).
7. Marketing cost as a % of sales.
8. Gross profit ($).
9. Gross profit as a % of sales.

This information is presented both for the current year and the following year.

As plans are executed, the Financial Summary is used for comparing actual results with plans, or controlling the execution of the plan. The point is that advertising, sales, and financial plans are derived from objective-directed product marketing plans and *not* prepared independently by the separate functions: Advertising, Sales, and Finance.

DEVELOPING A SYSTEM OF CONTROL

A system of control should (1) establish standards, (2) measure activities and results, (3) compare these measurements to standards, and (4) report variances between measurements and standards.

Control is relevant to planning because control standards have a greater effect in determining actual results than the objectives of the plan. Therefore, it is necessary that the standards which *are* set, reflect very closely the objectives of the plan.

In addition, a system of control informs the planner of the results obtained from execution of his plans. This is helpful because it becomes possible to change plans if they are found to be ineffective either because (1) the cause and effect premise on which they were based turns out to be faulty, or (2) the actual environment is sufficiently different from the forecast environment.

In the first instance, the objectives are still valid, but the method of attaining them needs to be changed. In the second instance, the objective may no longer be appropriate. Therefore, new objectives and strategies may be required, and with them, new courses of action.

ASSIGNING RESPONSIBILITY FOR MARKETING PLANNING

In practice, the management decision of assigning responsibility for marketing planning is the first step performed. In this paper, we have postponed discussion of this topic until the end, because organization of the planning function may depend on the kind of planning to be done. Therefore, it was necessary to describe first the steps in marketing planning.

Writers on the subject of marketing planning organization have described several alternatives:

1. Delegation of planning to functional executives, such as managers of the advertising, sales, pricing, sales promotion, marketing research divisions of the marketing department.

2. Planning done by a planning staff group.

3. Planning done by everyone who has a part to play in marketing the brand, including outside organizations.

4. Planning done by brand or product managers.

However, criteria are lacking in the literature for selecting the appropriate planning organization.

Leading firms often rely on product, or brand managers for planning, although the practice is not universal, and where such managers are used, their responsibilities are not always the same.

To illustrate this point:

1. At the drug company discussed earlier, product managers plan advertising of two kinds, and personal selling.

2. At the household paper products company, brand managers plan consumer advertising and temporary reductions in price charged to retailers and consumers.

3. The telephone company, on the other hand, does not employ product managers. Instead, planning is assigned to sales and advertising executives, for their individual functions.

Possibly these differences in planning organization can be attributed to differences in the means used for communicating with the market. The telephone company needs to communicate with business market customers (that is, business firms, government agencies, and so on) on an individual basis. The reason is that no two customers (other than the very smallest) are likely to need exactly the same combination of products and services. Therefore, a centrally-conceived, uniform approach, used alone, would not be suitable. The household paper products company and the drug company deal with mass markets where the potential profit made from individual customers is small. This rules out the possibility of tailoring a specialized approach to each customer. In addition, the needs and desires of large numbers of potential and actual customers are relatively similar. Therefore, grouping large numbers of customers into a market for a brand is an economical way of approaching the planning problem.

It follows that the "brand" manager is really a *market* manager, the market being the totality of actual and potential consumers of the brand. We may conclude, therefore, that a brand or product manager has a role to play whenever there is an opportunity to use standardized appeals in communicating with numerous customers.

Nevertheless, not all firms require brand managers, even though they may use mass communication media. For example, the Interstate Telephone Company permits all the advertising planning to be done in its advertising department, and delegates the major part of its sales planning to sales executives. The question arises then: what are the key differences that cause such marked differences in planning organization?

The answer that suggests itself is that there are important differences in the marketing objectives of these firms. Two illustrations can be given.

1. At the paper company, two of the important objectives are increase in market share, and product distribution in certain areas. Programming for these objectives requires crossing of functional lines. Therefore there appears to be a need for a special planning executive.

2. At the telephone company the important marketing objectives are: (1) to increase auxiliary equipment and service billings; and (2) to increase location service life of auxiliary equipment. These objectives are interpreted to require that "communications consultants" survey the operations and premises of business market customers. To achieve this, the company tries to persuade customers to avail themselves of the free services of these consultants. Thus, we have three levels of objectives: (a) persuade the customer to invite the communications consultant, in order to (b) have the communications consultant advise the customer, in order to (c) increase billings and service life.

Achieving objectives (a) and (b), the objectives that can be achieved by direct action—(c) obviously cannot—does not require any coordination among functions. Objective (b) is achieved by the Sales Department, and objective (a), by the Advertising Department.

The conclusion is that the planning organization should mirror the hierarchy of objectives: a planning manager is needed wherever there is an objective whose achievement requires coordination of, or selection from among, several functions. In practice, the existing organization may satisfy this requirement, in which case, no new responsibilities need be assigned. However, if existing planning responsibilities do not allow for this type of selection, or coordination, new ones need to be created.

IMPLICATIONS FOR MARKETING MANAGERS

When a new idea or concept is presented to the business world, its *form* often receives more attention than its *substance*. While attempts are made to adopt the new concept, old habits of thought, and procedures, are continued even though they may not be consistent with the new idea.

The central idea of marketing planning is to develop marketing objectives that will lead to attainment to the objectives of the firm, and then to devise programs and controls that will help to achieve these marketing objectives. In deciding to plan its marketing activities, a business firm has to stand ready to scrap its traditional budgeting and functional planning procedures and to re-think and reorganize its marketing. Only those methods and procedures should be retained that fit logically with the pattern of starting with the highest objectives of the firm and refining successive steps of instrumental objectives until courses of action are specified. Any other approach, or procedure, will give inferior results.

Admittedly, it is much easier to go through the five steps outlined in the first few paragraphs, and say that marketing is being planned, than to follow the procedure described in the body of this paper. However, in this instance, as in most, there are no easy short-cuts to the development of good, effective, and profit-able plans. Also, there really is no escape from the need to plan conscientiously. Leading companies *are* planning in this way, with obvious financial success. Those who wish to attain similar success will have to apply themselves equally. Successful procedures will not be developed overnight, or even in one year. Most likely, it will take from three to five cycles of planning to establish an effective, smoothly-working procedure. However, nothing will be accomplished if a sincere beginning is not made.

QUESTIONS

1. What is a hierarchy of objectives? Why is this hierarchy so necessary?

2. What factors should the firm take into consideration when forecasting the future environment in which it will operate?

3. Explain the flow model of a marketing planning procedure.

4. Why is it necessary that the marketing plan have a developed system of control?

5. What are derivative plans?

Pricing a New Product

JOEL DEAN

New product pricing is important in two ways: it affects the amount of the product that will be sold; and it determines the amount of revenue that will be received for a given quantity of sales. If you set your price too high you will be likely to make too few sales to permit you to cover your overhead. If you set your price too low you may not be able to cover out-of-pocket costs and may face bankruptcy.

From *The Controller*, XXIII, No. 4 (April 1955), 163-165. Reprinted by permission of *Financial Executive*.

WHAT IS DIFFERENT ABOUT NEW PRODUCTS?

New products that are novel require a different pricing treatment than old products because they are distinctive; no one else sells quite the same thing. This distinctiveness is usually only temporary, however. As your product catches on, your competitors will try to take away your market by bringing out imitative substitutes. The speed with which your product loses its uniqueness will depend on a number of factors. Among these factors are the total sales potential, the investment required for rivals to manufacture and distribute the product, the strength of patent protection, and the alertness and power of competitors.

Although this process of competitive imitation is almost inevitable, the company that introduces the new product can use price as a means of slowing the speed of competitive imitation. Finding the "right" price is not easy, however. New products are hard to price correctly. This is true both because past experience is no sure guide as to how the market will react to any given price, and because competing products are usually significantly different in nature or quality.

In setting a price on a new product you will want to have three objectives in mind: (1) getting the product accepted, (2) maintaining your market in the face of growing competition, (3) producing profits. Your pricing policy cannot be said to be successful unless you can achieve all three of these objectives.

WHAT ARE YOUR CHOICES AS TO POLICY?

Broadly speaking, the strategy in pricing a new product comes down to a choice between (1) "skimming" pricing, and (2) "penetration" pricing. There are a number of intermediate positions, but the issues are made clearer when the two extremes are compared.

Skimming Pricing

For products that represent a drastic departure from accepted ways of performing a service or filling a demand, a strategy of high prices coupled with large promotional expenditures in the early stages of market development (and lower prices at later stages) has frequently proven successful. This is known as a skimming price policy.

There are four main reasons why this kind of skimming price policy is attractive for new and distinctive products: *First,* the quantity of the product that you can sell is likely to be less affected by price in the early stages than it will be when the product is full-grown and imitation has had time to take effect. This is the period when pure salesmanship can have the greatest effect on sales. *Second,* a skimming price policy takes the cream of the market at a high price before attempting to penetrate the more price-sensitive sections of the market. This means that you can get more money from those who don't care how much they pay, while building up experience to hit the big mass market with tempting prices. *Third,* this can be a way to feel out the demand. It is frequently easier to start out with a high "refusal" price and reduce it later on when the facts of product demand make themselves known than it is to set a low price initially and then boost the price to cover unforeseen costs or exploit a popular product. *Fourth,* high prices will frequently produce a greater dollar volume of sales in the early stages of market development than a policy of low initial prices. If this is the case, skimming pricing will provide you with funds for financing expansion into the big-volume sectors of your market.

A skimming-price policy is not always the answer to your problem, however. High initial prices may safeguard profits during the early stages of product introduction, but they may also prevent quick sales to the many buyers upon whom you must rely to give you a mass market. The alternative is to use low prices as an entering wedge to get into mass markets early. This is known as penetration pricing.

Penetration Pricing

This approach is likely to be desirable under the following conditions: *First,* when the quantity of product sold is highly sensitive to price, even in the early stages of introduction. *Second,* when you can achieve substantial economies in unit cost and effectiveness of manufacturing and distributing the product by operating at large volumes. *Third,* when your product is faced by threats of strong potential competition, very soon after introduction. *Fourth,* when there is no "elite" market—that is, a body of buyers who are willing to pay a much higher price in order to obtain the latest and best.

The decision to price so as to penetrate a broad market can be made at any stage in the product's life cycle, but you should be sure to examine this pricing strategy before your new product is marketed at all. This possibility certainly should be explored as soon as your product has established an elite market. Sometimes a product can be rescued from a premature death by adoption of a penetration price policy after the cream of the market has been skimmed.

The ease and speed with which competitors can bring out substitute products is probably the most important single consideration in your choice between skimming and penetration pricing at the time you introduce your new product. For products whose market potential looks big, a policy of low initial prices ("stay-out pricing") makes sense, because the big multiple-product manufacturers are attracted by mass markets. If you set your price low enough to begin with, your large competitor may not feel it worth his while to make a big production and distribution investment for slim profit margins. In any event, you should appraise the competitive situation very carefully for each new product before you decide on your pricing strategy.

WHAT SHOULD YOU LOOK AT IN SETTING A PRICE?

When you have decided on your basic pricing strategy you can turn to the task of putting a dollars-and-cents price tag on your new product. In order to do this you should look at at least five important factors: (1) potential and probable demand for your product, (2) cost of making and selling the product, (3) market targets, (4) promotional strategy, and (5) suitable channels of distribution.

Demand

The first step in estimating market demand is to find out whether or not the product will sell at all—assuming that the price is set within the competitive range. That is, you should find out whether or not this product fulfills a real need, and whether enough potential customers are dissatisfied with their present means of filling that need. To do this, you should make some estimate of the total potential market for the new product and all its competing substitutes and then estimate the portion of this potential that your product is likely to get.

Next, you should determine the competitive range of price. This will be easier when substitutes are relatively close or when customers are familiar with the cost and quality of substitutes and act rationally on the basis of performance.

The next step is to try to guess the probable sales volume at two or three possible prices within the price range. The best way to do this is by controlled experiments; next best is by a close estimation of buyers' alternatives in the light of market preference.

Finally, you should consider the possibility of retaliation by manufacturers of displaced substitutes. If your new product hits any one of your competitors hard enough, you may be faced with price retaliation. The limit to this price cutting is set by the out-of-pocket cost of the price-cutting competitors. Therefore, some knowledge of the out-of-pocket cost of making competing products will be helpful in estimating the probable effects of a particular price.

Costs

Before going ahead with your new product, you should estimate its effect on your investment, your costs, and your profits. First you should estimate the added investment necessary to manufacture and distribute the new product. This investment estimate should include estimates of increased working capital that will be required at various sales volumes. Then you should estimate the added costs of manufacturing and selling the product at various possible sales volumes. The way to estimate costs is to calculate what your total costs would be with and without the new product; the difference should be assigned to the new product. Allocations of overheads that you are already incurring should not be assigned to the new product because they will be the same whether or not you go ahead with the addition to your product line.

In building up your two sets of cost and investment figures—one showing the situation *without* the new product, and the other showing the contrasting situation *with* the new product added to your line—be sure to take into account *all* pertinent items. It often happens that companies which lose money on new products have run into trouble because of unanticipated costs or investment requirements which have absorbed most of or all the profits realizable from the new idea.

New product costs may be segregated into half a dozen main categories: direct labor, materials and supplies for production, components purchased outside, special equipment (such as jigs, dies, fixtures and other tools), plant overhead, and sales expenses.

Direct Labor Methods of estimating direct labor may be built up in one of three ways: (1) You can compare each operation on each component with accumulated historical data, from your files, on similar operations for similar components, (2) you can develop a mockup of the proposed work-place layout and actually time an operator who performs a series of manufacturing operations, simulated as accurately as possible, (3) you can apply one of several systems of predetermined, basic-motion times which are currently available from private sources.

Make certain, however, that you include any added time used for setup work, or needed to take the item from its transportation container, perform the operations, and return the item again to its transportation container. When the total direct labor time is determined multiply it by the appropriate labor rates.

Materials and Supplies for Production In developing reliable cost figures for materials and supplies make a methodical list of all requirements. Having listed everything in an organized fashion, you can enter the specifications and costs on a manufactured-component estimate form. Remember to include any extra costs which may be incurred as a result of requirements for particular length, widths, qualities, or degrees of finish. Allowances for scrap should also be made as accurately as possible and corrected by applying a salvage factor if the scrap can be sold or reused.

Components Purchased Outside Place your specification for parts purchased from other concerns with more than one reliable supplier and get competitive bids for the work. But in addition to price considerations be sure to give proper weight to the reputation and qualification of each potential producer. Moreover, if you use a substantial volume of purchased parts you may want to use a "plus" factor above the cost of the components themselves to cover your expenses involved in receiving, storing, and handling the items.

Special Equipment Take careful precautions against making a faulty analysis of your expense and investment in special jigs, dies, fixtures, and other tools which you will need to produce the new product. To avoid trouble in this area make a table showing all cases where special equipment will be needed. The actual estimating of the costs of such equipment is best done by a qualified tool shop—your own if you have one or an outside organization. Here again, competitive bidding is an excellent protection on price. Do not include costs of routine inspection, service, and repair; these are properly charged to plant overhead.

Plant Overhead The overhead item may be estimated as a given percentage of direct labor, machine utilization, or some other factor determined by your accountants to be the most sensible basis. In this way you can allocate satisfactorily charges for administration and supervision, for occupancy, and for indirect service related to producing the new product. Overhead allocations may be set up for a department, a production center, or even, in some cases, for a particular machine. In calculating plant overhead make certain that in setting up your cost controls, your accountants have not overlooked any proper indirect special charges which will have to be incurred because of the new product.

Sales Expenses Your estimates of sales revenue at various potential volumes can now be compared with your estimates of added costs at those volumes. The difference will be the added profits of introducing the new product. Although the costs themselves probably should not be used as a basis for setting price, you should not go into any venture that will not produce for you a rate-of-return on the added investment required that is adequate to compensate for the added risk and still be at least as high as the return you could get by investing your money elsewhere. If no price that you set will provide enough revenue to produce an adequate profit over your added costs, then you should either drop the venture, try to cut costs, or wait for a more favorable time to introduce the product.

Marketing Targets

Assuming that the estimates of market demand and of cost and investment have been made and that the profit picture looks sufficiently rosy, you are now in a position to set up some basic goals and programs. A decision must first be made about market targets—that is, what market share or sales volume should be aimed at? Among other factors, you should probably consider what effect it will have upon investment requirements, whether or not your existing organization can handle the new product, how it fits in with the rest of your present product line, and so forth. These decisions should be made after a cold-blooded survey of the nature of your new product and of your company's organization and manufacturing and distributive facilities.

Promotion

Closely related to the question of market targets is the design of promotional strategy. As an innovator, you must not only sell your product, but frequently you must also make people recognize their need for this kind of product. Your problem here is to determine the best way of "creating a market." You must determine the nature of the market and the type of appeal that will sell the product and secure prompt acceptance by potential buyers. And you should also estimate how much it will cost you to achieve this goal.

Channels of Distribution

Frequently, there is some latitude in your choice of channels of distribution. This choice should be consistent with your strategy for initial pricing and for promotional outlays. Penetration pricing and explosive promotion calls for distribution channels that promptly make the product broadly available. Otherwise you waste advertising or stymie mass-market pricing. Distribution policy also concerns the role you wish the dealer to play in pushing your product, the margins you must pay him to introduce this action and the amount of protection of territory and of inventory required to do so.

YOUR DECISION

These are the factors you should look at in setting a price. Estimating these factors shrewdly and objectively requires specialized training and experience. Good estimates will make your pricing more realistic and successful. But pricing cannot be established by formula. Combining these factors into a pricing policy requires judgment. In the last analysis you must pull all the estimates of the experts together and arrive at your own decision. You will want to make sure that the pricing analysis is guided by sound principles and that the activities of your specialists are all geared toward the same end—devising a sound, effective marketing and promotional program in conjunction with a price that will meet your objectives of market acceptance, competitive strength, and profits.

QUESTIONS

1. What are the three objectives that the manager should consider in setting a price for a new product?

2. Explain the difference between *skimming pricing* and *penetration pricing*.

3. Explain the five factors to be considered in the process of putting a dollars-and-cents price tag on a new product.

How Important Is Pricing in Competitive Strategy?

JON G. UDELL

In an effort to ascertain the key elements of business success in the market place, the author conducted a study among 200 producers of industrial and consumer goods. A sample of fairly well-known and successful manufacturing companies was selected from *Martindell's Manual of Excellent Management*. Listed are companies which are supposedly well managed, evaluated according to the criteria developed by the American Institute of Management. The use of the manual seemed appropriate in that the two most heavily weighted criteria are sales vigor and management efficiency.

From *Journal of Marketing*, XXVIII (January 1964), 44-48. Reprinted by permission of the American Marketing Association.

The present study attempted to answer the question: "What are the key policies and procedures common to successful marketing managements in various manufacturing industries?"

Management's interest in the study was reflected by a 75% response to a 4-page mail questionnaire. The first section of the questionnaire listed 12 general policy areas of marketing management—among them, sales research and sales planning, pricing, management of sales personnel, and product service. The respondent, usually the vice president in charge of marketing, was asked to select the five areas which he regarded as most vital in his company's marketing success.

Importance of Product Development

The results indicate that product research and development, selected by almost 80% of the respondents, is most important in modern-day competitive strategy. Four other policy areas, relating to either product or sales effort, were selected by more than half of the respondents. Table 1 presents a percentage analysis of the responses.

It appears that business management did not agree with the economic views of the importance of pricing—one-half of the respondents did *not* select pricing as *one of the five* most important policy areas in their firm's marketing success.

Also, the two major facets of nonprice competition (product and sales effort) were subdivided into a number of policy areas; for example, sales effort was subdivided into sales research and sales planning, management of sales personnel, and advertising and sales promotion. In short, *the competitive activities relating to the product and to sales effort were selected as most important in the success of these firms.*

Pricing

The emphasis on product and sales effort does not imply that price is unimportant. Three factors probably account for the relatively low ranking of pricing:

1. In today's competitive economy, *supply*—or production capacity—

TABLE 1. HOW MANAGEMENT RANKS THE FACTORS OF MARKETING SUCCESS

Rank	Policy Areas	% of Firms Selecting the Policy Area[a]
1	Product research and development	79
2	Sales research and sales planning	73
3	Management of sales personnel	59
4	Advertising and sales promotion	56
5	Product service	52
6	Pricing	50
7	Organizational structure	44
8	Distribution channels and their control	41
9	Marketing cost budgeting and control	17
10	Financing and credit	14
11	Transportation and storage	7
12	Public relations	7

[a]Based on a tabulation of 135 usable questionnaires. Percentages here are rounded.

generally exceeds demand; and, therefore, nearly all sellers are forced to be either completely competitive or almost collusive in their pricing. Because there may be little or no freedom for a company to deviate from the market price, heavy reliance must be placed on product differentiation and sales effort.

2. *The relatively well-to-do consumers of today are interested in more than just price.* They are interested in product quality, distinctiveness, style, and many other factors which lead to both physical and psychological satisfaction. Consumers not only can afford but want product differentiation and sales promotion. From them the consumer receives a great deal of psychological satisfaction and utility. It is only logical that consumer-oriented managements would choose to emphasize products and sales efforts in an attempt to satisfy consumer desires.

3. *It is through successful product differentiation that a manufacturer may obtain some pricing freedom.* Products known to be identical must be priced identically in the market place. A departure from identical prices would result in all patronage going to the seller or sellers with the lowest price.

MARKETING STRATEGIES ACCORDING TO PRODUCTS AND CUSTOMERS

Economists have proposed several theories that give recognition to the nonprice factors of competitive strategy.[1] However, they have not credited the nature of the product and the characteristics of the buyers as the dominant factors in explaining how companies organize to market their products. Instead, the dominant factor is usually assumed to be the market structure of the industry (competitive, oligopolistic, or monopolistic).

A producer of machine tools would not be expected to compete in the same manner as a producer of perfume; and a comparison of the structures of the machine-tool and perfume industries would not explain the differences in their marketing strategies. *Common business sense would lead one to believe that a company's use of nonprice competitive strategy should vary according to the nature of a firm's product and the characteristics of the buyers for that product.*

Accordingly, the data were classified according to the respondents' type of industry: industrial goods, consumer durable goods, and consumer nondurable goods.

Producers of Industrial Goods

The producers of industrial goods stressed the product facet of competitive strategy.

Two of the policy areas listed in the marketing management study pertain directly to the product—product research and development, and product service.

---

[1] Lawrence Abbott, *Quality and Competition* (New York: Columbia University Press, 1951); Hans Brems, "The Interdependence of Quality Variations, Selling Effort and Price," *Quarterly Journal of Economics,* Vol. 62 (May, 1948), pp. 418-440; C.A. Stocking, "Advertising and Economic Theory," *American Economic Review,* Vol. 21 (March, 1931), pp. 43-55.

(Product service refers to those activities performed by a manufacturer in the attempt to guarantee that a product gives satisfactory performance to its users.)

As shown in Table 2, both of these policy areas were selected by about 80% of the industrial users.

The policy areas relating to sales effort were relegated to a lesser role by the successful manufacturers of industrial goods. The average selection for the policy areas pertaining to sales effort was 50%, as compared with the average product selection of 80%.

The industrial-goods producers' primary emphasis on the product facet of marketing strategy was also emphasized in letters received from various respondents. A Pratt & Whitney Aircraft executive said: "Our two most valuable assets sales-wise are the technical excellence of our products, and our policy of rendering the best possible product service to our customers both before and after the sale."

Producers of Consumer Goods

The manufacturers of consumer goods placed a much greater emphasis on the sales effort facet of competitive strategy. This emphasis was especially great in the case of the firms producing nondurable goods.

As shown in Table 3, the nondurable goods producers had an average sales effort selection of 85%, as compared with an average product selection of 45%. Durable goods producers had an average sales efforts selection of 79%, as compared with the product selection of 60%.

The differences were accounted for by the low selection ratios for product service, in that most consumer goods manufacturers selected product research and development.

TABLE 2. POLICY AREAS SELECTED BY INDUSTRIAL GOODS PRODUCERS

Policy Areas	% of Firms Selecting the Policy Area[a]
Product:	
Product research and development	79
Product service	79
Average product selection ratio	79
Sales efforts:	
Sales research and sales planning	63
Management of sales personnel	49
Advertising and sales promotion	37
Average sales efforts selection ratio	50
Pricing	47
Other areas:	
Organizational structure	50
Distribution channels and their control	34
Financing and credit	18
Marketing cost budgeting and control	12
Transportation and storage	9
Public relations	7

[a]Based on the questionnaires of 68 industrial goods producers. Percentages here are rounded.

TABLE 3. POLICY AREAS SELECTED BY CONSUMER GOODS MANUFACTURERS

Policy Areas	Manufacturers of Nondurable Goods	Manufacturers of Durable Goods[a]
Sales efforts:		
Advertising and sales promotion	89	73
Management of sales personnel	64	91
Sales research and sales planning	82	73
Average sales efforts selection ratio	85	79
Product:		
Product research and development	83	75
Product service	14	36
Average product selection ratio	45	60
Pricing	50	46
Other areas:		
Distribution channels and their control	54	46
Organizational structure	39	27
Marketing cost budgeting and control	29	9
Financing and credit	11	9
Transportation and storage	4	9
Public relations	7	....

[a]Based on the questionnaires of 28 nondurable goods producers and 11 durable goods producers. Figures here are rounded.

It is understandable that consumer-goods producers selected product research and development with such a high degree of frequency in light of their emphasis on sales efforts. It is less difficult to promote a differentiated product than it is to promote an undifferentiated product.

Product research and development are important, but sales efforts are *most* important to manufacturers of consumer goods.

Product research and development was not broken down into research related to physical (real) product improvement and research related to psychological (fancied) product improvement. It would be immaterial to the consumer-goods manufacturer if a product change were *real* or *fancied,* so long as the change was regarded as an improvement by his customers.

The second section of the questionnaire subdivided the general areas of policies and procedures into more specific categories of business activities. When product research and development was subdivided into three categories of activities, the following selections were obtained:

	Manufacturers of		
	Industrial Goods	*Consumer Nondurables*	*Consumers Durables*
Technical research and development	75	54	56
Marketing research related to new products	30	62	56
Product evaluation	16	19	22

As might be expected, the technical development of products was most emphasized by the industrial-goods producers, whereas marketing research related to new products was most emphasized by the consumer-goods producers.

This analysis indicates that all three groups of manufacturers—industrial, consumer durable, and consumer nondurable—stressed the nonprice facets of competitive strategy, and that the *relative emphasis on product and sales efforts varied according to the nature of the products and the characteristics of the buyers.*

To further test this proposition, the questionnaires were grouped according to specific industries. If the proposition were valid, there should have been a high degree of similarity in the marketing strategies of respondents of a specific industry. That is, the respondents of a given industry, producing similar products for like customers, should select similar policy areas as most important in their marketing success.

Here are three examples that demonstrate the validity of this proposition.

Case No. 1—Capital Goods Industry

The most homogeneous grouping of companies with similar products and similar customers consisted of 12 producers of major installations—capital goods. As Table 4 illustrates, *all 12 producers selected product research and development and product service.*

Distribution channels and their control was selected by 8 of the 12 producers. This may be because sales servicing before and after is often performed by the distributors of capital goods.

The 100% selection for product research and development and for product service were high. Statistically one would expect such an occurrence only twice in 100,000 trials due to random sampling error.

Assuming that each policy area is actually of equal importance, there is a .00002 probability of getting a policy area with a 100% selection ratio due to random sampling error (binomial theorum used). The fact that *both* of the policy areas pertaining to product were selected by all 12 respondents provides further statistical proof that the selection ratios are *not* due to chance.

TABLE 4. SELECTION OF MAJOR POLICY AREAS BY TWELVE PRODUCERS OF MAJOR INSTALLATIONS

Rank	Policy Areas	Selection Ratio—%
1	Product research and development	100
2	Product service	100
3	Distribution channels and their control	67
4	Organizational structure	42
5	Management of sales personnel	42
6	Sales research and sales planning	42
7	Advertising and sales promotion	33
8	Pricing	25
9	Financing and credit	17
10	Public relations	17
11	Marketing cost budgeting and control	8
12	Transportation and storage	8

Case No. 2—Metals Industry

Another grouping of companies was comprised of producers of steel, zinc, aluminum, and other processed metals. The companies have similar markets and similar products, in that their products are the raw materials for the manufacture of other goods.

It would be anticipated that the product facet of competition would have prevailed in the competitive strategies of these companies; and Table 5 shows that this was true.

Case No. 3—Chemical Industry

A third grouping of companies highlights the importance of customers in determining marketing strategy. Of the six chemical manufacturers participating in the study, three produced for the consumer market and three for the industrial market.

All six firms responded by selecting product research and development, but at this point the similarities ceased.

As shown in Table 6, the average product selection ratio of the industrial chemical manufacturers was much higher than that of the consumer chemical manufacturers. The average sales effort selection ratio of the consumer products manufacturers was higher than that of the industrial producers.

HOW IMPORTANT IS SIZE?

To ascertain the influence of company size on management's selection of the facets of marketing strategy, the responses were classified according to the sales volume of each company: less than $50 million, $50 to $100 million, $100 to $500 million, and over $500 million.

The differences among the selection ratios of the various size classifications were so small that none was found to be statistically significant. Apparently

TABLE 5. SELECTION OF MAJOR POLICY AREAS BY EIGHT PRODUCERS OF METALS

Rank	Policy Areas	Selection Ratio—%
1	Product service	100
2	Product research and development	75
3	Sales research and sales planning	63
4	Pricing	63
5	Distribution channels and their control	50
6	Management of sales personnel	38
7	Organizational structure	25
8	Transportation and storage	25
9	Financing and credit	25
10	Public relations	13
11	Advertising and sales promotion	13
12	Marketing cost budgeting and control	....

TABLE 6. SELECTION OF MAJOR POLICY AREAS BY CHEMICAL AND DRUG PRODUCERS

Policy Areas	Selection Ratio of Industrial Chemical Producers (3)	Selection Ratio of Consumer Chemical Producers (3)
Product research and development	100	100
Product service	67	...
Average product selection ratio	83	50
Advertising and sales promotions	...	100
Sales research and sales planning	100	67
Management of sales personnel	33	67
Average sales efforts selection ratio	44	78

size had little influence on the relative importance that a company attached to the various facets of its marketing mix.

IN CONCLUSION

The ranking method provided only a rough measure of the importance of price, product, and sales efforts; *but it was a measurement.*

As for another possible limitation—lack of differentiation between responses related to "what is" and what the respondents felt "should be"—one might ask, "Who is better qualified to select the most important areas of a successful firm's marketing program than the firm's marketing management?"

The study reported illustrates two major points:

1. In today's market, the nonprice facets of competition occupy a prominent role.
2. The explanation of the roles of nonprice competitive facets does *not* lie solely in the structure of the industry (or the size of the firm), but instead primarily in the nature of the product and its market.

The importance of the nonprice aspects of the marketing mix and the variations among industries can be explained by the nature of today's economy. To compete successfully in a setting characterized by oligopolistic firms offering rival products to a customer-dominated market, the firm must be customer-oriented. In appealing to the customer, management finds success in utilizing the nonprice facets of competitive activity, adjusting its strategy to the needs and desires of the buyer.

QUESTIONS

1. Explain why pricing received a relatively low ranking in the questionnaire designed to discover the key areas of marketing success.

2. What policy areas were considered to be the most vital in a company's marketing success? Why?

3. Explain why nonprice competitive strategy would vary according to the nature of a firm's products and the characteristics of the buyers of those products.

Are Channels of Distribution What the Textbooks Say?

PHILLIP McVEY

Perhaps Wroe Alderson said as much as is safe to say when he described a marketing channel as a group of firms which "constitute a loose coalition engaged in exploiting joint opportunity in the market."[1]

THEORY AND ACTUALITY

Certainly too much is said about channel relationships in many published textbooks for businessmen and students, if one is to look for proof in current marketing practice. The picture usually given is one of long lists of various types of middlemen and facilitating agencies, which differ minutely but precisely in functions performed. Alignments of particular types are presented as "right" or "customary" for a given commodity or type of producer. Furthermore, it is often implied that it is the producer who selects all the links in the channel and establishes the working arrangements with them, down to and including the outlet which sells his goods to the final user.

Several popular college textbooks in marketing illustrate this manufacturer-oriented approach to channel planning.[2] One reason for fairly standard treatment of channel-building is that the growth of marketing knowledge has proceeded from a description of the activities of existing business firms, leaning heavily on data provided by the U.S. Censuses of Wholesale and Retail Trade. The framework appears orderly and well planned. But little recognition is given to the probability that some channel sequences "just grew" like Topsy, without direction or intent of known parents.

The Census method of counting, whereby each separate establishment is assigned to a single traditional category on the basis of a *major-portion-of-dollar-volume* rule, tends to produce more orderliness in the picture than probably exists. It tends to obscure a great deal of "promiscuous distribution" and channel-jumping. The Census rule, like the Procrustean bed of Greek mythology, effectively reduces the number of categories into which firms are sorted, and avoids hybrid, nondescript classifications.

Yet hybridity is too common among marketing firms to be ignored. For example, almost any wholesaler will do some business at retail; similarly, it is not

---

From *Journal of Marketing,* January 1960, pp. 61-65. Reprinted by permission of the American Marketing Association.

[1]Wroe Alderson, "The Development of Marketing Channels," in Richard M. Clewett (editor), *Marketing Channels for Manufactured Products* (Homewood, Illinois: Richard D. Irwin, Inc., 1954), p. 30.

[2]Examples are found in: T. N. Beckman, H. H. Maynard, and W. R. Davidson, *Principles of Marketing,* sixth edition (New York, The Ronald Press Company, 1957), pp. 44-45. C. F. Phillips and D. J. Duncan, *Marketing Principles and Methods,* third edition (Homewood, Illinois; Richard D. Irwin, Inc., 1956), p. 562. M. P. McNair, M. P. Brown, D. S. R. Leighton, and W. B. England, *Problems in Marketing,* second edition (New York, McGraw-Hill Book Company, Inc., 1957), p. 66.

uncommon for a broker to find himself holding title to a given lot of goods, thus becoming temporarily a merchant middleman. A realistic classification may require the use of relative terms to identify types of operation, according to a range of variables—for example, the *degree* to which a firm caters to a given customer group, or the *frequency* with which a function is performed.

Further study of marketing textbooks may lead a reader to conclude that: (a) middlemen of many types are available to any manufacturer in any market to which he wishes to sell, and within each type there is an ample selection of individual firms; (b) the manufacturer habitually controls the selection and operation of individual firms in his channel; and (c) middlemen respond willingly as *selling agents* for the manufacturer rather than as *purchasing agents* for a coveted group of customers to whom the middlemen sell.

Yet none of these conclusions is entirely valid.

In a product line such as fashion apparel, a garment maker may have an extremely limited choice of types of middlemen: the selling agent, the broker, the direct-buying retailer, or the chain store buying office. The general absence of service wholesalers from this line of trade is not correctible by manufacturers' *fiat*.

In a particular market area, the choice may be even more limited. Of individual firms of a given type, there may be no choice at all. These limitations arise, of course, because of the free choices made by the middlemen as to locations, customer groups, and product assortments they elect to sell.

IS THE "CHANNEL" AN ACADEMIC CONCEPT?

Integrated action up and down a channel is a rare luxury in marketing. Why? It may be that the "channel of distribution" is a concept that is principally academic in usage and unfamiliar to many firms selling to and through these channels.

Instead of a channel, a businessman is likely to concern himself merely with suppliers and customers. His dealings are not with all of the links in the channel but only with those immediately adjacent to him, from which he buys and to which he sells. He may little know nor care what becomes of his products after they leave the hands of some merchant middleman who has paid him for them and released him to return to problems involving his special functions. A manufacturer may not even consider himself as standing at the head of a channel, but only as occupying a link in a channel that begins with his suppliers.

Policies

Choice of a channel is not open to any firm unless it has considerable freedom of action in matters of marketing policy. Other areas of policy seem to be treated with more respect. For example, it is well recognized that a *price* policy is an authoritarian privilege open only to those sellers who possess power to withhold goods from the market in considerable quantities, or who have the choice of alternative markets and the means to solicit them. Usually a differentiated product is necessary. Therefore, a wheat farmer can seldom have anything resembling a price policy.

Likewise, a *design* policy is meaningful only when variations in product characteristics have been understood and accepted by customers to be of significance. Manufacturers of semi-finished or component parts, or of textile "gray goods" cannot enjoy this luxury in most cases.

Similarly, the selection of a multi-stage channel is not the prerogative of a manufacturer unless his franchise is coveted by the middlemen he seeks, as being more valuable to them than their franchise would be to him.

Names such as Sears Roebuck & Company, Macy's, or Kroger mean a great deal more to the customers of these retailers than do the brand names of most of the items sold in their stores. These firms control the channels for many products, even to the point of bringing into existence some manufacturing firms needed to fill gaps in their assortments. In the same manner some national wholesalers, holding the reins of a huge distributive system, are more powerful than either their suppliers or their customers. In such extreme cases the power position is obvious. The big company, regardless of its position in the channel, tries to make its plans and policies effective by taking the initiative for co-ordinated action.

UNCERTAINTY AMONG SMALLER FIRMS

As to the many thousands of middle-size and small companies that truly characterize American marketing, the power position is speculative, vacillating, and ephemeral. Strength in certain market areas, the temporary success of a product, ability to perform a certain needed type of financing or promotional effort—these and similar factors enable companies to assume power.

On the other hand, financial reverses, an unfortunate sales campaign, or even the lack of accurate market news—these factors can shift power elsewhere, possibly to another link in the channel or to another firm in the same link. In any case, the opportunity of any firm is contingent upon the willingness of others to use it as a link in the channel.

Comparison with Advertising Media

Selection of middlemen has been likened to the selection of advertising media. In both instances the task is to find a vehicle which has an existing coverage (or circulation) which coincides with the market desired. A region blanketed with a neat mosaic of distributors' territories will appear on a map much like the same region covered by television stations.

However, there is an important difference. Seldom does an advertising medium restrict its availability. The advertiser's product need not be sold first to the medium on the grounds of self-interest. Only occasionally will a middleman accept any product he is offered. The requirement that he invest his own money and effort forces him to be selective in terms of probable outcome or profit. No seller can afford to neglect the task of selling *to* the middlemen he seeks, as well as *through* them. Nearly every comprehensive campaign of consumer advertising allots substantial effort to dealer promotion and distributor promotion. Indeed, much consumer advertising is undertaken primarily for the stimulating effect it will have upon middlemen.

Middlemen's Reactions

Middlemen's reactions to new-product offerings probably deserve more attention from manufacturers than usual. Wholesalers and retailers, as well as agent middlemen, enjoy an excellent position from which to make keen judgments of a product's probable successes within local markets. Free from the manufacturer's proclivity to "fall in love with the product," but not primarily concerned with its ultimate usage characteristics, middlemen who are alert merchandisers can look at the product with an eye to salability alone.

Yet it is common practice for manufacturers to force acceptance with a heavy barrage of consumer advertising, introductory high-markup offers, free merchandise, combination deals, co-operative advertising schemes, and the like. These may have the effect of "mesmerizing" middlemen, and of clouding the issue of the product's own rate of initial acceptance.

Lack of effective vertical communication in most channels is a serious deterrent. Possibly no other proof of the weakness of manufacturers' control over channels is so convincing as their inability to obtain facts from their own ultimate and intermediate markets. Information that could be used in product development, pricing, packaging, or promotion-planning is buried in non-standard records of middlemen, and sometimes purposely secreted from suppliers.

Channels research is one of the most frustrating areas of marketing investigation, since it requires access to data collected by firms which are independent, remotely situated, and suspicious. Unless given incentive to do so, middlemen will not maintain separate sales records by brands sold. Extracting the needed figures by preferred units of measure is often a hopeless task. To get such data, one producer of pipe tools adopted a device commonly used with electric appliances: a "warranty registration" questionnaire attached to the tools. Ostensibly designed to validate users' damage claims, its true purpose was to discover where, when, how, and by whom the tools had been sold.

Communication downward from the manufacturer is also faulty, placing in doubt the claim that all links in the channel are bound together by common objectives. For example, it is seldom practical to disclose a forthcoming promotional plan in all its details and to ask the middlemen whether the plan will be timely, acceptable, and supportable by their efforts. To do so would jeopardize the advantage of surprise, usually a significant competitive stratagem. Yet the value of synchronized, co-ordinated action on any new plan by all firms in the channel is obvious.

MIDDLEMEN'S VIEWS

Channel Building

To the extent that any middleman can do so, he should think of himself primarily as a purchasing agent for his customers, and only secondarily as a selling agent for his suppliers. The planning of his product line will proceed from an analysis of a finite customer group in which he is interested . . . to the selection of goods capable of satisfying those needs . . . and then to the choice of available suppliers who can provide those goods. Of course, he may actually begin his assortment with one or more basic products, chosen by him as a way of defining the area of customer needs in which he elects to deal.

From that point on, however, his chief stock in trade becomes not the franchises of important suppliers, but rather his customer group. He is interested in selling any product which these customers desire to buy from him. The attractiveness of any new offering by a supplier is not to be judged by the size of the markup or commission, nor the unusual nature of the product, nor details of its manufacture, nor the promises of manufacturer's advertising support.

The key question is: Does it fit the line? That is, does it complement the other products that he sells, in terms of salability to precisely the same group of buyers? His list of customers is probably less subject to intentional revision than are many other aspects of his business. Is it not at this point, then, that channel building starts?

Some unusual product combinations may result from this approach. A manufacturers' agent selling baby garments in the Southwest took on a line of printed business forms, which the small retailers on whom he called were seeking. An Omaha wholesaler successfully added grocery products to his liquor business. A Cleveland distributor of welding equipment rejected a portable farm welder offered by his principal supplier, since he had no contact with farmers, but was interested in carrying a line of warehouse tractors and lift trucks.

Approach to New Prospects

In some cases a middleman may deem it worth-while to shift from his current customer group to a new list of prospects, in order to find a market for a particularly promising new product. In the main, however, he will not do so. His approach to new prospects is based on their close similarity to those now on his customer list. To all these persons he attempts to become known as a helpful specialist in a well-defined set of recurring needs. The scope of his line, and the interrelation of products in it, must be known to the bulk of his customers. Scrambled merchandising, or stocking of unrelated items, will tend to split his market into many small groups.

Assortment Sales

Furthermore, the middleman attempts to weld all of his offerings into a family of items which he can sell in combination, as a packaged assortment, to individual customers. His selling efforts are directed primarily at obtaining orders for the assortment, rather than for individual items. Naturally the greatest *numbers* of his transactions will seldom be made in this way; but often his greatest volume and more profitable sales to "blue-chip" accounts will be assortment sales.

Catering to assortment sales has considerable significance to channel operation, because the kind of sales service which a middleman can offer a single-product supplier is affected thereby. Since he is relatively disinterested in pushing individual items, the middleman is criticized for failure to stress a given brand, or for the poor quality of his salesmen's product knowledge, his disuse of suppliers' advertising materials, his neglect of certain customers (who may be good prospects for individual items but not for the assortment), and even for his unrefined systems of record keeping, in which brand designations may be lost.

THE MIDDLEMAN AS AN INDEPENDENT MARKET

The middleman is not a hired link in a chain forged by a manufacturer, but rather an independent market, the focus of a large group of customers for whom he buys. Subsequent to some market analysis of his own, he selects products and suppliers, thereby setting at least one link in the channel.

After some experimentation, he settles upon a method of operation, performing those functions he deems inescapable in the light of his own objectives, forming policies for himself wherever he has freedom to do so. Perhaps these methods and policies conform closely to those of a Census category of middleman, but perhaps they do not.

It is true that his choices are in many instances tentative proposals. He is subject to much influence from competitors, from aggressive suppliers, from inadequate finances and faulty information, as well as from habit. Nonetheless, many of his choices are independent.

As he grows and builds a following, he may find that his prestige in his market is greater than that of the suppliers whose goods he sells. In some instances his local strength is so great that a manufacturer is virtually unable to tap that market, except through him. In such a case the manufacturer can have no channel policy with respect to that market.

QUESTIONS

1. Explain why Phillip McVey thinks that the "channel" may be an academic concept.

2. Explain why many firms may not have a choice of a channel unless they have considerable freedom of action in other matters of marketing policy.

3. Why should the middleman think of himself primarily as a purchasing agent for his customers and only secondarily as a selling agent for his suppliers?

4. Why does McVey think that the middleman is an "independent market"?

Is Advertising Wasteful?

JULES BACKMAN

With some exceptions, economists generally have criticized advertising as economically wasteful. All the criticisms are not so extreme as one widely used economics text which states:

> *Overall, it is difficult for anyone to gain more than tempo-rarily from large advertising outlays in an economy in which counteradvertising is general. The overall effect of advertising, on which we spent $14 billion [actually $15 billion—JB] in 1965, is to devote these productive resources (men, ink, billboards, and so forth) to producing advertising rather than to producing other goods and services.*[1]

Most critics do not go this far in condemning advertising. However, they do emphasize that advertising may be wasteful in several ways: by adding unnecessarily to costs, by an inefficient use of resources, by promoting excessive competition, and by causing consumers to buy items they do not need. This article brings together the scattered criticisms of advertising and answers to them and thus presents an overview of the debate in this area. The nature of these criticisms and the significance of waste in a competitive economy are first reviewed. Attention is then given to the vital informational role played by advertising, particularly in an expanding economy. Advertising is only one alternative in the marketing mix, and hence its contribution must be considered among alternatives rather than in absolute terms.

VARIATIONS ON A THEME

The criticism that advertising involves economic waste takes several forms.

Competition in Advertising

The attack usually is centered on competition in advertising which some critics state flatly is wasteful.[2] Others have been concerned about the relative cost of

From *Journal of Marketing,* XXXII (January 1968), 2-8. Reprinted by permission of the American Marketing Association.

[1]George Leland Bach, *Economics,* Fifth Edition (Englewood Cliffs, New Jersey: Prentice-Hall, Inc., 1966), p. 437. See also Kenneth Boulding, "Economic Analysis," *Microeconomics,* Fourth Edition, Vol. 1 (New York: Harper and Row, 1966), p. 513.

[2]Nicholas H. Kaldor, "The Economic Aspects of Advertising," *The Review of Economic Studies,* Vol.18 (1950-51), p. 6.

advertising as a percentage of sales. Sometimes an arbitrary percentage, such as 5%, is selected as the dividing line between "high" and more "reasonable" levels of expenditure.[3]

Such cutoff points are meaningless, since the proper relative expenditures for advertising are a function of the product's characteristics. It is not an accident that relative advertising costs are highest for low-priced items which are available from many retail outlets and subject to frequent repeat purchases (for example, cosmetics, soaps, soft drinks, gum and candies, drugs, cigarettes, beer, etc.).

Particularly criticized are emotional appeals, persuasion, and "tug of war" advertising where it is claimed the main effect is to shift sales among firms rather than to increase total volume of the industry. For example, Richard Caves states: "At the point where advertising departs from its function of informing and seeks to persuade or deceive us, it tends to become a waste of resources."[4]

In a competitive economy competitors must seek to persuade customers to buy their wares. We do not live in a world where a company stocks its warehouse and waits until customers beat a path to its doors to buy its products. If this is all that a business firm did, we would have economic waste in terms of products produced but not bought as well as in the failure to produce many items for which a market can be created. In the latter case, the waste would take the form of idle labor and unused resources.

Inefficient Use of Resources

Economists have criticized advertising most vigorously as involving an inefficient use of resources. This criticism has been directed particularly against advertising where the main effect allegedly is a "shuffling of existing total demand" among the companies in an industry. Under these conditions, it is stated, advertising merely adds to total costs and in time results in higher prices. There undoubtedly is a shifting of demand among firms due to many factors including advertising. But this is what we should expect in a competitive economy. Moreover, there are many products for which total demand is increased (for example, television sets, radio sets, cars, toilet articles) for multiple use in the same home. In the sharply expanding economy of the past quarter of a century there are relatively few industries in which total demand has remained unchanged.

It must also be kept in mind that the resources devoted to competitive advertising usually are considered to be wasteful "in a full-employment economy" because they may be utilized more efficiently in other ways. Thus, the extent of "waste" involved also appears to depend upon whether the economy is operating below capacity. This point is considered in a later section.

---

[3]Joe S. Bain, *Industrial Organization* (New York: John Wiley & Sons, 1959), pp. 390-91. See also *Report of a Commission of Enquiry Into Advertising* (London, England: The Labour Party, 1966), p. 42. The Reith Report defined "substantially advertised products" at 5% or more.

[4]Richard Caves, *American Industry: Structure, Conduct, Performance* (Englewood Cliffs, New Jersey: Prentice-Hall, Inc., 1964), p. 102.

Adds to Costs

Sometimes, it is stated that if advertising succeeds in expanding total demand for a product, the result is a shift of demand from other products, the producers of which will be forced to advertise to attempt to recover their position. The net result of such "counter-advertising" is to add to costs and to prices.

But all increases in demand do not necessarily represent a diversion from other products. Thus, an expanded demand for new products is accompanied by an increase in income and in purchasing power flowing from their production. Moreover, during a period of expanding economic activity, as is noted later, the successful advertising may affect the rate of increase for different products rather than result in an absolute diversion of volume.

Creates Undesirable Wants

Another variation is the claim that advertising is wasteful because it "... creates useless or undesirable wants at the expense of things for which there is greater social need. When advertising makes consumers want and buy automobiles with tail fins, tobacco, and movie-star swimming pools, there is less money (fewer resources) available to improve public hospitals, build better schools, or combat juvenile delinquency."[5] It is claimed that many of these types of products are useless and anti-social. Criticism of advertising is nothing new. In the late 1920s Stuart Chase claimed: "Advertising creates no new dollars. In fact, by removing workers from productive employment, it tends to depress output, and thus lessen the number of real dollars."[6]

These are value judgments reached by the critics on the basis of subjective "standards" which they set up. "What is one man's meat is another man's poison," as the old saying goes. The real question is who is to decide what is good for the consumer and what should he purchase?

In a free economy, there is a wide diversity of opinion as to what combinations of goods and services should be made available and be consumed. Obviously, tastes vary widely and most persons do not want to be told what is best for them. In any cross section of the population of the country there will be a wide disagreement as to what constitutes the ideal components of a desirable level of living. Each one of us must decide what purchases will yield the greatest satisfactions. We may be misled on occasion by popular fads, advertising, or even advice of our friends. But these decisions in the final analysis are made by the buyers and not by the advertisers, as the latter have found out so often to their regret.

COMPETITION AND "WASTE"

The critics of advertising are really attacking the competitive process. Competition involves considerable duplication and "waste." The illustrations range from

---

    [5]"Advertising and Charlie Brown," *Business Review,* Federal Reserve Bank of Philadelphia (June, 1962), p. 10.
    [6]Stuart Chase, *The Tragedy of Waste* (New York: Macmillan Company, 1928), p. 112.

the several gasoline stations at an important intersection to the multiplication of research facilities, the excess industrial capacity which develops during periods of expansion, and the accumulations of excessive inventories.

There is widespread recognition that inefficiencies may develop in advertising as in other phases of business.[7] Mistakes are made in determining how much should be spent for advertising—but these mistakes can result in spending too little as well as too much.

We cannot judge the efficiency of our competitive society—including the various instrumentalities, such as advertising—by looking at the negative aspects alone. It is true that competition involves waste. But it also yields a flood of new products, improved quality, better service, and pressures on prices. In the United States, it has facilitated enormous economic growth with the accompanying high standards of living. The advantages of competition have been so overwhelmingly greater than the wastes inherent in it that we have established as one of our prime national goals, through the antitrust laws, the continuance of a viable competitive economy.

Informational Role of Advertising

Advertising plays a major informational role in our economy because (1) products are available in such wide varieties, (2) new products are offered in such great numbers, and (3) existing products must be called to the attention of new consumers who are added to the market as a result of expansion in incomes, the population explosion, and changes in tastes.

The most heavily advertised products are widely used items that are consumed by major segments of the population. This does not mean that everyone buys every product or buys them to the extent that he can. Some of these products are substitutes for other products. For example, it will be readily recognized that cereals provide only one of the many alternatives among breakfast foods. In some instances, heavily advertised products compete with each other like, for example, soft drinks and beer. In other instances, additional consumers can use the products so that the size of the total market can be increased (for example, toilet preparations).

Potential markets also expand as incomes rise and as consumers are able to purchase products they previously could not afford. As the population increases, large numbers of new potential customers are added each year. Continuous large-scale advertising provides reminders to old customers and provides information to obtain some part of the patronage of new customers. The potential market is so huge that large-scale advertising is an economical way to obtain good results.

In addition, the identity of buyers changes under some circumstances and new potential buyers must be given information concerning the available alternatives. It has also been pointed out that some of these products are ". . . subject to fads and style changes" and that ". . . consumers become restive with

---

[7]Committee on Advertising, *Principles of Advertising* (New York: Pitman Publishing Corp., 1963), p. 34; and Neil H. Borden, "The Role of Advertising in the Various Stages of Corporate and Economic Growth," Peter D. Bennett, editor, *Marketing and Economic Development* (Chicago, Illinois: American Marketing Association, 1965), p. 493.

existing brands and are prepared to try new varieties." Illustrations include cereals, soaps, clothing, and motion pictures.[8]

The consumer has a wide variety of brands from which to choose. Product improvements usually breed competitive product improvements; the advertising of these improvements may result in an increase in total advertising for the class of products.

When any company in an industry embarks on an intensified advertising campaign, its competitors must step up their advertising or other sales efforts to avoid the possible loss of market position. This is a key characteristic of competition.

On the other hand, if any company decides to economize on its advertising budget, its exposure is reduced and its share of market may decline if its competitors fail to follow the same policy. Thus, for some grocery products it has been reported that ". . . competition within a sector may have established a certain pattern with regard to the extent of advertising, and any company dropping below this level faces possible substantial loss of market share.[9]

These results flow particularly if the industry is oligopolistic, that is, has relatively few producers who are sensitive to and responsive to actions of competitors. However, as the dramatic changes in market shares during the past decade so amply demonstrate, this does not mean that the companies in such oligopolistic industries will retain relatively constant shares of the market.[10]

The informational role of advertising has been succinctly summarized by Professor George J. Stigler:

> . . . *Under competition, the main tasks of a seller are to inform potential buyers of his existence, his line of goods, and his prices. Since both sellers and buyers change over time (due to birth, death, migration), since people forget information once acquired, and since new products appear, the existence of sellers must be continually advertised. . .*
>
> *This informational function of advertising must be emphasized because of a popular and erroneous belief that advertising consists chiefly of nonrational (emotional and repetitive) appeals.*[11]

Elsewhere, Professor Stigler has pointed out that ". . . information is a valuable resource," that advertising is "the obvious method of identifying buyers and sellers" which "reduces drastically the cost of search," and that "It is clearly an immensely powerful instrument for the elimination of ignorance. . ."[12]

---

[8]Lester G. Telser, "How Much Does It Pay Whom To Advertise?", *American Economic Review, Papers and Proceedings* (December, 1960), pp. 203-4.

[9]National Commission on Food Marketing, *Grocery Manufacturing,* Technical Study No. 6 (Washington, D.C.: June, 1966), p. 14.

[10]Jules Backman, *Advertising and Competition* (New York: New York University Press, 1967), Chapters 3 and 4.

[11]George J. Stigler, *The Theory of Price,* Third Edition (New York: The Macmillan Company, 1966), p. 200.

[12]George J. Stigler, "The Economics of Information," *The Journal of Political Economy* (June, 1961), pp. 213, 216, 220. See also S. A. Ozga, "Imperfect Markets Through Lack of Knowledge," *Quarterly Journal of Economics* (February, 1960), pp. 29, 33-34, and Wroe Alderson, *Dynamic Market Behavior* (Homewood, Illinois: Richard D. Irwin, Inc., 1965), pp. 128-31.

Often this information is required to create interest in and demand for a product. Thus, it has been reported:

> *. . . to a significant degree General Foods and the U.S. food market created each other. Before a new product appears, customers are rarely conscious of wanting it. There was no spontaneous demand for ready-to-eat cereals; frozen foods required a sustained marketing effort stretching over many years; instant coffee had been around for decades, supplying a market that did not amount to a tenth of its present level. General Foods' corporate skill consists largely in knowing enough about American tastes to foresee what products will be accepted.*[13]

Similarly, J. K. Galbraith, who has been very critical of advertising, has recognized that:

> *A new consumer product must be introduced with a suitable advertising campaign to arouse an interest in it. The path for an expansion of output must be paved by a suitable expansion in the advertising budget. Outlays for the manufacturing of a product are not more important in the strategy of modern business enterprise than outlays for the manufacturing of demand for the product.*[14]

We live in an economy that has little resemblance to the ideal of perfect competition postulated by economists. However, one of the postulates of this ideal economy is perfect knowledge. Advertising contributes to such knowledge. Thus, in such an idealized economy, even though advertising may be wasteful it would still have a role to play. But in the world of reality, with all its imperfections, advertising is much more important. Advertising is an integral and vital part of our growing economy and contributes to the launching of the new products so essential to economic growth.

How Much Is Informational?

In 1966, total expenditures for media advertising aggregated $13.3 billion.[15] It is impossible to determine exactly how much of this amount was strictly informational. However, the following facts are of interest.

Classified advertising was $1.3 billion

Other local newspaper advertising, largely retail, was $2.6 billion

Business paper advertising was $712 million

Local radio and TV advertising was $1.1 billion

Spot radio and spot TV advertising was $1.2 billion

---

[13]"General Foods Is Five Billion Particulars," *Fortune* (March, 1964), p. 117.

[14]J. K. Galbraith, *The Affluent Society* (Boston, Massachusetts: Houghton Mifflin Company, 1958), p. 156.

[15]This total excludes a miscellaneous category of $3.3 billion.

National advertising on network TV, network radio, magazines and newspapers was $3.7 billion

Direct mail was $2.5 billion

Classified advertising and local advertising are overwhelmingly informational
in nature. Certainly some part of national advertising also performs this function.
These figures suggest that substantially less than half of total advertising is of the
type that the critics are attacking as wasteful;[16] the exact amount cannot be
pinpointed. Moreover, it must be kept in mind that a significant part of national
advertising is for the promotion of new products for which the informational role
is vital.

From another point of view, even if there is waste, the social cost is considerably less than suggested by these data. Thus, in 1966 about $10 billion was
spent on advertising in newspapers, magazines, radio, and television; another
$746 million was spent on farm and business publications. Without these ex-
penditures, these sources of news and entertainment would have had to obtain
substantial sums from other sources. It has been estimated that ". . . advertising
paid for over 60% of the cost of periodicals, for over 70% of the cost of newspapers, and for 100% of the cost of commercial radio and TV broadcasting."[17]
Thus, advertising results in a form of subsidization for all media of communication. Without it, these media would have to charge higher subscription rates or
be subsidized by the government or some combination of both.

ADVERTISING AND EXPANDING MARKETS

Economic growth has become a major objective of national economic policy in
recent years. Rising productivity, increasing population, improving education,
rates of saving, and decisions concerning new investments are the ingredients
of economic growth. In addition, there must be a favorable political climate
including tax policies and monetary policies designed to release the forces conducive to growth.

Advertising contributes to economic growth and in turn levels of living by
complementing the efforts to create new and improved products through expenditures for research and development. One observer has described the process as
follows:

> . . . *advertising, by acquainting the consumer with the values
> of new products, widens the market for these products, pushes
> forward their acceptance by the consumer, and encourages the
> investment and entrepreneurship necessary for innovation.
> Advertising, in short, holds out the promise of a greater and
> speedier return than would occur without such methods, thus
> stimulating investment, growth, and diversity.*[18]

---

[16]For the United Kingdom, the "disputed proportion" of advertising expenditures has been
estimated at about 30% of the total. Walter Taplin, *Advertising, A New Approach* (Boston, Massachusetts: Little, Brown & Co., 1963), p. 126.

[17]Fritz Machlup, *The Production and Distribution of Knowledge in the United States* (Princeton, New Jersey: Princeton University Press, 1962), p. 265.

[18]David M. Blank, "Some Comments on the Role of Advertising in the American Economy—
A Plea for Revaluation," L. George Smith, editor, *Reflections on Progress in Marketing* (Chicago,
Illinois: American Marketing Association, 1964), p. 151.

Among the most intensive advertisers have been toilet preparations (14.7% of sales), cleaning and polishing preparations (12.6%), and drugs (9.4%). The markets for these products have been expanding at a faster rate than all consumer spending.

Between 1947 and 1966, personal consumption expenditures for these products increased as follows:[19]

	1947	1955	1966
	(millions of dollars)		
Toilet articles & preparations	1,217	1,915	4,690
Cleaning, polishing & household supplies	1,523	2,480	4,487
Drug preparations & sundries	1,313	2,362	5,062

As a share of total personal consumption expenditures, the increases from 1947 to 1966 were as follows:
Toilet articles and preparations from 0.76% to 1.01%
Cleaning, polishing and household supplies from 0.94% to 0.97%
Drug preparations and sundries from 0.82% to 1.09%
These increases in relative importance are based upon dollar totals. However, the retail prices of these products rose less than the consumer price index during the postwar years.

Between 1947 and 1966, the price increases were as follows:
Total consumer price index   45.4%
Toilet preparations   14.6
Soaps and detergents   2.6
Drugs and prescriptions   22.8
Thus, the increase in relative importance of these highly advertised products has been even greater in real terms than in dollars.

Between 1947 and 1966, the increase in *real* personal consumption expenditures has been:
Toilet articles and preparations from 0.68% to 1.12%
Cleaning, polishing and household supplies from 0.87% to 1.05%
Drug preparations and sundries from 0.82% to 1.24%
Clearly, advertising appears to have contributed to an expansion in the demand for these products and to the growth of our economy with the accompanying expansion in job opportunities and in economic well-being. There may have been some waste in this process—although all of such expenditures cannot be characterized as wasteful—but it appears to have been offset in full or in part by these other benefits.

The charge of large-scale waste in advertising appears to reflect in part a yearning for an economy with standardized, homogeneous products which are primarily functional in nature. An illustration would be a refrigerator that is designed solely to be technically efficient for the storage of food. However, cus-

---

[19]*The National Income and Product Accounts of the United States, 1929-1965, Statistical Tables* (Washington, D.C.: United States Department of Commerce, August, 1966), pp. 44-49; and *Survey of Current Business* (July, 1967), pp. 23-24.

tomers are also interested in the decor of their kitchens, in convenience and speed in the manufacture of ice cubes, in shelves that rotate, and in special storage for butter. These are additions to functional usefulness which "an affluent society" can afford but which a subsistence economy cannot.

Advertising in a High Level Economy

The concept of waste must be related to the level achieved by an economy. Professor John W. Lowe has observed that "Perhaps a good deal of the 'wastefulness' assigned to advertising springs from the fact that a large part of the world's population cannot consider satisfying *psychological wants* when most of their efforts must be devoted to *needs.*"[20] (Italics added.)

In a subsistence economy, scarcity is so significant that advertising might be wasteful, particularly where it diverts resources from meeting the basic necessities of life. Such an economy usually is a "full employment economy" in the sense that everyone is working. But the total yield of a full employment subsistence economy is very low, as is evident throughout Asia, Africa, and South America.

Professor Galbraith has noted that "The opportunity for product differentiation . . . is almost uniquely the result of opulence . . . the tendency for commercial rivalries . . . to be channeled into advertising and salesmanship would disappear in a poor community."[21]

In the high level American economy, there usually are surpluses rather than scarcity. The use of resources for advertising to differentiate products, therefore, is not necessarily a diversion from other uses. Rather, it frequently represents the use of resources that might otherwise be idle both in the short run and the long run and thus may obviate the waste that such idleness represents.

The Marketing Mix

The concept of waste cannot ignore the question—waste as compared with what alternative? Advertising cannot be considered in a vacuum. It must be considered as one of the marketing alternatives available. Generally it is not a question of advertising or nothing, but rather of advertising or some other type of sales effort.

It is a mistake to evaluate the relative cost of advertising apart from other marketing costs. It is only one tool in the marketing arsenal which also includes direct selling, packaging, servicing, product planning, pricing, etc. Expenditures for advertising often are substituted for other types of selling effort. This substitution has been readily apparent in the history of the discount house. These houses have featured well-advertised brands which were presold and, hence,

---

[20]John W. Lowe, "An Economist Defends Advertising," *Journal of Marketing,* Vol. 27 (July, 1963), p. 18.

[21]John K. Galbraith, *American Capitalism: The Concept of Countervailing Power* (Boston, Massachusetts: Houghton Mifflin Company, 1952), pp. 106-07.

virtually eliminated the need for floor stocks and reduced the need for space and many salesmen.

Advertising is undertaken where it is the most effective and most economical way to appeal to customers. It is a relatively low cost method of communicating with all potential customers and this explains its widespread adoption by many companies. To the extent that less efficient marketing methods must be substituted for advertising, we would really have economic waste.

SUMMARY AND CONCLUSIONS

There is wide agreement that the informational role of advertising makes a significant contribution to the effective operation of our economy. There is also agreement that inefficiency in the use of advertising is wasteful, as are other types of inefficiencies that are part and parcel of a market-determined economy. The gray area is so-called competitive advertising, largely national, which is the main target of those who insist advertising is wasteful. Although precise data are not available, the estimates cited earlier indicate that the charge of competitive waste applies to substantially less than half of all advertising expenditures.

Competition unavoidably involves considerable duplication and waste. If the accent is placed on the negative, a distorted picture is obtained. On balance, the advantages of competition have been much greater than the wastes.

Advertising has contributed to an expanding market for new and better products. Many of these new products would not have been brought to market unless firms were free to develop mass markets through large-scale advertising. There may be some waste in this process, but it has been more than offset by other benefits.

Where burgeoning advertising expenditures are accompanied by expanding industry sales, there will tend to be a decline in total unit costs instead of increase, and prices may remain unchanged or decline. In such situations, it seems clear that advertising, while adding to total costs, will result in lower total *unit* costs, the more significant figure. This gain will be offset to some extent if the increase in volume represents a diversion from other companies or industries with an accompanying rise in unit costs. Of course, such change is inherent in a dynamic competitive economy.

Advertising expenditures have risen as the economy has expanded. At such times, the absolute increase in sales resulting from higher advertising expenditures need not be accompanied by a loss in sales in other industries. This is particularly true if a new product has been developed and its sales are expanding. In that event, new jobs probably will be created and help to support a higher level of economic activity generally.

The claim that resources devoted to advertising would be utilized more efficiently for other purposes ignores the fact that generally we have a surplus economy. All of the resources used for advertising are not diverted from other alternatives. Rather, it is probable that much of the resources involved would be idle or would be used less efficiently. Even more important would be the failure to provide the jobs which expanding markets create.

Finally, advertising does not take place in a vacuum. It is one of several marketing alternatives. The abandonment of advertising could not represent a net saving to a company or to the economy. Instead, such a development would require a shift to alternative marketing techniques, some of which would be less efficient than advertising since companies do not deliberately adopt the least effective marketing approach. On balance, advertising is an invaluable competitive tool.

QUESTIONS

1. Explain the difference between informative advertising and competitive advertising.

2. What role does advertising play in expanding product markets?

3. Is it possible to have a high level of economic activity without the use of advertising?

4. Does advertising add to the price the consumer pays for the products he purchases?

Scouting the Trail for Marketers

Say you are a manufacturer of perfume. It's a president's business to look ahead. If you take your job seriously—and assume that your subordinates will do the same—there are three fundamental questions that you need to answer:
☐ What will women want to smell like five years from now?
☐ How much will they be willing to spend to make themselves glamorous—and who besides the perfumers will be competing for a share of that spending?
☐ What sort of retail outlets will be doing the bulk of perfume sales? Department stores? Discount houses? Drug stores? Suburban shopping centers? Downtown salons?

These are pertinent questions but broad ones. The brand managers of the different perfumes you sell will have questions of a different sort to answer. Each will want to know:
☐ This square bottle my scent comes in—what does it convey to the customer?

Is it exotic? Tweedy? Expensive? Sexy? Would we be better off with something slinky in swirls and gold leaf?

☐ When do most of my sales take place? I advertise my stuff as a light summer scent, but most of the orders seem to come in around Christmas. Is that the time to be talking about creamy shoulders and drugged summer nights?

☐ Would retailers push the brand harder if I sweetened the deal, increased the cooperative advertising allowance, or just gave the clerks more push money?

If you have 12 brands that means your brand managers have 36 questions among them. Add your own three, and like the Church of England with the historic 39 Articles of Religion on which it is founded, you have an equal number of points on which you must take a stand. Unlike the Church of England, however, you cannot take your 39 points as a matter of faith.

So at this stage you buy yourself some market research.

The Finder Outers

It is you and several thousand manufacturers and marketers like you who have made market research an established part of the U.S. business scene. There are about as many definitions of market research as there are active market researchers today, but they all have one thing in common: Market research is the arm of marketing that finds out things and thereby lays the basis for marketing strategy.

It is concerned with the facts of what people buy, when they buy, where they buy, why they buy.

Altogether, U.S. business spends something more than $200-million a year to support this question-asking. That doesn't seem like much when you compare it with a total of $246-billion retail sales annually. And even the $200-million figure drags in a number of purely statistical, figure-juggling functions, on analysis of warehouse reports, for instance, that have to be assigned to somebody's budget, so why not to the marketing department?

Keeping Up with Jones Co. Nevertheless, the market researchers feel that the future is all on their side. The rough and tumble of today's competition makes old-fashioned seat-of-the-pants marketing prohibitively expensive. The unprecedented outpouring of new products in search of a market can make it not only expensive but a breeder of red ink.

The pace at which new products move onto the market is breathtaking. Within a few months, a company such as General Electric may put on store shelves or in dealer showrooms (1) an electric knife, (2) a new 11-in. TV set, (3) an improved caulking compound for sealing windows, (4) and a "self-cleaning" electric oven priced at $575. On a single day, Bristol-Myers Co. offered the American consumer three new products—Score hair cream, Ban cream deodorant, Softique bath oil.

It's a costly process at best. In a two-year introductory period, it can take something like $10-million—not counting development expenses—to put into retail distribution a product retailing for just 49¢. If the product fails, that's money down the drain.

Yet today four out of five new products fail after launching.

Beating the Game It's to forestall such expensive failures that so many companies have turned to market research. As yet, it's not a bandwagon rush—though you'll find it some places where you might least expect it—and the lure of market research varies from industry to industry.

New York's Seventh Avenue either tests its fashions by inviting buyers to town and waiting for orders, or goes direct to the public. Cosmetics manufacturers don't yet do much market research, but their use of it is growing along with their advertising budgets. All the big food companies, on the other hand, have taken it up as routine procedure—as well they might, since any product on the average supermarket shelf competes with some 6,500 others to get into the housewife's cart.

Detroit is something of a special case. The auto companies run elaborate research programs, but they make up their minds on styling according to their own peculiar logic, which usually revolves around the idea of continuity of design from one year to the next and the continuation of an already defined styling trend. Necessarily, the auto stylists have to go on their own judgment, since a $2,500 automobile is hardly an item that can easily be put into test markets—when it's a question of styling, not something radically new like Chrysler's gas turbine engine [*Business Week* Mar.28'64,p74]

On such matters as what kind of transportation the public will buy—economy, luxury, sport, family, suburban—marketing research has been used heavily by Detroit. General Motors' market research section, which jumped its research budget 75% since 1959, and which does most of its work at the behest of the company's top-level distribution committee, has contributed greatly to the notable success of the divisions in recent years.

It's no accident that Chevrolet's four successive nameplate introductions, from Corvette to Chevelle, have hit their market niche just right—and without taking sales away from the standard, and more profitable, Chevrolet.

Lusty Growth For the companies that use market research it is already a way of life; they take it for granted that someday everyone will have to do the same. A big outfit like Procter & Gamble Co., the grand panjandrum of consumer goods selling, will put as much as $4-million a year into its own research and spend another $2-million on outside advice. A smaller marketer will shoot $12,000 a year just to get a report every 60 days on how its product is selling.

As management's purse strings loosen, more and more companies are joining this trend toward serious use of marketing research. A new survey of the field by the American Marketing Assn. offers some evidence of this dramatic growth:
☐ In the five years since AMA's last study, 502 companies responding to the questionnaire formed market research departments. That's more than in the 10 preceding years from 1948 to 1957 combined.
☐ Industry's outlay in the field is climbing. The mean annual expenditure for marketing research among consumer goods manufacturers nearly doubled in the five-year period—to $265,000. Four spent more than $1.7-million each. Among industrial goods makers, annual expenditure went up 44%, to $75,000.

Broader Ambitions As the market research expert finds more takers for his services, his confidence grows. He talks less and less in terms of modest fact-finding. More and more his vision expands to broad "information systems" that can be integrated into day-to-day management.

The market researcher's ambitions reach not only outward but upward. Today, he is not only answering broader and broader marketing questions; he is also taking a hand in framing the questions. He is not bashful, either, about suggesting the conclusions that should be drawn from his findings.

Thus, he is rapidly promoting himself, or being promoted by force of circumstances, to a place in management itself.

The top dog in market research today is the consultant—either on or off the payroll—who frames a theory of marketing, checks it out, pretests it, and watches as it is put into effect. Such a man cannot be classed as a mere technician. He is a strategist, and he is not content with a subordinate role.

WHO DOES WHAT IN THE FACT FACTORIES

The industry that serves the developing corporate appetite for market research is a fragmented affair, an industry of small businesses with only one sizable focus. The 300 or so companies and firms that make up its roster range from tiny (half a dozen employees) to large (5,000 employees). Most of the outfits grew up around a single, strong personality with a dominating idea, and most still retain the personal touch.

Their job is finding out things for marketers—and since there are so many pertinent things to find out and so many possible methods of doing it, it's not surprising that the industry is so split up.

Nor is it surprising that the biggest operator of them all is the one that performs the simplest and most basic function—keeping track of what goods are sold and where. This is the cornerstone of the business—the elemental, indispensable information that any marketer of fast-moving goods must have.

The company that purveys it is A.C. Nielsen Co. of Chicago. Its $45-million annual volume is nearly six times that of its nearest competitor, and a big hunk of the industry's $200-million-plus a year.

Counting, Counting Aside from its much-publicized broadcast measurement services—a relatively small part of its business—Nielsen offers a series of so-called Retail Indexes. The two largest measure the movement of goods in food stores and drug outlets, though Nielsen also pokes into appliance stores, camera retailers, and, most recently, discounters.

To represent the nation's food retailers, Nielsen uses a sample of 1,600 stores including units of every major grocery chain save A&P, which has always declined to cooperate. Teams of Nielsen field men are constantly in one store or another—counting packages on the shelf and cases in the back room, examining delivery invoices, noting special displays, cents-off deals, two-for-one offers, shelf prices.

Naturally, they count only products of Nielsen clients. Since these include all the top 50 food concerns, they count nearly everything in foods but meat and produce, plus a heaping handful of beauty and health aids, such as toothpaste and aspirin.

Charts and Tables   Every 60 days Nielsen reports. Early in May its account executives will stream out to marketing headquarters of clients, armed with charts and tables of the audit period ended Apr. 15.

In sessions averaging two hours, they will lay out a wealth of data: total inventory of a product as of Apr. 1; February and March sales and cases moved into retail stores during those months; distribution of a product broken down several ways—the maximum number of stores stocking it on date of audit and the number of stores stocking it analyzed by size. Clients get the same kind of information on competing products, lumped together or specified by name, as they wish.

Mounting Tab   The least you can spend on all this is about $12,000 a year, for a regional report covering about 25% of the national market. Cost for a national marketer averages $50,000 per "subject"—Nielsen's jargon for a single product group. A manufacturer of cold cereals buys one subject; if he wants data on hot cereals, too, that's another subject, and another $50,000. Prices vary as much as $20,000 up or down, depending on the data wanted; and a 10% discount for two or more subjects sweetens things for the multi-line producers.

That's the basic tab; on top of it the extras can really pile up. You can get monthly reports, data analyzed by as many as 20 sales territories, price and package-size differential studies on the effects of pricing under competitors or offering three package sizes instead of one—and so on until the annual tab per subject reaches $100,000. There are clients who shell out $2-million a year on retail indexes alone, before they even start on broadcast measurement.

Same, But Different   If Nielsen's reports are the bread and butter of market research, Audits & Surveys Co., Inc., one of its rising competitors, offers bread and butter with a little jam—or perhaps, some say, just margarine. It depends partly on your taste in figures.

Founded by statistician Solomon Dutka with a little money borrowed from his former boss Elmo Roper, A&S has rocketed in 10 years to No. 2 spot in the industry, with close to $8-million a year.

Its technique is to draw up a probability sample of business blocks in cities around the country and audit every store in these blocks. It counts by type of goods, not type of store, thus can pick up sales of razor blades, say, in candy, tobacco, and hardware stores and discount houses as well as in drug stores and supermarkets. This not only gives you a better reading on how goods are selling, Dutka argues, but also tells you how patterns of distribution are shifting.

The actual data clients get from the A&S sample of 5,300 stores are much the same as what Nielsen provides. The A&S service, however, is considerably less expensive. Where Nielsen's charges vary by size of client and number of brands reported, A&S charges a flat fee for each category, but sets a different price for each class. A good average figure is about $35,000 each. Extras can bring it up to $40,000.

Whose Figures?   Obviously, with such similar services, Nielsen and A&S have few clients in common. Yet, though Gillette Co. is a Nielsen client of long standing, its Paper Mate Div. uses A&S—because of the variety of outlets for pens.

Some find the Nielsen service too costly, or its reporting not broad enough for their distribution. Others criticize the A&S master sample. Nielsen's sample, heavily weighted toward large chain supermarkets, concentrates on the outlets that produce the high volume; so it gives reliable results for relatively small geographical areas as well as nationally. Critics say the A&S sample lacks this flexibility; if you want the sales of hair spray in a three-state Midwestern area, it may not pick up enough sales volume for an accurate reading.

To get around some of this A&S will over-sample in some market areas where requested. This seems to satisfy clients, because the list is large—and growing.

The Panel Show

Both Nielsen and A&S confine their counting to retail stores. Other market researchers prefer to count the customers. They do this, of course, by setting up a consumer panel consisting of a group of households, and keeping tabs on what these households buy and when they buy it.

The biggest panel operator, Market Research Corp. of America, uses the mails to keep track of 7,500 families every week. Each family submits a detailed diary of purchases in a broad range of product categories—food, household supplies, drugs, toiletries, and, most recently, textiles and clothing.

For a monthly report, and even more detailed quarterly summaries, MRCA gets anywhere from $25,000 to $60,000 a year per product class. It costs more for a product that's bought every week rather than once a month, more for a class with eight heavily competing brands, half a dozen sizes, and five flavors than for one with two or three brands.

A Fourth Dimension   What you get from MRCA looks on the surface much the same as what you get from Nielsen—total sales, share of market nationally and regionally. But the two-thirds of Nielsen's clients who also subscribe to MRCA obviously find something different. A panel taps a dimension of information unavailable to a store audit.

MRCA reports, for example, whether purchases are evenly distributed over the market or concentrated among a relatively small group, the economic level of purchasers, the amount of brand-switching. To a heavy user of advertising, it's apparent that this helps him pinpoint the kind of people who use his product —or are likely to—and to allocate his advertising dollars to the media that reach them best.

But an extra dimension can be tricky. The experts approach panel research with a grain of salt, because it depends on busy housewives remembering to put down everything in a diary and mail it in. A 5% gain or loss in share of market is phenomenal for packaged goods; but a diary sample can be subject to statistical variations up to 20%. When the sample error exceeds the fluctuation being measured, watch out.

The simple facts of who buys how much of what are basic; but to predict which way the customers will jump next you need to know why they make their decisions. If you can't quite rely on the customers themselves to tell you accurately, then what?

Head-shrinking

That's where the psychologists and sociologists of marketing research rush in, with their bag of clinical tricks with fancy names—projective techniques, depth interviews, semantic differential scales. They operate on the frontier of marketing knowledge, and turn up odd but often useful information.

Take the experience of the Nestle Co., which makes the little semi-sweet chocolate bits that go into tollhouse, or chocolate-larded cookies. Nestle proposed to use some excess bit-making capacity by fashioning bits of unsweetened chocolate and selling them for baking—so women wouldn't have to break up baking chocolate to melt it.

A little deep-dish research into women's attitudes disclosed that what they objected to wasn't the breaking up but the whole mess of melting. So the bit-making machines are still idle, but a semi-liquid baking chocolate is in the test markets.

From Couch and Clinic   Most of the techniques these researchers apply so assiduously stem, in one form or another, from pioneer work in academic psychology. The "depth interviewing" techniques, in which an individual is allowed to talk himself out for hours, without checklists or leading questions, is basically the tool of the psychoanalysts. People talk about how they feel: What do they think of when smoking? What kind of people do they think smoke cigarettes with filters?

Recently, a tobacco company commissioned just such a study among physicians. The aim: to find out what doctors really think about cigarette smoking and how hard they intend to push patients to give it up.

The so-called projective techniques are lifted intact from diagnostic clinical psychology. One—the semantic differential method—hands the subject a scale of words from good-to-bad, weak-to-masterful, lets him grade his feelings accordingly. This helps researchers measure subtle differences in thinking.

Some of the most striking results come from the thematic apperception tests, which acknowledge similarly that people may not reveal the truth about themselves in answer to direct questions, but often project their feelings onto another person. The classic example is the case of the lagging instant coffee sales, nearly a decade ago, which showed marketers that housewives must have at least the illusion of participation before they will accept convenience products.

Groups of housewives, presented with two shopping lists identical except for ground coffee on one, instant coffee on the other, loudly branded the compiler of the instant coffee list as lazy, neglectful of her family, far less of a housekeeper than the ground coffee buyer.

This basic result accounts for TV commercials advising the housewife to simmer her instant coffee "to bring out the flavor," and for prepared cake mixes requiring a fresh egg and cup of milk (when the powdered variety pre-added at the factory would serve as well).

How We Behave   Burleigh B. Gardner, who left the University of Chicago in 1946 to launch Social Research, Inc. (with backing from Sears, Roebuck & Co.) was a pioneer in another approach, the sociological—examining how people behave in groups and in the mass. He tries to explain—and predict—consumer behavior largely in terms of social class. One study concluded, for example, that women pick department stores that way; a Bloomingdale woman feels Macy's has too much of the common touch and Bergdorf Goodman is above her aspirations.

Study of behavior from a more mechanistic angle—now growing in popularity —derives from the behavioristic experimental psychology of the late John B. Watson. He made his reputation before World War I, then launched a new career in the early 1920s as J. Walter Thompson Co.'s first research director.

Watson's descendants deal with physiological effects of what goes on in the mind. Their "eye-cameras," registering eye movements in reading an advertisement, are a case in point; a slow rate of eye-blink is supposed to indicate aroused interest. A somewhat newer eye-camera, developed by Dr. E. H. Hess of the University of Chicago for an ad agency, records instead pupil dilation. In one experiment, 10 men mostly went wrong in identifying their own cigarette brand in a batch with marks disguised. But the investigator, noting pupil dilation while smoking, matched brand to man nine times in 10.

Few Dollars Though there's a lot of this sort of thing going on (a firm such as Daniel Yankelovitch, Inc., zoomed from seven employees to 150 in three years), it still doesn't bulk large in dollar totals or, for that matter, in the esteem of most professional researchers; one expert figures that $10-million a year probably overstates what is spent on all psychological and sociological market research. One reason is that the dog still has something of a bad name, from the days a decade ago when "motivational research" seemed a panacea to some, just downright chicanery to others.

Another reason is that it takes less money. The head-shrinkers believe they get good results with few heads. Elaborate reports based on fewer than 200 interviews are common, and you'd be surprised at the edifice that can be erected on only 50. That makes costs a good deal lower than for massive population samplings by the head-counters.

There are signs, though, that the depth interviewers are getting more ambitious—and more expensive. Every company now has its own sociologist or psychologist doing small reports with a few dozen interviews, says Burleigh Gardner, "so our clients are no longer satisfied. We have to get into big samples— maybe 2,000 interviews—and we have to make more sense out of them. We've been pushed into large-scale computer analyses, would you believe it?"

Automating Research

Gardner is clearly amazed to find himself in professional relationship with computer technology—and he is not alone. Yet the computer is the market researcher's latest toy; it removes his old limitations of manpower and office space. An IBM 7090, ripping off 15-million computations a minute, can take all the questionnaires you want, break out the social and economic characteristics of the population 16 ways, and come up with enough percentages to snow the analysts under.

But will a print-out the size of the Chicago phone book give you enough statistically valid and meaningful results to be worth it?

To make more significant use of computers, market researchers are beginning to explore a variety of complex mathematical techniques.

There is something called Bayesian decision theory, for example [*Business Week* Mar.24'62,p54]—a method of forecasting actions by manipulating statistical probabilities mathematically. Its special contribution is that probability values can be assigned not only to observable facts but to an executive's seasoned judgment. Instead of multiplying consumer interviews to predict the success of a new product, you can interview an experienced sales executive and add his opinion to the formula.

Models The rage these days is mathematical model-building, which in theory lets a marketer test the consequences of his decisions without actually committing resources. One research company that has put most of its eggs in that basket is Simulmatics Corp., a rather uneasy alliance of mathematicians, psychologists, and economists.

A well-publicized computer model of the U.S. Presidential electorate, set up with a view toward helping elect the late John F. Kennedy, launched Simulmatics as a commercial venture. Then it went into public opinion and economics, and now marketing models. One of the last is a brand-switching model called Dyna-Mark I. Given the results of a consumer panel of at least 1,000—with demographic data on each, observed for at least three successive purchases of a brand category—plus about $8,000 in cash, Simulmatics says it can:

☐ Tell where your new product's market share will likely end up.

☐ Show which competing brands are most vulnerable to your ads.

☐ Tell you whether your market is made up principally of loyal purchasers or of occasional purchasers.

PIONEERS AND PRIMA DONNAS

Except for Nielsen and Audits & Surveys, the concerns engaged in these many lines of market research seem to stay at annual volumes of $3-million or less—sometimes much less. Some claim the industry remains one of such small units because the long shadow of the one relative "giant"—Nielsen—keeps the sun off everyone else.

There are other reasons, though. Aside from Nielsen, A&S, and the biggest panel operators such as Market Research Corp. of America, research services are mostly hired for custom work—single studies or groups of related studies. This generates a relatively low volume.

Market researchers, too, are by and large prima donnas. The head men are fundamentally intellectuals whose chief joy in life is finding ways to get people to tell them interesting things; they shun administration, tend to fear size. The men they hire are also prima donnas, and this breeds conflict of personalities. The tendency is for talented employees to strike out on their own.

Man or Organization? So it happens that Louis Harris and Solomon Dutka once worked for Roper; Willard Simmons and Lester Frankel came from Politz.

Politz is generally regarded as one of the super-salesmen of the research business. He has a faculty for putting complex concepts into clear language, an original turn of mind, and the ability—common to the best of the research fraternity—to look at problems from an odd angle, with deceptively simple results.

But what would happen to his business if Politz had to retire? Nothing, he says; it's not just a man, but an organization. To his colleagues in the field, it looks more like an organization tied to a man. Sometimes the strings break. In recent weeks, at least half a dozen of Politz' top people have left to set up a new research unit at an ad agency.

Most other research services are also extensions of one or maybe two personalities. Of the famous firms, only Opinion Research Corp., founded by the late Claude E. Robinson, and Crossley S-D Surveys, Inc., by the now-retired Archibald M. Crossley, are still significant factors though the top man is gone.

Still Active   Most of the founders, however, are still active, or influential, though growing older. The business is so young that its pioneer generation is still around. Marketing research of even the most primitive kind is little older than the formation in 1911 by Charles C. Parlin, a Wisconsin school teacher, of a research department for Curtis Publishing Co. Until the late 1920s research simply meant analysis—juggling government statistics.

It was not until Crossley founded Crossley, Inc., in 1926 that modern methods of opinion sampling really got rolling. Elmo Roper set out on his own in 1933, George Gallup formed his own business in 1935.

Pragmatists   These men are all positive personalities. They are also all pragmatists, who entered the business because someone had an urgent need to find out something specific about a market. The pioneer's reputations depended on personalities and results, not technique. The methodology—this kind of sample or that kind of questionnaire—developed along the way, empirically.

MOVING IN ON MANAGEMENT

The individualism of the research pioneers has permeated the business right up to the present. In recent years, however, the center of gravity in marketing research has been moving from the research services and the ad agencies—which formed the first research departments and offered the earliest support to the independent research practitioners—to client headquarters. That's because marketing research is becoming less and less a one-shot affair aimed at a specific problem, and is beginning to achieve status as a legitimate business activity conducted on a continuing basis. As with any such activity, management wants it in the house, where it can be controlled.

A typical consumer goods company with about $50-million sales will spend about $100,000 a year on market research—half on staff payroll, half on outside services. An industrial goods maker of similar size will spend approximately half that total.

Paying the Freight   As you might expect, the bulk of the internal research budget —salaries—is spent on activities with only a tenuous connection with market research. To organization chartists, a market research section looks like a perfect place to dump a lot of figure-churning activities that have roosted for decades in other departments—economic analysis of government statistics, warehousing studies, analysis of district sales reports.

Though valuable, these are not really what modern marketing research is about. The crucial distinction is that they are fundamentally desk-bound, while marketing research, to its modern practitioners, is a field activity. To find out things, you sally out and ask people.

Yet these older statistical disciplines often pay the freight. One research department manager says economic analyses—which chew up two-thirds of his staff's time—yield enough savings in sales-force allocation studies, warehouse sitting, and such, to cover his whole budget.

Accepted   How well the research department uses its opportunities depends almost entirely on the quality of the man who runs it. Time was, notes one research man wryly, when a number of research directors were just "superannuated salesmen."

Today, many top company research directors possess the restless, probing minds, the impatience with pat answers always characteristic of the best research men. Respected by management, they have been able to get marketing research accepted on its own, not as an adjunct to advertising or sales. In short, research is a tool of management.

Hurdle   This attitude will have to become far more widespread, though, if market research is ever really to mature. In all the long chain of marketing intelligence, from consumer through interviewer, tabulator, report writer, and research director to client management, the most tenuous link is the last. It boils down to a question of belief: Does the company president trust his research man's figures?

The automobile business provides the most dramatic example, simply because serious miscalculation there is at once the most public and the most expensive. Ford, building the Falcon, sought a car that could compete with the burgeoning foreign-car market; it mounted a massive fact-finding drive to discover exactly what the consumer wanted. His wants and needs were translated minutely into the finished design, down to a curb weight within pounds of what the market said it wanted.

Purely from a research viewpoint, the car was right on target; Ford sold 500,000 in 1960, the Falcon's first year. But Ford, clinging to a notion that the car would have limited appeal—as something in the nature of a "schoolteacher's car"—ignored some clear signals from the consumer research data. One research report, pointing to a wider market, said: "The idea of an economy car seemed to appeal more to the higher-income, college-educated, multi-car younger families."

To the researchers, at least, it was clear that the Falcon had an appeal far broader than Ford thought. And so it did. The market was broad enough to cut heavily into sales of the standard Ford and seriously affect the company's profits.

Louder Voice   This helps to explain why, more and more often, research professionals are rejecting a passive role an an instrument of management, and are clamoring for a louder and more active voice in the corporate councils where research findings are acted on.

Many marketing researchers are content now to leave the physical assembly of data to mammoth fact-gatherers like Nielsen and to piecework interviewers and tabulators—if they can control the research process at an earlier and more meaningful level. As outside consultants, they seek a permanent relationship with clients that plugs them in to day-in, day-out decision making. Inside research directors mount a parallel drive to increase their role in management. Both talk in terms of complete information systems, and a role in corporate strategy.

Like other technicians before them—from public relations men to marketing specialists—researchers look toward the day when their particular angle of vision will influence the way that management sees things.

QUESTIONS

1. What kind of work activities does market research perform?

2. How can computer technology be used in the market research function?

3. How can information supplied by the market researcher be used in setting corporate strategy?

4. Why is it necessary for business firms to spend more than $200 million a year on marketing research activities?

Motivation Research

AUDREY LANGDON

Dow Chemical is now distributing the results of a recent motivation research study on automobile service station operators. Aim: to boost private-label antifreeze sales. Dow reasons that its motivation insights will help private-label packers do a more effective sales job on this group—the principal retail antifreeze outlet.

Dow's case is a timely example of the growing acceptance and use of MR by chemical process companies. Some are applying it to marketing, others to product development, and still others to problems involving morale and efficiency

Reprinted from the April 19, 1958 issue of *Chemical Week* by special permission. Copyrighted 1958 by McGraw-Hill, Inc.

of personnel. In all three areas, the MR approach is basically the same—depth interviewing to determine why people behave as they do.

Thus far, motivation research has been used mainly to determine why groups of people buy soaps, toothpastes, autos, etc. But MR's usefulness isn't limited to the consumer field, or even to marketing. Buyers of chemicals and equipment, as well as industrial personnel of all kinds, are potentially rewarding subjects of MR.

At first glance, it may be difficult to see how subsurface motivations can influence industrial chemical sales, new product development, product improvement or employee productivity, for instance. Consider these cases:

□ Corn Products Refining Co. recently used motivation research (plus more usual marketing research methods) to learn more about prevailing attitudes in customer companies; how these attitudes influence the purchasing of industrial starch products. The company found that the purchasing, production and research departments each had their own special reasons—call them motivations—for responding to Corn Products' (or competitors') sales efforts.

Once it knew the factors involved, Corn Products re-evaluated its marketing approach, geared it more closely to purchaser expectations.

□ General Electric Co. used motivation research to discover why direct-current motors were rejected by engineers for jobs that logically called for such motors. The company found that many otherwise-astute engineers regarded direct-current motors as "old fashioned." GE profited from its MR study, began an institutional advertising campaign aimed at correcting this mistaken image. Result: increased sales of dc motors.

□ Rensis Likert and Donald Pelz, two well-known social researchers at the University of Michigan Institute for Social Research, used MR on 300 scientists at the National Institutes of Health. They found that companies would do well to form research teams with varied scientific backgrounds and varied work experiences. Conclusion: applied researchers and basic researchers should mix with one another, exchange ideas and points of view. The study indicates that researchers work best in a well-balanced team—a finding that challenges the picture of the lonely, but happy, scientist.

Motivation research applied to marketing is an extension of market research, which seeks to discover: (1) who buys, (2) what they buy, (3) when they buy, (4) where they buy, (5) how they buy. Motivation researchers seek the answer to another question—why do customers buy?

Why customers say they buy may be poles apart from why they really buy. Knowing the real reasons can help management plan its sales strategy more effectively—it can provide clues to developing and marketing products that meet customer needs more precisely. Similarly, knowledge of what triggers executive or employee group actions can help management boost individual and group performance.

Discussing Dow's recent motivation survey, Director Percy Black of Social Attitude Survey, Inc. (New York, the company that conducted the study), says, "A motivation study is a depth interview, which attempts to go beyond the usual, and perhaps prejudiced, answers that often appear in ordinary surveys."

Parker Frisselle, Dow's market research manager, adds, "In essence, all market research serves one purpose—the substitution of information for conjecture, market intelligence for hunches. This acquisition of information can reveal new areas of market effort, stimulate new ideas. Research of this nature provides an indispensable service to the marketer."

Most consumer motivation studies undertaken by advertising agencies or MR consultants aim at improving the client's advertising or market effectiveness. To a lesser extent, but with effective results, consumer product development managers have applied MR in their work. Many chemical specialty products (shampoos, detergents, dentifrices, insecticides, soaps and proprietary drugs, for example), now on the market, were shaped to some extent by MR studies. MR has also influenced design of such diverse products as automobiles, cake mixes and fountain pens.

Because motivation research serves as a link between customers (at any level) and the manufacturer, it can be useful for keeping the laboratory product-development team in touch with the needs and attitudes of many different customer groups. Today, this function of MR could be particularly important to chemical process management.

These days, more than ever, the high risks involved in developing and introducing new products heightens management's need for a measure of customer acceptance of proposed or revised products prior to marketing, even prior to development. Motivation studies can provide this measure.

Here's a case in point. MR told Foster D. Snell, New York consultant firm, that it was not advisable for one of its clients to develop and market men's plastic overshoes. Depth interviewing of men revealed that plastic overshoes wouldn't sell, because they would be regarded by men as "too effeminate."

MR takes on further significance for chemical marketers, because of its ability to provide useful marketing ideas in situations involving many similar competing products—e.g., soaps, cigarettes, dentifrices, automobiles, etc. The greater the similarity between products, motivation research has shown, the less important is reason in making a selection.

This, of course, applies to competing chemical products that have the same chemical analysis, the same physical properties and, often, the same price. Depth interviewing can reveal the reasons for customers' product selections—their opinions of different companies and their products vs. competitors' products and companies.

Motivation research probes for useful ideas rather than statistical data. As a result, its findings are likely to lead to fresh marketing approaches, or to development of new products. By the same token, it can point to fresh approaches in understanding and handling employees.

In today's rough and competitive economy, the "me too" approach to problems in any of these areas is wisely avoided.

FOUR FUNDAMENTALS

In the growing stacks of MR case histories and findings, four basic concepts keep recurring. Management men who have already tangled with MR will recognize them. Those who are thinking of utilizing motivation research would do well to remember them:

1) Human behavior isn't always rational.

2) Products, like people, have individual personalities.

3) Companies, like families, have their own personalities.

4) To sell, a product must fill or stimulate some psychological or sociological need.

Consider each of these basic points in more detail.

Irrational Behavior They may like to think so, but industrial customers don't invariably pursue logical economic or psychological goals. People are people, whether they are selecting a new automobile or functioning as purchasing agents of large corporations. They have different and often conflicting goals for each of their roles: consumers, workers, customers, executives, voters, parents. To reach each goal, they follow a rationale determined by the dynamic balance of many economic, social and psychological pressures.

Dow was seeking to pinpoint these factors in its motivation study of service station dealers. The findings revealed that dealers hoped to be regarded as a combination of small businessman, mechanic, and "good Joe." Fear of failure hampers the average dealer's relationships with his customers, dilutes his feelings of loyalty to the company whose product he vends, limits his initiative as a businessman.

These are the pressures that keep him from pushing his company's brand of petroleum products, tires, batteries and accessories. To increase the dealer's loyalty to his company and its products, Dow recommends that its customers take a new approach to the service station dealer—one that will convince him that he's a respected, independent businessman who will receive the fullest cooperation and understanding from his petroleum company (which sells antifreeze to him).

Similar needs for acceptance and approval by people in the same occupational groups have led farmers to try new agricultural chemicals and physicians to prescribe new drugs.

Product Personalities Products, like people, have individual personalities. A product develops its personality from its physical characteristics, its price, the way it's advertised, where it's sold, the personality of the producing company and the product's performance in actual use. In addition, part of its personality results from the history of the product's competition and the competition's standing with the customer.

Successful brands usually have well-integrated personalities. The product's physical characteristics seem to customers to be in harmony with the product's performance, as well as with its advertising, its distribution and its packaging.

Company Personalities MR studies show that companies, like families, have personality patterns. Even the "objective" engineer's buying choices are influenced by images of companies' personalities. G. M. Basford, New York advertising and public relations agency, used MR to learn the factors influencing the selection of an engineering firm to build a plant.

Basford's discovery: chemical engineers limit their choices to engineering companies that seem "progressive," hence inspire confidence. Impressions of company personalities are carried over from engineers' college days—e.g., from classroom aids supplied by the engineering firm. Early impressions of a company were reinforced by its advertising, reputation with other engineers, and the types of projects it handles.

Filling Customer Needs Du Pont's Petroleum Chemicals Division found through MR that customers buy automobile polish to avoid appearing inferior in the eyes of others. That GE study on electric motor purchases revealed that engineers felt more "modern" when they were specifying alternating-current motors.

These two cases emphasize that a product must fill (or stimulate) a need, must perform its function satisfactorily in terms of the customer's evaluation of performance. Because customers judge performance in their own terms, not necessarily the manufacturer's terms, some marketers and product development men make the mistake of regarding customers as being incapable of distinguishing quality. It all comes down to this: products are subject to many standards of evaluation.

As these examples suggest, customers expect products to fill more than their nominal functions. Industrial and consumer products are also purchased as extensions of the user's personality, even as symbols of position.

Suppliers of industrial chemicals can learn through motivation studies to see their own products and company as customers see them—Corn Products Refining did this.

Little has been done with motivation research to fully develop these four basic concepts as they apply to chemical marketing.

Chemical process management can learn more about why industrial customers buy, what the hidden factors are that make them choose between comparable products selling for the same price. Chemicals producers and marketers who know more about these subsurface factors will be able to sell that much more effectively.

PROGRESS OR POISON?

Depth interviewing is still as hot an issue among marketing experts as it was when it first gained prominence in advertising and marketing circles about 10 years ago. The controversy is still pitched around techniques and benefits. Some marketing experts hail the depth interview as a key to economic progress. Others condemn it as a weapon to rob consumers of their political and social freedoms, as well as their hard-earned dollars. Arguments have fanned from New York luncheon tables to corporation conference rooms in San Francisco. And more than one best-seller has been distilled from the controversy.

The label "motivation research" arouses controversy partly because of sweeping claims made for it by a few leading practitioners and partly because of the sweeping power attributed to it by critics. Thus Corn Products' Director of Commercial Research Larry Gibson objects to use of the term in reference to his company's pioneering efforts in studying chemical sales. And, like Gibson, many informed process industry men prefer to use labels without derogatory connotations—"exploratory research," "attitude studies," or "surveys of customer needs."

Since motivation studies do not produce quantitative data, but rather direction and insight, they are useful in guiding the creative aspects of product development and marketing. Such qualitative research can never replace sound market analysis, of course. Process company executives must still have access to facts and figures obtained from market research.

Depth studies have one of the limitations of market research—they cannot predict absolutely the success of a new product. New motivations may evolve rapidly with changing economic conditions, public moods or ideas. Such new motivations may evolve during the brief period between the study and the marketing of a product. Technological, advertising and styling changes and other such factors may increase or decrease acceptance of a new or improved product. Especially where chemical specialties are concerned, customers have learned they can expect technological change; yearly improvements are almost demanded of the manufacturer.

Motivation research is out of the question for companies that are dominated by management's preferences rather than customers' or employees' opinions and needs. It can contribute little to a company that considers its customers too uninformed to be knowledgeable. And it can contribute almost nothing to a company that prefers the doubtful security of following the lead rather than taking it.

THE MEN BEHIND MR

In any research effort, success is usually proportional to the researcher's skill. The same holds true for MR. The best motivation researchers have solid backgrounds in the social sciences—psychology, sociology, anthropology—plus practical experience with survey techniques. Previous experience in the product or subject area under study is an asset. So is previous experience in industry.

Motivation interviewers are careful to appear neutral, interested, receptive and passive in the depth interview, but remain alert to many cues. Group interviewers, on the other hand, usually try to appear energetic and extroverted. Opinion leaders (top executives, physicians, government officials, association officers) give the best response to an apparent equal in professional status—the MR study director, for example.

No interview is ever conducted by a person the interviewee knows personally, or by someone with a vested interest in the outcome of the study that is being undertaken.

In conducting studies related to chemical product development or marketing, the motivation analyst doesn't need extensive knowledge of chemistry or engineering. His function is to interpret people's reactions in a form that management can use. Often the motivation analyst has the problem of winning management's confidence on the validity of the findings because MR results de-emphasize quantitative data.

Most good analysts steer clear of their own technical jargon in interpreting findings to management. Instead of relying on psychological or sociological terms, they prefer to explain their results in everyday language. Extreme psychoanalytical interpretations (e.g., to a woman, baking a cake is like giving birth to a baby) are avoided.

Motivation researchers are usually retained by process industry firms for a specific project. There's a long list of MR consulting firms, private consultants, or advertising agencies that have MR experts on their staffs.

SETTING THE TARGET

In setting up a motivation study, the researcher's first job is to define whose motivations are to be probed and for what purpose. Compared to market research studies, there are few rules for designing MR studies. Approaches are determined more by the subject matter covered and anticipated difficulties in bringing motivations to light. Questions posed by company administrators (in personnel, product development or marketing, depending on the area being studied) often help the motivation researcher to pinpoint his study.

Besides talking with executives, analysts like to confer with as many people who are concerned with the study area as possible; they're anxious to hear everyone's hunches and impressions about the possible motivations involved in the problem. In addition, where product development or marketing problems are the issue, motivation analysts review available market data and product sales reports to orient themselves to the problem.

Design of the MR study helps determine its size. Studies vary in size from 25 intensive personal interviews to 500 interviews with people in groups. The average is 100 personal interviews—and there's a trend in favor of large survey groups that are statistically controlled.

FEELINGS, NOT FACTS

The depth interview, in which people are encouraged to speak freely, sets MR apart from market surveys in which the researcher strives for consistency of data and accuracy of detail.

Most MR studies use the survey method, gathering personal interviews from representative people; some studies use group interviews of three or more people. These group interviews occasionally turn up social influences, prejudices and fears which are not apparent in sessions with individuals. Observing customers' behavior is another technique that is particularly useful for appraising a product's ease of handling.

Probing people's thoughts and feelings is a difficult process at best, since most adults have spent a lifetime suppressing numerous emotions. Even in speaking to an anonymous and sympathetic stranger such as the interviewer, people tend to give stereotyped reasons for their behavior. Motivation researchers try to penetrate such stereotypes to find out what they really mean to each individual.

To get people to talk even more honestly than they often talk to themselves, researchers use a combination of these techniques:

Technique 1 The interviewer starts with factual questions that are easy to answer, so as to establish a sense of mutual confidence. As the interview progresses, the questions veer away from facts and concentrate more on the person's feelings.

Showing the interviewee new products, new advertising, samples of competitive products, and requesting he demonstrate how a product is used are normal parts of the interview. Questions about age, education, occupation and other personal data are asked at the end of the interview.

Many interviewers note everything that happens during the session, even if the occurrences seem unrelated to the study. Unrelated items, on closer analysis, often hold important clues to motivations.

Technique 2 Instead of asking a person how he himself feels about something, he is asked to tell how other people feel. People are prone to attribute to others the feeling they are, for various reasons, unwilling to admit to themselves.

Technique 3 Instead of asking questions, the interviewer requests the person to tell a story about a photograph or sketch. Occasionally he asks him to fill in the missing lines of a cartoon. For concepts that are tough to express, the subject is asked to match pictures, associate words, or complete sentences. These are all ways of gaining insight into a person's motivations.

Technique 4 Interviewing procedure varies slightly where product tests and demonstrations are involved. The interviewer asks questions of the subject before he's exposed to the product, and then again after he uses it. During the actual use test, the interviewer remains in the background, observing reactions. Often, several observations of each individual are needed in order to obtain a "normal" picture. Intensive questions (Why did you do this? How do you feel about that?) come after the use test, or even at the end of a series of such tests.

FINDING THE PAYOFF

MR studies also differ from market studies in the handling and interpretation of gathered data. In MR, researchers generally try to preserve the color of the interviews, use quotations and incidents to illustrate the conclusions. Wherever possible, the language and terminology used by those interviewed are carried into the report, along with some expression of the results in more familiar industry terms.

Opening "factual" questions are seldom taken into account in analyzing MR results, since their function is merely to set the stage rather than to establish motivations. Considerable attention is usually given to the reaction of "extremist" groups, like heavy users, in contrast to nonusers. Their opinions usually offer excellent clues to a product's appeal.

Statistical tables and charts are rare in motivation reports. A thorough study often has at least one major finding that "everybody knew all along" but "had forgotten in the course of doing business." In fact, some MR studies serve only to confirm an idea that management has felt was true all along, but couldn't quite prove. A good study challenges orthodox thinking in a company, sometimes in an industry.

COUNTING THE COST

To a company with a strong market research program, the yearly dollar outlay for a thorough motivation research program will probably seem small. On the other hand, the cost per interview may seem high. A typical MR survey of 100 interviews compares in cost with a mail survey of 2,500 completed cases, or a door-to-door survey of 500 interviews. By studying each case in depth, however, motivation researchers are able to make valid observations using a smaller number of interviews.

Motivation techniques offer time savings that are important to cost-conscious CPI management men. MR can turn up ideas in a relatively short time, often half that required for market surveys. A large MR study covering an entire product line of one company took about three months to complete. A small study that focuses on a specific product could probably be completed in less than a month.

Though quick results are possible with MR, the researcher must take up the valuable time of administrators. Few companies have MR men on their R&D or marketing staffs. The study director, whether a consultant or a regular employee, should report to the administrator who has final say-so in making decisions in the area of the study. This might be the head of R&D, technical service, marketing, market research, advertising, production or personnel.

After findings have been reported, it takes more time for management to take action on them. MR ideas are turned into prototype products, marketing campaigns, or changes in personnel policies. When management is satisfied with the prototypes, it can go full-speed ahead in applying the MR findings on a larger scale. Many management men who question the efficacy of motivation research are usually surprised to find that, with MR working for them, they can bring the thinking and feeling of their personnel, customers and the consuming public into their laboratories, offices and conference rooms.

AN ACTUAL INTERVIEW

What does an MR interview sound like? Here's a brief excerpt from an actual session with a development engineer in a firm that uses pigments in making rubber and plastic products for the building industry. The interviewer represents a pigment firm.

Interviewer. "Then you're very interested in setting up an automatic handling system. Will you tell me more about the problems you've run into in your work?"

Engineer. "Well, I've been having trouble developing automatic handling of pigments. I'd like to be able to control the amounts of pigment used per batch. For one thing, this would cut down on the amount of spoilage of finished materials."

Interviewer. "That sounds quite worthwhile. What seems to be the trouble?"

Engineer. "Dusting is a big problem. So far as I know, there's no machine available today that can handle finely powdered materials, like pigments. Somebody should make pigments in pellet form instead of powdered. That would be a great idea."

Interviewer. "If some company developed a line of pigments in pellet form, would you recommend buying them?"

Engineer. "I sure would. Any vendor who solves customer problems should be encouraged. Unfortunately, though, I don't handle purchasing and I never get to see salesmen. I don't even have much to say on raw material specifications."

Interviewer. "Who has the most to say about purchasing?"

Engineer. "The executive vice-president. Nobody ever comes to see me. Only one man counts, the executive vice-president. He's everybody's boss."

Interviewer. "Very interesting. What do you think of technical service programs?"

Engineer. "I don't know of any company that has one on pigments. Most companies have good chemists and engineers on their staffs, but they aren't familiar with my technical problems."

Interviewer. "Do you think technical service programs are for the benefit of the customer or the supplier?"

Engineer. "If they don't benefit the supplier, they don't last very long."

From this MR session, an interviewer would recommend, for example, that the pigment company's management consider: (1) making pigments in pellet and liquid form, (2) seeking to develop pigments that dust less, (3) more effective publicity on its technical service program, (4) a new sales approach directed to development personnel in various industries.

QUESTIONS

1. Explain why business firms spend millions of dollars each year on motivation research.

2. What are the limitations of motivation research?

3. What is the difference between market research and motivation research?

4. Compare and contrast the different motivation research interviewing techniques.

Systems Approach to Marketing

LEE ADLER

More and more businessmen today recognize that corporate success is, in most cases, synonymous with marketing success and with the coming of age of a new breed of professional managers. They find it increasingly important not only to pay lip service to the marketing concept but to do something about it in terms of (a) customer orientation, rather than navel-gazing in the factory, (b) organizational revisions to implement the marketing concept, and (c) a more orderly approach to problem solving.

In an increasing number of companies we see more conscious and formal efforts to apply rational, fact-based methods for solving marketing problems, and greater recognition of the benefits these methods offer. While these benefits may be newly realized, there is nothing new about the underlying philosophy; in the parlance of military men and engineers, it is the systems approach. For, whether we like it or not, marketing is, by definition, a system, if we accept Webster's definition of system as "an assemblage of objects united by some form of regular interaction or interdependence." Certainly, the interaction of such "objects" as product, pricing, promotion, sales calls, distribution, and so on fits the definition.

There is an expanding list of sophisticated applications of systems theory— and not in one but in many sectors of the marketing front. The construction of mathematical and/or logical models to describe, quantify, and evaluate alternate marketing strategies and mixes is an obvious case in point. So, too, is the formulation of management information systems[1] and of marketing plans with built-in performance measurements of predetermined goals. But no less vital is the role of the systems approach in the design and sale of products and services. When J. P. Stevens Company color-harmonizes linens and bedspreads, and towels and bath mats, it is creating a product system. And when Avco Corporation sells systems management to the space exploration field, involving the marriage of many scientific disciplines as well as adherence to budgetary constraints, on-time performance, and quality control, it is creating a *service* system.

In this article I shall discuss the utilization of the systems concept in marketing in both quantitative and qualitative ways with case histories drawn from various industries. In doing so, my focus will be more managerial and philosophical than technical, and I will seek to dissipate some of the hocus-pocus, glamor, mystery, and fear which pervade the field. The systems concept is not esoteric or "science fiction" in nature (although it sometimes *sounds* that way in promotional descriptions). Its advantages are not subtle or indirect; as we shall see, they are as real and immediate as decision making itself. The limitations are also real, and these, too, will be discussed.

From *Harvard Business Review,* Vol. 45, No. 3, May-June 1967, pp. 105-118. © 1967 by the President and Fellows of Harvard College; all rights reserved.
[1]See, for example, Donald F. Cox and Robert E. Good, "How to Build a Marketing Information System," [*Harvard Business Review,* Vol. 45, No. 3, May-June 1967, p. 145].

PROMISING APPLICATIONS

Now let us look at some examples of corporate application of the systems approach. Here we will deal with specific parts or "subsystems" of the total marketing system. Exhibit 1 is a schematic portrayal of these relationships.

Products & Services

The objective of the systems approach in product management is to provide a complete "offering" to the market rather than merely a product. If the purpose of business is to create a customer at a profit, then the needs of the customer must be carefully attended to; we must, in short, study what the customer is buying or wants to buy, rather than what we are trying to sell.

In the consumer products field we have forged ahead in understanding that the customer buys nutrition (not bread), beauty (not cosmetics), warmth (not fuel oil). But in industrial products this concept has been slower in gaining a foothold. Where it has gained a foothold, it expresses itself in two ways: the creation of a complete product system sold (1) as a unit, or (2) as a component or components which are part of a larger consumption system.

Perhaps the most eloquent testimony to the workability and value of the systems approach comes from companies that have actually used it. For a good example let us turn to the case of The Carborundum Company. This experience

EXHIBIT 1. MARKETING SUBSYSTEMS AND THE TOTAL SYSTEM

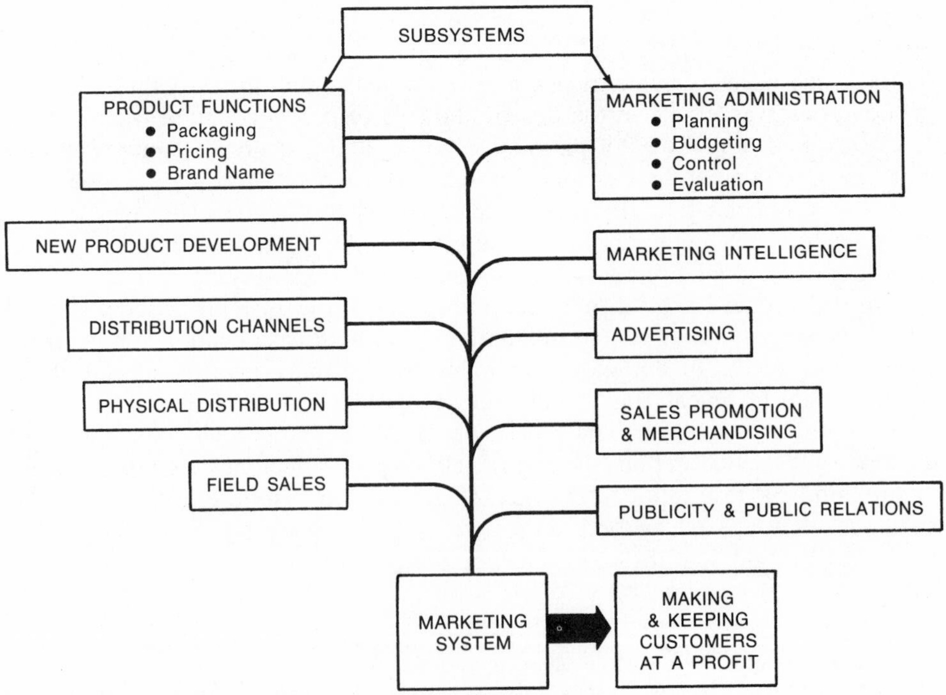

is especially noteworthy because it comes from industrial marketing, where, as just indicated, progress with the systems concept has generally been slow.

Birth of the Concept Founded in 1894, the company was content for many years to sell abrasives. It offered an extremely broad line of grinding wheels, coated abrasives, and abrasive grain, with a reputed capacity for 200,000 different products of varying type, grade, and formulation. But the focus was on the product.

In the mid-1950's, Carborundum perceived that the market for abrasives could be broadened considerably if—looking at abrasives through customers' eyes—it would see the product as fitting into *metal polishing, cleaning,* or *removal systems.* Now Carborundum is concerned with all aspects of abrading— the machine, the contact wheel, the workpiece, the labor cost, the overhead rate, the abrasive, and, above all, the customer's objective. In the words of Carborundum's president, W. H. Wendel:

> *That objective is never the abrasive per se, but rather the crea-*
> *tion of a certain dimension, a type of finish, or a required shape,*
> *always related to a minimum cost. Since there are many variables*
> *to consider, just one can be misleading. To render maximum*
> *service, Carborundum (must offer) a complete system.*[2]

Organizational Overhaul To offer such a system, management had to overhaul important parts of the organization:

(1) The company needed to enhance its knowledge of the total system. As Wendel explains:

> *We felt we had excellent knowledge of coated abrasive products,*
> *but that we didn't have the application and machine know-how*
> *in depth. To be really successful in the business, we had to know*
> *as much about the machine tools as we did the abrasives.*[3]

To fill this need, Carborundum made three acquisitions—The Tysaman Machine Company, which builds heavy-duty snagging, billet grinding, and abrasive cut-off machines; Curtis Machine Company, a maker of belt sanders; and Pangborn Corporation, which supplied systems capability in abrasive blast cleaning and finishing.

(2) The company's abrasive divisions were reorganized, and the management of them was realigned to accommodate the new philosophy and its application. The company found that *centering responsibility for the full system in one profit center* proved to be the most effective method of coordinating approaches in application engineering, choice of distribution channels, brand identification, field sales operations, and so forth. This method was particularly valuable for integrating the acquisitions into the new program.

(3) An Abrasives Systems Center was established to handle development work and to solve customer problems.

---

[2]"Abrasive Maker's Systems Approach Opens New Markets," *Steel,* December 27, 1965, p. 38.
   [3]*ibid.*

(4) Technical conferences and seminars were held to educate customers on the new developments.

(5) Salesmen were trained in machine and application knowledge.

Planning   A key tool in the systems approach is planning—in particular, the use of what I like to call "total business plans." (This term emphasizes the contrast with company plans that cover only limited functions.) At Carborundum, total business plans are developed with extreme care by the operating companies and divisions. Very specific objectives are established, and then detailed action programs are outlined to achieve these objectives. The action programs extend throughout the organization, including the manufacturing and development branches of the operating unit. Management sets specific dates for the completion of action steps and defines who is responsible for them. Also, it carefully measures results against established objectives. This is done both in the financial reporting system and in various marketing committees.

Quantitative Methods   Carborundum has utilized various operations research techniques, like decision tree analysis and PERT, to aid in molding plans and strategies. For example, one analysis, which concerned itself with determining the necessity for plant expansion, was based on different possible levels of success for the marketing plan. In addition, the computer has been used for inventory management, evaluation of alternate pricing strategies for systems selling, and the measurement of marketing achievements against goals.

It should be noted, though, that these quantitative techniques are management tools only and that much of the application of systems thinking to the redeployment of Carborundum's business is qualitative in nature.

Gains Achieved   As a consequence of these developments, the company has opened up vast new markets. To quote Carborundum's president again:

> *Customers don't want a grinding wheel, they want metal removed. . . . The U.S. and Canadian market for abrasives amounts to $700 million a year. But what companies spend on stock removal—to bore, grind, cut, shape, and finish metal— amounts to $30 billion a year.*[4]

Illustrating this market expansion in the steel industry is Carborundum's commercial success with three new developments—hot grinding, an arborless wheel to speed metal removal and cut grinding costs, and high-speed conditioning of carbon steel billets. All represent conversions from nonabrasive methods. Carborundum now also finds that the close relationship with customers gives it a competitive edge, opens top customer management doors, gains entree for salesmen with prospects they had never been able to "crack" before. Perhaps the ultimate accolade is the company's report that customers even come to the organization itself, regarding it as a consultant as well as a supplier.

---

[4]"Carborundum Grinds at Faster Clip," *Business Week*, July 23, 1966, pp. 58, 60.

Profitable Innovation

The intense pressure to originate successful new products cannot be met without methodologies calculated to enhance the probabilities of profitable innovation. The systems approach has a bearing here, too. Exhibit 2 shows a model for "tracking" products through the many stages of ideation, development, and testing to ultimate full-scale commercialization. This diagram is in effect a larger version of the "New Product Development" box in Exhibit 1.

Observe that this is a logical (specifically, sequential), rather than numerical, model. While some elements of the total system (e.g., alternate distribution channels and various media mixes) can be analyzed by means of operations research techniques, the model has not been cast in mathematical terms. Rather, the flow diagram as a whole is used as a checklist to make sure "all bases are covered" and to help organize the chronological sequence of steps in new product development. It also serves as a conceptual foundation for formal PERT application, should management desire such a step, and for the gradual development of a series of equations linking together elements in the diagrams, should it seem useful to experiment with mathematical models.

Marketing Intelligence

The traditional notion of marketing research is fast becoming antiquated. For it leads to dreary chronicles of the past rather than focusing on the present and shedding light on the future. It is particularistic, tending to concentrate on the study of tiny fractions of a marketing problem rather than on the problem as a whole. It lends itself to assuaging the curiosity of the moment, to fire-fighting, to resolving internecine disputes. It is a slave to technique. I shall not, therefore, relate the term *marketing research* to the systems approach—although I recognize, of course, that some leading businessmen and writers are breathing new life and scope into the ideas referred to by that term.

The role of the systems approach is to help evolve a *marketing intelligence* system tailored to the needs of each marketer. Such a system would serve as the ever-alert nerve center of the marketing operation. It would have these major characteristics:

☐ Continuous surveillance of the market.
☐ A team of research techniques used in tandem.
☐ A network of data sources.
☐ Integrated analysis of data from the various sources.
☐ Effective utilization of automatic data-processing equipment to distill mountains of raw information speedily.
☐ Strong concentration not just on reporting findings but also on practical, action-oriented recommendations.

Concept in Use   A practical instance of the use of such an intelligence system is supplied by Mead Johnson Nutritionals (division of Mead Johnson & Company), manufacturers of Metrecal, Pablum, Bib, Nutrament, and other nutritional specialties. As Exhibit 3 shows, the company's Marketing Intelligence Department has provided information from these sources:

EXHIBIT 2. WORK FLOW AND SYSTEMS CHART FOR MANAGEMENT OF NEW PRODUCTS

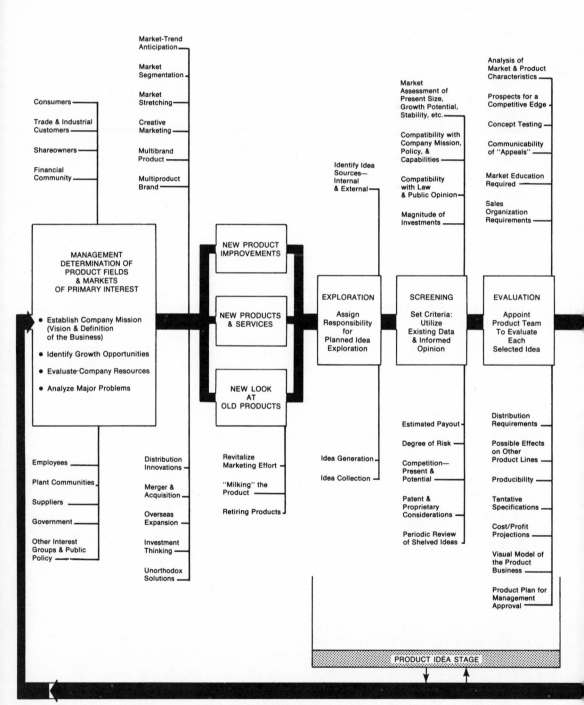

Note: This flow diagram was developed by Paul E. Funk, President, and the staff of McCann/ITSM, Inc.

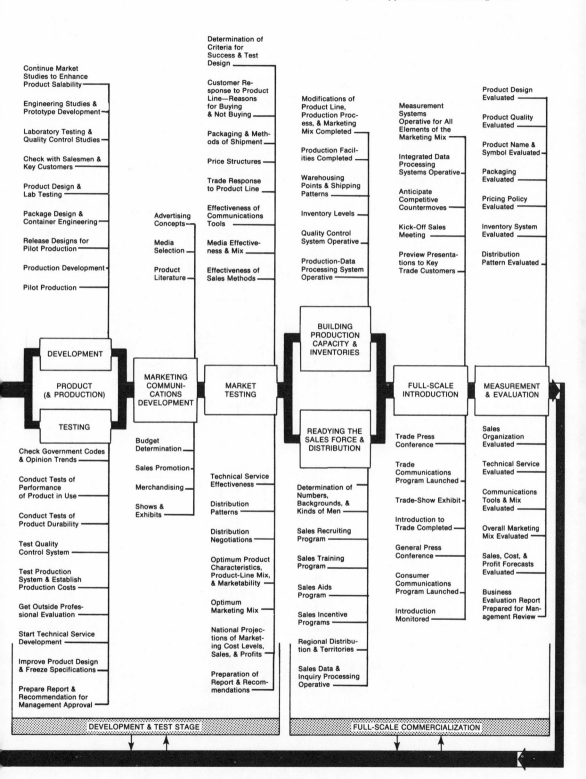

Determination of Criteria for Success & Test Design

Continue Market Studies to Enhance Product Salability

Engineering Studies & Prototype Development

Laboratory Testing & Quality Control Studies

Check with Salesmen & Key Customers

Product Design & Lab Testing

Package Design & Container Engineering

Release Designs for Pilot Production

Production Development

Pilot Production

Customer Response to Product Line—Reasons for Buying & Not Buying

Packaging & Methods of Shipment

Price Structures

Trade Response to Product Line

Effectiveness of Communications Tools

Media Effectiveness & Mix

Effectiveness of Sales Methods

Advertising Concepts

Media Selection

Product Literature

Modifications of Product Line, Production Process, & Marketing Mix Completed

Production Facilities Completed

Warehousing Points & Shipping Patterns

Inventory Levels

Quality Control System Operative

Production-Data Processing System Operative

Measurement Systems Operative for All Elements of the Marketing Mix

Integrated Data Processing Systems Operative

Anticipate Competitive Countermoves

Kick-Off Sales Meeting

Preview Presentations to Key Trade Customers

Product Design Evaluated

Product Quality Evaluated

Product Name & Symbol Evaluated

Packaging Evaluated

Pricing Policy Evaluated

Inventory System Evaluated

Distribution Pattern Evaluated

DEVELOPMENT

PRODUCT (& PRODUCTION)

TESTING

MARKETING COMMUNICATIONS DEVELOPMENT

MARKET TESTING

BUILDING PRODUCTION CAPACITY & INVENTORIES

READYING THE SALES FORCE & DISTRIBUTION

FULL-SCALE INTRODUCTION

MEASUREMENT & EVALUATION

Check Government Codes & Opinion Trends

Conduct Tests of Performance of Product in Use

Conduct Tests of Product Durability

Test Quality Control System

Test Production System & Establish Production Costs

Get Outside Professional Evaluation

Start Technical Service Development

Improve Product Design & Freeze Specifications

Prepare Report & Recommendation for Management Approval

Budget Determination

Sales Promotion

Merchandising

Shows & Exhibits

Technical Service Effectiveness

Distribution Patterns

Distribution Negotiations

Optimum Product Characteristics, Product-Line Mix, & Marketability

Optimum Marketing Mix

National Projections of Marketing Cost Levels, Sales, & Profits

Preparation of Report & Recommendations

Determination of Numbers, Backgrounds, & Kinds of Men

Sales Recruiting Program

Sales Training Program

Sales Aids Program

Sales Incentive Programs

Regional Distribution & Territories

Sales Data & Inquiry Processing Operative

Trade Press Conference

Trade Communications Program Launched

Trade-Show Exhibit

Introduction to Trade Completed

General Press Conference

Consumer Communications Program Launched

Introduction Monitored

Sales Organization Evaluated

Technical Service Evaluated

Communications Tools & Mix Evaluated

Overall Marketing Mix Evaluated

Sales, Cost, & Profit Forecasts Evaluated

Business Evaluation Report Prepared for Management Review

DEVELOPMENT & TEST STAGE

FULL-SCALE COMMERCIALIZATION

☐ A continuing large-scale consumer market study covering attitudinal and behavioral data dealing with weight control.

☐ Nielsen store audit data, on a bimonthly basis.

☐ A monthly sales audit conducted among a panel of 100 high-volume food stores in 20 markets to provide advance indications of brand share shifts.

☐ Supermarket warehouse withdrawal figures from Time, Inc.'s new service, Selling Areas-Marketing, Inc.

☐ Salesmen's weekly reports (which, in addition to serving the purposes of

EXHIBIT 3. MEAD JOHNSON'S MARKETING INTELLIGENCE SYSTEM

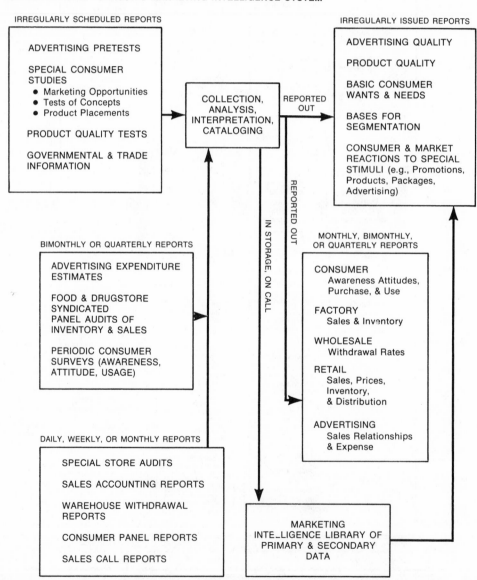

sales management control, call for reconnaissance on competitive promotions, new product launches, price changes, and so forth).

☐ Advertising expenditure data, by media class, from the company's accounting department.

☐ Figures on sales and related topics from company factories.

☐ Competitive advertising expenditure and exposure data, supplied by the division's advertising agencies at periodic intervals.

☐ A panel of weight-conscious women.

To exemplify the type of outputs possible from this system, Mead Johnson will be able, with the help of analyses of factory sales data, warehouse withdrawal information, and consumer purchases from Nielsen, to monitor transactions at each stage of the flow of goods through the distribution channel and to detect accumulations or developing shortages. Management will also be able to spot sources of potential problems in time to deal with them effectively. For example, if factory sales exceed consumer purchases, more promotional pressure is required. By contrast, if factory sales lag behind consumer purchases, sales effort must be further stimulated.

Similarly, the company has been able to devise a practical measurement of advertising's effectiveness in stimulating sales—a measurement that is particularly appropriate to fast-moving packaged goods. By relating advertising outlays and exposure data to the number of prospects trying out a product during a campaign (the number is obtained from the continuing consumer survey), it is possible to calculate the advertising cost of recruiting such a prospect. By persisting in such analyses during several campaigns, the relative value of alternative advertising approaches can be weighed. Since measurement of the sales, as opposed to the communications, effects of promotion is a horrendously difficult, costly, and chancy process, the full significance of this achievement is difficult to exaggerate.

Benefits Realized   Mead Johnson's marketing intelligence system has been helpful to management in a number of ways. In addition to giving executives early warning of new trends and problems, and valuable insights into future conditions, it is leading to a systematic *body* of knowledge about company markets rather than to isolated scraps of information. This knowledge in turn should lead ultimately to a theory of marketing in each field that will explain the mysteries that baffle marketers today. What is more, the company expects that the system will help to free its marketing intelligence people from fire-fighting projects so that they can concentrate on long-term factors and eventually be more consistently creative.

Despite these gains, it is important to note that Mead Johnson feels it has a long road still to travel. More work is needed in linking individual data banks. Conceptual schemes must be proved out in practice; ways must still be found to reduce an awesome volume of data, swelled periodically by new information from improved sources, so as to make intelligence more immediately accessible to decision makers. And perhaps the biggest problem of the moment, one underlying some of the others, is the difficulty in finding qualified marketing-oriented programmers.

Physical Distribution

A veritable revolution is now taking place in physical distribution. Total systems are being evolved out of the former hodgepodge of separate responsibilities, which were typically scattered among different departments of the same company. These systems include traffic and transportation, warehousing, materials handling, protective packaging, order processing, production planning, inventory control, customer service, market forecasting, and plant and warehouse site selection. Motivating this revolution are the computer, company drives to reduce distribution costs, and innovations in transportation, such as jet air freight, container ships, the interstate highway network, and larger and more versatile freight cars.

Distribution is one area of marketing where the "bread-and-butter" uses of the computer are relatively easily deployed for such functions as order processing, real-time inventory level reports, and tracking the movements of goods. Further into the future lie mathematical models which will include every factor bearing on distribution. Not only will packaging, materials handling, transportation and warehouse, order processing, and related costs be considered in such models; also included will be sales forecasts by product, production rates by factory, warehouse locations and capacities, speeds of different carriers, etc. In short, a complete picture will be developed for management.

Program in Action The experiences of the Norge Division of Borg-Warner Corporation point up the values of the systems approach in physical distribution. The firm was confronted externally with complaints from its dealers and distributors, who were trying to cope with swollen inventories and the pressures of "loading deals." Internally, because coordination of effort between the six departments involved in distribution was at a minimum, distribution costs and accounts receivable were mounting persistently.

To grapple with this situation, Norge undertook a comprehensive analysis of its distribution system. Out of this grew a new philosophy. A company executive has described the philosophy to me as follows:

> *An effective system of physical distribution cannot begin at the end of the production line. It must also apply at the very beginning of the production process—at the planning, scheduling, and forecasting stages. Logistics, in short, is part of a larger marketing system, not just an evaluation of freight rates. We must worry not only about finished refrigerators, but also about the motors coming from another manufacturer, and even about where the copper that goes into those motors will come from. We must be concerned with total flow.*

To implement this philosophy, the appliance manufacturer took the following steps:

(1) It reorganized the forecasting, production scheduling, warehousing, order processing, and shipping functions into *one* department headed by a director of physical distribution.

(2) The management information system was improved with the help of EDP equipment tied into the communications network. This step made it possible to

process and report data more speedily on orders received, inventory levels, and the actual movement of goods.

(3) Management used a combination of computer and manual techniques to weigh trade-offs among increased costs of multiple warehousing, reduced long-haul freight and local drayage costs, reduced inventory pipeline, and the sales value of an improved "total" product offering. Also assessed were trade-offs between shorter production runs and higher inventory levels, thereby challenging the traditional "wisdom" of production-oriented managers that the longer the run, the better.

(4) The company is setting up new regional warehouses.

As a result of these moves, Norge has been able to lower inventories throughout its sales channels and to reduce accounts receivable. These gains have led, in turn, to a reduction of the company's overall investment and a concomitant increase in profitability.

It is essential to note that even though Norge has used operations research as part of its systems approach, many aspects of the program are qualitative. Thus far, the company has found that the development of an all-encompassing model is not warranted because of (a) the time and cost involved, (b) the probability that the situation will change before the model is completed, (c) a concern that such a model would be so complex as to be unworkable, and (d) the difficulty of testing many of the assumptions used. In addition, management has not tried to quantify the impact of its actions on distributor and retailer attitudes and behavior, possible competitive countermoves, and numerous other factors contributing to results.

Toward Total Integration

The integration of systems developed for product management, product innovation, marketing intelligence, physical distribution, and the other functions or "subsystems" embraced by the term *marketing* creates a total marketing system. Thus, marketing plans composed according to a step-by-step outline, ranging from enunciation of objectives and implementational steps to audit and adjustment to environmental changes, constitute a complete application of systems theory. Further, as the various subsystems of the overall system are linked quantitatively, so that the effect of modifications in one element can be detected in other elements, and as the influences of competitive moves on each element are analyzed numerically, then the total scheme becomes truly sophisticated.

PLUSES & MINUSES

Two elements underlie the use and benefits of systems theory—order and knowledge. The first is a homely virtue, the second a lofty goal. Marketing is obviously not alone among all human pursuits in needing them; but, compared with its business neighbors, production and finance, marketing's need is acute indeed. The application of the systems concept can bring considerable advantages. It offers:

☐ A methodical problem-solving orientation—with a broader frame of reference so that all aspects of a problem are examined.

☐ Coordinated deployment of all appropriate tools of marketing.

☐ Greater efficiency and economy of marketing operations.

☐ Quicker recognition of impending problems, made possible by better understanding of the complex interplay of many trends and forces.

☐ A stimulus to innovation.

☐ A means of quantitatively verifying results.

These functional benefits in turn yield rich rewards in the marketplace. The most important gains are:

A deeper penetration of existing markets—As an illustration, the Advanced Data Division of Litton Industries has become a leader in the automatic revenue control business by designing systems meshing together "hardware" and "software."

A broadening of markets—For example, the tourist industry has attracted millions of additional travelers by creating packaged tours that are really product-service systems. These systems are far more convenient and economical than anything the consumer could assemble himself.

An extension of product lines—Systems management makes it more feasible to seek out compatibilities among independently developed systems. Evidence of this idea is the work of automatic control system specialists since the early 1950's.[5] Now similar signs are apparent in marketing. For example, Acme Visible Records is currently dovetailing the design and sale of its record-keeping systems with data-processing machines and forms.

A lessening of competition or a strengthened capacity to cope with competition—The systems approach tends to make a company's product line more unique and attractive. Carborundum's innovation in metal-removal systems is a perfect illustration of this.

Problems in Practice

Having just enumerated in glowing terms the benefits of the systems approach, realism demands that I give "equal time" to the awesome difficulties its utilization presents. There is no better evidence of this than the gulf between the elegant and sophisticated models with which recent marketing literature abounds and the actual number of situations in which those models really work. For the truth of the matter is that we are still in the foothills of this development, despite the advances of a few leaders. Let us consider some of the obstacles.

Time & Manpower Costs First of all, the systems approach requires considerable time to implement; it took one company over a year to portray its physical distribution system in a mathematical model before it could even begin to solve its problems. RCA's Electronic Data Processing Division reports models taking three to five years to build, after which holes in the data network have to be filled and the model tested against history. Add to this the need for manpower of exceptional intellectual ability, conceptual skills, and specialized education— manpower that is in exceedingly short supply. Because the problems are complex

---

[5]See *Automatic and Manual Control: Papers Contributed to the Conference at Cranford, 1951,* edited by A. Tustin (London, Butterworth's Scientific Publications, 1952).

and involve all elements of the business, one man alone cannot solve them. He lacks the knowledge, tools, and controls. And so many people must be involved. It follows that the activation of systems theory can be very costly.

Absence of "Canned" Solutions   Unlike other business functions where standardized approaches to problem solving are available, systems must be tailored to the individual situation of each firm. Even the same problem in different companies in the same industry will frequently lead to different solutions because of the impact of other inputs, unique perceptions of the environment, and varying corporate missions. These factors, too, compound time and expense demands.

"Net Uncertainties"   Even after exhaustive analysis, full optimization of a total problem cannot be obtained. Some uncertainty will always remain and must be dealt with on the basis of judgment and experience.

Lack of Hard Data   In the world of engineering, the systems evolved to date have consisted all or mostly of machines. Systems engineers have been wise enough to avoid the irrationalities of man until they master control of machines. Marketing model-builders, however, have not been able to choose, for the distributor, salesman, customer, and competitor are central to marketing. We must, therefore, incorporate not only quantitative measures of the dimensions of things and processes (e.g., market potential, media outlays, and shipping rates), but also psychological measures of comprehension, attitudes, motivations, intentions, needs—yes, even psychological measures of physical behavior. What is needed is a marriage of the physical and behavioral sciences—and we are about as advanced in this blending of disciplines as astronomy was in the Middle Ages.

Consider the advertising media fields as an instance of the problem:

A number of advertising agencies have evolved linear programming or simulation techniques to assess alternate media schedules. One of the key sets of data used covers the probabilities of exposure to all or part of the audience of a TV program, magazine, or radio station. But what is exposure, and how do you measure it? What is optimum frequency of exposure, and how do you measure it? How does advertising prevail on the predispositions and perceptions of a potential customer? Is it better to judge advertising effects on the basis of exposure opportunity, "impact" (whatever that is), messages retained, message comprehension, or attitude shifts or uptrends in purchase intentions? We do not have these answers yet.

Even assuming precise knowledge of market dimensions, product performance, competitive standing, weights of marketing pressure exerted by direct selling, advertising and promotion, and so on, most marketers do not yet know, except in isolated cases, how one force will affect another. For instance, how does a company "image" affect the setting in which its salesmen work? How does a company's reputation for service affect customer buying behavior?

Nature of Marketing Men   Man is an actor on this stage in another role. A good many marketing executives, in the deepest recesses of their psyches, are artists, not analysts. For them, marketing is an art form, and, in my opinion, they really do not want it to be any other way. Their temperament is antipathetic to system, order, knowledge. They enjoy flying by the seat of their pants—though you will never get them to admit it. They revel in chaos, abhor facts, and fear research. They hate to be trammeled by written plans. And they love to spend, but are loathe to assess the results of their spending.

Obviously, such men cannot be sold readily on the value and practicality of the systems approach! It takes time, experience, and many facts to influence their thinking.

Surmounting the Barriers

All is not gloom, however. The barriers described are being overcome in various ways. While operations research techniques have not yet made much headway in evolving total marketing systems and in areas where man is emotionally engaged, their accomplishments in solving inventory control problems, in sales analysis, in site selection, and in other areas have made many businessmen more sympathetic and open-minded to them.

Also, mathematical models—even the ones that do not work well yet—serve to bolster comprehension of the need for system as well as to clarify the intricacies among subsystems. Many models are in this sense learning models; they teach us how to ask more insightful questions. Moreover, they pinpoint data gaps and invite a more systematized method for reaching judgments where complete information does not exist. Because the computer abhors vague generalities, it forces managers to analyze their roles, objectives, and criteria more concretely. Paradoxically, it demands more, not less, of its human masters.

Of course, resistance to mathematical models by no means makes resistance to the systems approach necessary. There are many cases where no need may ever arise to use mathematics or computers. For the essence of the systems approach is not its techniques, but the enumeration of options and their implications. A simple checklist may be the only tool needed. I would even argue that some hard thinking in a quiet room may be enough. This being the case, the whole trend to more analysis and logic in management thinking, as reflected in business periodicals, business schools, and the practices of many companies, will work in favor of the development of the systems approach.

It is important to note at this juncture that not all marketers need the systems approach in its formal, elaborate sense. The success of some companies is rooted in other than marketing talents; their expertise may lie in finance, technology, administration, or even in personnel—as in the case of holding companies having an almost uncanny ability to hire brilliant operating managers and the self-control to leave them alone. In addition, a very simple marketing operation—for example, a company marketing one product through one distribution channel—may have no use for the systems concept.

APPLYING THE APPROACH

Not illogically, there is a system for applying the systems approach. It may be outlined as a sequence of steps:

1. *Define the problem and clarify objectives.* Care must be exercised not to accept the view of the propounder of the problem lest the analyst be defeated at the outset.

2. *Test the definition of the problem.* Expand its parameters to the limit. For example, to solve physical distribution problems it is necessary to study the marketplace (customer preferences, usage rates, market size, and so forth), as well as the production process (which plants produce which items most efficiently, what the interplant movements of raw materials are, and so forth). Delineate the extremes of these factors, their changeability, and the limitations on management's ability to work with them.

3. *Build a model.* Portray all factors graphically, indicating logical and chronological sequences—the dynamic flow of information, decisions, and events. "Closed circuits" should be used where there is information feedback or go, no-go and recycle signals (see Exhibit 2).

4. *Set concrete objectives.* For example, if a firm wants to make daily deliveries to every customer, prohibitive as the cost may be, manipulation of the model will yield one set of answers. But if the desire is to optimize service at lowest cost, then another set of answers will be needed. The more crisply and precisely targets are stated, the more specific the results will be.

5. *Develop alternative solutions.* It is crucial to be as open-minded as possible at this stage. The analyst must seek to expand the list of options rather than merely assess those given to him, then reduce the list to a smaller number of practical or relevant ones.

6. *Set up criteria or tests of relative value.*

7. *Quantify some or all of the factors or "variables."* The extent to which this is done depends, of course, on management's inclinations and the "state of the art."

8. *Manipulate the model.* That is, weigh the costs, effectiveness, profitability, and risks of each alternative.

9. *Interpret the results, and choose one or more courses of action.*

10. *Verify the results.* Do they make sense when viewed against the world as executives know it? Can their validity be tested by experiments and investigations?

Forethought & Perspective

Successful systems do not blossom overnight. From primitive beginnings, they evolve over a period of time as managers and systems specialists learn to understand each other better, and learn how to structure problems and how to push out the frontiers of the "universe" with which they are dealing. Companies must be prepared to invest time, money, and energy in making systems management feasible. This entails a solid foundation of historical data even before the conceptual framework for the system can be constructed. Accordingly, considerable time should be invested at the outset in *thinking* about the problem, its appropriate scope, options, and criteria of choice before plunging into analysis.

Not only technicians, but most of us have a way of falling in love with techniques. We hail each one that comes along—*deus ex machina*. Historically, commercial research has wallowed in several such passions (e.g., probability sampling, motivation research, and semantic scaling), and now operations research appears to be doing the same thing. Significantly, each technique has come, in the fullness of time, to take its place as one, but only one, instrument in the research tool chest. We must therefore have a broad and dispassionate perspective on the systems approach at this juncture. We must recognize that the computer does not possess greater magical properties than the abacus. It, too, is a tool, albeit a brilliant one.

Put another way, executives must continue to exercise their judgment and experience. Systems analysis is no substitute for common sense. The computer must adapt itself to their styles, personalities, and modes of problem solving. It is an aid to management, not a surrogate. Businessmen may be slow, but the good ones are bright; the electronic monster, by contrast, is a speedy idiot. It demands great acuity of wit from its human managers lest they be deluged in an avalanche of useless paper. (The story is told of a sales manager who had just found out about the impressive capabilities of his company's computer and called for a detailed sales analysis of all products. The report was duly prepared and wheeled into his office on a dolly.)

Systems users must be prepared to revise continually. There are two reasons for this. First, the boundaries of systems keep changing; constraints are modified; competition makes fresh incursions; variables, being what they are, vary, and new ones crop up. Second, the analytical process is iterative. Usually, one "pass" at problem formulation and searches for solutions will not suffice, and it will be necessary to "recycle" as early hypotheses are challenged and new, more fruitful insights are stimulated by the inquiry. Moreover, it is impossible to select objectives without knowledge of their effects and costs. That knowledge can come only from analysis, and it frequently requires review and revision.

Despite all the efforts at quantification, systems analysis is still largely an art. It relies frequently on inputs based on human judgment; even when the inputs are numerical, they are determined, at least in part, by judgment. Similarly, the outputs must pass through the sieve of human interpretation. Hence, there is a positive correlation between the pay-off from a system and the managerial level involved in its design. The higher the level, the more rewarding the results.

Finally, let me observe that marketing people merit their own access to computers as well as programmers who understand marketing. Left in the hands of accountants, the timing, content, and format of output are often out of phase with marketing needs.

CONCLUSION

Nearly 800 years ago a monk wrote the following about St. Godric, a merchant later turned hermit:

> *He laboured not only as a merchant but also as a shipman . . . to Denmark, Flanders, and Scotland; in which lands he found certain rare, and therefore more precious, wares, which he carried to other parts wherein he knew them to be least familiar, and coveted by the inhabitants beyond the price of gold itself, wherefore he exchanged these wares for others coveted by men of other lands. . . .*[6]

---

[6]*Life of St. Godric*, by Reginald, a monk of Durham, c. 1170.

How St. Godric "knew" about his markets we are not told, marketing having been in a primitive state in 1170. How some of us marketers today "know" is, in my opinion, sometimes no less mysterious than it was eight centuries ago. But we are trying to change that, and I will hazard the not very venturesome forecast that the era of "by guess and by gosh" marketing is drawing to a close. One evidence of this trend is marketers' intensified search for knowledge that will improve their command over their destinies. This search is being spurred on by a number of powerful developments. To describe them briefly:

☐ The growing complexity of technology and the accelerating pace of technological innovation.

☐ The advent of the computer, inspiring and making possible analysis of the relationships between systems components.

☐ The intensification of competition, lent impetus by the extraordinary velocity of new product development and the tendency of diversification to thrust everybody into everybody else's business.

☐ The preference of buyers for purchasing from as few sources as possible, thereby avoiding the problems of assembling bits and pieces themselves and achieving greater reliability, economy, and administrative convenience. (Mrs. Jones would rather buy a complete vacuum cleaner from one source than the housing from one manufacturer, the hose from another, and the attachments from still another. And industrial buyers are not much different from Mrs. Jones. They would rather buy an automated machine tool from one manufacturer than design and assemble the components themselves. Not to be overlooked, in this connection, is the tremendous influence of the U.S. government in buying systems for its military and aerospace programs.)

The further development and application of the systems approach to marketing represents, in my judgment, the leading edge in both marketing theory and practice. At the moment, we are still much closer to St. Godric than to the millenium, and the road will be rocky and tortuous. But if we are ever to convert marketing into a more scientific pursuit, this is the road we must travel. The systems concept can teach us how our businesses really behave in the marketing arena, thereby extending managerial leverage and control. It can help us to confront more intelligently the awesome complexity of marketing, to deal with the hazards and opportunities of technological change, and to cope with the intensification of competition. And in the process, the concept will help us to feed the hungry maws of our expensive computers with more satisfying fare.

QUESTIONS

1. What are the advantages in using the systems approach to marketing?

2. How are the various subsystems integrated into one overall marketing system?

3. Can the systems approach to marketing be utilized by a small firm?

4. What are the limitations of the systems approach to marketing?

5

The Production Function

The production function of a business is concerned with the creation of a product. It is a line function, as defined in Part Two of the text, because it contributes directly to the accomplishment of the objectives of a business.

The production function involves a wide variety of activities, ranging from the location of a manufacturing plant to the final preparation of products to be distributed by the marketing department.

Modern techniques of production are the result of the slow evolution of technology. The modern evolution of the production function began during the period of the Industrial Revolution. The invention of machinery such as the steam engine by James Watt and the spinning jenny by James Hargreaves revolutionized methods of production. These and other machinery inventions and innovations slowly brought to a close the handicraft stage of production in the United States. The new machinery gave rise to new industries, larger firms, and the era of mechanization. One of the characteristics of this age was the standardization of products and parts. Eli Whitney is given credit for developing the idea of product standardization when he first applied it to the manufacture of pistols.

The major impetus to the improvement of the production function after 1880 was the advancement in management methods.[1] Among the most famous contributors of management theory to the production function was Frederick W. Taylor, the "father of scientific management." He recognized production problems and analyzed them scientifically; this analysis led to their solution. Observing the variations in performance among the workers, Taylor established time standards to improve productivity and reduce costs. Although workers resented Taylor's "speed-up" practices, they were partially satisfied when permitted to earn higher wages through an incentive pay system designed by Taylor. In studying operational problems Taylor developed a number of management principles.

Other names associated with the development of scientific management are Henry Gantt, Harrington Emerson, and Frank and Lillian Gilbreth. Gantt is credited with the development of the Gantt Chart, a device used in production scheduling. Harrington Emerson was a pioneer efficiency expert. Frank Gilbreth is noted for his work in time and motion study. His wife, Lillian, was an early industrial psychologist.

---

[1]See Robert T. Hof, "Contemporary American Management," *Business Perspectives,* Winter, 1967, pp. 5-10. (This article is reprinted on page 68 of this text.)

Through 1920, workers were viewed as a factor of production that could be engineered like a machine. During the 1920's, however, workers began to be viewed as human beings that responded to things other than economic incentives. This was emphasized by the findings of the famous Hawthorne experiments, which gave rise to a theory of human behavior in organizations that emphasized the psychological and sociological aspects of work.

AUTOMATION

The era of mechanization led to *automation,* the automatic performance and control of productive processes. Different stages in the evolution of automation may be identified. First, there is *Detroit automation,* which is the initial stage beyond mechanization. In Detroit automation a series of machines are hooked together and the material to be produced moves automatically from one machine to the next.

The second stage of automation is *feedback control.* This type of automation includes the utilization of self-correcting devices. The self-correcting, or feedback, principle can be illustrated by the common household thermostat. After selecting the desired temperature, 72 degrees, for example, the temperature in the house is continuously monitored. If the thermostat indicates that the temperature has fallen below 72 degrees, it "tells" the furnace to start. When the temperature reaches 72 degrees, the furnace automatically shuts off. This continuous interchange of information between the thermostat and the furnace typifies the feedback principle.

The third stage of automation is that of *computer technology.* Computers are used not only to receive the feedback information but also to analyze all the data related to the situation. Following this analysis, the computer can issue orders to make the necessary adjustments in the production system.

Several factors have led to the development of automation. First, the cost of labor has been rising for many years. Second, there has been, and continues to be, a shortage of skilled labor. Finally, as technical complexities increase, the frequency of human error also increases. Through automation, these problems are partially overcome. However, automation has created problems of its own. First, where automatic machines were introduced and men displaced, social and economic problems developed. From these isolated occurrences a second problem evolved—the fear of automation, which in many respects has been unfounded.

Today, knowledgeable managers are overcoming the problems created by automation. Techniques of automation must be increasingly utilized if our society is to reach its desired social and economic goals and if American business is to compete successfully in foreign markets.

PLANT LOCATION

A crucial managerial decision pertaining to the production function is where the production facilities should be located. The objective is to select the location where production and distribution costs are at a minimum, yet where sales volume and price will provide maximum profits. The primary factors to be considered in plant location are transportation, labor, and operating expenses.[2]

Transportation as a factor in plant location is important from the point of view of cost and availability. The cost, convenience, and speed of receiving raw materials and supplies and shipping out finished goods is, in part, dependent upon the transportation facilities available (rail, truck, air, and water).

Management should also evaluate the *labor market* before deciding on the location of a plant. The labor market refers to the immediate quantity of persons available for employment. It also refers to the potential labor force, the quality of the labor, and the history of labor-management relations.

Among the more important costs included in *operating expenses* are the expenditures for utilities. The availability of utilities such as water, electricity, and fuel varies in different areas. They also vary in cost. Today, water is one of the scarcest resources, and its wide use in production processes is making it a critical factor for analysis in the selection of a plant site.

Miscellaneous factors such as climate, topography, political environment, and the social and cultural atmosphere of the community also affect the location decision. These secondary factors often have an influence on the primary factors. For example, in recent years many firms have placed increasing emphasis upon the availability of quality education and recreational facilities in selecting a plant site.

PLANT LAYOUT

While determining the location, management should also be considering the type of plant layout, or arrangement of machinery and facilities. A good layout is one that allows materials to move through the production operations at the speed desired and at the lowest cost.

The type of manufacturing process used is a major determining factor in the selection of the plant layout. Three types of manufacturing processes can be identified.[3] First, in *continuous* process industries such as an oil refinery, production is carried on twenty-four hours a day. The *repetitive* process industries produce items in specific quantities or lots. The manufacture of men's shirts is an example of the repetitive process. *Intermittent* process industries produce items only after orders are received. A large machine shop that produces specially designed manufacturing equipment is an example of an intermittent process industry. A thorough understanding of the manufacturing processes is crucial to the planning of the plant layout.

Manufacturing plants may utilize either product, fixed material, or process layout.[4] *Product layout* is used in the production of a standardized product that is typically produced in large quantities. The production of automobiles is an example of product layout. *Fixed material layout* is a production setup where

---

[2]Gordon B. Carson, ed., *Production Handbook* (New York: The Ronald Press Company, 1958), Section 19.

[3]*ibid.*, Section 19.

[4]Howard L. Timms, *The Production Function in Business* (Homewood, Illinois: Richard D. Irwin, Inc., 1962), pp. 309-314.

the item being manufactured remains stationary while men and machinery are brought to it. Heavy, bulky, awkward, and usually low-volume items use fixed material layouts. The manufacture of a jet airliner is an example of fixed material layout. *Process layout* is used when the sequence of manufacturing operations changes from product to product. Work centers form departments, and the product moves from one department to another to receive the process performed there. Machine shops are usually structured with a process layout so that the product can be moved from one department, such as drilling, to others, such as grinding, bending, or polishing, in any sequence required.

PRODUCTION PLANNING AND CONTROL

Production planning and control involves the determination and regulation of the production process. It includes the functions of routing, scheduling, and dispatching. The objective of production planning and control is to bring the elements of production together (labor, materials, machine, and money) to achieve the desired manufacturing results.

Routing establishes the path which production will take. The route outlines the operations to be performed and their sequence. *Scheduling* is fitting specific jobs into a timetable. *Dispatching* is the authorization to begin work. Once the production orders are dispatched, specific jobs will be performed according to the route and schedule.[5]

Production control is concerned with whether the production plan was achieved. The control process, as noted in Part Two, measures actual performance against the planned performance. If deviations from planned performance occur, the production manager has the responsibility to initiate corrective action.

RESEARCH AND DEVELOPMENT

In order to add to our body of knowledge, firms conduct research. Research is the critical investigation into natural sciences with the objective of acquiring new knowledge. The types of research are classified as pure and applied. *Pure research* seeks to add knowledge in some area with no immediate expectation of application to practical problems. *Applied research* seeks new facts and information with a definite practical use in mind. Applied research often results in the creation of a new product.

The *development* stage tests new products and examines the methods of producing them. Therefore, development is often considered to be a later stage of applied research. The Bell Laboratories of American Telephone and Telegraph Company have done a considerable amount of applied research and development to improve communication equipment.

Although some firms perform pure research, the major interest of most business firms has been in applied research and development. The reason for

[5]Richard N. Owens, *Management of Industrial Enterprises* (Homewood, Illinois: Richard D. Irwin, Inc., 1961), pp. 609-635.

this is that the firms in seeking profits see a more immediate and substantial gain from applied research. The specific goals of applied research and development are the improvement of existing products, the development of new products (product research), the improvement of production process (process research), and the possibilities of cost reduction. These goals, if achieved, contribute to the company objectives of profit and an increased share of the market.

Research and development is costly. By 1970, industry will be spending over $20 billion a year. Applied research and development will account for approximately 90 per cent of the total outlay. Industry is not the only supporter of research and development. The government, through its agencies and departments such as the Departments of Defense and of Health, Education and Welfare and the Atomic Energy Commission, exceed the expenditures of industry for research and development by over $2 billion a year. Universities perform a significant amount of the government-sponsored research.

The article by John Diebold states that automation is the agent of our current industrial technological revolution. The *Nation's Business* article shows how automation changes and creates jobs. Laurence O'Donnell reports in the *Wall Street Journal* on how companies are purchasing land as an investment that they may never use. Henry De Vos discusses the symptoms and scope of poor plant layout. Donald DeSalvia outlines some of the latest managerial techniques that are being applied in the production function. The article from *Financial World* points out that companies must engage in research and development to remain competitive.

Automation: Perceiving the Magnitude of the Problem

JOHN DIEBOLD

We have yet to perceive the magnitude and the true nature of the momentous change automation is effecting in our lives, in our businesses and in our society.

The potential and the problem are both far greater and *quite different* than yet perceived. The problem is grave and requires far more *private,* as well as public, action than has yet been proposed.

The speed of this technological change is so great that we must today do far more than even yet proposed to ascertain:

From *Advanced Management Journal*, April 1964, pp. 29-33. Reprinted by permission.

1. The true nature of the future that is cast for us by today's innovations;

2. The true magnitude and character of the problems posed for mankind by automation; and

3. The alternatives open to us to cope adequately with the changes automation is making in our world.

Automation is perceived only as a manpower problem—involving changes in labor requirements; changes in skill as jobs change; retraining and worker mobility. Managers and workers who have experienced automation in practice know that it is more than this—that it is more often than not introduced to make possible wholly new ways of performing a task, whether that task be controlling a business, a government agency or passenger air traffic.

Automation is all of these things. But my point is that it is much more.

Machines have always been important to us primarily in their role as *agents for social change.* We use the very term *industrial revolution* not because of the revolutionary machines of James Watt and Richard Arkwright, but because they created a whole new environment for mankind—a whole new way of life. What they gave to history was much more than the steam engine and the cotton gin, the railway and the power loom. Their machines gave society a whole new tempo, a whole new outlook.

Today's crop of machines is a far, far more powerful agent for social change than was that of the first industrial revolution. For today's machines result from a new found ability to build systems which: process and communicate information; translate from one language to another; respond to the human voice; devise their own route to goals that are presented to them; machine systems which improve their performance as a result of encountering the environment (machines in other words which learn in the normal sense in which that term is used); machine systems, in short, which deal with the very core of human society—with information, its communication, and use. These are developments which augur far more for mankind than net changes in manpower, more or less employment, or new ways of doing old tasks.

These are developments which mean that mankind will undertake new tasks, not merely perform old tasks in a new way. This is a technology which vastly extends the range of human capability and which will fundamentally alter human society.

The very nature of today's technology, its concern with the building blocks of human society, will in the course of the lifetime of students now graduating from universities—and perhaps in the lifetime of many businessmen today—force us to reconsider our whole approach to work, to society, and to life itself.

The technology of automation casts before it shadows of far greater social change than were brought about by the industrial revolution set in train by James Watt and Richard Arkwright.

Let us look, for example, at automation as perceived from three viewpoints: the individual; the manager; and public policy.

The *individual* perceives automation as a job threat or, if he be a mathematician, engineer or otherwise situated to benefit, he perceives it as a challenge and an opportunity.

Yet automation is going to force the individual—and all of mankind—to reconsider his very conception of himself. As Professor Herbert A. Simon, of Carnegie Institute of Technology, states: "The definition of man's uniqueness has always formed the kernel of his cosmological and ethical systems. With Copernicus and Galileo, he ceased to be the species located at the center of the universe, attended by sun and stars. With Darwin, he ceased to be the species created and specially endowed by God with soul and reason. With Freud, he ceased to be the species whose behavior was—potentially—governable by rational mind. As we begin to produce mechanisms that think and learn, he has ceased to be the species uniquely capable of complex, intelligent manipulation of his environment."

Man will find a new way of describing his place in the universe. Machine systems certainly show no signs of many of the fundamental human qualities such as imagination, volition, purposefulness, compassion or love. Yet my point is that man's ability to build machines which learn and which already possess so much of the quality we today call "intelligence" means that we have the most fundamental of changes in store for the individual and for our conception of our role as humans.

The manager, public administrator and private businessman, today perceives automation as a labor saving device and as a means for exercising tighter control on his enterprise and making it more responsive to rapid change. The great theme in today's business literature is that automation represents an opportunity to do a better job of managing.

This is all well and good as far as it goes. But in itself it tells only a small part of the story. For the significance of automation to the manager is not so much the new methods it gives him for managing—the new kit of professional tools so to speak—but the fact that the enterprise he manages will change totally due to the changes automation is effecting in our society.

The real potential, and the enormous problem, automation poses to the manager is that the environment in which the enterprise exists is changing, rapidly and completely. As the goals, aspirations, needs and wants of the individual shift, and shift again and again through the human social change induced by automation, the economic realities that sustain the enterprise will change.

In other words, the great meaning of automation to the manager is to be found in the social change induced by automation. This holds a far more profound meaning to the manager and businessman than the procedural revolution taking place today in management methods. For it is in its role of serving human wants that lies the entrepreneurial raison d'être of business and government organizations alike.

Rapid and major social shifts mean an entirely new and more day to day role for strategic planning in guiding the enterprise. It is here that automation is making profound change and it is here that we must look for the essence of the managerial meaning of this new industrial revolution. For here lies the heart of enterprise—ascertaining and filling human need—not the techniques of management, however important the latter may be in today's giant and changing organizations. Vitality and survival are determined by the ability of the organization—whether private or public—to perceive and fulfill these, now rapidly changing, human needs.

Public policy perceives automation as a problem of unemployment, retraining and change in manpower requirements. Altogether correct as far as it goes, and of critical importance. The additional and accurately perceived need for increased productivity occasionally produces in public policy a schizophrenic impression of calling in effect for "more technology—but go slowly!" But the public policy perception of automation is only too clear—if far too limited.

The reality of the public policy question is that the problem is much greater than yet perceived by all but a very few.

International political as well as economic forces will require us to increasingly press for world leadership in these new technologies—which are correctly perceived by the remainder of the world as a tomorrow in which they intend to live. This necessary drive for technological leadership—on which increasingly rests our economically privileged position—will sharpen and intensify the as yet largely unperceived social problems of automation.

It is significant, I think, that with increasing frequency and forcefulness statements of Soviet political and economic theory refer to automation as the means by which mankind will achieve the highest of estates. No shilly-shallying here. No confusion over whether to move forward. Rather, a firm determination to lead tomorrow where our country leads today.

Employment shifts and retraining may be easier in the Soviet, but I think we would be foolish to write it off at this. Marxist Leninist doctrine has long valued technology as a determinant of social change. It is positively *embracing* automation. Premier Khrushchev has stated, "Automation is good. It is the means we will use to lick you capitalists."

But even leaving the Sino-Soviet bloc aside, the international pressure is still there to force us to pursue the technology even more aggressively than we do today. The developing nations as well as the highly developed countries of the world look to the new technology of automation as a major solution to today's problems. In addition—and this is of great significance—many of them correctly perceive automation as the key to a very different kind of tomorrow.

We have no corner on this technology—even though we lead today. We can look forward only to increasing pressure from all parts of the world to move very much more rapidly in order to hold our leadership. The revolution of information technology is a revolution moved by human brains—and there is precious little built-in advantage to us other than our educational system and our major institutions of research. We will feel increasing pressure to keep ahead with both.

The solution to this public paradox is the creation of an environment conducive to technological leadership and rapid change. The first step must be the removal of all reason for fear over individual harm due to technological change. But the problem cannot be solved backwards—the proper role of public policy is to create the conditions necessary to leadership in the human use of this new technology.

The electronic computer—today's crude precursor of the machine systems automation is so rapidly bringing into existence—is important not nearly so much because of the things it does today—however much we have already come to rely upon it in our daily lives—but because it represents a new-found human ability based upon the most powerful of theoretical insights into the nature of information and its uniquely important place in our lives.

As this ability is expressed in machine systems that abstract as well as translate documents; help physicians to diagnose disease, lawyers to prepare briefs, teachers to develop better the capabilities of their students, the world will become a far different place than it is today.

Major *social* innovation seems to me to be called for to cope with such technological innovation. It must be as rapid and as great as is the technological innovation.

Last time we ignored the need for social innovation. One result was Karl Marx. His ideas have had more to do with shaping the lives of all of us than we would care to believe true.

The very magnitude and importance of the problem mean that we should not look to government for *the* solution. It is a task which should involve all of us, our best minds and hearts. It is a problem to be solved by the *private* as well as the public sector.

Pope John XXIII made a notable contribution to showing what must be done by the private sector in his encyclical *Mater et Magistra*. Governments can do much to ameliorate the human toll of transition and to help create an environment that will encourage technological leadership. But the shape of tomorrow's world is surely a problem to which we all can usefully contribute as individuals and working through private organizations as well as through our governments. We have hardly yet begun to face up to these aspects of the problem.

For example, the foundations and professional societies such as the Society for Advancement of Management, nourished in large part by increasingly automated industries, have thus far been conspicuous in their avoidance of interest in what the late President Kennedy characterized as "the major domestic challenge" of the Sixties. The private foundations and the professional societies are institutions to which we might reasonably look for help and guidance as the private sector contemplates these critical problems. The Society for Advancement of Management is to be commended for this present compendium on the critical issues of automation and management. Through such explorations will come more understanding of the problem. From this illumination new insights should be generated by management responsible for organization change.

Let me revert one last time to that upheaval of two centuries ago that we now call the industrial revolution. No one in the middle of eighteenth century England, least of all Richard Arkwright or James Watt, thought that they were changing civilization itself. Yet, for us, looking back, that is precisely what was *revolutionary* about the inventions they made.

They took men off the fields and out of the small shops and put them for the first time into factory life. Hence they gave us mass production, and through mass production the first civilization in history in which luxury was not confined to a few.

Like the pioneers of the industrial revolution of the eighteenth century, we face today a world in which only one thing is certain: change, fundamental change.

But unlike those earlier pioneers, we live in an age of the greatest sense of social responsibility in all history.

Our task today is to wisely use our technology, our knowledge of history, and our compassion to make the age of automation a golden Periclean age in

which a society based on the work of the machine—not the human chattel—
rises to the full heights of which the human spirit is capable.

QUESTIONS

1. How can machines be an agent of social change?

2. How is automation viewed by the individual, the manager, and legislators?

3. How are social and technological innovation related?

4. What must we do to make this era of automation a success?

New Look at How Machines Make Jobs

What happens when automation forces a person to change jobs?

For most people, it's a disaster—at least for awhile.

But for others such as cheery-voiced Dorothy Levendosky, it may be one
of the best things that ever happened to them.

She worked for 16 years processing dental X-ray film at E. I. du Pont de
Nemours & Co.'s Parlin, N.J., plant. Then came a decision to change the manufacturing process at Parlin. Miss Levendosky and a group of other women production employees took a four-month secretarial training course at company
expense, with full pay. Now she's happy as a secretary-stenographer for the
plant's photo products sales-service group.

"It's like a complete new life now," Miss Levendosky told *Nation's Business*. For one thing, she now works in daylight instead of semidarkness. "It
seems that I'm doing something really worthwhile."

Automation, of course, is many things to many people. To some, it means
simply the use of computers to do things many people used to be needed to do.
To others, it is the use of almost any machine to produce things humans used to
produce; in other words, one more extension of the mechanization of labor that
has been going on since invention of the wheel.

However you define automation—computerization, technological advance or whatever—it unquestionably means concern or hardship for a number of people as well as for their employers. New methods of doing things always have.

"That labor-saving machinery, so called, but which more properly should be called labor-making or labor-assisting machinery, displaces labor temporarily cannot successfully be denied. All men of sound minds admit the permanent good effects of machinery; but these good effects do not prevent the temporary displacement of labor. . ."

So reported the government's Commissioner of Labor back in 1886. And that is the essence of today's sound and fury: How to ease the problems of industrial transition for individuals caught in it.

Indeed, there's even little genuine debate over the broad value to the economy and over-all employment of what's come to be called automation—the advancing technological revolution is substituting machines for men in making and processing things.

As one of the government's most respected authorities on automation—Ewan Clague, Commissioner of Labor Statistics—puts it: "Technology as such does not result in a net loss of jobs in the economy. It does destroy the jobs and occupations of individual workers; but it creates new jobs and occupations which require workers."

"In a word," asserts George Terborgh, research director of the Machinery and Allied Products Institute, in his new book, "The Automation Hysteria," "technological progress is favorable to employment in the net, or over-all, and at least so far as process improvement is concerned, it causes far less personal dislocation and hardship than the alarmists would have us believe."

Even the top men of big labor—though not always their local leaders—embrace the virtues of this new industrial revolution.

"We don't oppose automation," insists Nat Goldfinger, top economist of the AFL-CIO. He declares the union simply wants job protection for workers in jobs affected by the new ways of doing things during the transition and a share of savings due to automation.

What's often overlooked is this:

Automation in its broad sense of technological advance is opening the door to easier, better-paying and more desirable jobs for many workers, enabling others to perform tasks for which they previously lacked skills and creating jobs which never would have existed otherwise.

Consider the case of the deposited carbon resistor and how Western Electric Co. automated jobs out of existence for a group of Winston-Salem, N.C., women.

The resistor is a tiny device about the size of a pencil which helps regulate current in amplifiers and other complicated electronic equipment which Western Electric makes for its parent American Telephone & Telegraph Co. Latest-model juke boxes use about a dozen of them. They must be extremely precise.

When the deposited carbon resistor was first developed, the women laboriously made it by hand processes. Their speed wasn't so dramatic but the big problem was quality. "We always had an extremely high reject rate because the tolerances had to be so exact," says a company official.

Clever engineers then devised a block-long machine that can be run by just a few technicians and spews out top-quality resistors. This brought down the cost of the resistors to economic levels, opened the way for creation of new applications of the technique to move electronic equipment and expanded jobs of many sorts at the Winston-Salem plant.

The women? Western Electric provided new job openings for all assembling other electronic components. In addition more jobs were created for others because of the new development.

Another bit of more or less automated equipment in Western Electric's Columbus, Ohio, plant doesn't cause workers to switch jobs but enables unskilled workers to do tasks they couldn't do nearly as well—if at all.

It's something called a wiring assist machine used by women wiring tiny pieces of electronic gadgetry into a memory unit for the Bell Telephone System's new electronic switching stations. A diagram tells the woman where to connect wires to terminals. When she completes the task properly, a light switches from red to green and she moves to the next step in the production process.

"A mistake in wiring can mean tearing down a $10,000 piece of equipment later on," says a Western Electric official in explaining how the machine enables workers to accomplish difficult tasks, thereby opening more jobs to more workers, as well as reducing costs.

From the worker's standpoint, the machine can mean more money because she is paid on a piecework basis under union contract and the machine permits faster work with fewer errors. Workers don't get paid for rejected equipment.

Similarly, a worker in General Motors Corp.'s precise maze of conveyors which forms its Willow Run Chevrolet assembly plant near Detroit is able to balance wheels for Corvairs expertly by reading a code of colored lights on an automatic tire-inflating machine. In the adjacent Fisher Body Division of General Motors, an automatic spotwelding machine welds together the front of Chevrolet bodies. To operate this automatic equipment properly requires little previous specialized training.

In Marion, Ind., white-gowned women push buttons on a semiautomatic line which enables them to mass produce extremely complex color television tubes for Radio Corp. of America. Without such cost-cutting production facilities, it is all but unthinkable that color television sales would have taken off as they have this year, providing jobs for many of the more than 10,000 workers at Marion and other Indiana and Pennsylvania cities where RCA makes its sets.

HOW AUTOMATION SAVES JOBS

And technology preserves jobs, too. One such instance is at Pima Mining Co.'s open pit copper mine near Tucson, Ariz., where new mining techniques and equipment will prolong production an additional 20 years by making low-grade ore economical to process.

American industry, with the help of advancing technology and automation, is thus reshaping the country's economy by providing new jobs for many and creating openings in new occupations for others who find little demand today for their skills.

Labor union officials in their Washington headquarters recognize the value of automation to the nation's economy. But they argue that the new job patterns downgrade the skills required by men on many production-line jobs.

"Take a millwright," argues Mr. Goldfinger. "There is now less need for a topnotch millwright to do specialized repair work in a plant. There is a general dilution of skills. He has to be more of a jack-of-all-trades, master of none. If you talk to a worker, he is unhappy because he is no longer a highly skilled man in one trade."

But, say the union men, if automation lessens the need for high skills, it increases the responsibility of the worker running or working with a new machine. Therefore, they contend, employees working with this equipment deserve higher pay to match their responsibilities for a costly machine.

Business, of course, is giving greater and greater attention to the human problems involved in automation's impact on employees.

Increasingly, companies are retraining workers due for replacement by automated processes, offering them employment at company plants in other cities, providing re-employment aid for workers who choose to leave, enabling older workers to retire earlier than normal and, whenever possible, letting attrition take care of any necessary job reductions by failing to replace workers who quit or retire on their own. The result is an easing of the transition and, in most cases, employment for the workers involved.

Ford Motor Co.'s Malcolm L. Denise, vice president for labor relations, boasts, for instance, "We have found it impossible to identify any group of laid-off Ford employees with unemployment that is attributable to automation as such."

Reports Joseph L. O'Brien, vice president for personnel relations of the Air Transport Association of America, "One of the nation's major airlines has adjusted successfully to its automated passenger reservation system through the process of attrition. The instant the system went into operation, the jobs of about 1,000 reservation clerks and 85 supervisors became obsolete. But not a single individual lost his job in the changeover. In fact, since the adoption of the new computerized reservation system, the carrier has more people on the payroll than before the system was installed. This is because business has grown so fast—partially because of automation—that new jobs have been created."

Not all companies are able to give their displaced workers that painless treatment but the Singer Co. dramatizes how automation means jobs for many of its employees—instead of the reverse.

Singer is halting production of sewing machines at its Bridgeport plant because its costs there were too high to compete with foreign manufacturers.

"In effect, the plant is being closed by automation," explains a company official. "If we could have automated sewing machine production, we'd still be making them in Bridgeport. We have to go into a different line of business, instead."

The new line of business at the plant is production of a wide line of electronic test devices and similar equipment which can be produced with more or less automated processes. One production aid is a small television set which an assembler watches and controls. It tells her when to take what steps in order to assemble an elaborate electronic device.

Some sewing machine workers have transferred over to this kind of work.

Many other workers lined up jobs with other manufacturers in the region who set up recruiting offices in the Singer plant at the invitation of Singer's management.

MANY ARE TOO SMART FOR THE JOB

And a number of other workers will take the opportunity to break away from their old trade into new work which may mean even better opportunities for them.

Dr. V. Donald Schoeller, president of the Foundation for Re-Employment, an organization helping Singer place its discharged workers, asserts that studies show 75 to 80 per cent of employees in industry have talents greater than they need for their job.

But these workers refuse to seek jobs which make use of these additional abilities until forced to when automation eliminates their jobs. The organization's experience finds that 30 per cent to 40 per cent of workers who lose their jobs to automation wind up changing careers by switching to new types of occupations with other employers.

Such a man is a 52-year-old machine operator for Singer who, over the years, had picked up a talent for making and designing tools. The closing of the Singer operations put him in line for a job with another industrial firm as a tool designer for about $4 an hour compared to the approximately $3.50 an hour he has been making under the title of machine operator, reports Dr. Schoeller.

"Individuals today shift more frequently from one job to another than in the past," points out Martin R. Gainsbrugh, vice president and chief economist of the National Industrial Conference Board. "Increasingly this shift is to a better job as vacancies multiply from the intensification of research and the accompanying acceleration of product innovation and product improvement."

Some forecasters believe today's new generation will change careers three times during their lifetime.

A prime example of what Mr. Gainsbrugh is talking about has been happening over recent years at the Indianapolis plant where Western Electric makes practically all of the telephones used by the Bell System. At the request of *Nation's Business,* officials took a close look at how technical advances have changed individual jobs in that factory.

Their findings: Over the past 10 years, machines have taken over many of the menial jobs in the plant. Jobs in which men used to drop rivets in holes or put a bolt through two pieces of metal before passing the assembly along for the next man to tighten have now been taken over by machines. Materials handling has also been largely mechanized.

Men who were doing these basic tasks—and there are many—now have mainly progressed to such jobs as inspector, operator of a battery of machines or troubleshooting repairmen. Total employment has risen, shooting up to 9,000 workers from 6,500 in the last 18 months, despite attrition whenever new automation procedures took over.

Significantly, the average overall wage in the plant is now considerably higher than it was before automation. Part of this wage rise is due to the general upward push of pay—but not all—say officials. A major part of the increase comes from the general upgrading of jobs as menial tasks have been automated and individuals have moved ahead in job classifications.

Company officials say it is impossible to pinpoint which or how many workers have moved into better-paying positions because of automation. Many men would have advanced through the regular escalator of seniority, experience and old-fashioned initiative whether or not automation was present. But, say the men on the spot, there is no question but that automated equipment enabled men who may have been in a rut doing menial jobs to try for better, more skilled jobs that opened up on the new machines.

WHITE COLLARS BY '75

This is the kind of change going on in factories across the nation. One indication of what it means to workers in the future comes from the U.S. Department of Labor. It estimates that by 1975, nearly half the nation's employed persons will work at white-collar jobs while the number in blue-collar, laboring jobs will shrink to about 33 per cent. As recently as 1956, these two types of employment ran neck-and-neck at just under 40 per cent.

If white collar—managerial and desk—jobs are as desirable as most people consider them, this means an improvement of the lot of the individual worker as the economy automates.

Industry and government are also trying to get a clear look at exactly how automation is changing the economy and jobs in general. A start will come when the National Commission on Technology, Automation and Economic Progress reports on its recent studies at the end of the year. Perhaps the farthest-reaching study, however, is a $5 million, 10-year look at the impact of automation being undertaken by Harvard University and financed by International Business Machines Corp., a firm in the forefront of automation and computerization.

What these studies find is certain to be significant. But none of the outcome will be so important as the fact that automation and technological progress today are bringing a more prosperous economy and better jobs for more workers.

QUESTIONS

1. How does automation make jobs? Save jobs?

2. Are unions completely opposed to automation? Why or why not?

3. What is management doing to solve the problems of automation?

4. What kinds of jobs are most likely to be eliminated by automation?

Corporate Land Rush

LAURENCE G. O'DONNELL

Which company is getting the most out of its capital-spending dollars:

The one that buys land only when it finally decides to build a new plant, and buys only as much as it needs?

Or the one that buys several times as much land as required for any factory it sets out to build—and goes on to snap up sites it can't see itself building on for years or even decades?

Many companies now think the second course is the wiser. Booming business, and especially booming plant-building, are making undeveloped industrial sites increasingly scarce and costly, they note. So, they believe, any company with even vague thoughts of future expansion ought to assemble the land now—before a competitor grabs it, and before the price goes out of sight.

UNION CARBIDE, FARM LANDLORD

Thus, Union Carbide Corp. this year acquired 800 acres in Newcastle County, Del., for which it has no specific plans. Last summer it rented most to tenant farmers. The purchase was the latest of a series. Since 1958, Carbide has paid $5 million to assemble 3,300 acres in three "strategic areas."

Prior to 1958 Carbide bought land only "with a fairly specific purpose in mind," says A. L. Foscue, vice president. But now, he says, it "realizes that plant sites in strategic areas are not to be had overnight."

Bethlehem Steel Corp. similarly says industrial sites big enough to hold major integrated steel works "have become a rarity"—and apparently it is setting out to line up some before they disappear. Last year it agreed to pay over $13 million in cash (and other land) for 1,800 acres owned by Atlas Chemical Industries, Inc., at Pinole Point near San Francisco. Atlas had torn down a dynamite plant that occupied the site several years earlier. Bethlehem has announced no plans to build immediately at Pinole Point—nor on 1,700 acres it has just finished assembling adjacent to its Sparrows Point, Md., works.

More prevalent than such land "stockpiling" is deliberate "overbuying." That is, a company planning a new plant will buy not only the land immediately needed, but enough extra acreage to hold all possible future extensions—and then some, perhaps. Currently, Bethlehem and Jones & Laughlin Steel Corp. are building only on portions of respective 6,000-acre sites they have assembled in Chesterton, Ind., and Hennepin, Ill.

DOUBLING THE FIGURE

"One company I know provides for space for the building, for anticipated extra buildings, for Parkinson's Law in the parking spaces—and then they double the

Reprinted with permission of *The Wall Street Journal*, December 8, 1965, pp. 1, 18.

final figure," says J. C. Clamp, vice president of Allis-Chalmers Manufacturing Co. He heads the Industrial Development Research Council, a group of 130 company site selectors.

But suppose a company winds up holding land it concludes it won't ever use? Then, too, it can profit. Already, some firms that joined the land rush early, and found themselves with unneeded or unusable acres, have begun reselling the excess at huge profits.

Chemway Corp. is quite undisturbed at the threat that a proposed highway will isolate a portion of a 230-acre site it had assembled in Wayne, N.J. The drug and cosmetics maker has sold 15 or 20 acres at prices up to four times its original per-acre investment, clearing a $92,000 profit. "Looking around" at the rest, "I get a very comfortable feeling," says a Chemway executive.

Other companies holding usable land are being tempted by rising prices to sell some rather than build on it. American Hoist & Derrick Co. was offered $385,000 for 8 of its 78 acres in Irwindale, Calif.—80% more per acre than it paid a year ago. It said no, but Harry W. Moberg, treasurer, says the company eventually may sell half the Irwindale land.

Are some manufacturers, then, turning into land speculators? Companies bristle at the question, and real estate men agree that most really are trying only to provide now for future expansion needs.

But land experts suspect at least some companies are assembling sites bigger than they ever will need, intending from the beginning to resell some acreage. If such a company could sell at a profit big enough to cover acquisition costs of the land it keeps to build on, it would in effect get a factory site free.

"In talking to industrial brokers, one company said it needed 10 acres but wanted 40 to 60," relates J. D. Sawyer, a Middletown, Ohio, land broker. "That's much more than their expansion needs of the next 10 years, so they must be buying to sell off some. They not only figure they'll end up with their site free, but with a major profit."

Statham Instruments, Inc., intended eventually to use the 23 acres it bought five years ago in Southern California. But the value of the site has more than doubled, to about $1 million now, says Lawrence T. Lindgren, vice president. So, he says, Statham is toying with the idea of swapping the 23 acres for a 67-acre site in Oxnard that it now rents. It won't need that much land in Oxnard, he says, but "ultimately we could sell off some, so it would be a good investment."

A series of land resale deals, however, could raise a tax problem for a manufacturer. Generally, profits an industrial firm makes selling land are taxed at capital-gains rates. But the Internal Revenue Service says that if a manufacturer has a history of buying more land than it needs and selling the surplus, it likely would be classified as a "real estate dealer." Then, its land profits would be taxed at much higher ordinary-income rates.

Partly because of this tax angle, partly because they shy from even the possibility of being called speculators, and partly because they distrust the economics of land "stockpiling," some of the nation's biggest corporations are resisting the new land fever. American Telephone & Telegraph Co., General Electric Co. and General Motors Corp. all say they still buy only the land they need when they need it—though GM does so much of that it has long operated a real estate division, Argonaut Realty.

AT&T engineers believe land values generally don't rise fast enough to repay the expense of carrying idle land with borrowed money. If real estate taxes and income taxes on any eventual resale profit are calculated as part of the carrying costs, "you find these 'windfall profits' aren't windfalls at all," another company contends.

But apart from any expectation of "windfall profits," many other companies find the case for acquiring land when it becomes available rather than when it is needed to be compelling. "The nation's inventory of unused prime industrial land is definitely shrinking," says Robert E. Boley, an official of the Urban Land Institute. He estimates there are about three million acres of land zoned for industry in the nation's major urban areas, but adds, "you can assume most of the prime land is already developed."

One result, Mr. Boley says: "There are quite a number of examples of companies buying prime land on rivers because they don't want it pre-empted by other users—or competitors."

As the supply shrinks, prices soar. "Surveys show prices have gone up as much as 10 times in the last 15 years around some metropolitan areas," says Mr. Sawyer, the Middletown broker. Farm land, increasingly demanded by companies that want to assemble bigger sites than can be had near cities, isn't cheap either. In the past 10 years farm realty values have risen 70%, to $146 an acre, according to the U.S. Agriculture Department.

Buyers grumble that some prices now are much too high. "We have seen some land in 10 years go from $3,000 an acre to $13,000 because of transactions between one entrepreneur and another who did nothing to the land but inflate the price," says Otto Pongrace, director of industrial development for the New York Central Railroad.

But many manufacturers are convinced prices will go still higher in the future, so they'd better buy now. Accordingly, they're snapping up land offered by a variety of sellers—other industrial firms, farmers and other individual owners, universities, some 1,500 to 2,000 industrial park developers, an estimated 2,000 community industrial development groups, and many small syndicates among them.

Railroads and utilities, too, often buy or help develop factory sites to woo prospective shippers and electric-power customers. New York Central Railroad and Cleveland Electric Illuminating Co., in a joint venture with a bank, currently are sponsoring the 750-acre Mentor Park industrial development in Mentor, Ohio.

Pennsylvania Railroad has acquired 70% of Great Southwest Corp., which is developing a 6,500-acre industrial park in Dallas and a 3,000-acre industrial park in Atlanta. In the past five years the Pennsy also has sold about 4,000 track-side acres to land-hungry companies for a total of $17 million. It has bought 2,000 more track-side acres for about $5 million in the same period, to offer for resale.

As industrial-land sellers have developed a more professional approach, so have the buyers. Many manufacturers are adopting standard techniques of the professional real estate dealer, notably including the purchase of options to tie up sites they are interested in while studying zoning, soil conditions and the like. "It is ridiculous to buy land without the proper zoning, so you take options on several sites in case one doesn't pan out," says an official of a large New York chemical firm.

Real estate brokers say a few companies have adopted a further refinement of option dealing. To cover the costs of buying options on sites they may wind up rejecting, they simultaneously sell options to other firms on land they already own but don't plan to use.

Not all the land deals manufacturers line up by these and other methods turn out happily. A New England manufacturer spent $700,000 to buy several hundred acres and get the zoning changed, but then decided not to use the site. Now the new zoning is hindering its efforts to get rid of the land. "It is hard to sell because no one wants it for that particular use," says Joseph Lund, Boston real estate consultant.

Atlas Chemical unexpectedly has had to turn residential land developer to rid itself of an abandoned Pocono Mountain, Pa., plant site. It proposes to cut the 778-acre tract into half-acre lots, and sell them for $1,100 to $5,500 each, as sites for vacation cottages and the like.

More commonly, however, companies stockpiling land they won't use for a while, if ever, have found it such a good investment that some appear to be doing considerable boasting about it within the financial community.

"A lot of companies say they have big paper profits on land they own," reports Eldon A. Grimm, senior vice president of Walston & Co., New York securities firm. A Minnesota manufacturer adds: "We know some people have made more money by revaluing their properties (that is, marking up their asset value on the balance sheet) than by operating them."

QUESTIONS

1. Why are companies purchasing more land than they will need?

2. What is this doing to the price of real estate?

3. Can companies legally buy and sell land without any problems?

Management Controls and Information

HENRY DE VOS

PLANT LAYOUT AND SPACE UTILIZATION

It is not uncommon for a practitioner to follow the flow of a requisition, invoice, or what have you, in an office, and mentally note a very erratic procedural movement. For example, the document might have started in one corner of the office, traveled clear across the room, returned to the point of origination, then out to the center of the office, and so forth.

This erratic movement will not only cause long delays in preparation of the documents due to unproductive travel time, but also put the office in a constant state of confusion. Most CPAs would rise to the occasion by recommending in a supplemental report to the client, that office procedures be reviewed with a view toward creating a more efficient office. In the course of such an engagement, the CPA cannot help becoming involved in office layout. To what degree becomes merely a matter of opportunity and sophistication. The principles of office layout apply to plant layout problems as well.

Similarly, a CPA may become involved in plant layout while observing work-in-process inventory, during systems and procedures engagements or through cost reduction programs. Most often, however, the latter is the rule because plant layout engagements attempt an optimum solution involving the lowest operating costs plus a desirable return on invested capital. In most situations, however, the solution must be limited to existing conditions. That is, the engagement really becomes a re-layout problem rather than one of developing blueprints for a new plant building. It is noteworthy that the same layout principles are involved whether it be an office or a plant layout engagement. The only difference between the two engagements is one of application. In fact the same symptoms often prevail.

SYMPTOMS OF POOR LAYOUT

As in an office layout problem, poor plant layout may be evidenced by a slow process, accident hazards, bottlenecks or perhaps just plain bad housekeeping, among others. Plant layout problems may also be caused by changes in product design, revisions in the sequencing of operations, new operations, replacement of equipment and the like. Further, every time an analysis is made of work standards or work methods at a cost center, any recommended change may involve the possibility of improving methods by rearranging the facilities involved.

Reprinted with permission from *The Journal of Accountancy,* April 1964, pp. 77-79.

SCOPE OF PLANT LAYOUT ENGAGEMENTS

In a plant layout engagement, the CPA must also concern himself with materials handling. While the end result of a layout assignment is to develop a flow of production that represents the most effective utilization of available space, it must also achieve a desirable level of efficiency. Therefore, alternative material handling methods must be considered. Suppose for an example that material flows from cost center 1 to cost center 2 utilizing pallets and fork-lift trucks. The CPA must not take the incumbent method for granted. He must question himself whether the material can be moved more economically, and perhaps create more space by using some other media. Perhaps one of the many types of conveyers or overhead cranes would be more economical under the circumstances. The use of conveyers might provide faster movement of material and would not require the extra space allowed for the operation of fork-lift trucks.

The speed of material flow from one cost center to the next cost center must, however, be tailored to existing conditions. For example, if the second cost center cannot absorb the flow of materials from cost center 1, at a faster rate, the practitioner may be creating a queuing problem by solving a layout problem.

ELICIT THE CLIENT'S HELP

The determination of what is to be laid out is the initial step in a plant layout analysis. Although this sounds elementary there are actually two broad classifications of layout assignments. The one considers the entire layout while the other case consists of making minor adjustments.

The very nature of plant layout engagements precludes a completely objective approach. While some principles have been developed, judgment plays an extremely important role. Therefore, the CPA should have the client supply him with information concerning product and production details, optional or interchangeable equipment, machinery operational sequencing and timing, future needs, process or product obsolescence possibilities, etc.

It is not unusual to consider sales forecasts and capital budgets especially when considering an entire layout engagement. In fact, it is not unusual to project five or more years into the future because of the expense involved in rearranging existing layouts.

DETERMINATION OF SPACE REQUIREMENTS

Before cost centers or work spaces can be arranged, the practitioner must estimate the space the respective areas will command. At this time, future additional production or service departments should be considered.

In determining space requirements, departmentalization will invariably arise. Most practitioners are aware that there are only two basic department layouts, the product and process layouts. Greater insight can be gained by referring to a standard production management book.

The CPA should next gather data on the existing buildings and current layout of the buildings. Plot plans will give the location of the building in relationship to existing roadways or rail sidings. This will give the practitioner some indication of what flow raw materials or finished goods must take under existing conditions. It will also be the determining factor in locating receiving and shipping docks. In addition, the practitioner should develop operation process or flow charts in order to get the proper perspective of what the current procedures are. These charts begin with the delivery of raw materials and continue through the entire process up to and including final shipment of the finished product. While noting operations, it is also important to check the approximate size and timing of all material movements. Under complicated situations, the practitioner may require the aid of standard templates or dimensional models. In any case a flow chart is a must to summarize operations and evaluate plant layout proposals.

LAYOUT OBJECTIVES

A good plant layout will generally achieve one or more of the following objectives:

1. Rapid movement of material through a plant
2. Provide a more convenient location for service centers
3. Avoid or localize objectionable conditions
4. Eliminate congestion
5. Reduce material handling and transportation
6. Provide optimum space under existing restrictions
7. Determine the best possible grouping of departments or processes

While every CPA will not get involved in all of the aspects implied in the term "plant layout" or "re-layout," he can become versed and perform in a less sophisticated manner.

While check lists are not wholly adequate in that they have a tendency to restrict freedom of thought, the accompanying questionnaire appeared in the Small Business Administration's *Technical Aids for Small Manufacturers* and may be helpful.

SPACE UTILIZATION CHECKPOINTS IN YOUR OWN PLANT

In the Receiving Department	Yes	No
1. Are materials standing around—piled up in the yard or on the receiving platform—waiting to be moved into the plant?.	☐	☐
2. Are there idle man-hours between material-handling jobs?	☐	☐
3. Can labor-savings be effected by such equipment as car-dumpers and portable conveyers?	☐	☐
4. Are materials unloaded in the yard, stacked, then moved to a receiving platform before finally moving into the plant?....	☐	☐

SPACE UTILIZATION CHECKPOINTS IN YOUR OWN PLANT

(Continued)

In Production Areas	Yes	No

    5. Is the production area cluttered with parts and materials waiting to be used? . . . . ☐ ☐

    6. Are "live storage" conveyers and tiering trays needed to facilitate the flow of materials and parts in production? . . . . ☐ ☐

    7. Does the scheduling of materials need streamlining? . . . ☐ ☐

    8. Do materials handlers have to wait long for an elevator (if you have a multistory plant) to move materials between floors? . . . . ☐ ☐

    9. Are materials moved criss-cross from one machine to another? (Small chutes, conveyers, lifting devices, and the like, offer excellent opportunities to speed production and cut costs.) . ☐ ☐

    10. Do tote boxes, bar stock, or parts of machinery project out into aisles? . . . . ☐ ☐

    11. Is every part, pallet load, or tote box clearly labeled? (In complicated operations, tags should show where they have come from and where they are going; to what order they apply; and what special handling is required.) . . . . ☐ ☐

    12. Is scrap disposed of efficiently—so that you can realize on its reconversion value, if any? . . . . ☐ ☐

    13. Are aisles clear, smoothly paved, and well-marked so that traffic can flow freely and safely? . . . . ☐ ☐

    14. Has traffic movement been studied recently to work out the shortest routes? . . . . ☐ ☐

    15. Has the use of vertical space in the production area been considered? . . . . ☐ ☐

In Storage Areas

    16. Are storage areas well-lighted to permit rapid movement of equipment? . . . . ☐ ☐

    17. Are storage areas marked off into sections, and are these sections numbered or lettered for quick and easy identification? . . ☐ ☐

    18. Is a record kept of what is stored in each area to facilitate receiving, production, and shipping, and, at the same time, reduce inventory costs? . . . . ☐ ☐

    19. Are products stored in the most easily handled form and in units in which they will be shipped? (If, for example, orders generally call for a dozen items, they should be packed and stored by the dozen.) . . . . ☐ ☐

	Yes	No

20. Is full use made of overhead space by stacking loaded pallets with appropriate materials handling equipment? . . . . ☐   ☐

21. Are related items placed in areas next to each other? . . . ☐   ☐

22. Are aisles wide enough to permit free movement of men and mobile equipment? . . . . ☐   ☐

23. Are storage areas located as close as possible to the production areas they serve? (Establishing small "branch" storage areas for in-process parts often can save a good many miles of travel in a year—and more than pay for any extra cost involved in establishing them.) . . . . ☐   ☐

In the Shipping Department

24. Are outgoing products ready when trucks and railroad cars arrive? . . . . ☐   ☐

25. Is the shipping area uncluttered with products and packages waiting to be moved? . . . . ☐   ☐

26. Is every package clearly labeled as to destination and mode of shipment? . . . . ☐   ☐

The special situations in each plant preclude the possibility of definite "yes" or "no" answers to the above questions. To score 100 per cent, answers to the first ten queries should be "no" and the balance should be answered "yes"; still, 100 per cent need not be your goal in all cases, for many situations will not justify going "all the way." Regardless of your answers, these questions provide guidelines to effective space utilization.

QUESTIONS

1. What are the symptoms and causes of poor plant layout?

2. Why and how are CPA's concerned with plant layout problems?

3. What are the objectives of a good plant layout?

A Review of Developments
in Production Management

DONALD N. DESALVIA

The topic of production management developments immediately suggests an examination of current changes in manufacturing methods and management. In surveying the current scene one is inclined to first notice the major technological changes which have occurred in recent decades.

Certainly the most prominent development in the minds of most people is automation. Without getting involved in a technical debate, we may briefly define automation as involving automatic transfer and self-correcting features which permit fully automatic control of an operation. In visualizing automation one usually thinks of fully-automated large-scale continuous-production plants in highly industrialized nations. Automation, however, has made inroads in such small scale operations as job-shops.

Numerically controlled machines are an example of automatic highly-flexible equipment suitable for small volume operations. Essentially, numeric control involves the automatic control of machine tools by means of numbers stored on magnetic or punched tape or cards. Through a computer these numbers dictate the machine's movement. A positioning system locates the tool at specified points where an operation is to be performed. Where the location of points is of importance and not the path between them, such as in drilling operations, a point to point system is employed. Where a shape is to be produced a continuous path system is employed. The tape or card input controls the actions of the machine through electronic impulses. Each instruction is followed until the entire operation is finished. With this type of system a single part may be produced or the cycle may be repeated to produce any number of parts.

While this type of equipment requires specialized labor skills to convert information on blueprints to a tape or card input it does lessen lead time by reducing set-up-time. It also reduces scrap, eliminates the need for large inventories of tools, jigs, and fixtures, and provides extreme accuracy on complicated shapes.

New methods of machining also have been developed. Machining with light has become possible with the development of the laser which is a beam of intense light which may be focused by a lens. Electron-beam methods have been developed for micro-machining and microwelding of "superhard" materials. Electrical discharge machining removes metal by sparks which erode the material and electrochemical machining consists of deplating material from the workpiece. These modern techniques of machining have the potential of becoming much more efficient than mechanical methods.

Space technology has resulted in the development of "superhard" metals that are readily machined and formed. Plastic and ceramic materials which in many ways are superior to metals also have been developed. Another outcome

From *Advanced Management Journal*, October 1964, pp. 79-84. Reprinted by permission.

of space research has been the development of high-energy-rate forming of different types. In one method, explosives are detonated against sheet metal blanks forcing them into dies which are much cheaper than those used in conventional methods. Forming now also may be accomplished by high-energy sparks or electro-magnetic fields.

Certainly, in even a brief listing of technological changes one would have to mention electronic data processing. Developments and applications in this field are progressing at an accelerating rate.

There have certainly been a number of technological evolutions in recent decades. It seems to me, however, that we should be more concerned with trends in the management of production rather than in techniques of production.

LONG-RANGE PLANNING

To some extent trends in management reflect underlying technological changes. Increased automation has necessitated greater emphasis on long-range planning to insure continuous operation of costly and complex equipment. This, I believe, may be expected to reverse the previous trend toward decentralization as more planning is done.

Electronic data processing is bound to have an impact on management. Space-age technology has already created an increased emphasis on quality and reliability. The complexity of modern technology may be expected to call for greater specialization in management. Numerical control, for instance, will increase the need for engineering knowledge in shop operations.

In addition to trends which arise from technological change we can isolate at least two other trends in management thinking. One is a greater emphasis on analytical methods and the other involves visualizing the internal and external environmental factors that the firm faces as an integrated whole—that is a systems approach.

Most managers tend to think in terms of specialized functions. The complexity of modern manufacturing, however, increasingly calls for an approach which cuts across lines of functional authority. A systems approach to materials management traces the movement of product from raw material to final consumer. Rhochrematics is the term given to this approach by Brewer and Rosenzweig.[1] Manufacturing of a single complex product often involves the simultaneous development and production of a vast array of individual components. Successful completion of the product requires integration of the various components and the various inputs used in producing them. PERT is a systems approach to planning and controlling this type of a program. Let us review these two approaches as illustrations of the systems concept.

Converting raw materials to a finished product and distributing products to consumers is a highly complex task in a modern firm. In the typical organization, the product in various forms passes under the control of a large number of functional departments. A brief listing of the functions involved would include:

---

[1]S. H. Brewer and James Rosenzweig, "Rhochrematics and Organizational Adjustments," *California Management Review* (Spring 1961) p. 61. See also Richard A. Johnson, "Rhochrematics— A System for Production and Marketing," *Advanced Management* (February 1961) p. 16.

1. purchasing
2. traffic
3. receiving
4. raw material storage
5. inventory control
6. manufacturing departments
7. production control
8. inspection
9. packaging
10. warehousing
11. shipping
12. marketing

Within each of the departments, controls are set up to insure the attainment of the specialized objectives of the department which often have little consideration of the functions performed by other departments or the overall objectives of the firm. Thus, there tends to be an optimization of separate departments which does not result in optimization for the entire operation. Material flows horizontally across the vertical structure of functional organization.

A systems approach to this problem views the flow of materials through the entire process and establishes controls to insure optimum flow rather than optimization of individual departments. The system results in lower total cost, better customer service, and better management control and coordination.

PROGRAM EVALUATION AND REVIEW TECHNIQUE

Program evaluation and Review Technique is a type of network analysis employed to recognize, identify, and control all interconnected links in a complex system over an extended period of time. Events and activities are the basic building blocks of a PERT network. Activities are time consuming elements in a program and in a PERT diagram they are represented by arrows. Activities begin and end with an event which indicates the completion of a distinct portion of a program. They are illustrated by a circle. Each event is numbered and connected by activities to those events which must precede it and those which follow it. A typical PERT network may consist of thousands of interconnected events.

Once the network has been diagrammed, the next step consists of developing an expected time for the completion of each activity. The expected time for the completion of each activity is obtained from three separate estimates—a pessimistic estimate, an optimistic estimate, and a most likely estimate.[2]

In the next step, all possible paths along the network are evaluated to determine the one with the longest expected time. This is called the critical-path. Any delay in activity on the critical-path will cause a delay in completion of the project. Since all other paths are shorter, they have some slack time. A delay in the accom-

---

[2]time expected = $\dfrac{\text{pessimistic estimate} + 4 \text{ (most likely estimate)} + \text{optimistic estimate}}{6}$

plishment of an event not on the critical path may not cause a change in the completion date.[3]

What help does this type of approach provide? First of all, just diagramming the network forces a great deal of planning. Once the critical path is recognized, management can divert resources from activity with slack times to activities on the critical path in order to reduce the time to complete the project. The approach permits management by exception by isolating the critical items which should be given the most attention. It also allows continuous evaluation and replanning as the project moves ahead. It is based on taking a systems viewpoint of a project.

While the most dramatic application of PERT programming has been in space developments it holds promise for some manufacturing programs. Planning and coordinating model changeovers, introduction of new processes, and relayouts could be assisted by the PERT techniques.

FORMAL ANALYTICAL METHODS

Another major trend is the increased use of formal analytical methods for studying managerial problems. The original exaggerated claims of early operations research enthusiasts have given way to slow but steady gains. As more theoretical knowledge is accumulated, increased applications may be expected.

Perhaps the best known and most widely applied analytical technique is linear programming.[4] It is a simplified method of finding from a large number of alternatives an optimum combination of limited resources to achieve a given objective. Some typical applications include determining optimum product mixes, machine loadings, schedules, assignments, allocation of capital, and location of warehouses.

Quadratic and dynamic programming are techniques of a similar nature. Other formal methods of analysis include simulation, queing theory, information theory, game theory and input-output analysis. In production problems simulation has been employed to improve scheduling of production and assembly through use of a mathematical model of the production facilities. Queing theory involves analysis of waiting lines which develop before service facilities. It may be employed to determine the optimum size of maintenance crews. It also has been applied to routing and sequencing problems, and to the determination of tool crib size. Quadratic programming has been employed in adjusting production to changes in sales. Information theory provides a means of examining communications problems in complex organizations.

The systems approach and formal analytical methods have produced some remarkable results and their full potentials have not yet been realized. These techniques, however, should not be expected to replace the need for judgment in management. They will never be able to solve all the problems faced by a man-

---

[3]For a more detailed explanation see R. W. Miller, "How to Plan and Control With PERT," *Harvard Business Review* (November-December 1956) pp. 93-104.

[4]See S. Stockton, *Introduction to Linear Programming* (Boston: Allyn & Bacon, Inc., 1963).

ager. The line balancing problem illustrates the limitations of these techniques at their current level of sophistication. Although considerable research has been devoted to this problem and some computer programs have been developed, no entirely satisfactory method has been found to replace the older trial and error methods. Nonetheless, they have had a considerable impact on management and the future promises an even greater impact. This suggests that future managers will have to have greater competence in these areas.

Besides changes in methods of manufacturing and trends in management thinking there have been significant changes in many of the standard tools of the production manager.

INDIRECT STANDARDS

With increasing world competition, cost reduction has become a major problem. Time standards have long been used on direct work but the irregularity and long cycles of indirect work have made it difficult to measure. With increasing cost pressure more attention has been devoted to setting indirect standards. One successful technique developed for indirect standards combines work sampling with performance rating. In this approach normal work sampling is accomplished and the result is leveled by a performance rating found by applying MTM to one portion of the study. This results in a standard adjusted for worker performance.[5]

Another development in the time study area is Master Standard Data which promises to greatly reduce the cost of setting standards. It combines the motions used in MTM into seven larger basic motions. Distance values have been reduced to the most frequent four. As a result, this system employs only 10% of the original MTM card figures. For jobs with a cycle time greater than 0.66 minutes, Master Standard Data is much faster (and therefore cheaper) than MTM and almost as accurate.

Combining Master Standard Data with a computer produces a system known as autorate. When there is a change in a job, the revisions are described on a punch card and the computer processes it to determine the new time standard. This method is particularly useful in plants where standards have to be frequently revised due to methods changes.[6]

In quality control, costs have been reduced and quality levels improved by shifting emphasis away from inspection to eliminate rejects to the prevention of defects by considering quality all the way from design and purchasing of materials to packaging and shipping finished products.[7] Considerable attention also has been given to automatic methods of testing.

To the well known fields of repair and preventative maintenance has been added a new subject—predictive maintenance.[8] It involves the use of sensing or measuring devices such as vibration analyzers to determine whether there has been a significant change in the physical condition of the equipment. This allows

---

[5]"Two New Twists in Performance Rating . . ." *Factory* (June 1962) pp. 71-73.
[6]"Work Measurement Scores Again," *Factory* (October 1962) pp. 84-85.
[7]A. V. Feigenbaum, "Total Quality Control," *Harvard Business Review* (November 1956).
[8]James Quinn, "The Real Goal of Maintenance Engineering," *Factory* (June 1963) pp. 91-93.

extension of operating time to maximum service life without increasing the risks of failure.

The modular design concept also has greatly reduced the down-time costs of maintenance. Another development is the design of equipment which will analyze and indicate the reason for its failure and thereby greatly reduces repair time.

The many changes that have been discussed are only a sampling of all the innovations in manufacturing and management techniques. New developments are constantly appearing. The new methods of a few days ago rapidly become standard procedures and are soon replaced by even better methods. This never ending process of change is one of the dynamic elements that makes production management a challenging field.

QUESTIONS

1. How have technological advancements affected the development of management?

2. What is the systems approach to materials management?

3. What is PERT? What does it force management to do?

4. What is the objective of linear programing?

Explore or Expire

"I don't need a great deal of money, Mr. Clemens," the tall, spare man said after explaining his invention. "You can have any part of it you want for $500."

Mark Twain, who had lost considerable sums of money on what he thought were sounder schemes, declined politely but firmly. Then, as the man turned away, the humorist asked, "What did you say your name was?"

"Bell," the inventor replied, "Alexander Graham Bell."

True or not, stories of this kind were fairly common until quite recently.

Albert Einstein's famous $E=MC^2$ and the Manhattan Project it made possible changed all that. Ever since the Federal Government's successful development of atomic energy in World War II, Uncle Sam has been the foremost patron of applied science.

Industry does most of the work, but the Government foots most of the bills. Private corporations—for the most part investor-owned—account for 67% of all research and development activity and government laboratories perform only 19% of the tasks (leaving 14% to be conducted by universities and nonprofit organizations). The Government pays for 70% of the work, industry picks up most of the remainder of the tab and the institutions contribute only a very small part of the cost.

With total expenditures running around $19 billion a year, industry as a whole is laying out funds at a rate of some $5.7 billion annually in its search for new products and technology. The growth of these efforts has been phenomenal. The present total of $19 billion contrasts with $5.5 billion spent ten years ago. In the manufacturing field, the expansion of R & D spending over the past decade has been half again as much as the growth in total sales.

Hard figures for specific companies are difficult to come by. Many firms guard their expenditures as information that might be helpful to competitors; in others—aircraft-aerospace, for instance—it might be difficult to know where R & D leaves off and production begins.

Among as representative a group as the 30 corporations whose stocks are in the Dow-Jones industrial average, only two make known their annual outlays for this purpose. Allied Chemical spent $29 million last year, slightly less than 3% of sales, and Union Carbide allocated $80 million, something better than 4% of every sales dollar.

These figures are probably high for industry in general. The chemical industry is by far the most active in this field, judging by National Science Foundation statistics which rank chemistry as employing more of the nation's scientists than the two nearest categories combined. With the Government's reach into space it is not surprising that physics and astronomy edge out the biological sciences as the disciplines that use up the second largest number of scientifically trained personnel.

Space exploration, as well as the endeavors of oil and mining companies, accounts for putting earth sciences in the fourth position as a user of talent. It is interesting to note that mathematics and statistics still keep more scientists busy than does psychology.

Over-all, some 800,000 scientists, technicians and engineers are at work on research in this country. This figure would have to be multiplied, perhaps several fold, to include all the back-up personnel that are engaged in the search for new products and new ways of doing things.

The figures are growing and will continue to do so at perhaps an even faster pace. General Electric's Missile & Space Division started ten years ago with six men working on the re-entry of space vehicles into the atmosphere. Today, some 1,200 people are at work in this division.

Anyone who thinks this sort of thing can't happen again need only look at the computer field alone. The first electronic "brain" was launched in 1946. It took eight years before the first one went to work for industry. Now, more than

20,000 of them are installed across the country and about as many more are on order. The Labor Department estimates that by 1970 there will be a need for more than 200,000 programmers to keep the computers in industry and government going.

The benefits that have accrued to business from research and development are too apparent to need elaboration. That more are in the offing seems almost a certainty. But obviously this is not an unrelieved boon. Everyone knows about the carriage makers who were put out of business by the gas buggy. Most people also know, however, that not all of them fell by the wayside. The Fisher Brothers proved remarkably adaptable and General Motors still brags about "body by Fisher."

The lesson for the investor should be clear. As part of the consideration of an equity's potential some thought must be given to the ability of the company it represents either to conduct its own program or adapt the available fruits of other efforts to its own products and processes. For, although R & D is not a magic formula for success or growth, no company can ignore research and prosper in today's competitive market place.

QUESTIONS

1. Who conducts most of the research? Who pays for most of it?

2. Has spending on research and development increased significantly in the past decade?

3. Why are the dollar expenditures on research and development by many companies not disclosed to the public?

6

The Personnel Function

There is one element common to all business firms regardless of their size, purpose, location, or importance. This is the human element. Every business requires people to staff its offices, factories, or stores. In many cases the use or misuse of the human factor has determined the success or failure of a company. Because of the complexity of the individual person and his importance to the firm, dealing with him has become an increasingly specialized function. The personnel function can be broadly defined as the management of people.

Most firms employing over one hundred people have personnel departments. In firms not having personnel departments, line managers, from the president to the foremen, handle the various personnel functions. In the larger firm, the personnel department is a staff department performing several functions. The major functions generally include the following: selection, education and training, wage and salary administration, and labor relations. A more global area in which the personnel department is particularly interested is that of the personal relationships and interactions of employees—human relations.

SELECTION

A continuing problem for most companies is the filling of its manpower needs. Various sources of labor are utilized in filling these needs. The sources of labor supply typically are classified into internal and external sources. When a job vacancy occurs, a firm may choose to fill the vacancy from an *internal source*. This would involve the transfer or promotion of an individual already employed by the company. *External sources* are utilized when a position is filled by hiring a new employee. Common outside sources include state employment services, private employment agencies, and schools and colleges. Some companies having strong promotion-from-within policies give initial preference to qualified current employees before seeking personnel from outside sources, but most firms use both sources to some extent.

The initial step in developing a selection program, regardless of the source used, is that of job analysis. *Job analysis* is an intensive, direct method of obtaining the important facts about jobs. It attempts to determine the specific tasks that comprise the job and the skills, abilities, and knowledge that are required of a worker to successfully perform the job. The important facts concerning the job are placed in the *job description*. The *job specification* lists the various qualifications needed by the worker. The development of job descriptions and specifications forms a standard against which the personnel manager can measure job applicants.

Several methods are used to aid the personnel manager in evaluating a job applicant's qualifications for a position. Application blanks, psychological tests, and personal interviews are among the most common techniques.

Application blanks are forms used to obtain biographical information from the applicant. Information usually gathered includes personal data such as name, age, sex, marital status, height, and weight. The applicant's work history is also an important part of the application form. He is required to list those positions he has held in the past, the duties involved, and the reasons for leaving these positions. References of previous employers and personal acquaintances are also requested. These references are usually investigated through letters or personal conversation.

Psychological tests are being used increasingly in the selection process. A psychological test may be defined as a "systematic procedure for sampling human behavior."[1] In sampling human behavior, the tests attempt to measure such attributes as the person's abilities, personality, and interests. The most commonly used test is the *ability test*. Ability tests measure general mental ability (or intelligence) and special abilities (or aptitudes). *Achievement tests* measure a person's current knowledge in a subject area. *Personality tests* attempt to describe various aspects of a person's personality such as his attitudes, temperament, and personal adjustment. The difficulties in administering and interpreting this type of test restrict their use to companies having trained testing experts, usually psychologists. Because of this limitation and the fact that the tests themselves have limitations, personality tests are not as widely accepted as ability tests. A subclass of personality tests are the *vocational interest tests,* which measure the likes and dislikes of individuals in regard to occupational activities. The interest test is used more in vocational guidance than in personnel selection.

The most widely used selection technique is the *interview*. The employment interview is used to gain additional information about the applicant, usually amplifying the data gathered on the application blank. Also, it allows the interviewer to form a general impression of the applicant, particularly how he interacts with another person. It should be remembered that the interview is only as reliable as the person conducting it.

TRAINING

With today's constantly changing technology and mobile labor force, a continuing managerial problem is maintaining a supply of competent personnel. To insure this, training is necessary, for both new employees and those needing improved techniques to continue to perform their old jobs adequately. Common training methods include orientation, on-the-job training, vestibule training, classroom techniques, and apprenticeship training.

---

[1]Dale Beach, *Personnel: The Management of People at Work* (New York: The Macmillan Company, 1965), p. 223.

Orientation aims at introducing the new employee to the company and to his new job. This introduction should be as complete as possible, giving the employee all the information he needs to adjust as quickly as possible to his job.

On-the-job training involves teaching the worker specific aspects of his job in the actual work situation. It is the most common type of training and is effective where the skills being learned are not complex and can be learned in a relatively short period of time. On-the-job training is often used in the learning of unskilled and semi-skilled jobs and various types of clerical work. The training is usually done by the employee's supervisor. Where either complex skills or theoretical material is being taught, on-the-job training falls short. Usually only individuals or small groups are trained in this way. *Vestibule training,* on the other hand, attempts to teach the skills needed for semi-skilled or clerical jobs in a classroom situation. This allows larger groups to be taught in a more intensive manner by a qualified instructor.

Classroom techniques include the traditional teaching methods employed in formal educational settings. The more important techniques are lectures, conferences, and the study of realistic sample cases. These techniques are used at virtually all levels of training. However, they are used to a greater extent at the various managerial levels than elsewhere in the organization. *Apprentice training* involves the training of skilled craftsmen through rigorous on-the-job and classroom experience. The apprentice programs typically involve intensive training over a period of two to six years.

Training is a personnel function that affects the great majority of employees in American business. The current attempts made by business to train their employees contributes to both improved business effectiveness and the continued personal growth of the employee.

WAGE AND SALARY ADMINISTRATION

Among the most important factors influencing a person in his consideration of a new job are the wages offered. Wages are also an important source of motivation for employees to perform their jobs effectively. For the firm, wages are a major cost, often the largest single cost of doing business. *Wage and salary administration* is the common term used to refer to the establishment of policies and methods of employee compensation.

Several factors may affect a firm's wage policy.[2] They include wage levels in the local labor market, the financial status of the firm, labor-management agreements, and wage and hour legislation. Prevailing wages in the local labor market are an important criteria as firms are in competition for workers; if other factors are equal, an employee will usually select the job with the highest pay. The financial status of the firm affects its ability to pay. If a firm is financially healthy, it will be able to pay higher wages than a marginally successful firm. Labor contracts set wages through the process of collective bargaining. Wage and hour legislation has established minimum wages above which a firm must pay. (This legislation affects those firms involved in interstate commerce.) In most busi-

---

[2]For a complete discussion of wage and salary administration, see David W. Belcher, *Wage and Salary Administration* (Englewood Cliffs, N.J.: Prentice-Hall, Inc., 1962).

nesses all of these factors, in addition to others of less importance, are considered in the formulation of wage policies.

The majority of American workers are paid in one of three ways: time wages, piece wages, or salary. With *time wages,* an employee's pay is dependent upon the number of hours worked. If his pay rate is $2.50 per hour, he would be paid $100 for a forty-hour week. However, if he worked only thirty hours in a week, he would receive only $75 for that week. Under the *piece wages* plan, the employee is paid for each unit he produces. However, a minimum hourly rate of pay is usually guaranteed. For example, a worker receives 5 cents per piece machined. He is also guaranteed a minimum of $1.50 per hour. If the worker machined forty pieces in an hour, he would receive $2.00 per hour. However, if he were able to produce only twenty-eight pieces in an hour, he would receive his minimum guarantee of $1.50. As can be seen by this example, it is to the worker's advantage to produce as many units as possible in order to exceed his minimum hourly wage. *Salaried employees* receive compensation which is uniform from one pay period (usually a week or a month) to another. It is dependent neither on time worked nor units of work produced. A salaried employee if his wage were $150 per week would receive $150 if he worked thirty-eight, forty, or forty-two hours per week. Methods of payment usually follow this classification, although the distinctions between the methods break down somewhat in actual practice. For example, some firms do pay overtime based on hourly rates to salaried workers.

Employees receive many benefits that are not in the form of direct pay. These benefits, usually referred to as *fringe benefits,* add substantially to an employee's compensation. They include such benefits as life and health insurance, pension plans, paid vacations and holidays, and social and recreational programs. Firms vary as to the type and extent of their benefit programs.

LABOR

Over 17 million Americans belong to labor unions. This fact of industrial life has important implications for business firms in our country. This group of workers, which is approximately one quarter of the nation's total labor force, exerts a tremendous influence on all areas of American life.

Union members, who are collectively referred to as *organized labor,* come primarily from manufacturing firms. The labor union has the primary function of negotiating agreements between its members and their employers concerning various conditions of employment such as wages, hours, and working conditions. The union also attempts to protect the individual worker from unfair treatment by management. The basic idea behind the labor union is that a large number of workers acting together can influence management, whereas the workers individually would have little power.

The history of the labor movement in this country dates from the early Colonial Period. During the early years of our country, craftsmen such as shoemakers and printers formed organizations to bring about some improvements in working conditions. These organizations were weak and short-lived, however. The early 1800's saw further attempts at organizing labor with the formation of local unions. In 1869 the first national labor union, the Knights of Labor, was founded. Beginning in Philadelphia as a local union of garment workers, the Knights of Labor quickly expanded in size and geography. It also extended its membership to workers in other occupations. After reaching a peak membership of over 700,000 in 1886, internal conflicts led to its decline. In 1886 Samuel Gompers formed the American Federation of Labor (AFL) from a number of craft unions, many of which had seceded from the Knights of Labor. During the next three decades the AFL grew rapidly, concentrating on the achievement of better working conditions for its members. The AFL admitted relatively few industrial worker unions into its federation. In the early 1930's eight of the industrial unions, after forming a strong vocal committee within the AFL, were expelled from the AFL. They were expelled because the AFL member craft unions were threatened by the possibility of a large inflow of other industrial unions.

The expelled unions under the leadership of John L. Lewis formed the Congress of Industrial Organizations (CIO). The CIO, focusing on the organization of workers, was immediately successful. Following this success, competition for additional union memberships began between the CIO and the AFL. This competition was ended in 1955 when the two national federations merged into the AFL-CIO. Nonaffiliated unions are referred to as independent unions. The largest independent union in the country is the Teamsters.

One of the most important functions of labor organizations is *collective bargaining*. Collective bargaining is a process in which union representatives negotiate with management over the terms of labor agreements or contracts. The principle upon which these negotiations are based is that the union is the authorized bargaining agent of the workers. The major provisions of a labor contract are wage rates, hours of work, employee benefits, working conditions, disciplinary methods, grievance procedures, and the length of the contract.

The labor-management relationship is affected not only by labor agreements but by labor legislation. Three major pieces of legislation currently affect labor policy: the National Labor Relations Act of 1935 (Wagner Act); the Labor-Management Relations Act of 1947 (Taft-Hartley Act); and the Labor-Management Reporting and Disclosure Act of 1959 (Landrum-Griffin Act).[3]

The Wagner Act sets forth regulations insuring the right of workers to organize and bargain collectively with employers. It also established the National Labor Relations Board to certify bargaining units as representatives of employee groups. This board (the NLRB) rules upon complaints of unfair labor practices committed by unions or management. The Wagner Act was seen by management to be strongly prolabor, and the Taft-Hartley Act was passed to establish a better balance between management and labor. This act attempts to equalize the rights and privileges of management with those guaranteed labor by the Wagner Act. The Landrum-Griffin Act was passed to aid in the control of abuses within organized labor. It has proved to be difficult to enforce and interpret, although its presence as law has helped to control some of the more flagrant problems.[4]

---

[3]See Edwin F. Beal and Edward D. Wickersham, *The Practice of Collective Bargaining* (Homewood, Illinois: Richard D. Irwin, Inc., 1963), for an analysis of labor legislation.

[4]Edwin B. Flippo, *Principles of Personnel Management,* 2nd ed. (New York: McGraw-Hill Book Company, 1966), p. 461, and Herbert J. Chruden and Arthur W. Sherman, Jr., *Personnel Management,* 2nd ed. (Cincinnati: South-Western Publishing Company, 1963), p. 510.

HUMAN RELATIONS

The understanding and direction of employees is among the most difficult of the businessman's tasks. If the objectives of the firm are to be met, managers must be able to deal effectively with their personnel. To do this, a knowledge of employee motivation is necessary. Also, the supervisor must know how to lead his employees.

The study of the "whys" or causes of behavior is called the study of *motivation*. Psychologists often discuss motivation as having three elements: needs, actions, and incentives. For example, a person who has gone several hours without eating has a *need* for food. When this need is great enough, it will cause him to seek food. At this point the need has become an *action*. The food which the person seeks is the *incentive*. In a similar case, a worker desiring a higher standard of living (need) will work harder (action) to increase his pay (incentive).

Needs or motives are generally classified as primary (unlearned) or secondary (learned) needs. *Primary needs* are inborn and include needs for food, water, sex, and sleep. They are basically biological in nature. *Secondary needs* can be either social or personal. Social motives involve our desire to associate with other people. They include needs for companionship, love, and the respect of others. Personal motives refer to those acquired needs concerning an individual's view of himself. Among the important personal needs are those for self-respect, freedom, and self-accomplishment. The strength and type of secondary needs vary considerably from one person to another.

Most employees in American business have satisfied their primary biological needs. Hence, managers focus on the secondary needs as the possible sources of satisfaction and dissatisfaction in their employees. If these needs are met, high employee morale will usually result; if not, low morale is likely. The complex nature of human motivation and the differences in motivation between individuals makes solving motivational problems difficult.

In addition to understanding the motives of employees, the ability to lead them is also necessary. *Leadership* is the process by which a person influences a subordinate to act in a certain way.[5] In the business environment a manager exercises leadership by influencing his employees to act in such a way that company goals are achieved. Three factors influence the leadership process: the leader, the followers, and the situation. The personal traits of the leader can affect his ability to lead. In a similar manner, the personalities and abilities of the followers will often determine the type of person who can lead them successfully. The situation or environment in which the leader and followers are acting can often change their behavior. For example, one person may have the ability to lead a Boy Scout troop and yet not be able to lead a group of skilled workmen. Another person might be a successful military leader, but a poor political leader. The interaction of all three factors—leader, follower, and situation—is important in studying leadership in the constantly changing business environment.

People do not only act as individuals when at work, but also as groups.

---

[5] Warren G. Bennis. "Leadership Theory and Administrative Behavior: The Problem of Authority," *Administrative Science Quarterly*, Vol. 4 (1959-1960), p. 295.

Employees are usually parts of formal work groups organized by management. Many may also be members of formal bargaining groups—the labor unions. However, informal groups are created apart from the formal organization when people of similar interests, likes, and dislikes gather together in a working environment. The informal group often meets its members' needs for companionship, friendship, and security. As the members of informal groups become close, membership in the group can affect the members' attitudes and behavior toward their employer, supervisor, and other workers. To effectively direct one's employees, a manager should be sensitive to the individual needs of his employees and also recognize the needs of the formal and informal groups under his supervision.

The readings included in this section attempt to give a broad view of the personnel function with the emphasis on current behavioral influences. The article by Harvey G. Foster briefly discusses the initial screening of a job applicant. Saul W. Gellerman investigates the proper role of psychological testing in the selection process, giving several guidelines as to their proper usage. George M. Davey's article focuses on seven problem areas in industrial training programs. "Appraisal by Results" is discussed by Walter S. Wikstrom, in an attempt at differentiating this concept from its correlate, "management by objectives." "The Meaning of Money," by Richard Stull, discusses the psychological aspects of money and the effect they might have on compensation systems. The *Nation's Business* article broadly describes a number of important practical labor problems. Harold Rush introduces the reader to the behavioral sciences, showing their importance in the business world.

Employee Screening

HARVEY G. FOSTER

It is generally accepted that a company is no better than its employees. A company with a high caliber of employee finds employee screening as necessary to maintain its standards as the company which desires to raise them.

Employee screening starts with the application. The company's application should be reviewed to determine that all information about the applicant which the company desires, will be set forth on the application itself, or secured in personal interview. What can be secured on an application today is restricted by the various State and Federal laws designed for the purpose of avoiding dis-

From *Personnel Journal*, July-August 1965, pp. 351-352. Reprinted by permission of the *Personnel Journal* of Swarthmore, Pennsylvania.

crimination against applicants, by reason of color, race, or creed. But basically, an application should contain the full name of the applicant, as well as any nicknames or aliases; the age, date, and place of birth, citizenship and such descriptive data as height, weight, social security number, address and telephone number. If the permanent address is different than the present address, this also should be included. The application could well include the full names of the applicant's parents, their addresses and employments. In addition, it should contain the full name, address, and place of employment of the applicant's spouse, if married. It should, of course, contain a record of past employment by date, address, and name of immediate supervisor, together with wage rate, information concerning the type of work performed, job title, and reason for leaving. A full educational background should be included, names of associations in which the applicant is active, together with the address of the association. It is necessary to include information concerning U.S. Armed Forces record, Selective Service record, and Military Reserve status. References, together with address, phone number, occupation, and length of association with applicant, are necessary. Relatives or acquaintances in the company should be listed.

Most helpful, too, is a listing for the preceding ten years, if feasible, of all residences of the applicant, including school residences. Of assistance are bank accounts, charge accounts, whether or not the applicant owns own home, rents, or resides with parents, information as to whether or not the applicant owns an automobile, driver's license, or licenses, including the type, state or states wherein issued, and the expiration date. Questions concerning whether or not the applicant has ever been arrested, including traffic violations, are, of course, pertinent.

It will be seen from the above, that the application should be quite detailed. This will provide excellent background information for the personnel department's use in conducting a personal interview.

PERSONAL INTERVIEW

The personal interview should be used to evaluate the applicant and make some determination as to whether or not he or she will be an asset to the company. In addition, it should be the means of exploring any questionable information set forth in the application. The interviewer should explore the patterns of employment and determine what conclusions can be drawn from them, and, just as important, exploration should be made of the gaps in employment record. Some indication, too, can be secured as to whether or not the applicant is living within his or her means.

The interviewer should have a check list which will summarize his opinion of the applicant and should make a positive recommendation as to whether the applicant should be given further consideration. If this is the case, further consideration should be given to any further testing at this stage.

VERIFICATION OF EMPLOYEE'S BACKGROUND

An extremely important phase of employee screening is verification of the information the applicant has furnished. Most companies, in one way or another, attempt to verify the past employment, altho many companies stop at this point. A company looking over its employee screening program should carefully consider its method of verification of past employment. The best method, of course, is an actual, in person investigation accomplished by company investigators or contract investigators. The minimum requirement should be a written query of the past employer, references, and law enforcement agencies. From an investigative standpoint, this could well start with the supervisors responsible for the applicant in his past employment, as well as a check of the past employers' personnel records. The investigation could continue with verification of the applicant's education, which should include academic standing and the evaluation of the applicant by some of his or her teachers. A credit check in the areas where the applicant and his spouse have resided is many times most revealing. Contact with local law enforcement agencies where the applicant has resided and gone to school is a must.

Record of Motor Vehicle Bureaus concerning the applicant's driving record is a necessity in certain types of employment and indicative of the applicant's stability in any event. Where possible, military record, with any type of questionable discharge, should be explored. Personal contact with references is desirable and surprisingly enough references are often the first to indicate that the applicant is questionable. In positions warranting it, contact with the applicant's neighbors as to his character and reputation in his neighborhood is also most helpful.

The company will, of course, have to make a determination as to how much it feels it can afford in time and money in screening its prospective employees. Some companies have found that the institution of an investigative check of the background of applicants has turned up information resulting in as high as 22% being turned down. As a result of this, some of them have revised their application and interviewing procedures, making them much more painstaking. But even in these instances, the rate of rejections of favorably considered applicants will run as high as 8%. Therefore, it behooves a company interested in maintaining its high personnel standards to make a thorough review of its employee screening program. Such a review, with the institution of basic safeguards, will pay handsome dividends.

EVALUATION OF APPLICANT

A final step should be a complete evaluation of all information—the application, interviews, tests and the verification of the applicant's background. Then, and only then, can the applicant be fully evaluated and the best possible determination be made of his suitability for employment with the company.

QUESTIONS

1. What facts should be gathered in the employee application?

2. List the types of information that can be secured in an employment interview.

3. Discuss the various aspects of an applicant's background that should be investigated.

Personnel Testing: What the Critics Overlook

SAUL W. GELLERMAN

Personnel testing finds itself on the defensive today, largely because of the recent publication of widely selling books that have openly challenged its value.[1] On balance I think this criticism is a good thing, even though the authors of these books have given an unrealistically frightening picture of the way selection tests are used in industry.

In the long run such critiques will stand or fall on their own merits. Rather than attempt a detailed reply to them here, I should like to consider the central question they raise. It is a very blunt question: Is personnel testing so loaded with faults that we should discard it entirely?

It is common knowledge among psychologists and personnel managers alike that tests have been widely misused, that not enough attention is paid to their limitations, or to the qualifications of the people who interpret them. The literature of personnel management has for years been full of warnings about the need to use tests more cautiously, to develop better ones, and to continuously check their validity. Unfortunately, this attempt to set our house in order by preaching to each other has not tidied it very noticeably.

Perhaps, then, the pressures generated by outside criticism will be more effective in stimulating the much needed modernization and reform of testing practices in industry. What we have to guard against, of course, is the fact that some of the critics are advocating not reform, but abolition. It is by no means inconceivable that their views might prevail, given enough alarm on the part of their readers and an uncertainty on the part of personnel people as to whether there is, indeed, anything in testing worth saving.

Though many of the criticisms that have been leveled against testing are true or partially true, the critics have sidestepped the basic question—is there any suitable alternative to it? That is, given the massive screening jobs that industry, universities, and governments face every year in connection with recruiting and job placement, is there a procedure other than testing that can do as helpful a job as tests at a reasonable cost but without so many disadvantages? I think all the available evidence indicates that the answer is *No*.

Consequently, apart from all the sound and fury of arguments for or against testing, the practical problem we face is not whether testing is worth while, but how we can make the best possible use of these admittedly imperfect instruments until their imperfections can be corrected or better instruments can be developed to take their place.

This is a complex problem, and it has a complex answer. In order to arrive at that answer, we must first tackle several preliminary questions:

☐ What is the nature of the recruitment process, and how does testing fit into it?

From *Personnel,* May-June 1963. Reprinted by permission of the American Management Association, Inc.

[1]For example, see B. Hoffman, *The Tyranny of Testing,* McGraw-Hill, New York, 1962; and M. L. Gross, *The Brain Watchers,* Random House, New York, 1962.

☐ Under what specific circumstances, if any, do tests help to improve the re-sults of recruitment?
☐ What is a valid test?
☐ Are any tests valid?
☐ Must a test's questions be job-related and "non-fakable" to be valid?
☐ Is validity necessary?
☐ Are valid tests useful?
☐ Finally, are useful tests necessary?

Only after we have threaded our way through these fundamental questions can we give an informed and dispassionate answer to the challenges now being made by testing's critics.

Let's begin by taking a broad view of the recruitment process as a whole. Every recruitment decision involves three variables that can seldom be defined exactly: the available supply of candidates who are willing to take the job for a salary the company can afford, the actual requirements of the job in terms of human abilities, and the actual capabilities of the available candidates. The basic problem facing the personnel manager is to reduce the uncertainty in all three areas, so that his final decision is based as much on fact and as little on faith as possible. To do this he has specialized techniques, and one of these techniques is testing.

Here we encounter a very important rule of interaction, which is that effective control over any one of these areas of uncertainty reduces the need to control the others. For example, if the personnel manager could somehow get access to a good supply of highly talented, highly motivated candidates, it wouldn't really be necessary for him to have a highly sensitive testing and evaluating program. All he would need is an attractive "employer image" that lured these outstanding people into his company in sufficient numbers to meet his needs. These men would all be very likely to succeed, and it would be pointless to try to use tests for making fine discriminations among them.

Regrettably, such a glut of high-potential candidates is one problem most personnel managers don't have, and so the uncertainty in the selection process usually has to be reduced by evaluating both the individual and the job. Con-sequently, any process—including tests—that can help to identify the most prom-ising candidates in a market where promising candidates are rare pays off in the selection process.

JOB EVALUATION

A careful job evaluation can help to reduce our dependence on methods of evaluating people, since it gives us a clearer idea of the minimum standards to look for in our candidates, and surer guidance in tapping the available pool of candidates. But once again, accurate job evaluations are all too rare. So we can say of personnel evaluation methods in general that they derive much of their importance from our deficiencies in the skills of recruiting and job evaluation, and that if we made progress in those skills we would not need to lean so heavily as we do on our admittedly imperfect instruments for evaluating people.

There are a number of ways of evaluating a man's qualifications besides tests; for example, interviews, reference checks, biographical data, and work samples. It doesn't make much sense to seek one method that is "better" than the others, since they all tend to be sensitive to different aspects of the individual. Also, none of them (tests included) is so reliable that a forecast based on it would not gain accuracy by being supplemented with other methods. As a practical matter, therefore, the most realistic question to ask about tests is not merely whether they accurately predict performance in themselves, but whether they add any greater accuracy to the predictions we are able to make using non-test methods.

In certain circumstances tests *do* add to predictive accuracy, and in all other circumstances they do *not*. Tests, like any other evaluation method, will increase the accuracy of a forecast only when there is a lasting, significant relation between test results and performance results—or, to use the psychologist's term, when the tests are valid—and when the tests are measuring aspects of the individual that other methods do not measure or do not measure so well.

The concept of validity is crucial for tests and every other selection tool. Hence it is worth noting some features about validity that are sometimes overlooked when the value of testing is being scrutinized.

First, *validity is a statistical concept; it refers to large groups, and not to individuals.* This means that a test is valid when, in a large group of tested individuals, test scores correspond to job performance more often than they would be expected to by chance alone. It also means that a test can be valid generally and still be dead wrong in the case of any given individual.

Obviously, then, tests are useful chiefly as a means of screening large groups, and are less useful in distinguishing between small numbers of individuals or in making a prediction about a single person. (This is true regardless of whether the tests are scored mechanically or interpreted individually by a psychologist.) Even the most valid test tells us, basically, only one thing about an individual: It quotes odds on his apparent chances of success.

Second, *a test doesn't necessarily have to be very valid to be useful.* This fact was first demonstrated more than 20 years ago by H. C. Taylor and J. T. Russell, but it is not widely known.[2] One of the main advantages of having a highly valid test is that it is possible to define a score above which nearly everybody succeeds on the job, and below which nearly everybody fails. However, if the validity of the test is low, it is harder to pinpoint the right "cutoff" score, because too many potential failures will be above any score and too many potential successes will be below it. Nevertheless, if the personnel manager is in a position to be very selective he can still confine himself to the *very* high scorers.

WASTEFUL BUT USEFUL

Though this procedure is admittedly wasteful of good men who get low scores, it still enables the manager, by being fussy with a small proportion of the men who

---

[2]H. C. Taylor and J. T. Russell, "The Relationship of Validity Coefficients to the Practical Effectiveness of Tests in Selection: Discussion and Tables," *Journal of Applied Psychology,* 1939, No. 23, pp. 565-578.

take a test of low validity, to hire as many successful men as he could by not being fussy with a large proportion of the men who take a test of high validity. In other words, a test of low validity can do a useful screening job in an abundant labor market.

Third, *tests are often more valid than we can prove them to be*. There are two main reasons for this. One is that most job applicants who obtain low test scores are not hired; hence their job performance is never known and cannot be included in any calculation of a test's validity. In effect, validity usually has to be estimated on the basis of a narrow range of high scores. The formula used to compute validity is sensitive to this restriction; the result is a lower correlation figure than would probably be obtained if a wider range of scores were included.

The second reason why a test's validity is often greater than it seems is that the yardsticks with which we measure job performance are frequently unreliable themselves. Performance evaluations by supervisors are notoriously subjective; yet often they are the only practical criteria we have for "validating" tests. For example, a recent study in a large oil company showed that test scores that had an unimpressive correlation with supervisory ratings at the time they were given were actually better predictors of ultimate success than the performance ratings. The proof of the pudding, of course, is in the eating; but since human careers take years to reach fruition, we have to make do with more immediate yardsticks, such as performance ratings, in estimating a test's validity.

Fourth, *a test can be valid even when the test questions are not pertinent to the job*. This fact has probably caused more misunderstandings about tests than any other. The point to bear in mind is that if the test score gives a reliable indication of job capability, then it doesn't really matter whether the score was attained through knowledge, guessing, or even deception. For this reason, we can make good use of tests that ask questions on subjects that the testees know nothing about, as well as tests that are transparently easy to beat.

For example, the "general information" type of test covers a very wide spectrum of knowledge, and therefore favors the man with a broad-ranging curiosity and the ability to reason his way to answers he doesn't necessarily know. It is, in other words, a measure of "applied intelligence," and can be quite a useful addition to selection programs in which *all* candidates can be presumed to be intelligent, but not all are necessarily inquisitive or clever in their use of their intelligence.

SENSIBLE DECEPTION

Furthermore, many interest and personality tests that lend themselves rather easily to simulation by the testee can also be useful for selection purposes, because a certain degree of posturing and concealment of motives is not only normal, but often a necessity for effective social relationships. In effect, such a test shows whether the individual is sensible enough to portray himself in a reasonably acceptable manner, or whether he is so naïve as to be overly candid, or (in the case of the test faker who gets carried away with his deception) clumsy enough to present an unbelievably sterling self-appraisal.

The important point is that it is not an indication of "true" interests or personality that the test is seeking, but rather (in this case) a sample of common sense, naïveté, or clumsiness. Going a step beyond that, we are less interested in this particular sample than in knowing whether the candidate is at least as sensible as he must be to do the job—which is an estimate that a valid test enables us to make with at least some degree of confidence.

Even though validity can take some strange forms, we are well aware that not all tests or test batteries are valid. When validity exists at all, it is a highly specific thing: A particular test may be a valid predictor of performance for people doing a particular job in a particular company at a particular time, using a particular minimum score as the cutoff point. But the same test may not be valid at all in any other context.

The "Validity Information Exchange" in *Personnel Psychology* (a quarterly journal) has for years published validity data on various tests with various employee populations, and the files of company psychologists and consultants are probably full of similar demonstrations that particular tests are valid in particular instances.

NO UNIVERSAL VALIDITY

But there is no such thing as general validity for any test; its usefulness as a selection instrument has to be proven for every job in every company in which it is used, and periodically reproven, as well. It is precisely here that some of the greatest shortcomings in industrial testing practice have arisen. Too many companies have installed tests that had proved to be valid elsewhere without troubling to revalidate them locally. I will go so far as to say that failure to validate locally with established, time-honored tests probably causes more misclassification of human beings than all the charlatans and smooth-talking test merchants put together. Honest oversight, in other words, can cause a great deal more mischief than dishonest or incompetent testing.

Now, even if a test is valid, is it necessarily useful? Not always. Some tests are valid with only an uneconomically small proportion of the people who take it; for example, a very difficult test on which scarcely anyone gets a high score, though nearly all high scorers succeed on the job. Other tests may be valid but take too long to administer, or cost too much, or probe more deeply than some believe an employer should. Still other tests, particularly those using projective techniques, are sometimes valid and sometimes not, since their interpretation is more of an art than a science. Some tests are valid for most people but invalid for a critically important minority, such as exceptionally bright or creative people taking multiple-choice intelligence tests. Finally, a test may be valid but essentially duplicated by a cheaper, shorter, or less controversial test.

HOW DOES IT PREDICT?

In general, therefore, the usefulness of a valid test depends on whether it adds enough predictive power to the test battery to be worth its added cost in time, money, and potentially unfavorable reactions. There is obviously no pat formula to guide us here, but it is a sobering fact that by combining two or more valid tests into a battery we usually get only a modest return in added predictive power. This is simply because valid tests tend to overlap; that is, they measure essentially the same characteristics.

The next question we must ask is, even supposing a test is useful, is it necessary? Are there situations in which tests can, in fact, give an accurate, economical forecast of job performance, but aren't really needed? There certainly are. We use tests to predict job performance, but sometimes we already know perfectly well what it is, as in the case of experienced personnel who have handled comparable jobs with a demonstrated degree of competence.

In such cases the person's job history may be as reliable an indicator of future performance as a test and possibly more so, since it is by no means uncommon for people who are already successfully holding down a particular job to score poorly when they are given a selection test for a comparable position. Obviously, there is little sense in testing experienced people "just to be sure" they can do what they have already shown themselves capable of doing.

There is a practical difficulty here, though—how to determine whether the previous job is truly comparable to the one under consideration. Jobs that carry the same title or are superficially similar may actually have very different requirements and here, of course, a man's employment record may be an unreliable predictor. Plainly, the comparability of jobs must be carefully weighed before it is assumed that competence can be transferred from one job to another, but this is no reason for the ritual of insisting that *all* candidates be tested, regardless of experience. As it works out, this means that testing will usually be appropriate with young applicants or with older ones who lack relevant experience.

Another needless use of valid tests, though often resorted to, is their administration to applicants who, for reasons unrelated to their test scores, are definitely not going to be hired anyway. Companies often give tests in such cases, either to make the applicant feel that he has had a thoroughgoing evaluation, or with the secret intention of putting the blame for the rejection on the test results. It need hardly be said that such deceptions are an abuse of tests, and, far worse than that, of people, too.

TESTS FOR TESTING

On the whole, then, I think it fair to conclude that testing, despite its imperfections, is clearly worth while in certain circumstances and probably valueless in others. It follows that a sophisticated policy in this area will be based on an awareness of the circumstances in which tests can be most helpfully employed. From the above analysis, we can pinpoint 11 conditions that should be met to enhance the probability that testing will be worth while in any specific instance:

1. A high proportion of the available candidates is unlikely to meet the performance standards of the job.

2. Alternative methods of evaluating candidates are not equally valid, or do not measure the same attributes as tests or do not measure them as well as tests, or are less convenient, acceptable, or economical than tests.

3. The test in question has been shown to be valid (i.e., significantly correlated with an independent measure of job performance) in a recent study of a sizable sample of the present employees of the specific company in which it is being used.

4. It is understood by those who will make the selection decision that test results, no matter how they are expressed or interpreted, are always an actuarial estimate of the likelihood of job success for all persons attaining similar scores and never a specific prediction for a specific testee.

5. The test results are therefore treated as only a part, and by no means an infallible part, of the total information on which the selection decision is to be based.

6. The personnel manager is mindful of the relation between the validity of the tests he is using and the available supply of qualified candidates, and moves his cutoff point up or down in order to minimize both the selection of unsuitable candidates and the rejection of suitable ones.

7. Where "fakable" tests or tests with questions that are unrelated to the job are used, there is statistical evidence that these characteristics do not seriously detract from the tests' validity, range of usefulness, or acceptability to the testee.

8. The tests are valid for at least the majority of persons who are likely to take them, including "significant minorities," when there is a need to identify these reliably.

9. The tests are economical of time and money, in relation to the importance of the job being filled.

10. Reliable information on the applicant's performance in a job comparable to the one he is being considered for is not already available.

11. The applicant is a genuine candidate who may actually be selected for the opening.

While these are rather formidable conditions, before we say that they are *too* formidable we should expose all other available methods of evaluation (interviews, reference checks, and so on) to an equally rigorous appraisal. If this were done, I think it would be apparent that tests are a considerably more effective procedure, when used in appropriate circumstances, than their detractors would have us believe, despite all their criticism.

I would insist, however, that where any of these 11 conditions is not present, there is a very good chance that testing is *not* worth while. So, rather than waste further time anxiously inquiring whether the last 40 years of industrial psychology have been one huge mistake, I believe we should busy ourselves with the more practical task of using tests as appropriately as we can, and moving ahead much more vigorously than in the past to refine and improve them.

QUESTIONS

1. What is the place of personnel tests in the total recruiting process?

2. Discuss the four important features about validity listed by the author.

3. Is it possible for a test to have universal validity? Explain.

4. When should personnel tests be used?

5. List and explain at least five conditions that should be met to insure that testing is appropriate.

Seven Roadblocks to Effective Training

GEORGE M. DAVEY

The view of a training program from the "visitor's chair" is like getting far enough away from the trees to see the woods. A few general observations from that vantage point might shed some light on the strengths and weaknesses of industrial training programs.

Some of these observations stem from management policies. Others result from actions on the part of training directors.

1

The Training Director Is Subjected to Pressures Both from Within and Without the Company, So That He Often Overlooks Certain Fundamentals of Learning Admittedly, industrial training does not have to follow the pattern of formal education. Yet, so long as training involves the mental processes of the trainees (as formal education programs require), then the basic established factors of the psychology of learning equally apply.

Training cannot be done overnight, despite the pressure of management for immediate results, the general reluctance or resistance of the trainee to such learning, and the desire of the trainer to get the job done. Under the prevailing handicaps time must pass before the learning process can be effected. There are few, if any, miracles of speed in effective learning. Psychologists tell us that the human mind just does not seem capable of operating that fast.

Whether the program be long or short, it should be paced to be effectively absorbed by the trainee.

Quick and concentrated programs seem logical on paper. But beware of mental indigestion. It can have the same results as physical indigestion.

From *Factory*, CXII, No. 3 (March 1954), 234-246. Reprinted by permission of *Factory*, now *Modern Manufacturing* magazine.

It's quite true that a few of us mortals are blessed with vigorous mental fortitude just as some of us have strong intestinal fortitude. But not all.

2

There Is a General Tendency to "Spoon-Feed" All the trainee has to do is appear at a certain time and place together with a group of other trainees.

Then the training director, or someone under his guidance, starts the ball rolling. He may pass out information on what to do or not to do. He might give a case or a problem and ask "What do you fellows think?" He might show a movie or film strip, and follow it with a discussion. No advance preparation is required on the part of the trainee.

Sometimes this is called the *conference method* of training. Let us say quickly that there is much merit to such an approach. Many programs can be best handled in this way, and over a period of years, the method has accomplished a good deal of excellent training.

But, just as quickly, let us recognize the dangers. Here is how three different training directors have expressed it to me:

"All too often the conference method can be merely an exchange of ignorances."

"The trainee must put in some of his own sweat to get anything worthwhile out of the program."

"The conference method is much like pouring a pitcher of water over the trainee's head and hoping that some of the water soaks in."

Perhaps in his desire to "sell" the program or make it palatable, the training director finds this is the easiest way out. Then, too, management might hinder the use of any other method. Again, that "ole debbil"—the human factor—rears its ugly head. Rightly or wrongly, the conference method is the most popular one used in industrial training.

So, although a lot might be said for this "spoon-feeding" method, over the long pull its effectiveness can be questionable.

If this were not so, why would it be necessary to repeat and repeat the basic substance of so many programs? More and more training people tell me that they've had "that old stuff" before, although the training people have wracked their brains to disguise the "old stuff" as "new."

3

A Broad Basic Program Is Passed Over in Favor of a Short and Specific One All too often the attention of the training director stops with the appearance of a need and he concentrates on setting up a correcting program. Instead, it might have been better to search deeper to find out why that need arose in the first place.

For illustrative purposes we can take a typical supervisory training program. There will be sessions on techniques of supervision, improving human relations, morale building, production-line problems, and other subjects along these lines.

These may be called the specifics of a supervisory training program. Various training methods and devices are used to put over the program: conference method, case method, lectures, use of visual aids, etc. But, if we analyze each of these specifics to discover what they have in common, the answer is elementary psychology. Therefore, to my way of thinking, psychology is a prerequisite to a supervisory program, and should be the foundation upon which a program is developed. Not the psychology given in college, but practical principles of psychology as applied to industry.

To cite another illustration: There may be a need for better letter writing, better report writing, better verbal or written communications. What is basic to these specifics? A possible answer might be effective English usage—grammar, or techniques of clear expression.

The big point is that, after all training needs are listed, they should be carefully analyzed to find out what learning matter they have in common.

From the foundation of a good basic course, it would seem far easier to handle the specifics.

While quite a few training people appear to agree in principle with this observation, there may be reasons why they cannot implement it.

If the reasons are shown to be valid—usually based upon management or operating hindrances—we have to accept them. However, where it is at all possible, a happy compromise might be to operate two parallel programs: A short one to take care of immediate training needs, and a long-term one designed eventually to cut down these so-called immediate needs, and lead to a better over-all program.

4

The Training Director Often Misuses Training Aids, As Well As Methods Other Than Good Teacher-Pupil Classroom Techniques   Naturally the average training director is dealing with adults who have heterogeneous educational backgrounds and social environments. Then, too, he does not have all the time in the world to perform the training function. In some instances the trainees are there by sufferance, and the authority of the training director over the trainees is nil. What handicaps!

Frankly there is little reason why there should be any formal classroom atmosphere for any program. There is every reason why visual aids, flip charts, tried-and-tested teaching techniques should be utilized. The difficulty is that training people often think that these training aids are the whole program.

A well-selected film, a series of soundly developed charts, etc., which are well received at the moment, do not necessarily mean that the objectives of the training session have been accomplished. Aids to instruction are no more than aids. Knowing when, where, and how to use them is a technique that does not appear to be mastered in one easy lesson.

5

All Too Often the Wrong People Get the Training   Generally this is not the fault of the training director as much as it is the fault of management as expressed through its training policy. But to say that it is the exclusive fault of management could be questionable. Perhaps it is the human factor in so many of us. Or perhaps it is caused by circumstances beyond control.

If management desires that all supervisors be trained, then all supervisors are enrolled in the program. So the training director makes the course attractive in order to "sell" it. He must not put too much pressure upon the mental activity of the supervisor, and must more or less spoon-feed. No wonder training directors get tired of "leading a horse to water, only to find that they can't make him drink."

Unless a supervisor is willing to do more than just sit through a training session, or match his common sense with his contemporaries, it is questionable how much value he gets out of the program, in relation to the time, money, and effort required to put it on. We mean value as expressed in terms of sound, permanent help to do a better job, not just a bit of immediate help that frequently wears off fast. This observation does not apply to situations where it is necessary to set up a program to pass out information of one sort or another, such as interpretation of a union contract.

6

Top Management Itself Does Not Participate in Training To appear at the beginning and at the end of the program is, in many instances, all that management will do. But how can management really know how a program is going over unless it is willing to become an active participant throughout the program?

To illustrate:

A training director was conducting a human relations program for frontline supervisors. He showed a filmstrip, depicting a case problem, and asked the supervisors what they would do about this situation. A trainee piped up: "I'd fire the guy." The training director reminded him of some of the previous material he had presented, and asked if there was another answer. The trainee then replied: "First I'd get all the information, then I'd fire the guy."

Later, the president walked in to "check" on the training activity. The training director showed the same filmstrip, which ended with the question, "If you were Mr. Foreman, what would you do now?" The president said: "That's easy—fire the guy." Then he walked out.

The big question is, who really needed the training more—the president and his staff or the frontline supervisor?

7

Management Frequently Takes a Short-Sighted View of Its Training Policies, with the Result That the Over-all Effectiveness of Its Training Department Is Handicapped There is that constant battle for company time between requirements of training and production schedules. Training must be confined within the narrow limits of direct application to company benefits. If an employee wants a solid training course, there is the usual tuition-refund plan. Fear that a company would be paying for an employee's education on which a competitor might capitalize dominates the thinking of management.

It is my feeling that, where possible, some of the characteristics of an apprentice program should be adapted to all forms of industrial training. Apprentices are people. So are the production personnel, the supervisors, the vice-presidents, and the heads of any organization. Too many of us are prone to want something without putting forth the effort to acquire it.

Were management willing to apply the same thinking to its over-all training policy as it does to its apprentice program, training directors would be in a better position to do a better job. And the over-all effectiveness of the entire industrial training program might show more lasting benefits.

QUESTIONS

1. Is "spoon-feeding" an effective training method? Explain.

2. Should training methods extend to organizational levels above that of front-line supervisors?

3. Discuss the reasons why business is vitally interested in the behavioral sciences.

4. On what types of business-oriented problems is the behavioral scientist currently working?

Management by Objectives or Appraisal by Results

WALTER S. WIKSTROM

Management by objectives is making sizable inroads into management thinking. So many firms have adopted it that it would almost seem that a company cannot claim to be modern if it does not profess to practice management by objectives.

Executives extol the merits of this approach to management planning and control and especially to management performance appraisal. Indeed, "appraisal

From *Conference Board Record,* July 1966, © 1966, National Industrial Conference Board. Reprinted by permission.

by results" is often used synonymously with "management by objectives." Whatever the name used, the concept appears to be the hottest thing to hit the management methods market in years.

Yet, an occasional executive is heard saying that management by objectives is not all that it has been cracked up to be. They say "We tried it and it doesn't work." Usually the criticism is directed to its performance appraisal aspects.

Analysis of the claims and counterclaims, and of company experience good and bad, suggests that both points of view may be right. It seems to depend upon what is being emphasized, management by objectives or appraisal by results. Although these terms are often treated as if they were identical, they may be used more accurately to describe two different emphases given to the concepts. "Management by objectives," in the experience of a number of firms, has been an extremely valuable approach to total management planning, organization, motivation, and control. Performance appraisal is merely one part of this total approach. "Appraisal by results" may describe a performance-appraisal technique and little more.

WHAT IS "APPRAISAL BY RESULTS"?

Appraisal by results is a four-stage process which, at the risk of oversimplification, may be described as follows:

1. An individual manager reviews the nature of his responsibilities and determines the important key results that he should reach in the year ahead if he is to make his expected contribution to the firm's goals. These are his proposed targets.

2. The manager and his boss confer about the proposed targets. Adjustments may be made so that the targets of one manager are coordinated with those of other managers and so that the efforts of the whole unit will blend into a unified contribution to the goals of the next higher unit. The individual manager and his boss reach agreement on a final set of targets that are challenging but attainable.

3. The manager goes to work, doing those things necessary to reach the targets he has agreed to reach.

4. At the end of the year, the manager's performance is appraised on the basis of his results. Consideration is given to the way in which he worked toward his targets as well as to whether or not he reached them. On the basis of the year's experience, another set of targets is drafted for the next year.

Appraisal and Development

Even this simplified sketch of the concepts of appraisal by results suggests some of the advantages claimed for it as a method of performance appraisal and management development.

Appraisal by results provides a climate for employee motivation. Behavioral science research indicates that management personnel are motivated by a "sense of belonging," a recognition that they have meaningful membership in a group that has significance for them. They respond to recognition of their accomplishments and to the opportunity to work toward their own goals.

The involvement of an individual manager in setting his own goals (even though they must be approved, and perhaps modified, by his boss) seems to provide some of these motivational elements. He sees that his thinking and his plans have significance in the total management scheme. He knows that he will be judged on the basis of his own efforts to reach goals that he has helped to set. He has the chance to become really involved in the management process—and, behavioral scientists state, involvement is a precondition for motivation.

It is said that management by objectives leads to improved management performance through clarifying responsibilities. The typical managerial position guide lists a great many responsibilities, usually describing them in terms of activities. Not all of these activities are equally important to the firm's welfare; not all of them contribute equally to its success. But statements of activities alone may not make the priorities clear. When a manager has to think of his work in terms of the results he will produce, it becomes easier to separate necessary activities from the merely desirable and to separate both from the unimportant. With a clearer concept of his responsibilities, a good manager has a head start on achieving meaningful results.

Appraisal by results is objective, or at least it starts with an objective set of facts. Previous appraisal systems usually started with a superior's judgments of the characteristics or traits of a subordinate. These judgments were then related to the subordinate's work performance. Unfortunately, the subordinate did not always agree with his boss's judgments of his character or see their relationship to the job he was doing. Indeed, he sometimes viewed the appraisal as both unfair and completely irrelevant.

Bringing Judgment into Play

When agreed-upon work goals are the standard against which performance is appraised, the starting point is less ambiguous: Either the targets were reached or they were not reached. Judgment comes into play as superior and subordinate analyze the reasons for the performance, good or bad. They consider whether the targets were set too high or too low, whether unforeseen circumstances made the targets inappropriate, and whether opportunities were seized or allowed to pass by. Judgment is involved in all these considerations. Differences of opinion may arise between the two men. But the basic facts are clear and relevant; the targets were hit, or exceeded, or missed. If the subordinate disagrees with his boss's interpretation of the facts, he is challenged to come up with more convincing explanations.

This points to another advantage claimed for management by objectives. The appraisal interview lends itself to realistic coaching by the superior. Instead of playing psychologist and counseling the subordinate on the development of a better managerial personality, the superior can help the subordinate to find more effective ways of getting the job done. (Presumably, the average manager knows more about how to manage than he does about the psychology of personality development.)

Further, the coaching can be done within a framework of managerial responsibilities—planning, organizing, leading, and controlling. The boss can review the subordinate's work in terms of the way he *managed*. Was the planning adequate—did it take all possibilities into consideration and develop alternatives? Did the subordinate properly delegate responsibilities to his own men? How did he go about gaining the wholehearted cooperation of his men? Did he make adequate provision to keep informed about the progress of the work necessary to reach his targets? In short, the manager can be appraised *as a manager.*

So What's Wrong with It?

When the advantages claimed for appraisal by results are set forth, it may sound like *the* answer to performance appraisal problems. Nonetheless, there are the executives who say they have tried it and it just has not worked.

The complaints are varied. In some companies, managers have obtained results all right but at the expense of desirable objectives that were not on the list of targets. Cost-reduction goals have been met by deferring needed maintenance. Sales-volume goals have been met by pushing easily sold but low-profit items. So much emphasis has been placed upon reaching the agreed-upon goals that everything else is sacrificed in the attempt to reach them. In these companies overemphasis upon the getting of specific results has led to the exercise of poor managerial judgment.

Akin to this is the complaint that some managers have pursued their stated goals even when events indicated that a change in objectives was desirable. While constant change of targets defeats the purpose of setting them in the first place, some firms have found managers who stick rigidly to their targets even when they have become inappropriate.

At least one firm abandoned appraisal by results because of the way the managers reacted to what they considered an unfair "speed-up." The company made it a practice to raise almost all the targets proposed by individual managers. They would tell men in one unit that another unit had set higher goals and that these would have to be matched. Some executives in this firm have admitted that most of these goals were really unattainable—they were targets that might be aimed at but that probably would be missed. The company thought that the managers could be motivated to high performance by making them stretch for difficult objectives. Instead of striving for them, however, most of the managers gave up trying to reach the goals because they knew that they were bound to fall short no matter what they did.

Some companies have geared their salary administration to appraisal by results. In a number of cases they have found that this defeated the developmental aspects of this program. Appraisals have been fudged to justify the salary action that a superior wished to take. All sorts of extenuating circumstances have been advanced to excuse the poor performance of a subordinate to whom the boss wanted to give an increase. Even worse, there are reports of cases in which boss and subordinate have set easy goals to make sure that "results" will justify pay increases at appraisal time.

Trait Appraisal Persists

Another complaint is that appraisals are still being made on the basis of personality traits and human characteristics, rather than results. The bosses are still making judgments about their subordinates as *men* rather than as *managers*. The appraisals abound with such trait judgments as, "he's a good man but should learn to be more aggressive," and, "he needs to display more initiative." This may result from habit and years of conditioning; the managers have not yet learned to concentrate upon measuring results and how they were achieved. But in a number of cases the persistence of trait appraisal has come about because their "targets" really were not specific, measurable goals in the first place.

In drafting targets or goals, managers have rewritten their statements of responsibilities to *sound* like targets rather than set down concrete results that should ensue from the carrying out of the responsibilities. A manager might have the responsibility for production costs. He might set as a target "producing at minimum cost." But that is not a goal in the same sense as "lower the cost of producing widgets 6% by September 30." When trying to appraise results against a vague and unmeasurable standard, managers may feel forced to fall back upon judgments of traits rather than measures of results.

The difficulty of drafting meaningful and measurable goals is often mentioned in connection with staff groups. It is argued that the staff exists to help the line accomplish its ends; in doing this "helping" work, the staff deals in unmeasurable areas. It may be all well and good to measure a line manager's performance on the basis of his concrete results, but the staff man can only be judged in terms of whether or not he is properly discharging his specialized "professional" duties.

The final—and possibly most significant—criticism is that the targets set by an individual manager may not tie in to the objectives of the unit of which he is a part, or that the unit's objectives may not tie in to those of the corporation as a whole. In either event, the individual managers cannot be measured by their results because the work they do to carry out the company's business is not really relevant to the goals they had set. This situation, it is said in a number of cases, arises because the company has not really identified its corporate goals.

Analysis of these complaints suggests that management by objectives, among many of the companies in which the complaints are generated, has meant performance appraisal and little more. And company experience seems to show that if that is all it is, appraisal by results may not amount to much, even as an appraisal system.

What more companies are discovering is that being able to appraise by results seems to depend upon really managing by objectives. If the targets that are set are used only for the year-end appraisal, they may be very wide of the mark. But if the objectives of individual managers are closely tied in to the objectives of the company as a whole, and if they are backed up by careful planning of the operations so that they will be met, then the performance of managers can be measured by the contribution their work makes to the achievement of company goals. In these cases, however, the real pay-off has been generally improved *management,* of which improved performance appraisal has by no means been the most important part.

MANAGING BY OBJECTIVES

Among companies that emphasize managing by the objectives that are set at all levels, the difficulties mentioned above are minimized, or don't appear at all.

Targets set by individual managers are relevant to the company's goals because the entire management group is involved in a total planning process. Mechanisms have been evolved to ensure that individual plans contribute to larger goals. In setting targets, managers develop detailed plans, perhaps with several alternative contingency plans, for achieving the targets. If totally unforeseen events require a change in direction, all concerned are aware of this long before the annual appraisal period, and the required adjustments are made. Appraisals are not fudged for salary purposes because too much is at stake; the management success of the company depends upon the achievement of individual goals.

In short, where management by objectives and appraisal by results has been successful, the appraisal phase is part of a continuous process of control—primarily self-control—in an on-going management process of planning and operating to achieve success.

Those companies, however, that are most enthusiastic in reporting their experience with management by objectives almost always mention the tremendous problems it has caused. When a company begins to manage by objectives, it finds it has a tiger by the tail. Wrestling the tiger into submission becomes a major effort. But the companies are quick to add that the rewards far exceed the difficulties.

What Are the Objectives?

In many cases, the problem that first becomes apparent is that of identifying corporate objectives. As managers at lower levels try to formulate their own objectives, it becomes apparent that they can do so only if they are clear about the objectives of the larger unit of which they are a part. This need for clarity runs up to the top of the corporation. It begs the question to state that managers *should* know what their responsibilities are, and *should* be able to develop meaningful targets in carrying out these responsibilities. Experience has shown that even a clear statement of an individual manager's responsibilities does not take the place of a clear statement of the broader objectives toward which his own goals must contribute.

Indeed, a number of companies have found that they have not really known what their short- and long-term objectives are. This has been true even in some firms that have prided themselves on their planning. Managers have tended to develop plans in terms of their responsibilities and activities; their objectives have been the results expected from that work. But management by objectives begins with the results to be achieved; then the activities necessary for achieving them are decided upon. This is a switch in emphasis that apparently can be very difficult for many managers.

Policy Considerations

A company may find that it has to identify not only corporate objectives but corporate policy. In trying to achieve their individual objectives, managers may take actions which were not contemplated by top management and which are not acceptable to them. Yet it is clearly impossible for every action contemplated by every manager to be approved in advance by top management.

How, then, can top management give to lower managers the freedom of action essential to the achievement of their individual objectives and still retain sufficient control to bar their taking steps that cannot be approved?

The solution that some firms have adopted is to carefully think through those crucial areas in which they can set forth corporate policy. These policy statements do not dictate the precise actions managers are to take. Rather, they serve as general guidelines to be followed in reaching decisions. They set forth the direction the decision should take, rather than the decision itself.

At least one company has found that it must also clarify those things that are *not* policy. It found managers protesting that they could not achieve their objectives because company "policy" prevented their taking the most effective action. In many cases no policy really existed. The managers had merely assumed the existence of policy when they had observed long-standing company practice. This company now attempts to clarify the distinction between policy and longstanding practice. Managers may not violate policy to reach their objectives but they are given complete freedom to change practices, however venerable, that stand in the way of more effective management.

Is the Organization Sound?

Management by objectives may also uncover problems of organization in individual jobs, or in particular units, or even in the company as a whole. A given manager may not have sufficient authority to take needed action. The responsibilities within a unit may not be delegated to the various positions in the most effective pattern. The over-all structure of the corporation may be a stumbling block to the reaching of broad corporate goals. Organization planners formerly talked of grouping work on the basis of homogeneity of activities. Now they have found that it is more effective to group work on the basis of homogeneity of objectives. The importance of this distinction was driven home to several firms when they began trying to manage by objectives.

As a result, they found themselves involved in the turmoil of restructuring units, changing assigned responsibilities, and delegating greater or lesser authority. One firm found it necessary to eliminate several vice-presidential positions, although the very competent vice presidents themselves were retained. The jobs had seemed necessary so long as they were viewed as a set of activities. But no one could identify any results that were produced. Rather than waste the talents of good men in purposeless though traditional activity, the company created other jobs that could produce genuine contributions to corporate goals.

Control

One of the advantages claimed for management by objectives is that it makes possible a high degree of self-control by individual managers. This idea is usually welcomed by top management. When the implications of the idea begin to sink in, however, they sometimes have second thoughts.

Control requires two things—standards against which to control operations, and feedback of information about the state of operations. The manager's statement of expected results or targets provides the standard. Operating statements of various kinds may provide the feedback, if they are timely and adequate.

To enable them to achieve effective self-control, a firm may have to give its lower-level managers far more information about the company and its affairs than it has ever provided in the past. As mentioned earlier, a manager can set realistic and meaningful goals for himself only when he has information about the goals of higher-level units toward which his goals must contribute. Some firms have done considerable soul-searching before making information about corporate or divisional objectives available at lower levels in the organization.

Firms have had less trepidation about supplying lower-level managers with information about on-going operations. Nevertheless, some have discovered that they were not well set up to provide the kind of information that was needed for control. For example, financial information has been delayed in many cases until it could be correct to the last penny. Yet, for controlling operations, a reasonably accurate estimate that is timely can be more useful than a completely accurate statement that is too late to prompt needed corrective action when things go wrong. Again, control reports may have been sent to a manager's superiors so that they could check on his work. But it may be more important to get the information directly to the manager, so that he can be aware of problems and handle them.

A Long-Term Effort

Firms that have tried to introduce a "program" of management by objectives have had to change their approach to be successful. It appears that this is not a program in the sense of a standard practice that can be developed and then implemented. Rather, it is an approach to managing. Managers at every level must learn to manage this way. Evidently, it takes some time to learn to do so effectively.

For this reason, some firms start out by setting goals for periods shorter than a year—for a half year, say, or a quarter. This provides more practice at goal-setting and faster feedback in formal appraisal interviews. As men become more skilled, the time periods are lengthened, although some firms retain a quarterly review of a rolling one-year projection of goals.

WHY DO THEY LIKE IT?

Ironically, the reason why companies like management by objectives is related to the problems just mentioned. While this approach to managing may force a company into efforts to clarify objectives and policy, and into the creation of new organizational alignments and different control and information procedures, it also provides an extremely valuable tool for analyzing these problems and finding solutions.

Objectives become the standard against which alternative courses of action can be weighed. Which of several possible organization structures will be best adapted to meeting a unit's objectives? What is the relative value of allocating $10 million to one division rather than another, in terms of the objectives toward which these possible investments will contribute? Which short-term goals best fit the long-term growth plans of the company? The objectives framework not only makes clear that there are problems to be solved, it helps to solve them.

What is often stressed by enthusiastic executives, and what may be its most significant advantage, is that management by objectives creates a climate in which all the company's managers get into the act of solving the company's problems. Freed to make genuine contributions to the company's planning, they respond with an enthusiasm that has frequently been astounding.

The late Douglas McGregor said, in *The Human Side of Enterprise:* "The motivation, the potential for development, the capacity for assuming responsibility, the readiness to direct behavior toward organization goals are all present in people. Management does not put them there. . . . The essential task of management is to arrange organizational conditions and methods of operations so that people can achieve their own goals best by directing their own efforts toward organizational objectives."

Few companies have attained McGregor's ideal. For that matter, few companies feel that they have a full-blown management-by-objectives approach in the sense that this philosophy has completely permeated the entire management group. To the extent that it has permeated, however, they report that it has gone a long way toward bringing about the atmosphere that McGregor described.

QUESTIONS

1. What stages exist in the appraisal-by-results process?

2. Discuss the advantages and disadvantages of appraisal by results.

3. Explain the differences between an evaluation program based on results and one based on traits.

4. Management by objectives is discussed by the author as the foundation of an appraisal-by-results program. Discuss management by objectives.

5. Why do companies using management by objectives as a philosophy of management like it?

The Meaning of Money

RICHARD ALLEN STULL

One psychologist has defined money as the sixth sense—without it you can't enjoy the other five! We all know the importance of money in our particular society in this country. But did you ever stop to think of the meaning of money? Why it is so significant in many different ways?

Personnel people in considering motivation, wage and salary administration, benefit and incentive plans, and counseling problems face daily the need to understand money and its many uses in the business situation. In the normal course of events, every person, unless he is altogether dependent upon others, contributes something to the common store of goods and services—the economic system. In return, he receives through the medium of money, the right to a certain share of that common store. The system is complex and rests on such institutions as property and contract, the division of labor, competition, and combination. Behind these are the laws of human nature, of social relationships. These laws, working through the needs and drives to acquire, to possess, and to provide for family and loved ones, operate to turn the boundless resources and powers of the earth into human services.

Money is usually defined as anything which is universally acceptable in final payment for goods and services. It serves four important functions in commerce and business:

1. Medium of exchange for goods or services
2. Standard of value, a means of measuring the value of goods and services
3. Storehouse of value by which the results of providing goods or services can be conveniently preserved for future use if paid for with money
4. Standard of deferred payment as the basis for credit and installment purchasing

In early America, Benjamin Franklin who was considered the essence of practicality, the embodiment of common sense, included in his famous list of virtues—*Frugality*. Said Franklin, "Make no expense but to do good to others or to yourself; i.e., waste nothing." Our grandfathers grew up on such sayings as, "A penny saved is a penny earned" and "Save for a rainy day." The attitude towards savings, however, has changed greatly in the last 25 years. There have been two world wars, a severe depression, a stock market crash, a bank holiday, and mounting inflation. And fortunes have been lost by persons who never speculated a dime. William H. Whyte, Jr. in *The Organization Man* asks "How can the organization man be thrifty? Other people are thrifty for him . . . for the bulk of his rainy-day saving, he gives his proxy to the financial and personnel departments of his organization."

Personnel people still tell the story of the "good old days" before psychological testing when more natural ways were used by some to "test" the qual-

From *Personnel Journal,* April 1965, pp. 187-188, 213. Reprinted by permission of the *Personnel Journal* of Swarthmore, Pennsylvania.

ifications of a young man for various jobs. It illustrates the change that has taken place. A boy is applying for work in the office of a merchant. The boss who is interviewing him is called to the telephone and asks the boy to undo a parcel for him during the interruption. The question is: will the boy carefully untie the knots, roll up the string, neatly fold the paper? Or, will he cut through the cord, tear off the wrapping, and throw both into the wastebasket?

If he did the latter, one kind of employer would consider him wasteful of materials, but another employer might think of such a boy as one who valued his time and presumably that of his employer too highly to waste it on the trivial saving of wrapping materials. How far have we moved from the preservation of materials to the saving of moments? Is one old-fashioned, and the other modern? Times have changed, but it is still true, as the sign on the banker's long desk indicated, "There's one thing money can't buy—poverty."

Employees want their compensation to reflect their responsibilities. They are interested in fair play based on merit. They want their performance reviewed periodically and appropriate increases granted. At the same time, they also want the assurance that the range will be adjusted when necessary, to keep pace with wage increases granted to hourly people and kept in line with area salary practices.

Money is a symbol. As such can be used in many ways. Its value depends upon representing something for which it can be exchanged. This includes not just things but such values as power, prestige, achievement and security. Psychologically, too, we know that money can become the root of many emotional problems. This would seem to stem largely from early training. Money has to be important to parents, and children become aware of this, especially as it is used by parents as a means of control, of reward and punishment. To understand the use of money, we must understand its meaning to the individual, and this frequently varies with his emotional need.

Think of the strange ways money is used to get rid of feelings, to punish, to hold on to married children. Careless spending, too, is often an indication of inner tension, if not simply poor habits. Gambling and begging get at basic influences in the emotional development of people. It is revealing in how many divorce cases, credit cards and charge accounts are used extravagantly to punish one or the other party just before the final decree. Money is a source of fear, and also great pleasure. How a person uses money and how he tips are important clues to his or her personality and character.

An executive in San Francisco, who, on a moment's notice, was called East one morning for an important meeting at the home office of his company, could not reach his wife at home to tell her. Accordingly, he called the leading department stores to cancel her charge accounts. Within the hour his wife had phoned!

Research has been scarce in money matters. Only a few studies stand out:

1. The Harvard Psychological Clinic, in 1953, learned that the lure of profit in mature managers is often that of an objective measure of success in accomplishing difficult tasks rather than one of making the most money for the least risk and effort.

2. Cornell University, in 1955, found that incentive plans are effective not because of money alone, but because:

a. Meeting the quota can be an effective way for workers to get the foreman off their backs—an achievement in some cases as important as the monetary reward.

b. By setting a quota, there is a game, with a score, and even fun thrown in.

c. Experienced workers learn that producing at a brisk pace is less fatiguing, in fact, than an erratic, slow production rate.

3. The University of Pittsburgh, in 1958, discovered that the traditional bread and butter motivators are not nearly as important to the growing professional work force of engineers, accountants, and scientists. Professionals who find their jobs challenging and exciting can often tolerate a poor manager.

4. More recently, Kaiser Steel Corporation is finding that group incentive plans for production may be more productive than individual incentives. In addition, a group plan provides a healthy atmosphere in which both management and workers can lose their misconceptions and prejudices about one another.

5. Small and large companies are re-thinking compensation of the exceptional junior executive. Often it is simpler to lose one of these "comers" through inadequate salary than it is to replace him. Many a young and competent manager is more interested in his immediate salary level than in sophisticated stock options and deferred compensation schemes. Bonus and cash incentive systems help him at a time when he needs it most for his family obligations. He is then in a position to plan his own investment program and estate. Retirement is losing some of its enchantment for many executives. Too many have learned that when the day does come for the better than average executive, he already owns his own home, has two cars, his children are through college, and he is too tired to make an eight hour day of collecting stamps, writing letters to the editor, or traveling all over the world with an ill wife. Later in his career, however, when he reaches the higher tax brackets, company controlled retirement plans take on more realism and are appreciated.

Personnel people continue to be alert to the psychological meaning of money. In the process they learn a lot about employees and themselves.

QUESTIONS

1. What four important functions does money serve in the business world?

2. Money is discussed as a symbol in the article. What does money symbolize?

3. What facts have research studies discovered about money and its importance to the individual?

What Executives Should Know About Labor

You sit at the bargaining table arguing heatedly over a labor contract. The strike deadline is bearing down on you. Tempers are getting short. For the first, and probably the last, time in your life you, a businessman, are actually championing the demands of the union.

Although the real names of the company and the union involved have been disguised, there is nothing phony about the intensity of your arguments or the experience you are getting in handling labor problems.

This mock negotiating session is part of the highly varied training you get as a participant or "AMP" in Harvard University's Advanced Management Program, the much-acclaimed course for men about to enter the top ranks in business and public organizations.

After hours of haggling and compromising, you and three other AMPs playing the role of union representatives think you are about to reach an agreement with the four management representatives, who also are AMPs.

But you get a telegram from "union headquarters," reading:

"THE CHICAGO ASSOCIATION NEGOTIATIONS WHICH WE EXPECTED TO BE EASY SAILING THIS YEAR HAVE TURNED SOUR. LOOKS NOW AS IF WE'LL HAVE TO TAKE A STRIKE. IMPORTANT THEREFORE THAT YOU SETTLE IF POSSIBLE. THIS DOESN'T MEAN YOU CAN'T TAKE A STRIKE IF THEY'RE UNREASONABLE BUT WITH ALL THE CHICAGO AREA PLANTS OUT IT WOULD BE TOUGH GOING—HARRY"

About the same time, unknown to you, company representatives get a confidential message of their own. It says that the company is likely to land a fat contract with the Navy Department.

The message continues: "It is likely that our existing equipment will be inadequate for the handling of all this work and that some subcontracting will be essential. I understand that arbitrators rule all over the lot on subcontracting when there is no clear management rights clause in the contract. So let's be sure we're protected on this one.

"But above all, now that we have the Navy contract in the bag, do everything within reason to avoid a strike, even if it takes more than 15 cents. Obviously don't let our friends (?) from the union know of this good fortune. They'd murder us if they knew."

ALAS, A LEAK

But a faithless secretary in one of the firm's offices has sneaked a peek at the memorandum and told a union official what she saw. You are handed another telegram from union headquarters that now urges you to be firm on the matter of subcontracting. You are ordered to seek assurance that all men from your local are employed before the company subcontracts any work.

So, while the desire of both sides to avoid a strike increases, so do the differences between them and so does the temperature in the bargaining room.

"I can't let this mock negotiating go on for more than a few days," says Prof. Thomas Kennedy, who conducts the labor portion of the 13-week AMP program. "The tension gets too strong."

For years Prof. Kennedy, who has a jolly Irish cop look about him, has been breaking up labor scraps, both mock and real. He has taught labor relations on and off since 1940, served as consultant to several companies and sat on scores of labor disputes as a professional arbitrator. He was industrial relations director for a major chemical company before moving to Harvard in 1956.

"Few AMPs have negotiated or ever will negotiate a real labor contract," Prof. Kennedy admits. "However, as future general executives it is they who will have to give the final answers to such difficult labor questions as, 'Should we take a strike on this issue?'

"In order to answer such questions intelligently, they must be able to communicate effectively with their company's labor experts. You mention the word 'union' to some businessmen and they're as quick to take offense as the king's musketeers.

"We're not trying to sell the AMPs a prolabor or antilabor view. We expect, however, that they will leave the program able to think and act more intelligently on labor relations without getting emotional."

You begin by studying the nature of collective bargaining and the legal framework within which it occurs in the United States. One of the first important laws controlling industrial labor contracts was the 1932 Norris-La Guardia Act. Management no longer could require a man to sign a contract not to join a union. It also made it hard to get an injunction against a union.

In 1935 the National Labor Relations Act, or Wagner Act, was passed, supposedly to encourage collective bargaining. It really gave organized labor a leg up. It declared that men were free to join unions and to be active in union organization, and that employers must not interfere with such activity.

The Wagner Act also guaranteed that employees would not be discharged or discriminated against for union activity. It provided an election procedure whereby the majority of the employees in a bargaining unit can select the union they want to represent them.

It required that once the employees have so selected a union, management must bargain with it in good faith.

Under the Wagner Act unions were able to organize workers as never before. In 1947 the Taft-Hartley or Labor Management Relations Act was passed over tremendous union opposition. It outlawed the "closed shop," so that an employer no longer could be required by a contract to hire employees only from a certain union.

The act's famous Section 14 (b) further provided that states could pass right-to-work laws which prevent not only the closed shop but any kind of compulsory union membership.

Taft-Hartley also declared that foremen and supervisors can be discharged for joining a union; supposedly assured the employer of his rights of free speech; provided for suing unions, and required that unions bargain in good faith.

In 1959 the Landrum-Griffin Act strove to protect the rights of union members from union bosses and to prevent misuse of union funds.

WHY A UNION?

Through a chain of labor cases, you see how these laws come into play as a nonunionized company evolves into a unionized company.

"What would you have done in the case in which a union tries to organize the employees of the Andre Cookie Co.?" Prof. Kennedy asks, waving his hand in a "come on" fashion to draw responses from the AMPs.

The best first move, the AMPs agree, is to find a good labor lawyer.

The next step is to ask yourself, "Why do the workers want a union in the first place?" Have they been misled by union organizers? Do they feel perhaps that wages are too low, that they have no way of communicating gripes, that they don't have enough fringe benefits, that vacations are too short, that their supervisors are incompetent, or that management is not handling certain social problems well enough?

The law restricts what you can do to prevent unionization. Although you are supposedly free to talk to the workers and express your opinions, you cannot use promises or threats, and the National Labor Relations Board (NLRB) has interpreted this severely.

Breaking this law for the first time usually results only in a cease and desist order.

If the Board upholds a complaint by a union that has lost an election, the most it can do is to order another election. Once a union has been beaten, even in a contested election, however, it is difficult for it to muster the strength to win the second time around.

BOARD CAN GET TOUGH

There is the possibility of heavier penalties in other cases. If the Board determines that management has discharged an employee for his union activities, for example, it could order the man reinstated with full back pay plus six per cent.

Refusal to do what the Board says could result in a court order, and violation of that would be contempt of court.

"How often should you break the labor law?" Prof. Kennedy asks. "Never? Just when there is a principle involved? Or whenever it's to your advantage and the penalties are minimal?"

All three suggestions find supporters. Some AMPs are highly disturbed at positions taken by fellow classmates.

"This is good," Prof. Kennedy remarks. "These are issues you will face later as top managers. They will not be completely new to you from now on, so you are less likely to panic when you face them."

Once a union has won certification and a contract has been signed, the major concern—at least until the next contract negotiation—is settling employee grievances.

A contract may say, for example, that a man is to be discharged or disciplined "only for just cause." Your interpretation of what "just cause" is in one grievance serves as a precedent for future cases.

Prof. Kennedy shows you a film that follows a grievance from start to finish.

He stops the film at six points where management must make decisions. During these breaks you comment on what management has done and you decide what you, if you were in charge of the company, would do now.

The film is about a man in an auto shop who refuses to handle some parts. "They're too hot," he claims. "I'll get burned."

He argues with the foreman and then takes his complaint to his shop steward. The shop steward turns in a report to union headquarters. Union and management representatives sit down together to solve the problem. By this time the problem has developed political complications and neither side will budge. The union chooses arbitration.

The film is temporarily stopped at this point for a discussion of arbitration. Prof. Kennedy points out that 94 per cent of today's labor contracts provide that disputes that can't be solved by union and management be taken to arbitration.

Many contracts provide that if union and management can't agree on an arbitrator, either the Federal Mediation Service (FMS) or the American Arbitration Association (AAA) is to be called in. These groups keep panels of arbitrators.

The film resumes. The case of the man who claimed he feared being burned by auto parts is before an arbitrator. Reports from scientists are presented showing the temperature of the parts at various times when the complaining worker was supposed to handle them. Doctors agree that the worker could not safely handle the parts at those temperatures. The film ends with the arbitrator ruling in favor of the worker.

The vital lesson here for management, Prof. Kennedy says, is to get the facts and to try to settle grievances early without letting them grow to enormous proportions. The foreman and the shop steward could have decided this case with a few simple tests on the spot.

You move now to a series of cases on major substantive grievances that especially plague top management these days. As with many Harvard business cases, the names of the firms are disguised.

The Dependable Tire case asks how a company can subcontract effectively under a union agreement.

Five years ago subcontracting was not the big issue it now is. Recent NLRB decisions, however, have given unions a stronger hand. Now if you wish to subcontract, the NLRB says you may have to bargain first with the union.

In the Seneca Co. case, a paper company can't expand production for fear of polluting a river. Costs are rising and Seneca must either automate or die. If it automates it would have to cut 500 men from a 2,000-man work force in a one-company town. How, you are asked, should you deal with the union in such a situation?

In the Glidden and Darlington Mills cases you consider whether or not companies must bargain with unions before shutting down or moving plants. An official of one firm that was moving told employees they would have to apply for jobs at the new plant just like any new employees. You discuss the wisdom of such a decision.

The Faraday Steel case considers the current problem of changing local working conditions. The difficulty arises because Faraday, a major steel producer, signs a general contract with the union, but terms of the contract are interpreted differently by local Faraday units.

At the base of the problem is the clash of two theories. The "residual rights theory" maintains that any powers that management has not turned over to employees in the contract remain in the hands of management. Some contracts spell out this theory in a "management rights clause."

Unions champion the "status quo" theory in which they assume that all working conditions will remain the way they have always been, unless the changes are specified in the contract. Some contracts embody this theory in a "past practices clause."

To further confuse matters some contracts have both management rights and past practices clauses.

You now get to test out the concepts developed up to this point in the labor course. The AMP class is broken into four-man bargaining teams to consider a grievance case. As in the mock negotiations, half of the team plays the management role and half labor's role.

First you read over the case. Fite, a veteran worker in the Rocket Chemical Co., has been passed over for advancement to a mechanic-carpenter No. 2 job. Management claims Fite has been put in a similar job many times and never done well in it.

The company claims it has the right to promote the best man, despite Fite's seniority.

You meet with other members of your team to map strategy. Your team agrees that the case is clear cut: Fite is a goldbrick, a no-good.

But when you meet face-to-face with AMPs representing the labor group, you find the two of you are miles apart in your views. Your job is not to see how hard a bargain you can drive, but to try to reach a "fair and workable agreement" by 8:30 the next morning.

The grievance sessions go on into the night all over Hamilton Hall, your living quarters, and in small conference rooms off tunnels connecting buildings on the campus of Harvard's Business School.

To those AMPs on the labor side of the table, this is an especially new experience. Many of them for the first time are convinced that the union is right and that management's contentions are absurd.

You may not realize it now, but you are getting valuable experience in the art of negotiating, an important tool in many aspects of business. AMPs from past classes have written Prof. Kennedy that they are now negotiating all the time in their new positions and find the mock sessions one of the most useful parts of Harvard's program.

If the two sides can't agree, the labor team must decide whether to take the case to arbitration or to drop the matter.

The next day in class each AMP is expected to be ready to defend his team's agreement or failure to agree. Some groups decided to promote Fite. Some ordered him to take training first. Some decided not to promote him.

In each AMP session a new way of handling the grievance comes up. This session one group decided to give Fite the promotion but to fire him if he didn't work out.

The class tries to find out why some groups ended up sending the case to the arbitrator. In a few cases a personality clash was the cause.

"Well, when this guy made that remark," one AMP reports, "we'd had it."

GRIEVANCE SKILL IMPORTANT

Prof. Kennedy points out that the variety of settlements suggests that skill in handling grievance procedures can give important gains to one side or the other— gains it could not have made during contract negotiations, a subject you study next.

In the United States, unlike the situation in some foreign cases you study, there are no labor courts to settle disputes over the negotiation of contracts.

The great motivation for settling in America, of course, is that a strike costs the company profits and the workers wages.

"Is this the best kind of system?" Prof. Kennedy asks. "Should we have labor courts or compulsory arbitration rather than allow strikes?"

Most AMPs say no. Some of their comments:

"Management's economic power is much more effective than its political power. There are more of them than there are of us. Putting the settlement of contracts in politics rather than in economics is not good for management."

"Where will government draw the line? How can the courts set wages on the one hand and not prices and profits on the other?"

"As far as the government's concerned, we of management already are second-rate citizens."

"There would be the problem of enforcing any compulsory arbitration, a problem you don't have when parties settle disputes among themselves. Maybe you can force 100,000 miners to go to work, but you can't make them dig."

"You eliminate the threat of the strike, which is the greatest incentive for reaching an agreement."

"The courts will be loaded down with contract disputes."

COURT DEFENDERS RESPOND

Comments favorable to labor court or compulsory arbitration include:

"How can the government otherwise avoid strikes that could cause a national emergency, such as those in shipping, railroads, steel and airlines?"

"You shouldn't assume that the judges will be unfair. Compulsory arbitration will avoid loss of production and the public inconvenience of strikes."

You now tackle a battery of cases involving major contract negotiations. Among them are the steel negotiations of 1956 through 1965.

You spend a good part of one of the hour-long classes discussing the firm offer made to Steelworkers in 1956 by U.S. Steel, Bethlehem and Republic.

This type of offer is a form of what has come to be called boulwarism, after Lemuel R. Boulware, General Electric Co.'s former employee relations chief. In boulwarism management decides what it considers to be fair, based on all the information it can gather. Its offer is firm. It will change the offer only if the union can present new and pertinent information.

Many of the AMPs feel boulwarism is the only honest, sincere way to carry out bargaining.

"This business of the big demand by the union and the little offer by management is like buying blankets in Mexico," says a Canadian bank superintendent.

"The price is set at 300 pesos and you offer 60 pesos and you finally settle at 120 pesos. This is a phony, time-consuming type of bargaining and, moreover, it's immoral and dishonest."

Other AMPs say boulwarism forces union leaders to lose face. They are not given a chance to bargain. It looks like an attempt to destroy a union and just make things tougher generally.

They further argue:

"The union men really catch it from the membership if they accept a take-it-or-leave-it offer.

"Under boulwarism, the companies put themselves in difficulty, too, because they don't have room to move during bargaining.

"Boulwarism also is dangerous, because if management can dictate the terms in collective bargaining, then labor must search for other means to get what it wants."

In the 1962 steel negotiations, the union made a big issue of U.S. Steel's ability to pay more. You are asked if the ability to pay should enter into negotiations.

"Should you penalize the efficient company by making it pay higher wages?" Prof. Kennedy asks. "Should you, in other words, subsidize the inefficient?"

In President Kennedy's Administration the government set up so-called price-wage guideposts. It said if wages increase faster than productivity the result would be inflationary. But if wages stay within the guidelines there should be no price increase.

You are asked to compare the attitude of the Kennedy Administration with that of the Eisenhower Administration in earlier labor negotiations.

The government certainly got into collective bargaining during steel negotiations of 1965. I. W. Abel had ousted David McDonald as president of the United Steelworkers, promising he would bargain differently. The vote had been close, so Mr. Abel was anxious to make a good showing.

After getting the strike deadlines postponed, President Johnson called negotiators to Washington and had Secretary of Labor Willard Wirtz and Secretary of Commerce John Connor recommend a settlement which both sides finally accepted reluctantly.

AMPs COMPARE CONTRACTS

It is at this point, after getting a better feel for the atmosphere under which contracts are negotiated, that you sit on union's side in the mock negotiation of a labor contract.

Most AMP negotiating groups decided the tough subcontracting issue by compromise.

"We fought hard against the union shop," explains one management AMP, "because we believe it is unAmerican. But we gave them a lot of fringe benefits because we were interested in the health and welfare of our employees."

"We got a whole mess of fringe benefits," boasted a labor member of another negotiation, "and we also got a union shop."

"With all those fringe benefits," commented another AMP, "you don't need a union shop."

One management group consented to an agency shop in which new employees would not have to join the union but would have to pay dues anyway.

DEVELOP CREDIBILITY

Good contract bargaining, Prof. Kennedy points out, boils down to developing credibility on the other side without getting so committed that you can't move any more.

"Language is awfully important in convincing the other side that you can't withdraw. You must be careful that you don't give a sense of ultimatum to the other side. Opponents are unlikely to succumb to a clear ultimatum. But you can skillfully get around to the same thing with the right language."

These techniques can be applied to all types of negotiations, not only to collective bargaining. You can use them when selling or buying land, for example.

On the subject of ethics in labor relations, you read part of the Teamsters Union hearings held in 1957 by the Senate Subcommittee on Improper Activities in Labor and Management, better known as the McClellan Committee.

Prof. Kennedy asks:

Should unions be permitted to own stock in, or make loans to, companies whose employees they represent?

If a union leader sends you a Christmas gift, would you accept it?

If a union leader says he has a boy in college who needs a summer job, would you give him some preference over the boy who comes in off the street? What about the son of your banker? Or the sons of those who grant you licenses?

Would you have a drink with a labor man after negotiations?

Do you have certain personal principles for which you are willing to lose your company? What about your duty to the stockholders?

AMPLE ANSWERS

Some of the AMPs' responses:

"You'd better not do anything unless you're willing to have it printed on the front page of the local paper."

"Union and management are like a minus and a plus. If they come together the sparks will fly. I wouldn't take gifts or help them get jobs."

"As management people and civic leaders, we must set the moral tone for our community."

In this final class with you, Prof. Kennedy describes some general trends in labor relations.

The first is a decrease in union membership as a percentage of total employment. This is due to a number of reasons:

1. There has been a sudden spurt in automation, especially in the coal, steel and auto industries, which had been heavily unionized.

2. The number of white-collar workers is increasing and the number of blue-collar workers decreasing.

3. Many firms have moved their plants to areas of the United States where unions are comparatively weak.

4. Companies have developed sounder personnel programs, and some nonunion companies are paying higher wages than unionized firms.

5. Management is better at skimming off the best leaders for its ranks.

6. The old fighting spirit has left the labor movement. It is not too convincing any more to talk about trying to improve the lot of the steel worker who already has two cars.

7. Union scandals have disenchanted many would-be labor supporters.

8. The Teamsters are out of the AFL-CIO. Nothing helps a local threatening a strike like having the Teamsters on its side.

9. Right-to-work laws have encouraged men who don't want to be union members.

10. Employers have sharpened their skills in avoiding unions.

11. There has been an improvement of management's public image in collective bargaining as opposed to labor's image.

12. As a result of automation, there has been a decline in the effectiveness of the strike weapon in a number of industries. Supervisors can run the plants.

At the same time that union power declines, paradoxically the scope of collective bargaining expands.

Subcontracting, plant-moving and plant-closing are matters that until recently management alone could decide. Now government is forcing management to bargain such decisions with the union.

"Is collective bargaining working in the United States?" Prof. Kennedy asks.

More than 98,000 of the 100,000 labor union contracts that come due each year get settled without strikes. Most strikes that do occur are short.

A second paradox in labor relations today is that although great improvement has been made in the whole system of free collective bargaining and we have a better system for settling conflicts, in the past five years there has been increasing pressure for government handling of bargaining.

"Hopefully we are not moving toward compulsory arbitration," Prof. Kennedy says. "You don't want to throw the baby out with the bath. If we go to government for settlement of hours, wages and working conditions, we're going to have a lot of difficulties. The government eventually would want to set prices, profits and even executive salaries."

QUESTIONS

1. List and briefly describe four laws affecting labor-management relations in the United States.

2. Discuss the various steps in the arbitration process.

3. Explain the arguments for and against the formation of labor courts or compulsory arbitration in our country.

4. Define and discuss boulwarism as a method of labor-management bargaining.

5. What are some of the current trends in labor relations? Do the trends appear to be increasing or decreasing union power?

What Is Behavioral Science?

HAROLD M. F. RUSH

"Nothing is permanent except change," contended Heraclitus back in the sixth century, B.C. Succeeding generations have echoed this sentiment, especially in this century of unprecedented change. The business world has taken on so completely new a face in so relatively short a time, that the business manager often finds it difficult to keep abreast with the ever-increasing developments in his field. He may even find that the management concepts he has put into practice for most of his working life are under re-examination.

The conscientious manager who prides himself in being conversant with newer trends probably hears or reads a lot about the widening interest of businessmen in behavioral science. And he may be even a little embarrassed that he isn't quite sure what it's all about. Well, in the most elementary terms, what is it?

A good starting point is to examine the word "behavior." Webster defines it as: "Mode of conducting oneself; the way in which an organism, organ, or substance acts, especially in response to a stimulus."

Behavioral science is interested in studying behavior, specifically human behavior, in response to various stimuli—internal and mental or external and physical. The term came into popular usage because men working in the field considered it more descriptive than the formerly used "social science." The word social, they felt, was associated too much in the layman's mind with sociability, and, possibly more to the point, social science was often confused with socialism.

Behavioral science connotes all the factors that go into man's fundamental personality—his needs, his emotions, his thinking, his ability to relate his thoughts and feelings. His actions are a result and a composite of all these factors.

WHO IS A BEHAVIORAL SCIENTIST?

The group of academic disciplines which constitute the behavioral sciences is large. In one sense, any person who engages in the study of human behavior is a behavioral scientist; but so broad a definition could be carried to the absurd. (An internal auditor is interested in how people spend money. Is he, then, a behavioral scientist?) A behavioral scientist is simply someone whose *primary* concern is the study of how and why people behave as they do.

The first profession that comes to mind when considering the role of the behavioral scientist is psychology. By definition, psychology is concerned with the study of the mind and its inter-relation with an *individual's* behavior. The second profession is sociology. Sociology is concerned with the evolution of society, or the forms, institutions, and functions of human *groups*. In the study of groups, these two areas, for example, overlap so much that it is sometimes

From *Conference Board Record,* September 1965, © 1965 by the National Industrial Conference Board. Reprinted by permission.

difficult to ascertain which of the two disciplines does what. It would be unprofessional to call these situations jurisdictional disputes; but, as an example of overlap, there is an area of specialization within psychology that is interested in groups also. This is called social psychology. The essential difference between a social psychologist and a sociologist is that the former is primarily interested in studying the behavior of an individual as he relates to, or is affected by, the groups in which he lives and functions, while the latter is more concerned with the group as a whole and one group's relationships with another. When directed to "work situations," the efforts of both the psychologist and the sociologist have applicability to the business world.

The behavioral scientist label also has been applied, under certain circumstances, to the economist, the political scientist, the human engineer (who seeks to adapt the work environment to the man), and to a host of other specialists. What the person is called is of less importance than what he does. Social psychologists, industrial psychologists, industrial sociologists, labor economists, educators, physicians, anthropologists, and many more professionals come under the umbrella of behavioral sciences because all are concerned, to varying degrees, with human behavior.

WHAT DOES HE DO?

In its raw form "science" refers to knowledge obtained by study and practice or to any department of systematized knowledge. By this definition the behavioral scientist is a scientist, although his counterparts in the natural or physical sciences sometimes may balk at the use of the term as applied to psychologists, sociologists, cultural anthropologists, *et al.* Strictly speaking, the behavioral scientist works within the framework of scientific method, and he applies tests of statistical and clinical validity to the evidence he collects. He approaches a problem in much the same way as the physical scientist: he does basic research by measuring and counting and by observing existing phenomena; he performs experimental work based on a given thesis and postulates a system or approach based on the evidence he gleans. In describing his basic methodology he borrows the language of the physical scientist. He speaks in terms of research, development, and application. But his data, unlike those of the physical scientist, can rarely, if ever, meet the criterion of indisputable universality: he cannot work in the perfectly controlled environment of a laboratory; he cannot extrapolate with rigid authority; he does not deal with properties and conditions that remain constant; he cannot control the quality or quantity of his variables. In short, the properties he is working with are the most complex of all organisms, physically, mentally, and emotionally—people.

Even the most scientifically oriented behavioral scientist recognizes that his field is not at this point an exact science. Still, through adherence to principles of scientific method, through constant observation of his subjects, and thorough validation of his findings, he attempts to predict what is likely to happen to a given person or groups of persons within a given situation.

Most behavioral scientists recognize that they may never reach the point of axiomatic certainty—the variables and complexities of people are great. But their efforts have already produced considerable knowledge about how and why people behave as they do, how their strengths and weaknesses can be evaluated, what their needs and wants are.

There are even persons working within the framework of behavioral research (and particularly as it applies to the business world) who do not follow strict rules of scientific method and inquiry. Many businessmen feel, however, that their theories or philosophies have contributed much to the understanding of people at work and generally of the management process.

Some of the disciplines that are lumped together as behavioral sciences are relatively young; psychology as a modern system was still considered to be an embryo as late as the beginning of this century, for example. But the studies, major ones, have been made possible by an increasing level of sophistication over the past couple of decades. As techniques become refined, many expect that a more finite contribution will be made by the behavioral scientist, particularly to the world of work.

WHO IS INTERESTED IN HIS WORK?

There has been a recent surge of interest in behavioral science on the part of people in business. But the question may arise: "After all, hasn't industry managed to survive and even thrive without behavioral science in the past?" Business *has* survived and thrived, but not without behavioral science in some form.

Human behavior and its effects upon productivity have been the interest of management for a long time—long before anyone coined a term for the study of this subject. From the early studies on employee learning, in the 1890's, to the first time-and-motion studies, to the development of tests and a more sophisticated approach to employee selection, to on-the-job training, to supervisory training, and on to the advent of management development, companies have become more and more sensitive to how the employee acts and reacts, how he functions in various situations, how his innate abilities can be matched with the job requirements, how to create a work environment conducive to job satisfaction, harmonious relations, and a higher level of production.

Most earlier behavioral scientists were concerned with the physical factors that make for higher levels of production (well designed machines and work areas, healthy working conditions, illumination, temperatures at the work place, job analysis and selective placement, use of color and music to induce efficiency). They were also interested in keeping the employee loyal and content (rates of pay, paid vacations, insurance benefits and pensions, recreation, coffee breaks, etc.). Broadly speaking, they were interested in manipulating the tangible and/or material environment; and they were, in the main, interested in the rank-and-file worker. Some modern behavioral scientists contend that these earlier studies were concerned with man as an adjunct to a machine, and thus may not be considered behavioral research at all.

It is doubtful whether all of the interest of business in its employees, even in the earlier stages, was initiated out of altruistic concern. Many social pressures, the rise and power of organized labor, the employer's obligation under workmen's compensation laws, and the ever-increasing industrial competition all may have had a part in "forcing" many companies to take a closer look at their relations with their workers. Outside pressures and influences aside, management began to realize that in a competitive free-enterprise economy its only permanent advantage lies in its human resources. With this growing realization, management has intensified its inquiry into the how and why of human behavior.

In this perspective the current activity in behavioral research is, for all practical purposes, a continuation of earlier studies with a new dimension added: the scope of concern.

Whereas early behavioral research concerned itself with workers *en masse,* today's focus is more on the manager and the management process. In the family-owned company the owner did the "hiring and firing," and frequently he kept in close touch with the actual manufacturing operation. In the large modern corporation the head of the company necessarily has a group of technical and administrative specialists who do the jobs the owner-manager used to perform. It has been demonstrated that a good machinist doesn't automatically make a good manager of a machine shop; a crack salesman doesn't necessarily make a good marketing manager. Successful managers need training and special experience in the administration of material and human resources. This need has given rise to the professional manager. The manager of today is rarely the "working group leader." Thus, more than ever, he must depend upon his subordinates to get the work done. Yet, he is accountable to the company for the work output, morale, and performance of those in his unit.

Other factors also have contributed to the change of emphasis. Some of them are: increasing automation; finer distinctions in occupational specialization; refinement of scientific and technical capabilities of the corporation; and the unparalleled affluence of the populace. Society is rapidly becoming one in which the emphasis is shifted from work done by hand to work done by the mind. In this computer age the human mind becomes a more valuable commodity. As machines do the work previously done by men, the professional manager makes his greatest contribution mentally: decision making and management of human resources.

The key to the performance of a manager and to that of his employee is "motivation," a point which is being stressed increasingly by the behavioral scientist in the university and by the businessman. Business has long been concerned about motivation but, for the most part, the interest has been confined to consumer motivation. Researchers have begun to move in their studies from motivation to buy to motivation to work.

What is this thing called motivation? Motivation is defined as a drive within the individual, rather than without, which incites him to action. What the behavioral scientist is interested in is *what* motivates the individual. What are the factors conducive to motivation?

What is involved—or the total concern—can be illustrated by the old saw "You can lead a horse to water but you cannot make him drink." In this folk proverb all the elements are present—you, the horse, the leading, and the water. These are all the external, physical, and material factors. The element missing is the thirst, or the need—or desire—for the water. While modern behavioral scientists recognize that man is infinitely more complex than a horse, the same principle applies. And some behavioral scientists contend that business has for too long tried to do the leading (or actually *has* been leading) without allowing the individual to aspire to or to satisfy his own needs in order to achieve self-realization.

What can the behavioral scientist do about it? For one thing, he can look for the factors that are conducive to motivation. For another, and this, perhaps, is more important, he can determine what the individual's needs *are*. It is an accepted maxim that man is forever a goal-seeking animal, and if it can be determined what those goals *are* and *why* he seeks them, society—or business for that matter—may not only be better equipped to help him reach them, but may also find itself better off.

Some established beliefs about what motivates a person on the job are now being questioned—for example, the long-held assumption that money paid for services is enough to keep a person happy and productive. With high employment and growing affluence, money seems to have lost much of its power as a motivator. Money obviously can be a stimulus to motivation if a man is unemployed and hungry, but it is not a motivator in the real sense. The motivation for the unemployed man is to feed, clothe, and shelter himself, so even then money becomes a means to an end. Some behavioral researchers have shown that above a certain level of responsibility compensation is not a motivating factor at all. If a manager is paid $20,000 annually, for example, it does not necessarily follow that he is more strongly motivated to do a good job if he is raised to $30,000. The salary he receives may make him more *satisfied* with the job, but it won't necessarily make him more highly motivated. A substantial amount of research indicates that compensation, at best, can provide satisfaction only *off* the job.

A prevailing trend in behavioral research as related to human motivation assumes that, in order to reach his inner-directed goals, a man must first know himself and be able to find an outlet for his needs. The atmosphere in which he lives and works must be one that encourages self-expression and self-realization. Furthermore, it is believed that a person's concept of himself determines his attitude toward his contemporaries and the groups in which he functions, because he looks at his world through the only eyes he has—his own. But objectivity about oneself is very difficult to achieve. For this reason much of the behavioral research conducted today is concerned with finding ways to help man know himself, his capabilities, his limitations, and his abilities to relate what is inside him to the external world. Part of his world is composed of the groups in which he moves: his community, his family, and his world of work. His world of work is made up of groups; it is made up of individuals, who make up groups and subgroups. The contemporary manager must communicate with, and work with and around a variety of persons with a wide range of personalities and skills.

WHAT'S HE WORKING ON NOW?

Many behavioral scientists, sensitive to the personal and social needs of the individual, are engaged in research on the nuances of human relationships and inter-relationships. As indicated earlier, they are trying to find the elements that create an environment conducive to personal growth and self-realization. Much of their research is designed to elaborate and elucidate on the individual and the group. A few current concerns with special interest for the business world include:

☐ *Communication.* Upward, downward, and lateral communication within an organization; keeping channels of communication open for flow of accurate and useful information; formal and informal methods of communication; improvement of personal skills in written and oral communication; verbalization of internal needs; "feedback" and effects of communication efforts within the organization.

☐ *Decision Making.* Development of skills in handling "open-ended" or problematic situations; degree of participation at various levels of the organization; rational versus impulsive (or intuitive) approaches; boundaries of "risk-taking."

☐ *Innovation and Change.* Effecting technological, managerial, and organizational change within an organization; implementing change when indicated and gaining acceptance of novel situations; barriers to innovation; effect of change on productivity and morale; innovation through high motivation.

☐ *Conflict.* How it arises in an organization; interpersonal and interdepartmental hostility and conflict; optimum resolution of conflict; effect on organizational goals and the group's ability to function under stress.

☐ *Leadership.* Qualities of effective leaders; development of leadership ability; relative effectiveness of "permissive," "supportive," and "autocratic" approaches to management of an organization; entrepreneurship.

☐ *Authority and Accountability.* Limits of power; relation of responsibility and authority; span of control, reaction to authority from peer, subordinate, and superior groups; degree of accountability; delegation of responsibility and authority.

☐ *Learning, Perception and Creativity.* Measurement of learning capacities; individuals and groups as perceived by other individuals and groups within the organization; development of potentialities; refinement of existing skills; creation of climate for personal growth and creative expression; personal creativity within the larger organization's goals and structures.

The above represents only a most cursory overview of the facets of human composition and behavior that occupy the professional behavioral researcher these days. Not only do these capsule listings comprise but a few examples of the topics that might be identified with contemporary behavioral research, but also within the topics there is much overlap.

HOW'S HE DOING?

With these interests, how is the behavioral scientist doing? At least, how is he doing in terms of the three stages of scientific inquiry, that is research, development, and application? All three warrant comment on the state of the art.

Research is defined as "diligent and systematic inquiry or investigation into a subject in order to discover facts or principles." The research stage seems to be the most active. There are foundations and other philanthropic organizations whose chief activity is the support of research in human behavior. Their encouragement (and their funds) is being used by an ever-growing number of behavioral scientists to do fundamental research in behavior of individuals and groups, increasingly aimed at the business environment. Some well-known social psychologists, sociologists, (and a few political scientists and econo-mists) have begun adapting older theories about intergroup behavior—previously concerned mainly with community, educational, and ethnic groups—to the world of work.

Aside from the intensive research in the departments of social science at major universities, there can hardly be found a respected business school without a division that is performing behavioral research of some sort, and there are springing up inter-disciplinary centers which surmount departmental boundaries for concerted effort in behavioral research.

Research is also being performed by the military services, either directly or through contract with behavioral science institutes, on many of the same problems that confront the business world, e.g., leadership, communications, etc. This reflects the growing realization that group problems are group prob-lems—regardless of where they exist.

Basic research is apparently thriving, judging from the outpouring of books on behavioral research and the numerous research reports in scientific and management journals.

This research most often takes place on the university campus or at some other place where the subjects can be observed closely and where data can be verified with a considerable degree of accuracy. The subjects are often students who contribute time to the experiments and then return to their regular work. Sometimes the subjects are businessmen, but the major extent of their partic-ipation is a laboratory session for a specified time away from their places of work. Occasionally behavioral research is conducted in an actual work setting, but most frequently the work force sample is small or restricted to companies whose orientation is in favor of behavioral research to the extent that some researchers question the validity of the findings of these experiments performed with "preconditioned" subjects.

EARLY APPLICATION

If one accepts the premise that earlier research in physical factors that affect productivity was actually behavioral research, then the application phase is widespread and evident in modern business. Changes in the work environment and production processes that were considered radical innovations a few years ago are now accepted practice.

Another example of popular acceptance and application of behavioral science is the use of employee selection aids, particularly psychological tests, the struc-tured interview, and the weighted application form.

There is some evidence that business is applying the additional findings of the modern group of behavioral researchers. Consumer motivation studies were cited earlier, but perhaps a more significant trend is the acceptance of work-motivation theories by some companies, noticeably in the management development area. Instances of full-scale adoption of current motivational theories are rare, but a few companies have changed complete organization structures in order to put into use some of the more recent theories. And a growing number of companies are enlisting the aid of the behavioral scientist to conduct "laboratory" sessions within the organization, all aimed at achieving a higher degree of communication and motivation among their executives.

While both development and application require removal "from the laboratory to the world," they are sometimes confused. Development implies further research and follow-up, always with the thought in mind that the thing being tried is still research, while application is the putting into practical use a principle or law which is accepted as a concrete phenomenon.

There are those, including some behavioral scientists, who decry application of theories about interpersonal and intergroup relationships until they are more fully developed. One psychologist asserted, "There are a handful of companies that are so concerned about their executives' mental health and performance that they are ready to embrace any new theory put forth. . . . They seem all too willing to try putting into practical application every new fad that comes along. . . . What we need is more developmental research."

Development means "to bring out the capabilities or possibilities; cause to grow or expand into a more advanced or effective state." Development for behavioral scientists, as for physical scientists, involves taking a piece of pure or theoretical research which has been refined in the laboratory and putting it through further tests in a given situation where the variables are not as strictly controlled. In other words, development is an expansion of a piece of basic research to see if it is pragmatic.

For the behavioral researcher concerned with people at work, it means trying out a theory in an actual work setting with constant observance, measurement, validation, and recording of data, with the hope that he will achieve universality.

THE NEED FOR DEVELOPMENT

The development stage is noticeably missing in the largest segment of business. Development often is indicated for a particular piece of research that already has had some development and application, because conditions for a specific company or type of business may not be the same as for business as a whole. An example of application without appropriate development may be found in the use of psychological tests for screening of employees. Some tests have gained so much in popularity that they have become the *sine qua non* for employment throughout the organization, even though the accepted scores have not been validated for the particular industry, the particular company, and the particular jobs under consideration. To ensure that "cut-off" scores are realistic for the situation in which they are used, development research is indicated in many cases.

Carrying this example further, some companies have begun to stress validation of employment tests. For the most part, however, these validations lack desirable accuracy. The usual procedure in validating a given test is to follow up on the work performance of people after they are employed. It is expected that persons scoring 90, for example, will turn out to be better workers than those scoring 70. In most validation efforts, however, an arbitrary "cut-off" score, say 50, is established, and applicants scoring below that point aren't hired. If the scores established for employment, and taken as an indicator of job success, are to be developed and validated fully, the company would have to hire some people who score in the lower percentiles as well as those who achieve a score in the upper percentiles. Then, the job success of those who scored 10 or 20 could be compared with the higher achievers. Even among those scoring in the upper ranges, the person with a 70 score may show more job success than the person with a 90, if they are in different jobs. If psychological tests are to be given much credence, the need for developmental research is apparent.

For another example of application without thorough development the businessman needs only to look at methods of performance appraisal as they are popularly and widely used. A great deal of basic research has been performed on systems of evaluating an employee's success on the job. The fundamental research showed that such reviews were desirable because they left both the superior and the subordinate with a sense of sympathetic understanding. It was further shown that mutual confidence and trust resulted from the feeling that both parties knew fully what the job required and what was expected of the subordinate in meeting the job's objectives, as well as what he could expect from his superior.

So, a major segment of the business community installed performance appraisals throughout their respective companies at all levels of responsibility.

Did anyone stop to ask: "What effect, if any, does the performance appraisal have on subsequent work performance?" There may have been questions in the minds of some businessmen, but only recently did a large multiplant company, working in collaboration with behavioral scientists from a leading university's school of business, decide to take a look at the effect of those frank, free-communication appraisals on the performance of the employee afterwards. (Incidentally, at least in the study cited, the effect of performance appraisals on subsequent work performance had a *negative* correlation.)

Employment tests and performance appraisals are only two examples of the work of behavioral scientists which has been accepted and put to use without adequate development. Much more fundamental research is at the stage where development is indicated and needed, if the knowledge gained through the basic research is ever to be meaningful for the business world. Why, then, is this developmental research not being conducted?

There are many reasons why the gap exists. Managements' (or organizations') resistance to change has been offered as one reason. Also, relatively few companies have been in a position to provide a climate conducive to behavioral research. Therefore, the developmental research has been restricted, almost exclusively, to a few large corporations with a management that is more likely to be sensitive to newer concepts and trends, and with the funds to sustain a staff to carry out the studies. In the main, these efforts have been further restricted to the corporate offices where product output and manufacturing schedules aren't paramount. Occasionally, development research in human behavior is conducted by smaller companies—usually very small companies dealing in services, rather than material products, where communication channels are relatively close and controllable.

The reluctance of most companies to participate in behavioral research may be understandable, even to the behavioral scientists, for many developmental projects can (and do) involve a complete rearrangement of interpersonal and intergroup relationships and functions. For this reason, many businessmen have been hesitant to "play around with profits" by encouraging innovation and change in the organization's structure. Granted that increased productivity and harmonious relations are still the goals of behavioral research as it relates to business, these changes may not be observable immediately. For men accustomed to thinking in terms of manufacturing schedules and year-end profits truly innovative experiments have often been shunned in favor of the "tried and true."

The behavioral scientist may feel, on the other hand, that he has produced theories which have been tested and worked out to their optimum in the atmosphere of fundamental research. It is, therefore, the hope of behavioral scientists that more and more companies will appear upon the scene with both the willingness and the desire to "pick up the ball" and develop the findings of this basic research. On the strength of their experience during the past few years, they feel that their optimism is justified.

QUESTIONS

1. List and describe the academic disciplines constituting the behavioral sciences.

2. What differences exist between the behavioral scientist and the physical scientist?

7

The Evolving Patterns of Business

The world of business is an exciting, dynamic one. Because of its constantly changing nature, the business world twenty years from now will differ significantly from that of today. The changes which are occurring are major in character; however, they appear to be evolutionary changes rather than revolutionary. These changes currently taking place are the ways in which business adjusts to its environment.

Three major factors stand out as being of vital importance in the evolution of business during the coming decades. They are: the changes constantly occurring in the field of management, the growth of international business activities, and the ever-increasing role of government in the business environment.

MANAGEMENT AND THE FUTURE

Management in the past was and, to a great degree, in the present is an art. Managerial skills, such as decision making, problem solving, and the direction of employees, have proved difficult to teach. The good manager, for the most part, possesses these skills, as does the pianist or the sculptor possess the skills of his art. Practice, training, and education at best sharpen the skills of those possessing them; in those not having these abilities, only a moderate degree of competence can be taught. Management in the future, however, will be more than an art. It will be an applied science. Managers today and even more so in the future must apply scientific knowledge and techniques to the various problems they face.

Technical and scientific advances have been taken advantage of as they have developed. The contributions of Frederick Taylor and his followers and the development of operations research during the Second World War are two examples. The future of management, however, promises even greater utilization of scientific advances than has ever been seen in the past. Whether one looks at the automated production line, the electronic computer, or the development of the laser, science will greatly influence management. Automation, as was discussed earlier, will change the nature of the workplace and the demands made on the worker. The electronic computer already gives the manager both a powerful decision-making tool and a huge storehouse of information. Advances in physical science, such as the laser, are opening doors to completely new construction, communication, and production techniques. The challenges and problems of the manager will be the effective and full use of these new tools.

The advances currently being made in the mathematical and physical sciences are being paralleled by those in the behavioral sciences. Sociologists, psychologists, and anthropologists are continuously finding out more about the worker and the effects of the working environment. Current studies in the behavioral area have led to the rejection of some myths concerning workers. Studies have also led to more realistic theories of worker behavior. Again, efficient application of knowledge developed by behavioral scientists will be the problem of the manager.

The current development of management as a science in its own right, and as a profession, will have a profound effect on its future. In addition to the application of knowledge taken from the physical and social sciences, management is using the scientific method to solve its own problems. The use of research techniques and scientific methodology will enable management to solve problems currently considered to have no solution. The rise of management to the level of a science will have strong secondary effects. These include increased status among the other social sciences and changes in the teaching of management.

The increasing professionalization of management is seen in many ways today, and this trend will probably continue more strongly in the future. This professionalization began as a result of the separation of ownership and management as the number of large businesses increased. As a company grows, there is increasing necessity for formal managerial education and training, the development of a firm base of scientifically proven management principles, and the adoption of a code of ethics. As management approaches professional status, many changes could occur—the setting of rigid educational requirements before the title "manager" could be used; the carrying out of punishments for unethical actions, similar to the disbarment of unethical lawyers. Certification or licensing procedures might be instituted, as they currently are for certified public accountants, lawyers, and physicians. However, many observers of the business scene feel that this professionalization will not occur.

The future of management is an exciting one. The changes that occur will affect every American business and, ultimately, every American. For students of American business, the future holds both challenge and promise.

INTERNATIONAL BUSINESS

International business is business operations by firms located in two or more independent countries. While the study of international business is a comparatively recent development, trade between nations is nearly as old as recorded history. There is proof of international trade taking place in the year 1000 B.C.

There are several ways in which international business can take place. First, a firm may be engaged in international business as an *exporter*. Exporting is the sale of domestic goods to another country. Second, a firm may be an *importer*. Importing is the purchase of foreign-made goods for resale or use in the United States. In both exporting and importing the companies involved do not have any tangible investment, such as a plant or machinery, in another country.

A third way in which international business takes place is through *international marketing*. A firm engaged in international marketing still may have no investment abroad but it does actively participate in marketing activities in the foreign country. Activities such as sales promotion, advertising, and market research are directed by executives of the firm stationed in the foreign country.

As the foreign business grows, a fourth level of international business usually develops. This generally includes the manufacture of the product in the foreign country. This may first be done under an agreement with a foreign manufacturing company which has the capacity to manufacture the product. Later, if the business develops to an appropriate size, the company may build a manufacturing facility in the foreign country and become what is called a *multinational business*. At this stage the domestic and foreign operations are often kept separate. That is, there are two management groups. One group makes decisions for domestic operations, the other for international operations.

The final stage in the expansion into international business is the *world enterprise*. This stage would integrate the entire operations of the business throughout the world under one management. Few firms have reached this level of international business activity, but many firms are actively moving toward the adoption of this business concept.

International business has a rather romantic and emotional appeal because of the melodious and intriguing names of distant places such as Bangkok, Rangoon, or Rio de Janeiro. However, business has very realistic objectives. The objectives of a firm in international business are the same as those in domestic business; namely, to maximize profit and capture a share of the world market.

The accomplishment of these objectives requires at least two things. First, greater effectiveness must be achieved in the organization of the operating units. Second, a management team must be built that can handle problems on a worldwide basis.

International business is vital to the survival and growth of our country. Because of the uneven distribution of resources, no country is self-sufficient. Consequently, while international trade accounts for only about 6½ per cent of our Gross National Product, this trade is made up of some strategic materials that make our prosperity possible. For example, we import iron ore, copper, and nickel. Our productive capacities would be severely restricted if such materials were unavailable. At the same time, we export materials that we have in abundance, which permits other countries to develop. The monetary value of United States imports and exports is greater than any other country in the world.

We measure the value of international trade and determine whether a favorable or unfavorable *balance of trade* exists. The balance of trade is the difference between our total imports and total exports. If total exports exceed total imports a country has a favorable balance of trade. The United States usually has a favorable balance of trade.

The balance of trade covers only imports and exports. The *balance of payments* is the tabulation of all economic transactions between residents of one country and the rest of the world. The balance of payments includes the exports and imports of a country plus the overseas receipts and expenditures of the government, private companies, and individual citizens. This comprehensive balance sheet of receipts and expenditures for such things as defense, foreign aid, new plants and equipment, and tourist expenditures, reveals whether a country spends more abroad than other countries spend in it. If receipts exceed expenditures, a country has a credit, or favorable balance of payments. If expenditures exceed receipts a nation has a debit, or unfavorable balance of payments. The United States has been operating with an unfavorable balance of payments for several years.

There are many differences that must be recognized by managers dealing in international business. The first difference is that products and money cross the boundaries of sovereign nations. Each nation has its own policies that affect trade. Tariffs, special marking of packages, and other regulations must be complied with if the goods are to be traded.

A country usually has its own monetary system. International trade requires transactions to be conducted in different currencies. It is, therefore, necessary to know the value of one currency in relation to another. This relationship is called the *exchange rate*. For example, a United States businessman buying goods in England would find prices quoted in pounds. The current exchange rate between pounds and dollars is one pound equals approximately $2.40.

Another significant difference for international business is marketing and market characteristics. The firm must tailor the product characteristics, pricing policies, channel of distribution, and promotional efforts to satisfy the demands of the foreign consumers. The differences in markets may be the result of the laws of the country, the customs of the people, and the economic resources of the nation.

Finally, the businessman must be informed about the special business practices, techniques, and documents of international operations. For example, bills of lading, consular invoices, and insurance documents must be processed before goods can move in international trade.

BUSINESS-GOVERNMENT RELATIONS

The Congress of the United States in 1946 passed the Employment Act. This act sets forth the economic objectives of our country. These objectives are full employment, full production, price stability, and growth in productive capacity.

In our economic system business has the primary responsibility for the production and distribution of the goods and services desired by the consuming public. As was explained in Part One, government has continuously regulated the activities of business, and this regulation has increased significantly since the 1930's.

In pursuit of the objectives of our economy as stated in the Employment Act of 1946, the federal government has used structural economic control. Through structural control, the government tries to bring about the type of business structure that will achieve the nation's stated economic objectives. The major tool of structural control is antitrust legislation (Sherman Act of 1890 and Clayton Act of 1914). Antitrust legislation was passed to insure the maintenance of competition in our economy. A number of economists feel that our present antitrust legislation and enforcement policy needs to be re-evaluated.

In addition to structural control, the government also uses functional economic control to aid in the achievement of its objectives. Fiscal and monetary policies are the two main tools used in functional economic control. Fiscal policy is concerned with the control of government spending and government receipts (taxes). Increased government spending enlarges the total demand for goods and services within the economy. For example, an order by the government for additional military aircraft stimulates business activity in many ways. Business firms will have to hire additional employees and purchase additional raw materials and supplies to produce the aircraft. Purchases by aircraft firms, in turn, stimulate additional business activity in other industries throughout the economy. Increased government receipts (taxes), unless offset by increased spending, will depress the total demand for goods and services. Thus, fiscal policy can be used either to have a stimulating or dampening effect upon total economic activity.

Monetary policy is determined by the Federal Reserve System's Board of Governors. The Governors seek to control the interest rate and the rate of credit expansion in the economy. In periods of inflation (general increase in the price level), the Governors will attempt to increase the rate of interest and reduce the amount of credit available in the economy.

Monetary and fiscal policies are to be preferred over direct price and wage control, another form of functional control. This is particularly true in a free-enterprise economic system such as ours. Direct controls over prices and wages represent extreme measures, usually reserved for times of national emergency (war). Even then, these direct controls must be supplemented by monetary and fiscal policies.

Sound monetary and fiscal policies are a key to the government's ability to achieve its economic objectives. Without the proper formulation and execution of these policies, business would constantly find itself faced with economic upturns and downturns. Thus, monetary and fiscal policy has done much to smooth out the so-called "business cycle." The last serious depression in this country occurred during the 1930's, although we have had several mild recessions or declines in the level of economic activity since World War II.

Historically, there has been conflict between business and government. Businessmen traditionally have felt that government has overextended its power and authority in its dealings with business. A number of observers of the business scene feel that business is undergoing a change in its attitude toward government and its policies. For example, Professor Theodore Levitt of the Harvard Graduate School of Business writes, "Business now has, for example, a remarkably tolerant and relatively friendly attitude toward the complex congeries of national fiscal, monetary, and social welfare programs inaugurated during Mr. Johnson's first three years as President."[1]

It is impossible to precisely predict the nature of the relationships between business and government in the future. In our society it is important that neither government nor business become all powerful. It would be desirable if business and government could work together in a manner that would enable the economy to achieve its objectives and perpetuate the values of our free-enterprise system.

The articles that follow were selected to provide a greater insight into some of the more important evolving patterns of business. Richard Stull gives his

---

[1]"The Johnson Treatment," *Harvard Business Review,* January-February, 1967, p. 114.

ideas on where management will be in the 1970's. The *Nations Business* article presents the predictions of Leo Cherne, Executive Director of the Research Institute of America, on the future of business. The article by Endel Kolde presents an overview of the changing nature of international business. The article "Better Is Not Good Enough" states that the slow reduction of the deficit in the balance of payments of the United States is not enough to maintain the needed rate of economic growth. James Daniel and James Shuman explain why the dollar is in danger. Thomas Fiske deals with the critical problem of the appropriate relationship between government and business. Henry Ford II discusses the role of the corporation in public affairs.

Management Challenges for the 1970s

RICHARD ALLEN STULL

The practicing manager is a busy man. In the press of operations, he needs to solve daily sales, production, and inventory problems through the people who report to him. The professional manager, however, has learned to periodically come to full stop and take time to review the probable future framework in which his firm will operate. He knows only too well that the insight and accuracy of his vision and that of his colleagues at all levels in his business spell out the prospects for survival and success. Right now management is adjusting its seatbelt for 1970.

In the history of management, knowledge without techniques has proved useless; techniques without knowledge has been dangerous. The new management movement includes today both a physical and mathematical science sector and also one grouping the behavioral or social sciences. The real difficulty has been one of how to absorb the methods and findings of both into a fundamental scheme of management. Only as we solve this problem will it be possible to take the advice of Thomas Edison to "stand on the shoulders of others."

Many are recognizing that one of the difficulties with management science has been that academic people have not really known business firsthand. Professors, consultants, and specialists of all sorts are quick to tell managers what they ought to do, but too few businessmen have been asked or said what they actually do while they are managing. More and more, the manager's realistic voice is being sought and heard. In the final analysis, management itself is not a science but a practice. The prime purpose of a science is to *describe* phenomena and behavior. The chief function of a practice is to *control* them. Certainly,

From *Advanced Management Journal*, January 1965, pp. 44-51. Reprinted by permission.

one of the most encouraging developments of recent years has been the growing application of scientific knowledge to the solution of practical management problems.

In our research, national and international seminars, and on consulting assignments, our managers and staff have personal contact with several thousand key managers in a broad cross section of companies of varied industries around the world. The following review focuses the lense of professional management on significant trends which numerous studies and the testimony of practicing managers tell us appear to be taking definite shape for 1970:

1. A fast paced market for 1970
2. Marketing recentralization
3. More rational decisions
4. Increased management specialization
5. Changes in merit compensation
6. Growth in project management
7. Management featherbedding
8. Formal education for managers
9. New management task forces
10. Lateral entry
11. Profit reconsidered
12. Emerging professional management
13. Science fact
14. A challenging future

FAST PACED MARKET FOR 1970

Barring a global war, uncontrolled inflation, or greatly increased government regulation of business, foreseen are:

a. Countless new products and materials
b. Fast changes in distribution channels
c. Higher selling costs and greater profit challenge
d. Increased competition at home and abroad

Certainly by 1970, it will be difficult for most companies to be in the running without a market-oriented approach to management decisions. This will involve long range marketing programs based on careful research. With an anticipated $750 billion gross national product, 210 million population, and 200 per cent rise in discretionary consumer spending, we shall have reached a fast-paced consumer market demanding high cost. New or improved products, materials, and processes will multiply. U.S. industry spent over $60 billion for research and development over the past decade and the bill will probably go up to $120 billion by 1970. "Brand loyalty" will no longer be a safe bet.

The production pace will be stepped up. There will be shorter periods between discovery of a product and its appearance on the market. The result will be a need for much closer coordination among the research, marketing, production, and engineering departments. Computers will take over much of production control and inventory control, resulting in greater capacity. Automation will probably consolidate production facilities and fewer plants will be needed.

The marketing-for-profit approach will dominate management thinking. Company plans will be predicated on buyers' needs. The profit rather than volume approach to selling will be almost universal. Marketing managers will not only participate in production and finance, but, in many companies, will be the strongest voices in planning. The top marketing man will often be a staff man who will coordinate field sales, advertising, merchandising, promotion, public relations and marketing research.

It is not likely that there will be substitution of products on such scale as occurred when natural gas and oil replaced coal, aluminum replaced copper in many uses, and paperboard packaging cut into the market for wood boxes. But there will be newness and improvement in many areas. An important shift in products and processes in the future will be generated by the current research and development efforts in the military and space exploration fields. Older, well-established industries will put up greater resistance to the introduction of new substitute products. For example, the steel industry has already limited the role of aluminum in some of its markets by introducing improved, thin tin-plate.

Of the estimated 35 million increase in population, about two-thirds will be among those under age twenty and those over age sixty. Products designed to meet their needs will be in increasing demand. The war babies of the 1940's will be marrying, creating several million new households. Heads of families will be better educated, with more cultivated tastes and a higher budget for discretionary spending with which to satisfy their desires. Mail order, house to house, club and party plan selling are expected to make substantial gains. Customer sovereignty will have come of age as competition increases at home and abroad.

MARKETING RECENTRALIZATION

Even companies adding new units that previously would have been granted considerable autonomy will depend on a strong central control, not only in operational planning but in the setting of operating and financial policy. A number of companies have gotten into trouble by over-decentralizing authority. Rheem Manufacturing Company is a case in point. This New York metal container manufacturer expanded into aircraft parts, home appliances, plumbing fixtures and a multitude of new areas in early 1950. It divided some sixteen plants among six regional managers and cut them loose without a well engineered organization structure and adequate controls. The company is still recovering. Raytheon Manufacturing Company is another example, not unlike General Dynamics on a much smaller scale, in attempting to operate a patch-quilt of decentralized divisions under a distant holding company. It had to be bailed out by Harold Geneen, new President of International Telephone and Telegraph Corporation.

Marketing particularly, has been gradually centralized in such companies as Mobil Oil Company, Elgin Watch Company, Olin Mathieson, and American Brake Shoe Company. These organizational realignments, while different in each case, have a common element which is a marked move toward corporate control over marketing and product planning, analysis, and strategy. This marketing direction from the top is very similar to the financial control found in General Motors and Du Pont, and may be anticipated as a consciously planned shift among a number of key companies by 1970.

While at first glance information technology has encouraged greater centralization because the relevant data for top management is more readily at hand, the same data can also be more quickly available for self-control to managers in decentralized operations. This is an area as yet insufficiently understood and explored. There will undoubtedly be much experimenting in the next few years to achieve an effective balance between centralization and decentralization.

MORE RATIONAL DECISIONS

Special interest is growing in increasing the rationality of management decisions at all levels. Such companies as Westinghouse, Kaiser Aluminum and Chemical Corporation, and Lincoln-Mercury Division of Ford Motor Company are already providing education in the decision making process to large numbers of their managers.

Business decisions will become increasingly complex because of:
a. time—the necessity for long range planning
b. scope—decisions are no longer local, but increasingly international
c. regulation—government power and control will in all likelihood increase
d. investment requirements—higher capital investment for success is becoming mandatory.

Computerized decision making will probably move the role of planning and performance measurement higher up the line in corporations. Just as the industrial engineer has, in many cases, taken over the production planning that was formerly left to foremen, so planning functions may be taken from middle managers and given over to technical specialists. This trend, however, will increase difficulties between business management and computer systems management. Concern here is in the possible transfer of operating control from accountable line managers to the computer organization. This shift is untenable for persons inexperienced in the actual business functions and may create serious organizational problems.

INCREASED MANAGEMENT SPECIALIZATION

Middle management functions are undergoing a continual specialization. The financial function as once handled by one manager is today broken up into a number of areas that require specialists on taxes, investments, fund raising, and the like. There will be a growth in the number of kinds of staff specialists. Line-staff functions will broaden, and managers will be needed who have the understanding and ability to work with these specialists in tune with the times. Moreover, there will be a sharp increase in staff functions. Executives in production, marketing, and engineering will be served by specialists in operations analysis, statistics, etc. so that new knowledge from any of these disciplines can immediately be brought to bear in making strategic decisions.

CHANGES IN MERIT COMPENSATION

Small and large companies are reconsidering compensation of the exceptional junior executive. Often it is simpler to lose one of these "comers" through inadequate salary than it is to replace him. Many a young and competent manager is more interested in his immediate salary level than in sophisticated stock options and deferred compensation schemes. Bonus and cash incentive systems help him at a time when he needs it most for his family obligations. He is then in a position to plan his own investment program and estate. Retirement is losing some of its enchantment for many executives. Too many have learned that when the day does come for the better than average executive, he already owns his own home, has two cars, has an electric razor, his children are through college, and he is too tired to make an eight hour day of collecting stamps, writing letters to the editor, or traveling all over the world with an ill wife. Later in his career, however, when he reaches the higher tax brackets, company controlled retirement plans take on more realism and are appreciated.

GROWTH IN PROJECT MANAGEMENT

Project management has arisen in U.S. industry to handle problems which confront the manager of Department of Defense and National Aeronautics and Space Administration projects. Companies doing business with the government have found the project manager a useful organizational position to encompass planning, control, supervision, and the engineering or manufacturing involved in producing a complex end-product such as a rocket. In achieving his objective, however, unlike the functional manager, the project manager usually has no line authority over the organizations producing the end-products he must deliver. His duties often cut across interdepartmental, interdivisional and even intercompany lines. They are further complicated by the prospect of involving one or more governmental agencies.

A number of large Department of Defense-National Aeronautics and Space Administration contracts, in fact, have hinged on whether bidding companies had or would set up a project management organization to handle the contract.

The project management concept was actually practiced by the government as early as World War II's Manhattan Project. It was eminently successful as developed by General Bernard A. Schriever in building the first intercontinental ballistic missile. A few industries tried the concept in the early 1950's and, by 1959, a number of companies had established such organizations. Project management coordinates the actions involved in producing projects deliverable on time, within estimated costs, at specific reliability and performance, at a profit to the contractor. The purpose of project management is to insure the achievement of these objectives through the already established functional organizations but without the latter's specialized interests upsetting the whole. Two companies which have used the project management organizational device most effectively are North American Aviation and Hughes Aircraft Company. It is anticipated that as the military and space exploration fields expand, project management will give organization charts a new look and make possible the production of amazingly complex products in record time.

MANAGEMENT FEATHERBEDDING

A common union policy, the practice of spreading the work, will possibly be adopted as policy by some companies at certain levels of management in attempting to overcome many problems attending automation and computer innovation. Plans must be made not only for management transfers and retraining but early retirements and severance allowances in special cases. Dislocations are bound to come which will mean reconsidering our standards for doing business, governing ourselves, and living together. The trend has shown up clearly in employment among the blue chip corporations during the past decade. The United States Steel Corporation, our number one steel producer, employed 300,000 persons in 1951. Today it employs 200,000. General Electric has increased its employee force from 214,000 to only 250,000 in the last ten years. E. I. du Pont de Nemours & Company, largest chemical producer, today has about the same number of employees it had ten years ago, 86,000. The Chrysler Corporation reduced its employment from 100,000 in 1951 to 75,000 in 1961.

FORMAL EDUCATION FOR MANAGERS

The place of formal education in preparing men for managerial positions will become increasingly important. This will be no substitute for the need for intuitive judgment and other important basic personal qualities. But the probability is on the upswing that one who is equipped with the classified knowledge, principles, and techniques of the specialized work of management will do a significantly better job of managing than the one who has not. The recruiting pattern of major industry is setting this trend because the men who have this education, buttressed by good business experience, are proving out. Moreover, managers as well as technical specialists will need mid-career training to keep abreast of new knowledge, methods, and procedures.

NEW MANAGEMENT TASK FORCES

An organizational device which is coming more and more into play is the *task force*. This concept is creating additional need for more middle managers with real leadership skills, men who are able to guide a group effectively towards a specific objective. A model example was initiated several years ago under Robert E. Brooker, then president of Whirlpool Corporation and now the energetic president of Montgomery Ward. Six promising young men were selected and came to be known as Whirlpool's Long Range Planning Task Force. The men were in an age bracket between 35 and 42 and their experience included manufacturing, engineering, sales and finance. Their assignment was working out a ten year plan for the growth and development of Whirlpool. The study was divided into six phases:
    a. Determination of objectives
    b. Agreeing on a method of analyzing the problems
    c. Securing background information
    d. Assigning specific projects to members of the group and, when necessary, enlisting outside support

e. Reviewing and discussing the findings on the individual projects and coming to an agreement on the recommendations

f. Summarizing their work and reporting to the chairman and the president.

The task force made forecasts of the market for major appliances for ten years. They studied invention and rate of change, aspects of technical development, and distribution. The latter resulted in an economic forecast of the geographic distribution of sales to be achieved by 1970. A mathematical model for distributional facilities was then set up to serve independent dealers most economically within this geographic distribution of sales. Developed was a gateway system of regional warehouses which brought stocks closer to the consumer and provided for the mixing of shipments of all appliances when shipment was made to the dealer. The gateway system also contributed a means of leveling factory manpower in securing maximum production economies.

Finally, as a result of the study a number of reorganizations were instituted, including manufacturing and the international division.

EMERGING PROFESSIONAL MANAGEMENT

Related to the changing trend is the rising importance of the professional manager. As the separation of ownership in management proceeds, professionalism will tend to take hold. A concept of trusteeship will, in all likelihood, develop and modify the traditional concept of directors as representatives solely of ownership but of the public as well. There will be new interest in the adoption of codes of ethics and professional standards.

As managers learn to master their specialized kind of work, classify their body of knowledge, develop a common vocabulary, identify and utilize principles, adopt and practice a code of ethics, they will approach professionalism. Capitalism was founded on *self-goals* characterized by the statement: "I want a bigger piece of pie, and it's my duty to create a bigger piece of pie." Today the emphasis has moved to one of *shared goals:* "Let's work together to make a bigger pie."

The growth and development of public relations shows the change in point of view. Originally, we had the *press agent* who was of the P. T. Barnum philosophy: "There's a sucker born every minute," and "The public be fooled." The transition came with the *publicity man* such as Ivy Lee whose objective was: "The public be informed." Today we have the *public relations manager* characterized by the approach: "The public be informed and its favor earned."

SCIENCE FACT

Computers and the behavioral sciences are learning to shake hands with one another in the nation's largest companies. And practical, smaller companies are adopting and using the new methods. Mathematics and model building techniques are only the beginning of a new interdisciplinary approach to operations which are on the march from production problems, inventories, scheduling and quality control to personnel, marketing research and management development applications.

Science fiction is becoming science fact. Experimental psychologists have found that pigeons can be trained to 99% accurate visual inspection of small parts. The birds can inspect about 1,100 parts per hour on a plant assembly line. The pigeon is a common laboratory animal, inexpensive, costing approximately $1.25 per bird and about $1.00 per month to feed. They have excellent eyes, learn fast, and live about 20 years.

While no applications have been made to date, this experiment augers for the unexpected possibilities in the future. Pigeons have been trained for inspection work several times in the past, but they were laid off at the last moment because of the fear of union repercussions. On another occasion, in a drug company, they were trained to pick out pills that were inadequately coated. The idea scared the sales department. Even though the birds were hermetically isolated from the pills, salesmen feared the association with pigeons would be just too much for the public to swallow!

Managing a modern oil refinery is one of the most complex in all industry and becomes more so every day. For example, computing a refinery's basic operating statistic, the stock balance (crude in and products out), until recently was manually completed monthly on about the 20th of the following month. Computerization has enabled several leading companies to provide a printed stock balance every morning to each foreman on the line.

No one knows where the technological revolution will lead. Some believe that great new industries will come into being which will create even more employment to the point where many arguments against automation may turn out to be academic. The manager's intellect will be released from data-collecting and analysis as these are taken over by machines. With this freedom for more creative contemplation, he can theorize and develop even greater technology. There is evidence that atomic energy may one day be used to melt ice caps, explore space, power industry, and change the weather. Newspapers and magazines may be transmitted by radio or television into one's living room. Pocket-sized walky-talkies will be able to keep everyone in constant communication. Advances in medical science may include diagnosis by computers and unheard of cures. Money may be eliminated, with customers presenting their thumbs to an electronic scanner that will automatically deduct the purchase price from their bank account. Also foreseen are submarine carrier ships that can cruise serenely beneath the surface of the sea, ignoring the weather conditions above.

A CHALLENGING FUTURE

In Dun and Bradstreet's practical and beautifully conceived annual report for 1963, the following striking paragraphs caught many a reader's eye:

> *Knowledge is the orderly accumulation of information. Truth is the perception of principles from which ideas are shaped. Wisdom is the skill with which knowledge and truth are combined in the exercise of judgment. Management employs all three in its daily review of the facts on which decisions are made . . .*

And, of the information revolution:

> *The electronic eye not only finds the needle in the haystack but threads it for instant use. However, no calculating or computing device is any better than the human control directing its use.*

Management moves into a new era as it adjusts its seatbelt for 1970. The computer has reduced the incidence of the margin for human error, but it cannot take the place of thinking. There can be no substitute for human judgment in setting up controls on the fast future highways of new information. This is management's challenge for 1970—and beyond.

QUESTIONS

1. Describe the changes predicted in marketing for the 1970s.

2. The author states that there will be a sharp increase in staff functions. Why will this occur?

3. Discuss a management task force. What can this system do for a company?

4. Is professionalism a foregone conclusion for management? Or is it possibly little more than a dream?

Preview of Change: From Now to 1980

The nation is now entering a new year, a new political administration and, in the belief of many, a potential new pivotal period in business.

Another punctuation mark in time will be the year 1980. Another election year, it will be a time of stocktaking and preparation for meeting the conditions of the final years of the Twentieth Century.

For a look at America in the period between now and 1980, the editors of *Nation's Business* interviewed Leo Cherne, executive director of the Research Institute of America, Inc., at his New York headquarters.

Mr. Cherne describes where he and his associates think business opportunities will lie. He talks of the challenges businessmen will face in their thinking. And he forecasts that the roles of governments will change as will the pace of daily life, both of which will affect your business.

Mr. Cherne, what will be uppermost in businessmen's minds in 1980?

Businessmen in 1980—that's only 15 years away—will be primarily pre-occupied with this particular question: How to keep up with the fantastic techno-logical change which is only now beginning the process of rapid acceleration—the introduction of advanced data processing, of infinitely more rapid and complete systems of communication, of fantastic electronic devices, of new ways of making things and new materials from which to make them.

It is enormously difficult to describe the impact of these and other tech-nological advances. This is at the very heart of the difficulty businessmen will increasingly have in dealing with these things: Understanding what it means, what is its magnitude, how do I use this technology?

Technology is moving faster than the human capability to apply it.

Does this mean, then, that the businessman who can learn to use this technology for his own purposes is going to gain an advantage?

I am saying that if the businessman is not well informed he will not even have a chance to exist as a businessman.

It will not be possible for the businessman to remain indifferent to the world of science.

Isn't this largely true already? What further changes can we expect, for instance, in production?

Almost without exception, new production processes by 1980 will achieve a quantum jump in precision, speed of operation and capability of being run with little or no human supervision.

Assembly operations will be drastically reduced. To a larger and larger extent, products or major segments of products will be made in one piece—often in one operation.

Engineers in 1980 will be able to set the theoretical specifications of a new product and then invent materials to meet these needs. As we see it, new materials will have many new properties: The ability to resist sudden and extreme changes in temperature without losing flexibility, transparency or workability, for instance. Color that can be changed by external means, such as an electrical impulse. The ability to be bonded instantly to many other materials. The ability to conduct electricity safely and convert it to light or heat at selected points in the material itself. Almost total absence of surface friction, without lubrication, under any operating conditions.

These are only some of the advances in technology which businessmen will have to learn to apply in this new era.

What goods will people want in 1980? How will consumers' demands change?

More durable goods, not as rapid a growth in the sale of nondurable goods. This is a reversal. In recent years, the trend has not been as favorable to durable goods.

These are products for the home and automobiles?

Yes, among other things. You also can't tell now what new products will come on the market.

It is very clear, for example, that home or family motion pictures on electronic tape, immediately playable back on the home television set, is a development attainable within the short-term future.

The picture phone will undoubtedly take hold. The only restraint will be how rapidly telephone companies can introduce them.

In addition, we foresee a very substantial increase in the desire for certain kinds of services. Travel is one of them.

The pressures of sheer crowding in constantly growing metropolitan centers will introduce a substantially increased desire for privacy of various kinds.

Better housing?

Better housing, better construction, more privacy in the walls.

But in addition to that, a greater tendency on the part of people to get away to the national forests, or other secluded areas, privacy that way.

Individuality of all kinds will see something of a rebirth as a result of the pressure of the mass. Mammoth markets for indistinguishable commodities will, of course, grow. But what has been ignored by many businessmen is that there is the simultaneous growth of substantial markets for unique and different things, for various elites within the community. These will be very important markets.

The vastness of the major markets is a fact which can be projected into the future. There is no doubt about it. But some of the most substantial opportunities will exist in the separate markets, the particular and special choices and the less general tastes.

Instead of planning for sales of many low-price models and a few deluxe models, merchandisers can figure on sales of as many or even more of their top-of-the-line numbers as of their standard items.

Who will buy these goods? How big will the market be?

By 1980, the nation's population will be about 245 million, some 50 million larger than today.

Over the five years immediately ahead, the wave of men and women who were the baby boom after World War II will be moving through college into the ranks of income-earners and into the family-forming age group. The boost for the economy will be impressive.

Finally, in the first half of the 1970's, they will be giving the birth rate another push upward, producing an echoing baby boom, with implications for housing, home furnishings, baby clothes, toys and food.

Not only will there be more families in 1980—82 million against 48 million today—but a great many more of them will be well off by today's standards. The typical family will have an income of about $9,800, more than half again as great as today's $6,400. Proportionately three times as many families will have incomes of $15,000 or more. The proportion with incomes of under $5,000 will shrink by nearly half. All of these figures are in constant dollars, of course.

Do you expect a steady boom between now and 1980?

Unfortunately, no. Economic growth will not come about smoothly and easily, with no crises. It's almost certain that, as in the past, the uneven rate of development will create periods of recession, serious unemployment and profit-less business operation between now and 1980.

What is the job outlook?

I think we will be coping with a job problem for the rest of our lifetimes. But we do not expect giant unemployment. A combination of factors will lead to a kind of suppressing of the problem, a certain amount of featherbedding or make-work—the addition of amenities and leisure-time activities on company payroll and less demanding attitudes about continuous work.

Interestingly enough, the major group that will press in this direction will be businessmen.

Why is that? Increasing social consciousness?

It is partly social consciousness, but it is by and large individual business consciousness. Businessmen do not relish handing out discharge notices. It is becoming part of the business culture, even now, that somehow or other the disemployment effects of automation ought not to be imposed on those now employed.

The manager is not thinking of society as a whole, he is thinking of his business, his people.

To be sure, this is far less than a complete answer, because while it may shelter employees from the effects of automation in that plant, it certainly does not open up opportunities for new employees.

When we talk of more leisure time, incidentally, we do not visualize a four-day week. That does not mean that a four-day week will not exist for a certain percentage of businesses or for certain crafts. But it is our judgment that it will be a more relaxed, shorter five-day week.

We visualize more three-day week ends. We visualize a longer vacation period. We visualize a spread of the sabbaticals that have been introduced in particular production industries where automation has had a dramatic effect, as, for example, in steel production.

Have people learned to cope with leisure?

Not yet. The human race has never had to. We are in a most remarkable period. Throughout all human existence, it has been utterly impossible, no matter how hard one worked, for the mass of the people ever to have enough to eat, ever to have enough of the physical necessities of life.

We in America are within just a very few years from the point where more dollars will be spent by the consumer on services than the sum total of all physical needs.

Work will increasingly drain only a part of man's energy, and for the first time he has to grapple with the question: What does one do with time and energy if work takes only a part of it? This is really a novel question.

Is it that it must be activity meaningful to the individual?

Yes. In a sense, when work is reduced, as it almost certainly will be, there is a very real crisis of values for people generally. Great groups of people have been trained by nothing in their whole culture, background, religion, philosophic conceptions, for anything other than work as a meaningful activity.

Does this open up new enterprises for people?

It opens up for business a wealth of new opportunities. There is an explosion already well under way in travel.

Certainly I think it is significant that the United States publishes more paperback titles than either we or any other group of nations ever have, the fact that there are more serious recordings sold, the fact that attendance at symphonies was larger than attendance at football games in 1963. These are manifestations of the fact that, given time and money, a substantial percentage of the population will learn to use them and certain groups will learn to satisfy their demands.

One of the great new opportunities for business is the sale of culture and education. And I think that much of education is not going to be conducted in schools. Initial education, yes, but a remarkable amount of it will be made available through the efforts of individual businesses.

Incidentally, I do not mean to be romantic. I am by no means suggesting that because there will be time available and, because there will be larger real dollar income, that most American families will be going to symphonic concerts, reading the best and most difficult paperback books published, going to schools or taking courses at home.

I think that for many the additional money and additional time will bring problems they can't absorb intelligently. Some people will get the bends and will do silly or dangerous things, because they will be disoriented by the availability of resources, time and money that they are just not emotionally equipped to handle.

Does all this bring a danger of inflation as wages rise and hours shorten?

None of this need, by itself, produce inflation. Inflation is a result of many things—the size of wage increases in relation to output, the whole cost-price wage equation, government policy.

There is no doubt at all that wages will increase. We conclude that in constant 1960 dollars gross national product, which ran between $620 and $625 billion in 1964, will in 1980 all but have doubled to $1.16 billion. The actual amount in 1980 dollars will be larger because, of course, there will be a continuing erosion of the dollar.

Personal consumption will double. In 1980 we expect that $745 billion, after taxes and savings, will actually be spent by the 245 million Americans of 1980. Bear in mind that $745 billion is about 20 per cent more than the total gross national product now. These are in constant dollars.

Will there be inflation? I would say that over this 15-year period to 1980, the annual percentage of inflation will, if anything, be lower than in the last 15 years.

Why?

First, the presence of people hungry for jobs will be an important moderating influence on excessive wage increases.

Second, the United States increasingly sees its economic survival depending on competitive prices in the international market place. That will operate as a restraint on the price increases among businessmen.

Third, the federal government will be a smaller influence for inflation than it has been at any time in the past 30 years, no matter what administration is in power in Washington. Federal government expenditures as a per cent of gross national product are dropping. This is not because of restraint on the part of a particular president. It is because the rest of the economy is going to grow faster. The federal government will have less leverage.

Do you expect that there will be further federal tax reductions?

Without any question. The only question is: What year? If I had to guess now, I would say that 1967-1968 will see the next round of income and corporate tax reductions, in addition to the excise tax reductions, which I anticipate will take place in 1965.

What do you see happening in relations between the federal government and local and state governments?

I see no abatement in the need for traditional services. I see some areas, in fact, of fairly obvious increase. The problem of air pollution is a new problem, or at least the dimensions are so increased as to make it an essentially new problem. That problem will involve government. And in my judgment it is going to involve local and state governments.

On the urgent problem of needs in education, we are just not going to have the educational plant that this country will require, even numerically. Let's assume no qualitative change in education—though I do visualize a substantial qualitative change—but even quantitatively we don't have enough schools.

We will need more medical facilities.

The doctor is a local instrument. So is the hospital. So are nurses. There is an urgent need for nursing homes, what with the rapid increase in older population groups and the increased ability to keep older folks alive. We have never been accustomed to grappling with that, and the answer, by definition, is local. So there is going to be a continued and expanding demand for more and more local and regional services.

Will state and local taxes continue to increase?

No question.

How does this affect the businessman? Presumably he is going to have to take a look at his relationship with state and local governments?

Businessmen more and more will develop increased concern and real anxiety about local government, and less and less preoccupation with the federal government. This is a product of the fact that business is a physical thing located in a place, and its needs are local. If business needs trained manpower, it is the local entity which is relevant, not the federal government.

In addition, businessmen are obviously deeply concerned with social order. It is generally assumed that the New York World's Fair did not have the attendance last summer that had been expected in part because of fear of crime in the streets. That also means thousands of businessmen did not have the income they expected to have. Businessmen have been the first to feel the effects of social discontinuity.

We saw in the tax bill last year an example of how the interests of both the federal government and the business community coincided. Do you foresee more examples of this happening in the future?

I think there will be two trends operating simultaneously. The federal government is a source of regulation of business, whether it is regulation of pricing practices or advertising, whether it is regulation conducted by the Federal Trade Commission or the National Labor Relations Board. The federal government as the source of regulation will, by virtue of that fact, be an irritant to many businessmen.

On the other hand, the federal government as an ideological source of hostility to businessmen will not be what it has been. This has already changed profoundly. I think it is not accidental that some of the business community found Lyndon Johnson less hostile than many of his predecessor presidents.

I think we have finally gotten the great depression out of our system, the economic warfare and political warfare of that period of time. I think we have gotten a kind of inverted Marxism out of our system, the sterile language of hostility between government and business, between labor and business. I think we have gotten some of the Franklin Roosevelt language out of our system.

In other words, we have gone through 30 years since the great depression, and even a Democratic administration now is remarkably sympathetic to many business objectives. Part of that flows from the fact that even Democrats have discovered in this period of time something they really did not know that clearly in the 1930's, and that is that if the federal government has any interest in maintaining prosperity and encouraging growth, government by itself at best is only a modest instrument in that direction.

QUESTIONS

1. What new types of products will be introduced in the coming years? How will these affect the job of the manager?

2. In what ways will the nature of work change by 1980? Will the ordinary worker find his life greatly different from what it is today?

3. Is inflation a great danger in the years ahead according to Mr. Cherne?

4. How will business-government relations change between now and 1980 according to the author?

Business Enterprise in a Global Context

ENDEL J. KOLDE

Since World War II, international business relations of the United States have undergone far-reaching changes in scope, composition, and structure.
☐ Foreign trade that used to comprise the bulk of transboundary business has shrunk to a minor fraction; total exports are now less than a third of the estimated overseas sales of United States companies.
☐ International intermediaries—export and import merchants, commission houses, and trading companies—have been submerged by new arrangements and are on the verge of disappearing from the institutional structure of United States business.
☐ Multinational corporate ventures have risen to remold not only the channels of international trade but also the internal organization, as well as the external relations, of the corporation itself.
☐ The spans of corporate incentives and impediments have shifted, widened, and diversified as more and greater impacts from foreign environments compound domestic norms for managerial behavior and action.
    And the changes continue.
    It is not my intention in this article to catalog the past or the prospective changes. They are too numerous to count and too elusive to classify. My purpose is to identify the main sources—the apparent prime movers—of this process of change and thereby to move a step closer to a conceptual scheme for the emergent

---

Reprinted from the *California Management Review*, Vol. VIII, No. 4, Summer 1966. Copyright 1966 by the Regents of the University of California.

multinational business system. To minimize any dogmatic prejudice which a narrow frame of reference might tolerate, the subject is viewed from a broad interdisciplinary perspective.

Environmental Systems

The primary distinction between international and domestic business lies in the environmental framework and the organizational and behavioral responses that flow from it. As a company transcends a national setting, its environmental framework changes progressively in countless respects. New ground rules as defined by law, custom, and culture; new values; new contradictions, inter-actions, and balances among external forces; and new opportunities as well as uncertainties arise. The wider the company's international scope, the greater become the environmental diversities and multiversities surrounding it. To make rational choices among the alternatives available to it in different countries, the company must be able to identify, understand, and anticipate the negative and positive forces of the international diversity.

From a global perspective, the international business environment consists of three major divisions:
□ The Industrial West, with a few sprouts scattered elsewhere.
□ The Subindustrial South.
□ The Communist East.

The geographic scope and positions of the three divisions are [as follows:] The industrial countries cluster around the North Atlantic with North America and western Europe as the two principal areas. Japan, Australia, New Zealand, and South Africa complete the industrially developed sector of the free world. All these are predominantly capitalist countries with market-oriented economies. Private property, free enterprise, and open competition form the trigonal founda-tion of their economic philosophy. Politically, they are guided by the principles of representative government, democratic processes, and the rule of law. In historic heritage, they all belong to the Western culture, with Japan the sole exception.

The Communist realm occupies most of the large Euro-Asian land mass and forms geographically a cohesive whole, its only detached outpost being Cuba. Primarily production-oriented, the Communist system substitutes state monopoly for private ownership and enterprise. All productive resources belong to the state; individual property rights being confined to nonproductive chattels, mostly personal effects. The market mechanism is replaced by compulsive national planning, administered through an unparalleled bureaucracy, and enforced through all agencies of the government not only as the Marxist mode of produc-tion but also as a means of socialist justice. Politically, these countries are ruled by autocratic, one-party dictatorships where due processes as well as laws them-selves are subjugated to the power of officials' actions. Culturally, the Commu-nist world is almost evenly divided between the Occidental and the Oriental. While the Communist leadership so far has come mostly from the Western cul-tures, the system itself has spread more toward the South and the East. As a result, Asians have surpassed Europeans and outnumber them by a 3 to 1 ratio in the Communist citizenry at the present time. (Peking's challenge to Moscow is, at least in part, a reflection of the shift in the ethnic and cultural balance of the Communist bloc.)

The subindustrial or underdeveloped sector of the global economy covers vast expanses of Africa, Central and South America, Oceania, and southern Asia. Unlike the other two, the underdeveloped world has no basic doctrine or economic philosophy of its own. However, as explained later, certain ideological contours are emerging which may provide these countries a common philosophical base. Politically, the underdeveloped world consists mostly of pseudodemocracies and outright personal dictatorships. The Philippines, Pakistan, and India are perhaps glaring exceptions to prove the generalization. Culturally and ethnically, these countries represent the widest possible range. However, the indigenous people far outnumber the Europeans. The cultural heterogeneity, which in the past was repressed by the disproportionate influence of the European elements, is now forging to the foreground and inviting anxious curiosity throughout the world.

The three business systems are vastly different in size: nearly half of mankind lives in the Subindustrial South, one-third in the Communist East, and only a little over a fifth in the Industrial West. If time dimension is added to the current profile by considering the natural growth rates, the population disparities among the three divisions are certain to grow rather than diminish in the future.

Lest a misimpression is created, it should be emphasized that the three sections of the global economy, or environmental systems as they have been called here, are by no means homogenous and harmonious. To the contrary, each is full of internal differences, tensions, and even contradictions. But their internal diversities are overshadowed by the sharp contrasts among them. As the environmental systems themselves, so also the enterprises within them exhibit sharp contrasts in character and behavior.

This is not the time or place to try to identify and catalog the specific contrasts. Suffice to say that be it legal status, ownership, organization, objectives, strategies, policies, practices, social responsibilities, or intracompany relations, they can develop and function only in the context of the environmental system under which the enterprise exists. What is more important, the specifics change in response to the changes in incentives and impediments which the system can offer or impose. Our focus is on the dynamic aspects of the global environment to uncover the sources and forces for change to which managements must be sensitive to succeed.

THE INDUSTRIAL WEST

International business relations in the industrial world are being transformed by a sweeping movement toward a closer integration of the different industrial economics. With a gradual shift from a bilateral to a multilateral trading system, spearheaded by GATT[1] and accelerated by the rise of supranational economic

---

[1]General Agreement on Tariffs and Trade, signed in 1948, and since then the main force for tariff and trade negotiations.

unions, arbitrary trade barriers—visible and invisible—have declined sharply, and the convertability of currencies, at least for external purposes, has become a reassuring reality.

However, the process goes far beyond the classical concept of trade liberalization. Its primary agents, the European Economic Community and the multinational corporation, are transforming the fundamental economic structure of the Industrial West. Since one is operating on the governmental and the other on the managerial plane, they are best discussed separately.

THE COMMON MARKET

International economic integration emanates from the western European continent where it took the form of the Schuman Plan in the early 1950's, which pooled the coal and steel industries of Belgium, France, Holland, Italy, Luxemburg, and the West German Republic into a supernational entity—The European Coal and Steel Community, subsequently expanded into the European Economic Community, popularly known as the Common Market.

The objectives and methods of the EEC are set forth in great detail and clarity in its constitution—the Treaty of Rome—which went in effect in 1958 and has in the short time since emerged, not only as a document of global consequence, but also as the blueprint for progress, prosperity, and industrial power.

What is the treaty about? Its basic dictate is to liberate business enterprise from all international hurdles and impediments and to harmonize national policies of the member countries so as to minimize economic differences among them. This freedom is not limited to trade alone, as often erroneously portrayed in the popular press or in anti-Common Market propaganda. In addition to a free flow of goods and services, the Rome plan provides also for a complete freedom of movement for capital, labor, and entrepreneurship, thus extending its influence to all aspects of economic endeavor.

The treaty is not a utopian scheme. It boldly deals with the problems which the exposure to competition will inevitably bring to industries and companies whose sheltered existence behind import tariffs and other protective barriers is now coming to an end. Many of these companies have found renewed vigor and vitality in the impending peril and have adjusted magnificently; others, however, have been unable to go it on their own. For the latter, the plan provides adjustment assistance to facilitate a gradual and orderly reallocation of the resources and manpower employed in the less efficient and noncompetitive sectors. By doing so, the Rome Treaty goes beyond all earlier international conventions, which at best grant to a foreign enterprise (goods or investments), the so-called *most favored nations treatment,* i.e., the rights and privileges which are accorded to foreign enterprise from the most favored country, but never what a domestic company enjoys.

Once in full force, the Rome Treaty will replace the most favored nations principle with the *national treatment principle,* under which discrimination against foreign products, investments, and companies is completely eliminated and all business transactions and institutions accorded equal treatment under similar conditions.

Effect on United States: 1962 Trade Expansion Act

That this precedent has already had a profound effect on international economic relations is clearly reflected in our own Trade Expansion Act of 1962, which is in part a reaction to, and in part an imitation of, the Rome Treaty.

This act, generally regarded as the greatest legislative achievement of the late President Kennedy, and a basic change in our foreign trade policy, empowers the President to cut import tariffs to one-half on any product and to zero on products in which the United States and the EEC together represent eighty per cent or more of world trade. Second, the act replaces the traditional American method of negotiating tariff agreements on an item-by-item basis with the so-called across-the-board approach used by other countries by which industrywide or even broader categories of products may be treated as a single unit for the purpose of tariff adjustment.

Third, and perhaps most importantly, the 1962 Act abandons the premise of noninjury to domestic business (basic to the United States tariff policy since the beginning of the nation) and substitutes for it the concept of adjustment assistance as employed in the Rome plan. Under the doctrine of noninjury, tariff cuts were permissible only so long as they did not result in import competition which was injurious to American industry; under the new concept, injurious import competition resulting from tariff reductions does not require the President to invalidate the new rates, but instead entitles the injured party to apply for federal assistance to find new ways of competing or to shift its resources into another activity. This assistance may take the form of long-term loans at low interest, technical and managerial help, tax relief, retraining of workers, transportation and moving allowances, etc. While the act still retains the President's traditional power of revoking a tariff reduction under an escape clause and thereby eliminating the import competition, this alternative is not likely to be used often.

Through the 1962 Trade Expansion Act, European economic integration can be expected to have its greatest effect on American business, despite the fact that its effect upon direct foreign investments and competition on world markets already overshadows most other aspects of United States international economic relations. The impact of the Trade Expansion Act has been delayed so far because it was predicated upon negotiations with the EEC to be carried out under the auspices and rules of the General Agreement for Tariffs and Trade (GATT). These negotiations, popularly referred to as the "Kennedy Round," started in May 1964 in Geneva, Switzerland, and are expected to last for several months. Unless they collapse completely, which contrary to newspaper headlines is highly unlikely to happen, a much greater flow of business across the Atlantic in the near future appears a certainty. This will both multiply and strengthen the economic bonds between the two areas, and greatly increase their interdependence on one another.

Effect on Other Areas—EFTA, LAFTA, CACM

In other countries, the Rome Treaty has caused similar responses. In the rest of Europe, trade liberalization, geared almost directly to the EEC, has become the central objective. To keep pace with the EEC, seven other countries formed the European Free Trade Association (EFTA)—also a supranational body. Its membership includes the United Kingdom, Portugal, Austria, Denmark, Norway, Sweden, and Switzerland. Strong forces are at work to amalgamate the two integrated areas into a Pan-European mass market of colossal dimensions. Although Franco-British political rivalries currently deter any further rapprochement between the two blocs, this situation can be expected to improve as both parties come to realize that neither can subjugate the other with or without United States aid.

In South America, a continental free market is being built on the basis of the Treaty of Montevideo which created the Latin American Free Trade Association. In Central America five countries have combined into a common market and are showing great earnestness in trying to make it a reality, despite rather limited complementarity among them.

In Africa and Asia, economic integration is debated with great passion and enthusiasm. The plans so far proposed have been drowned in the violent tides of nationalistic, racial, and tribal conflicts which have beset the ex-colonial societies. But it seems to be only a matter of time until workable plans for concrete action will emerge. In fact, the groundwork for such a plan on a wide basis was laid in the World Trade and Development Conference which was held in the spring of 1964 in Geneva, Switzerland. This conference, called under the auspices of the United Nations, was devoted almost exclusively to the economic problems of the underdeveloped countries and is expected to be of immense significance in the future, not only in having brought these countries closer together among themselves, but especially in the political pressure which they, in unison, can exert for a closer integration between the developed and underdeveloped parts of the world.

Economic Effects

While the Rome Treaty has served as the symbol and a precedent for the supranational integration movement, the real push has come from the impressive results which the European Common Market has actually produced.

According to the Eighth General Report of the Common Market Commission, officially presented to the European Parliament in Strasbourg on June 17, 1965, by its President, Dr. Hallstein, the growth of the Common Market from 1958 to 1964 (inclusive) is highlighted by these facts:

☐ The Community gross product (GNP) up by 38 per cent (for the U.S., up by 28 per cent; for the U.K., up by 21 per cent); industrial production up by 51 per cent (in U.S., 43 per cent; in U.K., only 28 per cent); intracommunity trade increased 168 per cent (due to tariff cuts); exports up by 53 per cent and imports by 66 per cent.

☐ In both exports and imports, the EEC has surpassed the U.S. The report further shows that, contrary to pessimistic predictions by some outside "experts," the rate of investment in the EEC has not slowed down: in 1964 it was 11 per cent higher than in 1963, absorbing 23.3 per cent of the community's GNP which is appreciably greater than in other industrial countries (in the U.S. it was about 16 per cent). As new means of accelerating the integrative process, the Commission proposes: the establishment of legal provisions for European companies as distinct from companies chartered by the individual member nations; the creation of a European patent; and the elimination of indirect restraints of trade such as discriminatory taxation, government monopolies, cartelistic schemes, and other internal practices which may tend to retard the integration process.[2]

Unlike the United States and United Kingdom, the EEC has had no unemployment. On the contrary, its progress has been hampered by overemployment and a shortage of workers. True, there is no way of telling what the progress would have been without the Common Market (such comparative experimentation is beyond the powers of economic analysis), but it is extremely difficult to argue that the EEC has been an unproductive force and utterly absurd to speculate that the area could have done better without the arrangement.

Since, in the international realm, nothing succeeds like success, economic integration has become a new force even behind the iron curtain. While denouncing EEC, the Soviets have broadened and intensified the program of the Comecon[3] in an effort to convert it into a communist version of a common market. Within the Soviet Union, integration is seriously considered to form larger and more closely knit economic units out of smaller states and regions.

In Latin America, too, international integration is gaining momentum. A common market was created among Costa Rica, El Salvador, Guatemala, Honduras, and Nicaragua by the ratification of the General Treaty of Central American Integration in 1960. This union has progressed rapidly and already shows significant results. The South American countries combined with Mexico under the Treaty of Montevideo, also signed in 1960, into the Latin American Free Trade Association (LAFTA) which aspires to amalgamate the entire South American continent into one gigantic market unhampered by trade restriction. In a longer perspective, the Montevideo plan is conceived as the first phase for a complete economic integration patterned after the EEC, once the trade union is complete. That is to say, free movements of capital, people, and economic institutions will be added to that of goods and services. That the two Latin American markets might merge after each has overcome the problems of its transition period appears more than plausible.

In addition to the indigenous forces, the dynamics of international integration in Latin America derives exogenous impetus from the United States through the Alliance for Progress program. As declared by President Lyndon B. Johnson on August 17, 1965, the Alliance for Progress program will, from now on, place great stress on international integration and the building of a multinational infrastructure as the bases for Latin American development. A separate fund will be set up to finance the international and multinational programs. In the words of the President:

> *First, we must step up our efforts to prevent disastrous changes in the prices of those basic commodities which are the lifeblood of so many of our economies. . . .*

---

[2]Cf. *European Community*, No. 83, July 1965.

[3]Comecon may be translated as the Council for Mutual Economic Assistance. Its membership includes Bulgaria, Czechoslovakia, East Germany, Hungary, Outer Mongolia, Poland, Rumania, and the U.S.S.R.

> *Second, we must try to draw the economies of Latin America much closer together. The experience of Central America reaffirms that of Europe. Widened markets—the breakdown of tariff barriers—lead to increased trade and lead to more efficient production and to greater prosperity. The United States will . . . contribute from its Alliance resources to the creation of a new fund for preparing multinational projects. By building areawide road systems, by developing river basins which cross boundaries, by improving communications, we can help dissolve the barriers which have divided the nations.*
>
> *In addition, I hope the American nations will consider the establishment of a program—patterned after European Coal and Steel Community—for the production and trade, on a continental basis, of fertilizer, pesticides, and other products that are needed to increase agricultural production. My country stands willing to help in such a venture. And thus, in ways that he never imagined, we can move closer to the dream of Bolivar.*[4]

It would be a gross oversimplification to leave the impression that economic integration is running its global course with smoothness and ease; on the contrary, its path is uneven and full of obstacles. Massive forces of East-West rivalries, political intrigue, and the backwash of decolonization in the underdeveloped world obscure and retard its progress.

While the progress of international economic integration can be retarded, it cannot be stopped. For it is not only another diplomatic device, but also a force that emanates from the fundamental dynamics of contemporary international economy. As science and automation push back technological frontiers, possibilities for more and better life are created—but only for those who can amass the investments and absorb the quantities required by the rescinding scale of the *optimal plant.* Neither small companies nor small countries can, therefore, qualify. Can any small country deliberately deny itself that which the large ones and integrated international communities can enjoy? Not for long. More than anything, the exploding expectations of the consuming public everywhere have provided the power to break the barriers that constrain the realization of its economic aspirations.[5]

THE MULTINATIONAL CORPORATION

The second fundamental change in international business has been the shift from foreign trade to multinational operations. While this may sound like a play on words, it has nothing to do with semantics; in fact we have, so far, failed to

---

[4]*Presidential Documents,* I:4 (August 23, 1965), 99.

[5]It is relevant to note that the prototype scheme for the international integration movement, the EEC, is the creature that defied, and still does, the established political dogma of international relations which holds that a solution and settlement of political issues is an absolute precondition for any such economic rapprochement as integration involves. Yet the breakthrough was made on the economic and not on the diplomatic front.

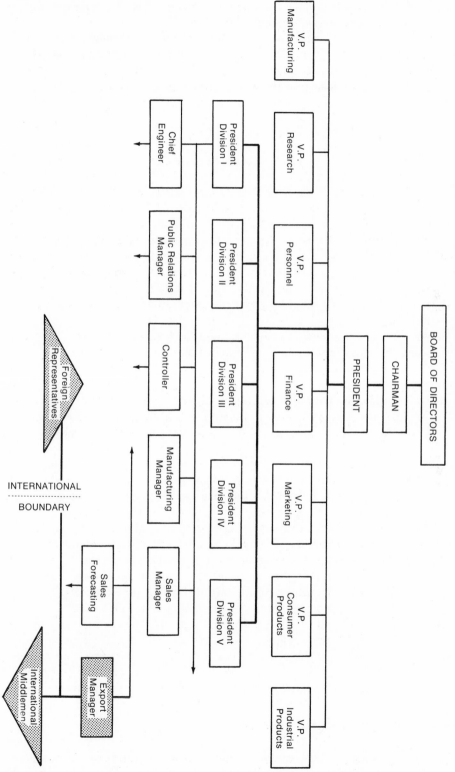

FIGURE 1. THE EXPORT DEPARTMENT IN A TRADITIONAL CORPORATE STRUCTURE

find a word to properly describe the new phenomenon. Clearly, the word "operations" is a clumsy and ill-suited term to describe it.

To measure the magnitude of the structural changes and their managerial consequences which the rise of the multinational corporation has engendered, a starting line or base is necessary. A description of the traditional or "normal" institutional model for foreign trade would provide such a base.

"Normal" Foreign Trade Institutions

The traditional way of doing business abroad used to be through exporting or importing, i.e., selling goods and services produced by the business firms in one country to the residents of another. Thus, international business dealings consisted primarily of the movement of goods across national boundaries and the resultant monetary transactions in the opposite direction.

These flows were channeled through business firms who specialized in serving as intermediaries between the business systems of different countries: export-import merchants, commission houses, export brokers, combination managers, etc. The export process, thus, required three separate transactions:

☐ Between the United States firm and the international intermediary such as the export house.

☐ Between the international intermediary and the foreign importer.

☐ Between the importer and the foreign consumer.

To be sure, several additional steps were often added. But these three constituted the basic linkages connecting the business systems of different nations.

If we visualize the entire process of production and distribution as the total task of export business, this process under the traditional pattern was divided among three independent companies: the American producer, the export intermediary, and the foreign importer. No one institution had control or jurisdiction over the entire process.

The international and foreign phases of this process were confined to marketing and transportation activities. Other managerial functions such as production, engineering, public relations, etc., were rarely affected by the export activity. Foreign business was a part of the sales department or division and was so situated in the corporate structure (Figure 1). Since most of the complexity of the export marketing was left to the international intermediary, the export department possessed few skills or capabilities which were significantly different from those of the domestic sales organization of the firm. In status and influence, the export department seldom equaled the domestic marketing department and often functioned as a subordinate unit to it as shown in Figure 1.

Except for petroleum, mining, and a few other extractive industries, the described model remained the characteristic or "normal" way of doing business with other countries until World War II. Since the war, however, a new scheme has emerged and a massive shift from the old to the new set in motion.

International Headquarters Company

In the new scheme, the international intermediary is replaced by company-controlled but operationally and often legally separate organizations, usually

FIGURE 2. A MULTINATIONAL CORPORATE STRUCTURE WITH FOREIGN OPERATIONS SEPARATED FROM PARENT CONCERN

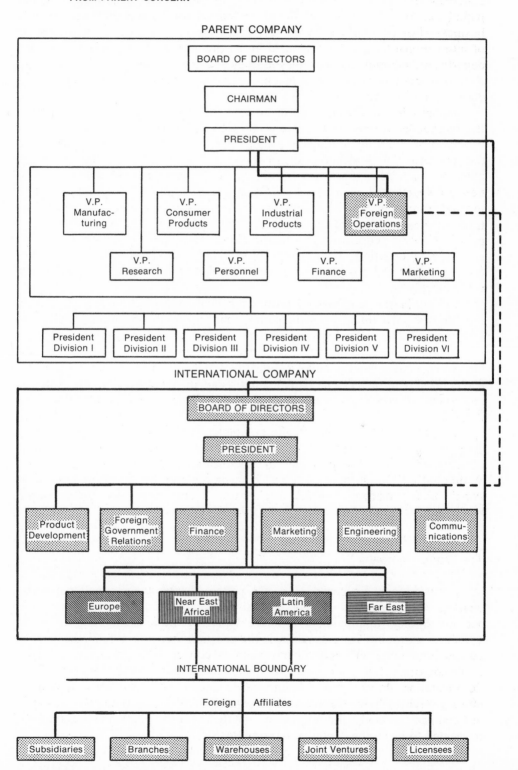

in the form of a Foreign Operations or International Operations Subsidiary Company. Its over-all function is to serve as the "State Department" for the parent, i.e., to assume responsibility for all international aspects of the company's business. (For a model, see Figure 2.) By this structural change, the management of international business is upgraded in the process: it is no longer an obscure department, subordinated to domestic sales and overshadowed by other aspects of the company business, but a much better defined and relatively autonomous entity in the corporate structure.

But this is not all. The subsidiary does not stop in the narrow confines of the independent export intermediary but goes far beyond them. In addition to exporting or importing, it tends to establish its own facilities in foreign areas for the purposes of production, distribution, and service. These foreign-based affiliates—branches, subsidiaries, joint ventures, and licensees—create many new problems which management must handle in an international setting. While the spectrum of international management responsibilities under the old foreign trade scheme was limited to selling and shipping tasks, they now may encompass not only a more complete multinational marketing program but also engineering, production, personnel, labor relations, investment, corporation finance, public and government relations, foreign business practices, and many other functions.

Indeed, in many a foreign operations subsidiary, the spectrum of management functions is wider than that of the parent concern. This is true because the subsidiary encounters problems which are peculiar to multinational activities: negotiations with foreign authorities; dealings with supranational bodies; and being able, on one hand, to adapt its objectives, policies, and methods to the social and cultural requisites of a particular country and, on the other, to create sufficient uniformity and continuity to enable effective coordination and control of the entire multinational structure.

Consequently, the new scheme completely changes the traditional notion of an international executive. At the same time, it underscores the need for a different term than "foreign trade" or "exporting" to describe the new pattern. Within business itself "foreign trade" is being replaced by "international operations"; in the academic world "foreign trade" has grown into "international business." Neither is fully satisfactory for its purposes.

The World Company

Most multinational concerns today are patterned after the international headquarters company model. But the process of change has not ended here. A new and still different multinational structure appears to be in the making. Its basic scheme is shown in Figure 3. While, in the previous model (Figure 2), the domestic and international affairs of the multinational concern were separated and most of the corporate staff of the parent company retained their inward-looking domestic orientation, the new model integrates American and international operations into a cohesive whole. The dualistic structure which the international headquarters company created is thus eliminated and the entire top echelon of the company reoriented to its multinational responsibilities.

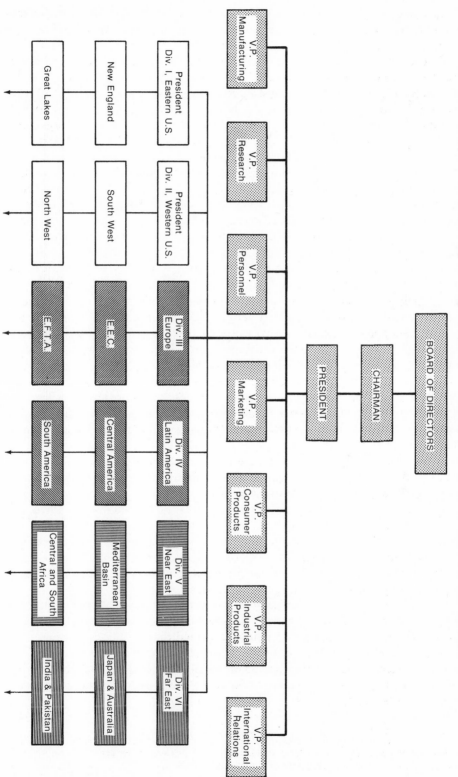

FIGURE 3. A WORLD COMPANY: MULTINATIONAL CORPORATE STRUCTURE WITH FULLY INTEGRATED FOREIGN AND DOMESTIC OPERATIONS

The large corporations are currently moving in this direction. But how widespread an adoption this integrative pattern will enjoy remains to be seen. To a significant degree, the conditions which business enterprise will encounter in foreign countries, especially in the so-called underdeveloped world, will determine the future course of this trend.

It seems, however, that among the industrial countries the integrative World Company is most likely to become the basic norm for business organization in the future. Space does not permit a full development of supporting arguments for this prediction. To observe that the World Company is, in principle, an aspect of the international economic integration discussed above and, as such, will derive momentum and continuity from a powerful movement, helps to place the argument into its proper perspective. That many administrative advantages and greater efficiency are possible through this model than through the traditional trade or the international headquarters model can be argued quite convincingly.

A survey of 104 international companies revealed that a firm derives four major types of advantages from a multinational structure.[6]

1. Marketing advantages. No tariffs or quotas; lower cost of transportation, lower inventory requirements and savings in warehousing (economic distances between points of production and points of consumption reduced); easier to service market, less sales resistance, and better efficiency of promotional companies.

2. Production advantages. Lower wage costs; easier-to-meet local standards of engineering, weights and measurements, and laws affecting product quality; procurement economies; transportation economies.

3. Financial advantages. Cover taxes; greater flexibility for moving earnings and assets from one country to another without incurring U.S. tax liability (e.g., from an unstable, high-risk, high-profit area to a stable country); higher rates of interest available for short-term holdings of company assets; easier access to local sources of capital.

4. General management advantages. More promising growth alternatives for company than at home; stabilization of earnings through diversification of markets and production facilities; additional outlets for technological slack (profitable re-employment of product ideas, processes, techniques, facilities, and management skills which domestically are threatened by obsolescence); better relations with supplier, distributors, customers, and governments; access to foreign technical innovations; "localization" of administrative practices and procedures in terms of national custom; an improved company image ("international" has come to mean the "major league" in business).

Viewed from a broader perspective, the growth of multinational companies brings with it political and social developments, which, in the main, have long been desired. From among them might be capsuled these:

☐ Stronger and more permanent bonds among different countries.

☐ More efficient utilization of natural resources, manpower, and capital.

☐ Built-in deterrent to international conflict in the form of industrial interties which cannot be broken as easily as the flow of trade.

---

[6]Cf. E. J. Kolde, "Functions of Foreign Based Affiliates in the Administrative Structure of International Business Enterprise," *Revue Economique et Social,* December 1962, pp. 155-182; and a follow-up survey now being prepared for publication.

☐ A surmounting pressure to rethink and redesign U.S. international economic policies and attitudes toward foreign affairs.

THE UNDERDEVELOPED SOUTH

The most significant characteristic of the underdeveloped world is poverty— poverty in the absolute sense of the word, i.e., inability to secure the physical necessities for sustaining one's life. This concept should not be confused with "poverty" in the relative sense as currently used in reference to the less privileged groups in this country.[7]

As explained by the late Professor Ragnar Nurkse, an underdeveloped nation finds itself in a vicious circle of poverty which can be depicted in the following diagram in which the arrows show the cause-effect relationships:

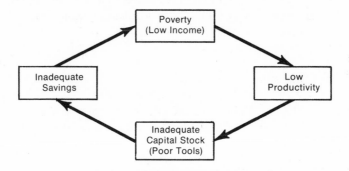

To improve their lot, these people must somehow break this circle. That they realize this and have come to regard it not only as an economic imperative but as a political and ideological maxim is a fact that no government, old or new, autocratic or democratic, can any longer ignore. Indeed, the tide of political awakening that in the last fifteen or so years has swept away what seemed invincible colonial empires (British, French, Dutch, Belgian, etc.) gained much of its immense force from the rising expectations that greater contact with the outside world has brought to those peoples.

The Urge to Industrialize

The same contact has helped to point also to what the underdeveloped world has not accepted as the only answer to this problem—industrial development. The faith in industrialization is so deep-rooted and profound that it is often looked upon not only as the basic economic objective but also as a political ideology; in some places it has become a fanatic devotion.

The urge to industrialize, to grow in economic strength and political stature, is the force which unites the underdeveloped world and propels it to mobilize

---

[7]Relative poverty is a subjective concept which varies with one's notions of dignity and justice rather than with biological necessity.

its energies on a global scale as happened in Geneva at the World Trade and Development Conference referred to above. One need not become a prophet to predict that this conference was but the first global manifestation of the potential power which the brotherhood-in-poverty-and-unity-in-goals-and-aspirations is placing in the hands of the underdeveloped countries, despite their differences in many other respects.

The fact that the governments of the underdeveloped countries are irrevocably committed to industrialization at all costs does not mean that they possess the capacity to bring it about or that they go about it intelligently. But they are not standing still; they are not only hoping, but acting. Discontent to wait until what, in the West, is considered "normal economic progress" runs its course, they are determined to force the pace and to shorten this process. This, they believe, can be accomplished by artificial insemination and spawning of industrial development on a crash program basis by government initiative and action. Inspirations for such beliefs come in great measure from the Soviet Union, partly as an example and, more importantly, as propaganda expounding the slogan of rapid results by Communist methods.

Central Planning and State Enterprise

As a consequence, the economic systems of the emerging nations are characterized by compulsive national planning *à la* U.S.S.R., which allocates the resources not according to the dictates of a free market, but according to the targets and goals set by government authority.

Along with planning on the national level has come state enterprise on the industry and company levels. However, only Cuba, by adopting a Communist regime, has completely eliminated private enterprise to this writing. In all the other emerging nations, the balance has shifted toward state enterprise but only to a limited extent and on a sporadic rather than a systematic basis.

Some observers attribute the growth of state enterprise to mistaken notions of the often inexperienced governments of these countries. They believe that, as the governments mature and the peoples initial intoxication with independence wears off they no longer will fall for Communist propaganda and the trend will be reversed in favor of private enterprise. At the moment, it appears that in certain countries the growth of state enterprise has, in fact slowed down or stopped completely. But such indications are too few to justify the claim that they reflect a turning point in the trend; at best they reflect a pause, perhaps a consolidation of the government sector, before further drives toward socialized enterprise are started.

Neither Capitalism nor Communism

What we have in the underdeveloped countries is neither capitalism based on free enterprise nor communism based on complete nationalization, but a peculiar brew of the two with characteristics all its own. As pointed out before, it is not a crystallized system with definitive principles and established values, but a volatile mix in which free enterprise must learn to live, or fall prey to Communist onslaught, or be discarded as antisocial. There is no other choice short of armed force and reinstitution of the colonialist system. Regrettably, the business community of the Industrial West has not possessed either the vision or the flexibility effectively to cope with the new environment in the underdeveloped areas. Instead of anticipating the course of the change and adapting to it, private enterprise too often has tried to resist or ignore the new forces and has discredited itself in the eyes of the indigenous public as the rearguard of colonialist power.

To be sure, there have been expropriations, nationalization, and lesser harassments of private enterprise which no amount of management's perspective and willingness to cooperate could have prevented. So long as there is political strife and social mobility, such things will continue to happen in the future as they have in the past. Indeed, the underdeveloped countries have no monopoly on nationalization or any other statist tactics but can follow the precedence provided by such industrial nations as Britain (coal, steel, radio, etc.), Sweden, and Italy, just to name a few. However, the important point to be made here is that a dogmatic, anti-government attitude freezes the managements of private companies into a rigid position which retards their capacity to swim with the current.

New Managerial Calculus

What seems to be needed is not more formal guarantees and legal contracts (many companies might have survived if they had not been lulled into a fictitious security by their faith in an "airtight" document), but a deeper appreciation of the realities of the underdeveloped societies and new criteria for management action. To come straight to the point: profit motive, either with or without the accessories of what, in this country, are called "social responsibilities," is not sufficient to guide management action in the environment of the backward countries. A new and far more embracive economic calculus has to be substituted for the traditional cost-revenue accountancy to measure the other dimensions which, in these new countries, have became equally decisive for the birthright and prosperity of a business enterprise.

What is this new calculus? And what other dimensions does it entail?

Professor Robinson of MIT provides an answer in his recent book entitled *International Business Policy.* The criteria for private enterprise to follow may be summarized as follows:

Impact of company operations on the country's social overhead, i.e., the demands that the project would create for various social services, such as water, welfare, health, housing, and power. Since the government of an underdeveloped nation is almost by definition operating with an inadequate budget to create the facilities and institutions necessary for basic services, it is compelled to look critically at any new strains that are placed upon its limited finances.

Effect on public revenue of the private firm, i.e., the taxes it will pay. This has been a particularly crucial factor for American as well as European multinational companies who often employ arbitrary prices in "selling" to other units of the same firm in some other country. The objective of setting these intracompany prices may be to minimize income taxes and/or import duties or to permit the company to take its profits in the currency of a country in which it wants to keep its surplus or use its funds. Thus, from the standpoint of profit maximization for the corporation as a whole, it may be desirable to show low profits or even a loss on the company's operations in an underdeveloped country.

But from the standpoint of that particular country such manipulations mean reduction of public revenues in the form of lost taxes and its government is likely to endeavor to recover these losses even if drastic action is necessary.

The company's effect upon the balance of payments of the country concerned is another important dimension, i.e., will it strengthen or weaken the foreign exchange position of the country?

All underdeveloped nations tend to suffer from a deficit in their balance of payments. This is due to their heavy dependence on imports from the developed areas to acquire the capital equipment and other manufactured products which they need for industrial development. Their governments, therefore, stress strongly the exchange-earning and exchange-using aspects of any enterprise, old or new.

If the American company depends on imported parts, subassemblies, or other ingredients which may be the most efficient method of acquisition from the company's profit standpoint, the effect from the country's standpoint will be a drain on the balance of payments—a possible disemployment of domestic resources which are displaced by, or remain undiversified because of, the imports. Add to this the intracompany pricing aspect discussed above, and there is enough incitement for a nationalist leader to move to stop this "neo-colonist exploitation" by expropriation or tight regulation of the industry.

Other variables to be added to this new managerial calculus are: *the company's effect on the economic growth of the country* (need for satellite industries, services, development of skills, etc.) and its *effect on employment and development of human resources.* This last point deserves further elaboration.

Human Resources and Underdevelopment

The bulk of the underdeveloped countries suffer from a disproportionate ratio of nonproductive to productive people. This is due first to the basic demographic structure as shown in Figure 4—relatively few people (small percentage) in the productive age bracket—and second, to the widespread underemployment of people engaged in agriculture and other extractive pursuits, e.g., a family of nine working on a farm that could be run by two or three people.

To be able to break the circle of poverty and to reach the point of sustained growth and development, the government of these countries must put their human resources to a better use. While, in the light of current trends in the United States (automation, layoffs, etc.), the underemployment problem in the backward countries may seem quite similar to our own, the facts and reasons are quite different. The unemployment and poverty problems that we face are caused by the displacement of human labor by capital equipment. In the economist's terms, the problem is caused by "too much capital and technology in relation to labor."

FIGURE 4. WORLD POPULATION DISTRIBUTION

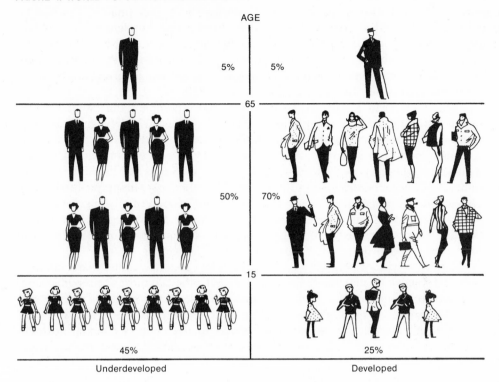

In the underdeveloped areas, the reverse is true: their underemployment is due to the lack of capital and technology to provide the infrastructure within which modern industrial civilization could merge. To build that structure, to create the basic social capital, they must mobilize their human resources by all and any means morally acceptable. This is not to say that modern automated facilities are contrary to the best interests of these countries. Often they are not. But more often a comparative analysis will show that the capital-intensive facility, although a productive and profitable venture as a separate entity, must be charged a heavier burden of opportunity cost than can be justified from a broader perspective. For example, a plant is 10 per cent more efficient than other plants but provides 20 per cent less employment and adds less to development of new skills and know-how.

American Strategies in Underdeveloped Areas

The United States and, to some degree, other Western countries have tried two strategies for promoting capitalist enterprise in the emerging countries. One has been to "buy" itself rights and privileges through loans in unprecedented amounts, and the second, to negotiate treaties and agreements which focus on provisions concerning the rights and privileges of the enterprise in the country concerned. Neither has brought the expected results.

The treaties have failed because, whatever their provisions, they cannot interfere with the internal affairs of a sovereign state; since unilateral proclamations such as used in colonial times are politically and morally obsolete, recent efforts through intergovernment instruments have accomplished little beyond conveying the official attitude of the United States government to the other country involved. That sometimes this has hastened, rather than deterred, antibusiness measures is an assertion that need not be debated here.

On the foreign aid front, the picture is more complex and blurred by religious, ideological, and other intense passions. The aid policy engendered a trend of alienation rather than cooperation between the United States and the recipient countries, not to mention the measurable effects on our balance of payments and gold reserves. Wooed by both the United States and the Soviet Union, underdeveloped countries soon discovered that their bargaining positions were considerably strengthened if they remained aloof instead of aligning themselves with either side. Thus, a new concept of neutrality or nonalignment was procreated. This is not to be confused with the long-standing policies of Sweden and Switzerland which represent a different concept altogether.

The new type of neutrality is, first of all, an economic rather than a military policy designed to maximize external aid and other countries' economic concessions to the neutrals. Second, it is a policy based on expedience and as such must be varied as the currents of East-West tension change. Thus, the label "nonaligned" by itself gives no real clue as to the country's actual attitudes and policies. One also needs to know who it is nonaligned against at a particular moment.

But as a group, the nonaligned have become a formidable force that can not be discounted any longer. Realizing the leverage which they gain by staying aloof and especially if acting as a bloc, they have turned their mock neutrality from an opportunistic manipulation into something approaching a doctrine which no amount of foreign aid can be expected to alter in the foreseeable future. Only if both the West and the East become convinced that halfhearted allies and part-time neutrals can be more of a bane than a boon and adjust their foreign policies and programs accordingly can there be hope for a stabilization of business climate in the underdeveloped world.

THE COMMUNIST EAST

In this section, I will not focus on the Soviet bloc as a potential market for American products. That a market potentiality exists behind both the iron and the bamboo curtains is a fact that only dogmatists and some professional bureaucrats fail to grasp. The question on this point is not really an economic one at all but political—not, "can we or can't we?" but, "should we or shouldn't we?" As such, it will be answered when the political questions are answered. The United States Chamber of Commerce recently passed a resolution urging the government to withdraw its embargo, and it will not be surprising to learn that new openings for East-West trade have been found and its volume increased.

My reason for discussing the Soviet bloc is its influence upon the business environment in the other two systems—the underdeveloped areas and the industrial world itself. A study of the international affairs of the postwar world with a view to causal relationships will reveal that the story for the last twenty years has been written in terms of a triangular dialectic which consists of Communist actions, Western counter-actions, and neutralist reactions to the two. *The prime mover in this global process has been the Communist camp; its initiative, ideas, and maneuvers represent a dynamic force which cannot be equalled.*

The political influence on the West of the Soviet bloc is probably plainer to most of us than we wish to admit. What is perhaps less so is the Soviet's role and especially its potential as competition in world markets. News of Soviet inroads into non-Communist markets has been scattered but occurs at an increasing frequency—Soviet oil, machine tools, development projects, etc. However, it is not their size or frequency that has startled the Western businessman, but their terms.

The Communist Concept of Costs and Profits

The prices that Soviets quote have at times confounded Western business. A few years ago, Soviet microscopes and other scientific instruments appeared in the American market at a fraction of the cost of making them here; oil from Baku and Kaspian basins is currently flowing to European refineries at prices far beneath the reach of any Western producer; these are just two of a number of such instances. Our business press, efficient as it otherwise is, has dismissed such sales as dumping practices which are motivated by political, rather than economic, considerations and which, as deficit propositions, cannot be sustained in any significant volume or length of time.

This is an erroneous interpretation. *The fact of the matter is that the Soviets, in many instances, can not only master the resources to undersell Western competition in world markets, but that they can make a profit by doing it.*

How is this possible? The answer lies in the Soviet system rather than in conventional economic analysis. All international transactions of the Soviet Union (or of any other Communist country) are centralized in one government agency, the Ministry of Foreign Trade, which is expected to conduct its operations so as to make the greatest contribution to the Soviet economy as a whole, i.e., maximize the output and minimize the cost. While this may sound quite capitalistic, it works altogether differently.

Take the case of the microscopes. To make a profit, American producers must sell their instruments at prices which exceed their costs; the Soviet Foreign Trade Ministry can sell its microscopes at almost any price, either above or below the cost of production, without suffering a loss, because its calculation is not based upon microscopes but upon the entire foreign trade of the Soviet Union. Suppose the Soviets need chemical equipment (which they in fact do) and that this can be bought from the United States for $50 million, from Germany for $59 million, from France for $65 million, or from England for $70 million. The United States is the most economical source, but it insists on payment in dollars or gold. Since the Soviet Union has no more uncommitted dollars or gold, it must earn the dollars to take advantage of the American offer on the chemical equipment. They have microscopes and find they can sell them in large enough quantities to earn the $50 million of United States currency if they price the instrument 15 per cent below its bookkeeping costs.

Thus, the microscopes appear on the world market (possibly including the United States) at what seems to Westerners a 15 per cent loss; on the $50 million sales this would amount to $7.5 million. But with the dollar exchange earned through these sales, the Foreign Trade Ministry now can buy the desired chemical equipment at a $9 million saving (United States over German). Thus, the Ministry has not only covered its costs but produced a net profit of $1.5 million by this double maneuver.

The same reasoning can be applied by the Soviets to decisions regarding whether to produce or to import a product. If importing offers substantial savings over domestic production, they will not hesitate to "sacrifice" another product (by selling it below cost) to make the imports possible.

This capacity of the Communist foreign trade to profit from a loss is a very real one and cannot be written off as propaganda or be expected to disappear. If anything, it will exert itself more and more as the bloc's trade with the outside world expands. This capacity arises not from a superior technology but simply from the fact that complete centralization gives the Soviet executives the scope and flexibility of discharging losses in one product line or industry against gains of another; under our competitive private enterprise, this system is impossible. To counteract this Communist power, the West has no choice but to reconsider its ideas about economic organization, especially antitrust actions and cooperation between government and business, at least to the extent to which world competition is concerned.

Foreign Aid

The second main area where Communist policies and actions have influenced American business is in foreign aid. Since the aid dollar tends to turn into a trade dollar, it acts as either a stimulus or a depressant on exports, depending on how much and to whom aid is granted.[8]

For many years, and to some extent even now, one of the primary criteria for the allocation of American foreign aid was the different countries' responsiveness to Soviet policies; those who leaned toward the sickle and hammer gained in priority for such aid while others lost. Since the response to the Soviet's imperialist policies tends to vary with the intensity with which they are pursued, the ironic result has been that Western foreign aid, and through it the trade and investment opportunities in the world markets, has been at times determined by Soviet policies and actions probably more than anything else.

Statism

The third effect of the Communist bloc upon business in other areas has been the Soviet model as an example—both real and illusory—of a completely nation-

---

[8]A grant of aid to Country X increases U.S. exports to it. But, unless the U.S. export industries involved have excess capacity or the imports of Country X have a completely different composition than those of Country Y, the latter will receive a smaller volume of U.S. exports as part of them are now directed to X. The effect of aid is even more pronounced if there is a re-allocation from Y to X.

alized and state-run economy. This has undermined the sanctity of property rights and perpetrated tendencies toward expropriations, national planning, and state enterprise throughout the world.

These trends are strongest in the underdeveloped countries, as previously indicated, but the Industrial West has by no means proved immune to them. The nationalizations in Great Britian (especially the Labour Party's 1964 program), the state-owned industries of Italy, Sweden, and Mexico, and the noises made by labor parties in other non-Communist countries illustrate the sweep of this current.

The fact that a planned economy can function and progress at a rapid rate, which the Soviets have demonstrated, is a great fascination in the underprivileged countries. That human rights and freedoms are part of the prices paid for Communist economic growth seems hardly to affect the attraction. The techniques and methods which have been developed and the experiences gained in the management of a planned economy as contrasted to the market economy have helped to uplift the concept of national planning from the gutter of radical irresponsibility, where it used to belong, to the level where it is taken seriously by influential leaders not only in Egypt, Ghana, and Indonesia, but also in Britain, France, and the United States.

Of particular interest in this connection is the concept of planning which is evolving in France. Described as indicative rather than compulsory planning, the French version is, in many ways, different from the Communist blueprint. Yet the idea of a managed economy, run according to deliberately set targets and allocation of tasks to substitute for the market-directed environment, represents the greatest challenge to the central doctrine of Western economic thought—the theory of competition—since the publication of *Das Kapital* a hundred years ago. The fact that the French model, unlike the Communist one, rejects compulsion and substitutes for it democratic and social processes makes it no less potent. Indeed, the contrary is true. It is watched with intense interest throughout the free world; United States congressional delegations and the President's economic advisers have made personal trips to Paris to study the matter. If the new approach endures, we may have reached the threshold of an era in which both Capitalist and Communist systems as we know them now will become passé.

SUMMARY

The global business scene is in a greater state of flux than in any previous period. Both integrative and disintegrative forces are at work. In the free world, there is a tri-level process of fusion—through multinational corporate structures, through supranational economic unions (EEC, EFTA, LAFTA, etc.), and through multilateral trade liberalization. The intermeshing of companies, industries, and economies of different countries which these movements produce open new opportunities for growth and productiveness of business.

In the colonial realm, the old order has suffered a near-complete disintegration, giving rise to scores of new nations which, as fragments of old empires, must redefine their role in the light of the new realities. In search for new definitions, they have started to shift toward a position of solidarity and a consensus of community among themselves and to acquire an attitude of political detachment and economic independence from the Industrial West. However, nationalism and racism, which in the West have rapidly declined, are on an upswing in the backward areas and will remain a source of tension and instability for a long time to come.

Heavy population pressures, coupled with an intense yearning for higher standards of living, exert irresistible pressures for an accelerated industrialization. Radical actions, including expropriations and direct state interference and competition, are, therefore, a serious hazard to private enterprise. To survive and to prosper in these areas, it is necessary for business to synchronize company strategies and policies with the national goals and aspirations of the country involved and to be sensitive to governmental concerns about public revenues, the balance of payments, social overhead, and infrastructure as a whole.

From the Communist orbit emanate both political aggression and economic imperialism. The competitive weapons which the Soviet states possess set a private company at a disadvantage, not only because of the national power and prestige that the Soviets can command, but also because of their capacity to absorb losses on one industry to gain on another.

Through its example and propaganda, the bloc presents a frontal attack to the free enterprise system as such. The spreading of socialization, state enterprise, and compulsive planning are evidence of the seriousness of this challenge.

QUESTIONS

1. Why is the global business scene in a greater state of flux than ever before?

2. Compare and contrast the organization structures of the multinational firm and the firm engaged primarily in export-import trade.

3. What is the "new managerial calculus"? Why is it needed in international business?

4. Explain why poverty is considered so significant in the underdeveloped areas of the world.

Better Is Not Good Enough

LAWRENCE F. MANSFIELD

The deficit in our international balance of payments last year was the smallest since 1957, according to a preliminary report by the Commerce Department released on February 11. Yet, only the previous day, President Johnson had sent a message to Congress requesting additional legislation to deal with "our continued imbalance of payments." Why?

The answer is simple enough. The improvement last year was so small that it was not worth crowing about. Like someone who has stumbled into a mudhole while walking across a field, we cannot feel very much elated when the next step sinks us only six inches into the ooze instead of seven. Preliminary figures indicate a deficit on "regular transactions" of about $3.0 billion last year, compared with $3.3 billion in 1963, $3.6 billion in 1962, $3.1 billion in 1961, and an average of $3.7 billion for 1958 through 1960.

The figures are not all in yet, but it is clear that the very large fourth-quarter increase in the deficit to $1.45 billion, seasonally adjusted, resulted from a massive increase in private, non-governmental lending to foreigners. We know this partly by direct evidence, partly by deduction. In the first place, we know that we exported more goods to foreigners than we bought from them. As a matter of fact, the surplus in our merchandise trade, $1.7 billion, was larger than at any time since 1947 and 1948, when most of the world was still recovering from war

FIGURE 1. U.S. BALANCE-OF-PAYMENTS DEFICITS, 1960-64

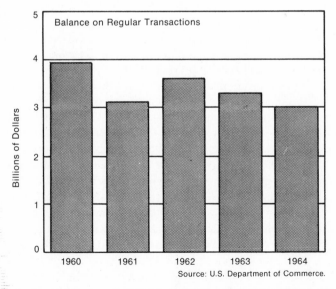

Source: U.S. Department of Commerce.

The deficit on regular transactions decreased slightly in 1964, but by much less than had been hoped.

From *Monthly Review of Federal Reserve Bank of Atlanta,* March 1965. Reprinted by permission.

TABLE 1. U.S. BALANCE OF PAYMENTS, 1964, BY QUARTERS (MILLIONS OF DOLLARS, SEASONALLY ADJUSTED)

	I	II	III	IV
A. Merchandise Trade (excluding military goods transferred under grants)				
Exports	+6108*	+6053	+6364	+6619
Imports	−4411	−4600	−4727	−4895
Balance	+1697	+1453	+1637	+1724
B. Selected Capital Movements				
1. U. S. Capital				
New issues of foreign securities	− 107	− 204	− 161	− 585
Redemptions	+ 54	+ 38	+ 38	+ 75
U. S. transactions in other foreign securities	+ 94	+ 40	+ 37	− 11
Capital outflows reported by U. S. banks:				
Long term	− 251	− 96	− 246	− 331
Short term	− 449	− 461	− 172	− 441
2. Foreign Capital				
Foreigners' transactions in U. S. securities	− 42	+ 12	− 37	− 28
Total of Selected Capital Movements	− 701	− 671	− 541	−1321
Total of Trade and Selected Capital Movements	+ 996	+ 782	+1096	+ 403
Other Transactions	−1242	−1415	−1776	−1850
Balance on Regular Transactions	− 246	− 633	− 680	−1447

* (−) indicates payment, (+) indicates receipt by Americans
Source: U. S. Department of Commerce.

devastation and the United States was practically the only source of supply for a great many things. So the deficit did not result from any sudden deterioration in our trade account.

In addition to our trade in goods, we buy and sell numerous services, the Federal Government makes loans and grants to foreign governments, and private companies and individuals lend and make gifts to foreigners and invest in their enterprises and securities. There is some flow of foreign capital into this country as well. Of all these many types of transactions, we have information on only a few. This information is summarized in Table 1. We know, for example, that Americans bought $585 million of newly issued foreign securities in the fourth quarter, more than were purchased in the first three quarters combined. They also bought, net, $11 million of previously issued securities, and American banks reported an increase in claims on foreigners on behalf of themselves and their customers. These claims of $772 million were in the form of bank loans, bank acceptances to finance foreign trade, and collections of debts owed to their customers. Foreigners sold, net, $28 million of U.S. securities they had owned and redeemed $75 million of old securities coming due for repayment or refinancing. Available data thus can account for $1,321 million of capital outflow from the United States. This is a very large figure when it is considered that in all of 1963 these types of capital outflows amounted to only $2,303 million.

On all these transactions for which we have data there is a surplus of about $400 million, made up of the $1,724-million trade surplus and the $1,321-million capital outflow. Yet, we know that there was a deficit in the fourth quarter. The deficit in our international payments is defined as the change in our monetary reserve assets plus the increase in the short-term claims of foreigners on us, minus receipts from any special government operations that are either exceptional or are designed to help in financing the deficit. We have information on all these items, and they add up to about $1,450 million. This means that we still have to account for an excess of payments of about $1,850 million.

The principal items in the balance of payments on which published figures are not yet available are estimated in Table 2 for the fourth quarter. Although we have no figures, we have a pretty good idea of how these items have behaved recently; and we know that very large changes from year to year or quarter to quarter in several of these items are not very likely. Military transactions, for example, regularly produce a deficit of $500-600 million a quarter. This has been slowly declining as foreign governments buy military hardware from us and contribute to the maintenance of our overseas military facilities.

Other services include: transportation, on which we come out about in balance; travel expenditures, which produce a deficit because more Americans travel abroad than do foreigners in this country; income from investments, on which we have a large and growing surplus as we bring home part of the dividends and interest earned on the tremendous amounts of our capital invested overseas; and miscellaneous services, such as insurance, royalties and fees for books and inventions, and so on, on which we have a fairly rapidly growing surplus. Conservative estimates of these service items produce a surplus of at least $750 million.

Federal Government grants and loans probably account for roughly a billion-dollar outflow. There may have been some increase in this item during the year, but in view of the emphasis that has been placed on holding down outflows resulting from our foreign aid programs, it seems unlikely that the increase could have been very great. Private remittances to people abroad (private charity and immigrants' gifts to the folks in the old country) plus government pensions to people living overseas account for another $200-225 million outflow.

Adding all these known and estimated items together and subtracting their total from the known deficit leaves $800-900 million that must be accounted for by capital outflows for which we do not yet have figures and by errors and omissions. These unidentified capital movements include such things as direct investment by U.S. businesses abroad—that is, the purchase or construction of new

TABLE 2. ESTIMATED U.S. BALANCE OF PAYMENTS (FOURTH QUARTER 1964)

Merchandise Trade Balance	+1724*
Military Transactions Balance	− 500
Other Services Balance	+ 750
Government Grants and Loans, Net of Scheduled Repayments	−1000
Pensions and Remittances	− 220
Private Capital Movements	
A. Selected Capital Movements Identified in Table I	−1321*
B. Other Capital Movements and Errors and Omissions	− 880
Balance on Regular Transactions	−1447*

* See Table 1. All other figures estimated.

production or distribution facilities—loans and credits to foreigners and investments in foreign securities and time deposits by nonbank businesses, and some direct investment and miscellaneous capital inflow into this country by foreigners.

This $800-900 million net outflow of capital in forms other than those listed in Table 1 is not a great deal larger than the average outflow for the first three quarters. Since we have assumed that the balances on military transactions, other services, Government grants and loans, and pensions and remittances were not vastly different from the preceding quarters, it follows that most of the increase in the deficit in the fourth quarter resulted from an upward surge in the capital outflows of the types listed in Table 1. In particular, the increase in new issues of foreign securities was quite extraordinary. From other sources, we know that the growth of bank loans to foreigners was unusually great in the fourth quarter.

EXPLANATIONS AND IMPLICATIONS

Since about 1956, U.S. private capital has been flowing in large amounts to the rest of the world. To a great extent, this outflow has contributed to the very large deficits we have experienced each year since 1958. In the first half of 1963, capital outflow reached such proportions that the Administration felt compelled to try to slow it down. In July of that year, President Kennedy proposed that an "interest equalization tax" be applied to sales in this country of all new foreign securities coming from the "developed" or "industrialized" countries, mainly those of Western Europe and Japan. The tax was graduated in such a way that it added about one percent to the rate of interest these securities would pay. The idea was to make it more expensive for Western Europeans to borrow in this country without at the same time raising interest rates to domestic borrowers, which might put a damper on business expansion. Canada and the "underdeveloped" countries were exempt from the tax.

Immediately after the IET was proposed, capital outflow fell off drastically; yet, in 1964, it began to creep up again and, after the actual enactment of the tax in September of last year, there was a flood of new security issues, particularly Canadian. Many foreign borrowers seemed to have been waiting for enactment of the tax to determine what its exact provisions would be. In addition, bank loans, to which the tax did not apply, were apparently used as a substitute for security issues. The bad fourth-quarter results led President Johnson to take several additional steps to curb the outflow of capital and propose others.

In the first place, when the IET was enacted into law, a provision was added to the original bill that authorized the President to extend the tax to bank loans to foreigners when the loans are for one year or more if he determined that such loans were defeating the purpose of the tax. This was the so-called "Gore Amendment," and the President invoked it when he delivered his message to Congress on February 10. Second, he proposed new legislation: (1) to extend the life of the IET two years, to December 31, 1967; (2) to extend the coverage of the IET to one- to three-year loans to foreigners by nonbank lenders; (3) to change the tax laws so as to encourage foreign investment in the U.S.; and (4) to reduce the value of merchandise that returning travelers can bring home duty free from $100 to $50.

In the third place, the President announced a program of voluntary restraint under which banks, nonbank institutional lenders, and other business with interests abroad would be requested to limit the loans and credits they make available to foreigners this year to five percent of the amount outstanding at the end of last year. He requested that preference be given in any credit to foreigners to financing of American exports. The Federal Reserve System has provided banks and other lenders with a set of guidelines with which to measure the amount of expansion of foreign credits that would fit the voluntary program. The Secretary of Commerce has requested nonbank business firms to reduce gradually their holdings of liquid funds abroad to the level they had reached on December 31 1963, and he has requested about 750 of the larger business firms with foreign interests to establish balances of payments for their own companies with a view to effecting a 15-20 percent improvement this year in their transactions with the rest of the world.

Finally, the President promised to push even harder the existing programs to expand American exports, to cut our military expenditures abroad, and to tie foreign aid to the purchase of American goods and services.

REPERCUSSIONS

For the past few years, there has been no lack of advice on how to solve our balance-of-payments problem. Recently, some of this advice has emphasized the virtues of monetary discipline. By this it is meant, apparently, that we should curtail bank credit in order to limit capital outflows and raise interest rates. Such higher rates would enhance the attractiveness of foreign investment in this country. This is similar to the classic mechanism of adjustment of the old gold standard, although it is hoped, apparently, that such a curtailment of credit would not have to be carried so far or proceed so fast as to slow the pace of domestic economic expansion. In any case, it implies that domestic economic policies must to a considerable extent be conditioned by the state of our balance of payments. In an interdependent world, this is probably inevitable in some degree. For these proposals to work satisfactorily, however, other countries must also follow the "rules of the game." If the surplus countries should, for example, resist the decline in their surpluses that is the necessary concomitant of a reduction of our deficit, then deflation might become a competitive game, with everybody the loser.

So far, we have managed to continue our economic advance for an unusually long period while making at least some progress on the balance-of-payments front. If the competitive position of the U.S. continues to strengthen, as it clearly has in recent years, and if the President's recently announced program is successful, we shall have gone a very long way toward eliminating our deficit. Once it is eliminated, however, the international monetary system must find a way of providing some progressive increase in international means of payment, which our overflow of dollars has heretofore provided, perhaps a little too fully. Hopefully, the studies under way at the International Monetary Fund and among the principal world trading nations can provide the answer to this problem too.

QUESTIONS

1. Why does the U.S. operate with a deficit in its balance of payments?

2. What items in our balance of payments cause the U.S. to have a deficit balance?

3. What changes in monetary policy would help our balance-of-payments position?

4. How is the International Monetary Fund trying to help the world with balance-of-payments problems?

Why the Dollar Is in Danger

JAMES DANIEL AND JAMES B. SHUMAN

Balance of payments, stability, gold reserves, exchange rates, the international monetary system . . . these words suddenly are no longer confined to Wall Street and the financial pages but are popping up in dinner-party conversations and political campaigns, in newspapers and magazines. Something's afoot. Simply and in the starkest terms, the free world's financial system is in danger of crumbling, and concern is spreading on both sides of the Atlantic. Only if we heed the danger signals, warns William McChesney Martin, chairman of the Federal Reserve Board in Washington, will we have "a chance to avoid another such disaster as the Great Depression."

In Great Britain, cracks in the system have already appeared. Last November the British pound, the medium of exchange for 40 percent of world trade, faltered and almost failed. It was saved only by an unprecedented international rescue operation in which 11 nations pledged up to $3 billion to keep Britain and the rest of the free world solvent.

And things are still shaky. In Washington, Treasury Secretary Henry Fowler has warned that the dollar may find itself in as dangerous a plight as the pound. For, like Great Britain, the United States has long been sending more money abroad than we have earned through export sales of our products. Since the monetary crisis could precipitate worldwide depression, vitally affecting the lives of millions of Americans—conveivably costing them their jobs, homes and all the trappings of prosperity—it is a matter of concern to everyone.

SOLID-GOLD BACKING

The "international monetary system" is, basically, the sum of all the financial agreements built up over many years to enable nations to do business with one another: to permit Americans, for example, to buy Japanese radios, German cars and French perfume, and in turn permit people in those countries to buy things we make.

Since every nation has its own currency, trade or investment or business dealings outside one's own territories would be virtually impossible without some way of knowing in advance how much the dollar, the pound, the franc, mark, lira and other currencies are worth in terms of each other. International commerce would be limited to barter. So, over the centuries, nations have developed "the system." At its heart is the requirement that each national currency be backed by "hard" reserves that all other nations will accept in payment. For many centuries this meant only one thing: gold. Then, because there just wasn't enough gold in the world to meet total needs, the British pound and later the U.S. dollar—each solidly backed by ample gold reserves and a strong economy—became acceptable substitutes.

In practice, the system of using paper money in place of gold works something like this: Suppose a tourist from Cedar Rapids goes to France on vacation. In Paris, he goes to a bank and exchanges $500 in U.S. money for an equivalent amount of francs. In effect, the dollars he turns over are like a bank check: they represent an amount of gold which the French central banking system can then claim from the U.S. government.

But because this kind of transaction goes on constantly, not only by tourists but also by businessmen and governments, most of these gold "checks" are never presented for payment. If, for example, the Paris bank to which our tourist goes has a French customer standing at the counter, buying the same number of dollars with his francs, the two transactions simply offset each other on the books.

$35 PER OUNCE

But sometimes it doesn't even out; there may be more people selling dollars than buying them. If there were no way to prevent it, the law of supply and demand would then take over and the price of dollars in terms of other currencies would drop, as far as necessary for the surplus to be sold. The result would be a drastic shake-up in the whole international price structure. U.S. industries dependent on imports would suddenly find themselves having to pay more for goods or raw materials imported from abroad. Exporting industries would temporarily enjoy an advantage—a cut-price effect—in selling abroad, until other nations in self-defense erected tariff walls or cut the value of *their* money. The last time the world had such a monetary breakdown the result was the Great Depression.

What prevents this today is a carefully constructed treaty signed at Bretton

Woods, N.H., in July 1944, by the United States, Britain, France and 41 other nations and since subscribed to by almost all non-communist nations. Under the Bretton Woods agreement every nation is supposed to declare *and then maintain* an official value of its money, regardless of supply and demand. All monetary values are expressed in terms of gold or of U.S. dollars (35 dollars to one ounce of gold). If any government holds a surplus of any other nation's money, which would push the price down, that nation is supposed to buy back the excess with gold or U.S. dollars. If there is a shortage, which would drive the price up and be equally disruptive, they are supposed to sell more of their money for dollars or gold.

The effect of all these rules is: 1. to bring gold or dollars—the basic reserves—into countries which have a favorable balance of trade; 2. to make the U.S. dollar the pivotal currency in the international monetary system.

DANGER OF CASHING IN

If a nation consistently buys more abroad than it sells, invests more in other countries than other countries invest in it, gives away more in aid than it gets back, the ledger won't balance. That nation will run a balance-of-payments deficit, and its currency will be in surplus in other countries.

This is what has happened to the United States for 14 of the past 15 years. Under our foreign-aid programs we have furnished more than $100 billion in grants, loans and military aid, first in Europe, then to Asia, Africa and Latin America. In addition, we have spent dollars abroad to support our own military forces essential for the defense of the free world.

Until 1958 our balance-of-payments deficits averaged about $1.5 billion a year. Then rising prices in the United States weakened our competitive position in world markets, just when Europe and Japan became once again formidable competitive forces, and this caused a relative drop in our exports. Also, Europe's economic resurgence began to attract growing amounts of American capital abroad. The result: our deficits doubled. They averaged almost $4 billion a year over the last three Eisenhower years, $3.3 billion over the Kennedy years, and $3.1 billion over the Johnson years so far.

Because of our commitment to take surplus dollars off the market by selling gold, our gold stock—which in 1957 amounted to almost $23 billion, or three fifths of the free world's monetary gold—now has dropped to less than $14 billion. Of even graver concern are the dollars held by foreign governments, which could be cashed in at Fort Knox for gold. These now amount to $13 billion, almost as much as our remaining supply.

THINKABLE VS. UNTHINKABLE

Of the three possible solutions, one is unthinkable—devaluing our currency by raising the price our government pays for gold. In theory devaluation contributes to prosperity by discouraging imports and making exports cheaper; in practice it only leads (as happened in the Depression) to competitive devaluations and breakdown. It would end forever the dollar as the world's pivotal currency.

This leaves two thinkable solutions: (a) monetary measures and (b) administrative measures. The first means, simply, using the *indirect* powers of the government—setting interest rates, varying the amount of federal spending and loans—to see to it that the nation's money supply grows only fast enough to finance actual economic growth, not fast enough to permit inflation, which raises the price of our exports in world markets. For example: if interest rates are allowed to go up slightly, it discourages unnecessary borrowing at home by making loans more expensive, and it attracts foreign capital by making investment here more profitable.

The drawback is that no Democratic or Republican administration has shown a firm enough resolve to take measures that would stop the steady erosion of the value of the dollar, which today, midway in the 1960's, has already lost ten cents of the purchasing power it had in 1957-59. The dominant philosophy is that mild inflation—now running at a not-so-mild 1.8 percent a year—is essential for rapid economic growth.

That leaves: administrative measures. These run all the way from promoting exports, to restricting the movement of capital, to "psychological" moves such as limiting the amount tourists can bring back into the United States without paying duty.

BELT-TIGHTENERS

President Eisenhower in 1960 sent Congress a trade-expansion act designed to increase exports. In 1961 President Kennedy added to the Eisenhower program by proposing greater use of federal tax funds to finance American sales abroad, plus stricter requirements that American aid dollars be spent for American goods. For the first time the public was asked to "sacrifice": the $500 duty-free tourist allowance was cut to $100. In 1962 President Kennedy again trimmed some overseas spending, got another trade-expansion act passed, and revised tax laws to encourage repatriation of American profits taking refuge in overseas "tax havens."

Despite these measures, the balance-of-payments problem only burst out in a new direction. Suddenly there was a sharp upsurge in American purchases of stock in overseas corporations. To discourage this, President Kennedy asked Congress for a special tax on such stock purchases. The tax simply caused a new, and larger, flood of surplus dollars to flow abroad in the form of loans from American banks.

At this point President Johnson called on American corporations either to postpone expansion of their overseas operations or to finance such programs by borrowing abroad. Banks were persuaded to cut back their foreign loans, and Congress extended the special tax on foreign stock purchases to cover bank loans as well. Even so, the most optimistic believe that in 1965 we will once again have a substantial overall deficit.

BEWARE OF "EASY MONEY"

Many observers agree with George Champion, chairman of Chase Manhattan Bank, that "the government's program consists of short-run measures aimed at achieving quick results. But the balance of payments is essentially a long-run problem."

Secretary Fowler has called for a free-world conference on the problem. Meanwhile, the American people need to be made familiar with the issues involved and with their stake in an early, complete cessation to the dollar and gold drain. In Congress, advocates of "easy money"—low interest rates, readily available cash—fret that ending American deficits will bring about a "liquidity crisis," reducing the amount of dollar reserves available to finance world trade. This, says Secretary Fowler, is economic nonsense. Unless American dollar outgo *is* reduced, he points out, other countries will lose confidence, convert still more of their dollars into gold, and then world liquidity will really decline.

An economically sophisticated electorate, aware of the dangers and able to make its wishes known, is the greatest boon our country could have in dealing with the problem. As Talleyrand said of war and generals, money is too important to leave to politicians.

QUESTIONS

1. What is the international monetary system?

2. What are "hard" reserves?

3. The U.S. dollar is a hard currency. How and why is it in danger?

4. What is devaluation of currency?

5. What monetary and administrative measures can be used to solve the monetary crisis?

Whose Responsibility — Business or Government?

THOMAS E. FISKE

The title of this article may well have raised a question: Responsibility for *what?* Let me answer that question at once. I shall discuss the obligation to maintain a workable and sensible relationship between business and government. And beyond that, I shall suggest a few ways by which the relationship can be improved.

Reprinted by permission from the July 1966 issue of the *Michigan Business Review,* published by the Graduate School of Business Administration, The University of Michigan.

In our times the business of business goes far beyond mere business. The businessman affects, and is deeply affected by, every aspect of American life. The same may be said on the government side: Government brings about change, and *is* itself changed, by nearly every phase of American activity.

SOUND RELATIONSHIP ESSENTIAL

Just who *is* responsible for maintaining a sound relationship between business and government and for improving it when necessary? Does the major burden fall on business or on government? If the major burden falls on government, how far should it go in seeking a better accommodation toward the needs of business? If business has the major responsibility, is there a practical limit to what it can do for this better relationship?

Obviously, these are complex questions, not easily answered. Simple, "instant" solutions to problems growing out of the relationship between American business and American government are few and far between. But it is certainly worth examining the questions and offering—however tentatively—approaches that may hold the promise of their solution.

In considering these questions, one is almost immediately drawn to the matter of government regulation. And from there the trail inevitably leads to a consideration of those all-important contemporary vehicles of government guidance—the regulatory agencies. They express, in their form and in their activities, nearly everything we mean by government control.

They are not the only expression of government control, but they furnish us with a good laboratory sample.

GOVERNMENT CONTROL TRIGGERS EXTREME VIEWS

The topic of government regulation triggers strong and voluble responses from two widely differing camps. One side shouts for new and more stringent restrictions on business operations; the other decries regulation of any kind. One faction sees rigid regulation as the cure-all to social, economic, and political problems; the other proclaims that unrestricted business activity is the only answer to the good society for all.

Both of these extreme viewpoints are, of course, only demonstrations of pronounced astigmatism. They fall far short of the target area of reality—that middle ground in which differences can be settled and realistic appraisals made.

The middle ground of public opinion—more populous and less vocal than the extremes—recognizes the validity of measuring proposed regulatory steps in terms of necessity and appropriateness and with a broad view toward the consequences.

To occupy this middle ground is to realize that progress depends on striking the right balance between too little and too much restriction.

Those with extreme convictions often overlook the fact that both business and government carry out similar functions. Both have a client to serve. Both handle someone else's money. Both can contribute to the general prosperity of the nation. To carry out these functions, there must be a certain amount of give and take on both sides. The amount of give and take can be established only through exchange of information, opinions, ideas. In this exchange, there is little room for inflexible viewpoints, for ironbound tenets that ignore social, economic, or technological change . . . or history.

MUST AVOID "TUNNEL VISION"

Too often in our modern society—with its emphasis on specialization—there is a propensity to develop "tunnel vision," to narrow one's scope to the area of immediate concern and operations.

This narrow viewpoint can be found in both government and business. When it becomes a determination for action—when smaller immediate objectives take precedence over larger, more comprehensive goals—then the public is not being served.

Let me present some rather simple and general examples:

☐ A labor leader may demand large wage increases without considering the effect on production costs, product prices and—ultimately—the health of the industry. The demands may end in elimination of jobs.

☐ A businessman may seek to restrict by legislation a competitor's quite legitimate actions because he is unable or unwilling to meet the competition openly. His attitude encourages inefficiency, invites outside control, and in the long run does his own business harm.

☐ A consumer may demand an unreasonably low price level for a product. By insisting on controls for an artificially low price, he is tinkering with the natural controls of the free market, and the effects of his action radiate to other areas. In the long run, he may end up paying . . . first through poorer service and, later, through even higher prices when the market situation violently forces a correction.

CONDEMNING ALL REGULATION NO ANSWER

Once a problem is at the government level, subject to government regulation, the same kind of tunnel vision can compound it. Being endowed with human frailties that all of us have, some government people tend to see a problem in terms of a narrow, special interest. In addition, only a few of those who are called upon to regulate business have substantial experience in the area of their concern. They sometimes deal primarily in directives—in regulations—in findings by examiners. An overall view of a problem may be lost in the shuffling of papers.

In the face of such facts, one may be tempted to condemn all regulation. Yet here we come face to face with one of those fascinating paradoxes of American life. As a people, we object to rules and regulations imposed by others. We believe that the last act of a dying organization is to get out a new and enlarged edition of the rule book. But historically, we have always demanded that exceptions be made. We have always recognized that some guidelines, backed with power, are essential if our kind of society is to work.

REGULATORY AGENCIES NEEDED

While freedom to market *products* and engage in commerce has been a corner-post of the American economic structure, the need for establishing some regulation in the marketplace is a historical fact of life. Thus we have created such regulatory agencies as the Interstate Commerce Commission, the Securities and Exchange Commission, and the Federal Trade Commission.

While good business-employee relations are important, and both employer and employee would like to have them, nearly everyone realizes they do not come easily. Thus we have created the National Labor Relations Board to act as referee.

While many business organizations are seeking to compete in world markets, and in theory accept the principle of free international trade, they recognize that some exceptions must be made. So they have a strong interest in regulations that affect domestic imports.

While all Americans recognize the importance of trust and confidence on the part of a patient toward his doctor, most of us recognize the need for professional standards. So we have a system of state medical licensing boards.

"PROOF OF THE PUDDING"

I think few business historians would contend that United States currency would be stronger if there were no Federal Reserve Board. Or that the American consumer would be healthier if there were no Food and Drug Administration. Or that the nation's industrial activity would be greatly accelerated if there were no antitrust laws.

We ought to recognize that in many areas regulation has been highly beneficial, even though at first there may have been those who didn't think it would be.

Decades ago, the financial community, for instance, bitterly opposed any regulation of the stock exchanges. But when regulation finally came with the creation of the Securities and Exchange Commission, public ownership of securities grew enormously, and far from Wall Street. Today, owning a share of American business, through ownership of common stocks, has become commonplace.

MUST LOOK AT TOTAL PICTURE

Four years ago, the government decided to take another close look at the securities markets. Congress authorized a Special Study. Out of it grew new regulations—worked out quietly in the conference room by representatives of the securities industry, and professionals on the SEC staff. They were able to do this because—over the years—both sides had learned to look at the total picture. They saw stock trading from the standpoint of investor, broker, corporation—and its role in the whole economy.

Perhaps, some day, all business-government relations will be this harmonious. Now, of course, they aren't.

In the field of air and water pollution, for example, extremely narrow vision is often exhibited by both business and government. Some segments of government cry for stronger and stronger regulation applied with scant consideration of the broad technical, economic, and even medical facts of life. Some businessmen are guilty of the same myopia when they plead for complete freedom to put anything into our air and water. Both sides are wrong. Neither perceives that while some restrictions are necessary, all factors in the broad picture must be taken into consideration.

GOVERNMENT NOT FREE FROM BLAME

Today, we in the petroleum industry witness still another example of tunnel vision—this time on the part of the government. I refer to the manner in which regulation is being applied to the natural gas producer. Under a concept of regulation tailored to public utilities, rigid and often arbitrary controls are being imposed on the price of natural gas at the wellhead. It is sold in competition, not under an exclusive franchise like that of a public utility. The flag of "consumer protection" is raised to explain regulatory actions. Yet with tight government regulation, the pace of discovery of new natural gas supplies has not kept up with the increase in demand. This is regulation without due consideration of an important part of the picture. The incentive to find new supplies of gas is weakened, and shortages of natural gas, and probably increased costs to the consumer, may well lie ahead.

MIDDLE GROUND MUST BE SOUGHT

Such instances demonstrate how important it is that business and government seek the middle ground. In accomplishing the all-important task of improving government-business relationship, it is evident that *both* government and business have a role. In the long run, each has the responsibility to contribute to this relationship, above and beyond their usual day-to-day routines. "Business as usual" and "government as usual" simply are not good enough for these *un*usual times.

We must remember that both government and business are responsible to the same people. Government officials are really the spokesmen for people. These officials owe their existence and survival to their perception—yes, and even anticipation—of public demands. I believe history shows that individuals in government are often better attuned to the demands of the public than is business leadership. The wise course for business and industry to follow, therefore, when new government proposals are made, is to listen carefully and remember that it really may be the people who are speaking.

BETTER COMMUNICATION ESSENTIAL

In the first place, business and government can both do a better job of communicating with each other. What can't be accomplished in the realm of honest communication can't be accomplished at all.

Businessmen must stand ready to explain, to discuss, to debate—and be more willing to do it than they have been in the past. And this willingness cannot be limited to critical periods as, for example, those times when a legislative proposal affecting business adversely is about to come up for a vote in Congress. Such firefighting tactics *are* necessary at times but there is a pressing need for *continual* communication with government. We cannot limit our contacts to times of crisis. By keeping government informed, educated on our everyday problems and accomplishments, we shall lessen the dangers of unsound legislation and regulation. We should strive to eliminate the possibility of tunnel vision in government by providing a broader view of ourselves and our problems. Government people also must be prepared to listen, to question, to view a problem as part of a larger picture.

ALL VIEWS DESERVE STUDY

Those who originate proposals and frame regulations need the benefits of all viewpoints, including the business viewpoint. They need the information that only businessmen can provide. As John Connor, Secretary of Commerce, said not long ago, "How many businessmen are going up on Capitol Hill to give their views on these subjects? I know some have done so, but not nearly enough. We in Washington need the benefit not only of your private criticisms but of your constructive alternative proposals, voiced loud and clear in public. If business wants to open the eyes of Americans as to its real needs and aims, it must launch a program of corporate communications far more intensive than anything yet undertaken . . . ."

CONTACTS MUST BE CLOSER

Second, a better footing must be found for the basis of contact between business and government. Business should be more aggressive in proposing constructive legislation, in policing its own problem areas, in contributing its expertise and talents. The day is long past when any industry can hope to succeed by flatly opposing the adoption of proposals it does not favor. Such simple negativism is out of keeping with our times. Our society demands fast solutions to its problems, and if we are not happy with a solution that is proposed, we must be prepared to develop and put forth a workable alternative, one that will be acceptable to all sides. Today construction—not obstruction—must be the basis for business-government relationships.

Finally—and most importantly—more businessmen are going to have to participate in government affairs. I mean active involvement—not passive interest.

The involvement must start on the local level. For when we analyze today's business-government relations, we can see participation at the local and state level is every bit as urgent as contributing our talents in Washington. Perhaps it is even *more* urgent.

MORE ATTENTION NEEDED IN STATE AND LOCAL AFFAIRS

As a practical matter we are going to have to realize that it is fruitless for business to go storming into Washington to complain about burgeoning federal agencies eroding states rights if we fail to go back to the state capital and support a government strong enough to exercise those rights. Government is a matter of practicality more than anything else. As Woodrow Wilson said, "Jefferson's Declaration of Independence is a practical document for the use of practical men . . . it is not a theory of government but a program of action."

It is inaction and inefficiency at lower levels of government that, more than anything else, have contributed to the expansion of the federal organization. If this is to be corrected we as businessmen are going to have to accept more of a responsibility for working for good government on the state and local level.

MORE BUSINESS PARTICIPATION REQUIRED

In the final analysis, government merely reflects the consensus of those participating in the governed society. And the more intensive the participation, the more accurately will government be able to mirror the wants and needs of society's many segments.

Whose responsibility, I asked initially, and I repeat—Business or Government? I hope I have made it clear that I consider it a question of sharing. And I'm sure that from both sides, it's susceptible to improvement.

Many of us are already putting our shoulders to the wheel in this respect. Maybe the answer lies in all of us trying even harder. We must understand government and help government to understand us and our problems. Only then will the right equilibrium be obtained.

QUESTIONS

1. Explain why federal government regulatory agencies are needed.

2. Explain how government-business relationships could be improved.

3. What role should state and local governments play in the regulation of business?

4. Why does "tunnel vision" develop among government officials and business leaders?

The National Alliance of Businessmen

HENRY FORD II

The National Alliance of Businessmen's charter was set forth in President Johnson's Manpower Message to Congress on January 23, 1968. In his message, the President called on American business to apply its talents to a critical national problem: finding jobs for the hard-core unemployed.

The President suggested a new partnership between government and industry, in which the government would draw on its informational resources to identify and locate hard-core unemployed, and industry would bring its resources to bear in preparing them for and placing and retaining them in productive jobs.

Some of the present hard-core unemployed can be assimilated in industry simply by changing existing entry barriers to their employment. But many others will require extra effort in recruiting, training, and counseling.

To underwrite the extra costs of this extra effort, the President has proposed to the Congress that $350 million be provided to support what he has called the JOBS Program (Job Opportunities in the Business Sector). $106 million will be provided from funds already available in fiscal 1968, with $244 million to be provided in 1969.

The goals of the Alliance are to help put 100,000 hard-core unemployed persons to work in productive jobs by the summer of 1969, and 500,000 by 1971. The Alliance has also been asked to find work for 200,000 needy youths this summer, and to advise the Secretaries of Labor and Commerce on how the government can be most helpful in reaching these goals.

The NAB Program stems essentially from the government's recognition that previous efforts to relate government job training programs to actual jobs and placements had not been fully successful because employers were not sufficiently involved. The basic function of the Alliance is to get employers involved and committed. As the first step toward our goals, we are asking employers in the 50 largest metropolitan areas to pledge that they will hire specific numbers of disadvantaged adults and young people.

Giving people who have been held back by prejudice and poverty a chance to earn a decent life is no longer solely a matter of justice and the principles of democracy. After the tragic events of the past few summers, we must finally recognize—if we didn't recognize it before—that our very national unity and the peace of our cities are at stake. As Governor Kerner's Commission on Civil Disorders has pointed out, our nation is being divided into two separate and hostile societies. That trend must be halted before the separation is complete.

Jobs are not the whole answer to the problems of poverty and racial discord, but they are an essential part of the answer. A man cannot respect himself unless he can use his God-given abilities to make a living for his family by doing some-

Reprinted by permission from the July 1968 issue of the *Michigan Business Review,* published by the Graduate School of Business Administration. The University of Michigan.

thing of value for other people. A man who cannot respect himself cannot respect other people, or the society which denies his manhood.

Business holds the key to equal job opportunity. Government cannot meet this need without major help from business, simply because business is where most of the jobs are. In the past, most of us in management have probably assumed that the hard-core are unemployed because they are unemployable. Our task now is to prove that we were *wrong,* that most of them have the potential to move into the mainstream of the American economy.

Securing job pledges is only the beginning of what we must do. This program will fail unless the people who are hired become permanent, productive members of the labor force. It is not a relief program or a make-work program, or a gimmick to cool things for the summer. Our efforts will do harm, not good, if we hire people, raise their hopes, and then let them slide back into idleness and despair. We are, therefore, asking employers not only to hire people they would never have hired before, but to see that they get whatever education, training, counseling, understanding, and support they need to become good employes.

This will mean important changes in employers' attitudes and in how they run their businesses—in whom they hire, how they hire, and what they do with people and for people after they are hired. And these changes will have to reach all the way from the chief executive to the lowest level of supervision. Training for members of management will be almost as important in this program as training for hard-core employes.

The normal business approach to community problems is to put up the money, as long as someone else is willing to work on the problems. But we can't buy our way out of this particular set of problems. In fact, we are not even being asked in this case to put up the money to pay the extra costs of hiring and rehabilitating the hard-core unemployed. The Federal government is putting up the money, and business is being asked to provide the jobs and the training.

The Department of Labor will work with the State Employment Services to find the people who need our help. The Labor Department has also worked out a simple contract procedure so that employers, as individuals or in groups, can be reimbursed for the extra costs of hiring and training the hardest of the hard-core.

There is really no precedent for this kind of undertaking. It will not be easy, but we are off to a good start. Companies all over the country have been responding magnificently. In only two months, we were able to put together a nationwide network of offices manned by borrowed executives who will be working for the Alliance for at least six months. More than 500 volunteer executives, whose talents command $15 million or more in annual salaries, are engaged full time in our Washington office, our eight regional offices, and our 50 metropolitan offices. An additional 7,000 business and professional people have been trained and are soliciting employers for job pledges and contract proposals.

As of May 21, the Alliance had received pledges from companies all over the country to provide 106,000 jobs for the hard-core unemployed. This, of course, represents 106 percent of our target of 100,000 hard-core jobs by the summer of 1969. Some cities had pledged for more jobs than they were asked to pledge. Detroit's pledges, for example, were more than three times its goal.

In addition, we had pledges for 70,000 jobs for poor young people this summer. This represents 35 percent of our target of 200,000 such jobs. However, some of the biggest cities, which were slow getting started, are now moving rapidly toward their goals. Jobs must be found for poor young people who otherwise would have nothing to do when school lets out, and we are now concentrating our efforts on this part of our assignment. Among other things, we are organizing an approach to thousands of small businesses on the basis of "each one hire one."

Businessmen will have to carry most of the burden of making the Alliance program a success, but the Alliance needs and welcomes all the help it can get. We, in turn, are determined to be as helpful as we can to existing organizations that are already working toward the same basic objectives.

The program has the fullest possible cooperation from the Federal government, which is lending the Alliance a substantial number of executives. Some businessmen may have doubts about entering into job-training contracts with the Federal government. But I can assure them that the Labor Department is doing everything it possibly can within the limits of the law to make these contracts simple, flexible and businesslike and to keep the paperwork to a minimum.

The National Alliance has also established good working relationships with state and city governments and such organizations as the Urban Coalition, the Chamber of Commerce, the National Association of Manufacturers, the Advertising Council, the Urban League, and the AFL-CIO—to name just a few. In fact, I have never before seen such a wide range of organizations united with such enthusiasm behind a single goal.

Finally, we are working to gain and to keep the confidence and support of organizations representing the ghetto community—the people we are trying to help. They are looking to business to prove that the rest of the country really cares about their problems and needs, and to provide reasons why they should have hope for the future. Businessmen must not and cannot let them down. Too much is at stake, for all of us.

QUESTIONS

1. What is the National Alliance of Businessmen?

2. What role can the NAB play in helping to prevent social unrest?

3. Why is it in the best interests of the business community to cooperate with the Federal government in finding jobs for the hard-core unemployed?

Correlation Chart

Listed below are the books used most frequently in introductory business courses.

This chart was prepared as a guide for interested instructors and students to facilitate maximum utilization of this book of readings.

The parts of *Modern Business Administration: Introductory Readings* are listed across the top of each column. The numbers below each heading indicate the relevant chapters in the textbooks cited at the left.

Gentry, Dwight L., and Charles A. Taft, *Elements of Business Enterprise,* 2nd ed. (New York: The Ronald Press Company, 1966).

Glos, Raymond E., and Harold A. Baker, *Introduction to Business,* 6th ed. (Cincinnati: South-Western Publishing Company, 1967).

Hart, Donald J., *Business in a Dynamic Society* (New York: The Macmillan Company, 1963).

Jucius, Michael F., and George R. Terry, *Introduction to Business,* 3rd ed. (Homewood, Illinois: Richard D. Irwin, Inc., 1966).

Keith, Lyman A., and Carlo E. Gubellini, *Introduction to Business Enterprise,* 2nd ed. (New York: McGraw-Hill Book Company, 1967).

Mauser, Ferdinand F., and David J. Schwartz, *American Business—An Introduction* (New York: Harcourt, Brace & World, Inc., 1966).

Musselman, Vernon A., and Eugene H. Hughes, *Introduction to Modern Business,* 5th ed. (Englewood Cliffs, N.J.: Prentice-Hall, Inc., 1969).

Ross, William D., *Business in a Free Society* (Columbus, Ohio: Charles E. Merrill Books, Inc., 1966).

Sielaff, Theodore J., and John W. Aberle, *Introduction to Business,* 2nd ed. (Belmont, California: Wadsworth Publishing Company, Inc., 1966).

Walton, Scott D., *American Business and Its Environment* (New York: The Macmillan Company, 1966).

Weimer, Arthur M., *Business Administration,* 3rd ed. (Homewood, Ill.: Richard D. Irwin, Inc., 1966).

Wheeler, Bayard O., *Business—An Introductory Analysis,* 2nd ed. (New York: Harper & Brothers, 1968).

	1 The Business Environment	2 Management and Organization	3 The Finance Function	4 The Marketing Function	5 The Production Function	6 The Personnel Function	7 The Evolving Patterns of Business
Gentry & Taft	1,2,5	4,6,8,27	7,23	15,16,17,18	9,10,11	12,13,14	3,21,26,28
Glos & Baker	1,2,27	4,5,6,25	18,19,20,22, 23,26	7,8,9,10	12,13,14	15,16,17	11,28,29
Hart	1,2,3,9,11	4,5,16,17	6	8	7	12	15
Jucius & Terry	1	4,5,6,23	13,14,15,16	7,8,9,10,11	17,18,19,20	2,3	12,26,27
Keith & Gubellini	1,2,3,27	4,5,6,12	11,18	8,13,19	9,15,22	10,16,17	25
Mauser & Schwartz	1,2	3,5,6	7,8,9,24	19,20,21,22,23	15,18	12,13,14	28,29,30
Musselman & Hughes	1,3	4,6,7,10	16,17	19,20,21,22	14,15	11,12,13	2,24,25
Ross	9,10,11,12, 13,14,15	4,7	5	6	5	6	8,16,17
Sielaff & Aberle	1,21,22	2,5,8	3,6,7	12,13,14	11	17,18	15,20
Walton	1,2,3,4,5,6, 7,8,10,11,12, 17,22	29	15	13,16	8	14	9,23,28,33
Weimer	1,5,8	2,4,9,10,11 12,13,14,25	17,23	15	16,19,20,21	3,18	7,22,26
Wheeler	1,2,3,26	5,6,7,8,22,25	18,19,20,21	9,10,11,12	14,15	16,17	13,27,28